CW01430724

The Complete Sales Guide

David Upsher

mitac
PERFORMANCE DEVELOPMENT

ISBN 0-9520207-1-8

Designed by Fox Design Consultants
Illustrated by Mike Roberts
Cover printed by Barwell Colour Print
Text pages printed and bound by Bookcraft

Dedication

For all the great salespeople, customers, teachers, friends and colleagues that I have met and learned from on my own journey through a lifetime of selling and teaching. This is your story and this book is dedicated to you.

David Upsher

INTRODUCTION
The Complete Sales Guide

"If something doesn't change,
we are going to end up
exactly where we are headed"

There are so many books and guides on selling available today. Who needs another one? Anyway you can't become a super salesperson by reading a book. You are born that way, aren't you? Yes, there are a lot of books on selling. Yes it's true, some great salespeople are born that way. It is also true that most great salespeople are made that way. They are born with a natural ability to communicate with people, and then they are made by learning how to use that ability to help people buy.

The Complete Sales Guide is probably the simplest guide to selling you will ever read and put into practice. You will share the experiences of many great salespeople in both story and 'how to do it' form. You can't be taught experience but you can learn it. By copying and using the skills of great salespeople, you can improve your own sales skills instantly.

This guide will show you the way. The content includes carefully selected, well established 'best sales practices' that great salespeople have used, are still using and will continue to use. These best practices have been broken down into easy to follow steps and then blended with simple, relevant and usable techniques from a branch of communications psychology known as Neuro Linguistic Programming (NLP).

NLP examines the different ways that people think and communicate with each other. It is also the study of what makes people who are good at doing certain things good at doing them. Once you have found out what the difference is that makes the difference, you can start to 'model' what it is that other people do in order to improve your own skills and abilities. By blending the recognised skills of great salespeople with simplified NLP techniques, this guide becomes unique. It contains a depth of knowledge not usually available to salespeople.

Yet another unique feature is that this is the very first guide to selling to incorporate the new Mitac 'F.A.S.T' way of learning. F.A.S.T stands for:

Focused, Accelerated, Sales Training

Focused

Very much on selling vehicles within the motor industry, although anybody selling anything will find this a very useful, practical and usable guide to finding, securing and retaining customers.

Accelerated

Through the use of illustrations and diagrams, metaphors and sales stories as well as 'how to do it' sections, the reader will be able to 'see' and 'hear' what needs to be learnt at both a conscious and unconscious level. This means that you can learn twice as much for half the effort; twice the gain for half the pain, so to speak.

Sales Training

Sales Training is the whole theme of the guide, but the emphasis is very much on 'helping people to buy' rather than just 'selling' them something.

Three chapters in particular will introduce you to some very exciting opportunities to improve your own communication skills dramatically when meeting and talking to anybody, not just customers. These are:

1. **Rapport and Opening Sales Relationships**
2. **Sensory Acuity and the Sales Process**
3. **Meta Programs and Sales Excellence**

1 Rapport and Opening Sales Relationships

Most salespeople have heard about the importance of having 'rapport' with customers. Most salespeople are **never taught how** to do this to any real degree. The chapter about *Rapport* takes the subject apart for you bit by bit. It explains how rapport occurs naturally when people meet. People have it, but most don't know they have it, since it is usually outside of conscious awareness. The techniques clearly and simply outlined in this chapter will show you how to **create rapport consciously**. This will enable you to establish and maintain a far better relationship with your customers; this in turn will result in high sales levels as well as job enjoyment and satisfaction.

2 **Sensory Acuity and the Sales Process**

This chapter takes selling in a new direction by explaining exactly how people communicate with each other. Did you know, for instance, that there is not just one English language, there are at least three: a 'visual' language, a 'sound' language and a 'feeling' language. This chapter will show you how to identify the best way to communicate with different people to ensure that they understand fully what you are saying or asking. Clearer communication results in a higher level of understanding and rapport. This in turn will have a **dramatic effect** on your personal sales ability.

3 **Meta Programs and Sales Excellence**

Most salespeople will not have heard of 'meta programs', although we all use them all the time to make sense of the world we live in. Meta programs are the 'filters' that the brain uses to select what information to pay attention to and what to discard. For example, people will:

- Move away or move towards things
- Pat themselves on the back or expect others to do it
- Make their own minds up or seek advice from others
- Be in a hurry or have all the time in the world

This chapter will identify seven generally recognised filters and show you how to use people's own filters when you communicate, so that you will develop the ability to literally **talk the customers own language.** This easy-to-learn ability will hone your personal sales ability into something far beyond recognised sales techniques.

You don't have to go through a lot of pain to be great. Look at the great salespeople you know or read about. They do it simply and elegantly. If you really want to be a greater salesperson, then this guide is the difference that will make the difference... for you. Think about this guide as a journey through sales time, then

Sit back... Take the journey... Learn... Enjoy.

CONTENTS

SECTION EIGHT That Extra Mile

SECTION NINE Walking Beyond Your Limits

SECTION TEN Out Into the Unknown

SECTION ELEVEN Endings

SECTION TWELVE Appendices

'He' or 'She' Unless gender is specified, the pronoun 'he' has been used throughout this book. The only motive for this is to remove the necessity to use 'he or she', which is disruptive and unwieldy.

SECTION ONE

Which Route to Follow?

'"*Where do you want to go?*" said the cat'

CHAPTER 1
Which Route to Follow?

"One day, Alice came to a fork in the road,

and saw a Cheshire cat in a tree.

'*Which road do I take?*' she asked.

'*Where do you want to go?*' said the cat.

'*I don't know,*' Alice answered.

'*Then,*' said the cat, '*it doesn't matter*'"

Selling has changed and is changing. Most of the changes have happened in the 1990s. The road ahead is one of change. It's no longer valid to say "*We've always done it that way*" or "*I've had thirty years' experience of retailing vehicles*".

In the latter case, quite often the person making that statement has had but one year's experience thirty times! That means they are trading mentally in the 1960s, going round and round, year after year, like a gramophone record stuck in a groove. (Look what happened to the gramophone!)

Western ideas regarding change are very much based on the philosophy "*If it ain't broke, don't fix it*". This is probably why Robert Dilts, in his book *Beliefs*, shares the thought with us: "*Success is as much a limitation to creativity as is failure.*" Eastern ideas regarding change appear to be based more on the philosophy "*If it ain't broke, make it better*". We have started the change process, but still have far to go.

Dilts shares the following unsourced statement regarding change in *Beliefs*:

"*If the automobile industry had changed as much and had come as far since it started as the computer industry has, a Cadillac would cost $2.75 and go a million miles on a tank of gas.*"

Picking the Route

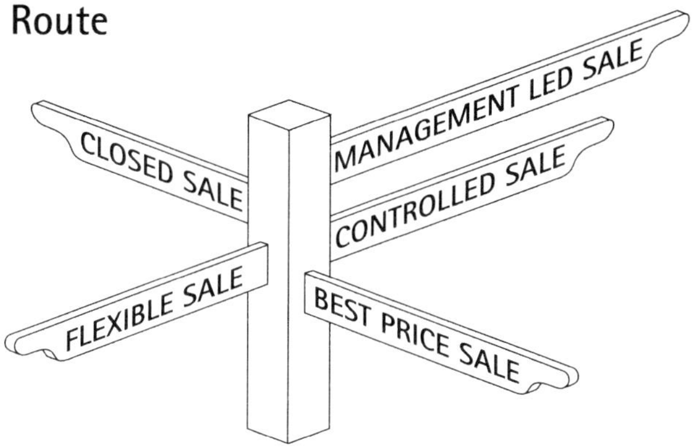

The pages that follow hold a multitude of ideas and techniques that will mostly be applicable irrespective of what system you currently use or will be using. One of the greatest secrets of success has to be in the words of Lewis Carroll:

> "One day, Alice came to a fork in the road
> and saw a Cheshire cat in a tree.
> "*Which road do I take?*" she asked.
> "*Where do you want to go?*" said the cat.
> "*I don't know,*" Alice answered.
> "*Then,*" said the cat, "*it doesn't matter.*"

There are basically five routes to follow in automobile retailing:

1. **The closed sale**
2. **The best price sale**
3. **The controlled sale**
4. **The management led sale**
5. **The flexible sale**

Which route you take is down to your company's individual circumstances, trading conditions and preferences.

- Pick the right route (for you) and you will make progress.
- Pick the wrong route (for you) and you will go out of business.
- Pick no route to follow and anything can happen!

So here are your options:

1 The Closed Sale

Sometimes referred to as the 'no sale'. This is like ice-creams on a hot sunny day. It's the classic seller's market. I worked with a salesman once who sold vehicles in the Middle East. His monthly, repeat monthly, sales target was 160 units.

"*How on earth do you manage to do that?*" I asked him.

"*It's simple,*" he told me, "*I open the door at eight o'clock, the customers form a queue at my desk, the order form is completed and signed, the money is paid in full, I give them the green docket and they pick up their vehicle three days later from the warehouse.*"

He hadn't the time to say "*Hello, how's your camel?*", let alone pass the time of day.

There are franchises in the United Kingdom, as in many countries, where this 'shop assistant' style would be most appropriate. The danger of the Closed Sale route is complacency. In time it can lead to a lack of interest in the sales process and in the purchasers. Just because goods are in short supply, we, the sellers, do not have the right to be off-hand with the buyers; we must not become custodians of 'couldn't care less' attitudes and givers of poor service.

The Closed Sale route is probably the shortest to success and the shortest to failure. If you can keep it customer friendly and user friendly, it is a very pleasant way of doing business indeed.

2 The Best Price Sale

Approximately 10% of the American automobile retailers have gone down the 'no hassle, no haggle' route during the 1990s. There has been a slight backlash of late, because dyed in the wool motor retailers of long standing find it very difficult to turn a deal down for the sake of another fifty dollars. "*It kind of sticks in your throat and doesn't seem natural,*" as one recently told me. Others take to it like hippopotami to mud baths!

The Best Price concept was born out of research at the University of Tampa in the late 1980s. A project was run to measure consumer attitudes toward vehicle dealer personnel, operation and advertising. Respondents answered 40 questions, and 750 questionnaires were analysed. One very significant finding was the dislike of high pressure, pushy salesmen and negotiating. Most customers were fed up with the hassle of having to haggle.

Similar research into buyer opinions, carried out in the UK market shortly after, showed that three out of five new vehicle buyers would prefer to be offered a lower fixed price than a higher one from which they were to negotiate an individual discount. This survey, on behalf of a major vehicle distribution group, covered nearly 1,300 drivers. Among them, only a minority were comfortable with haggling for a discount.

During the early 1990s, some North American dealers got together and decided to remove the negotiation process from the vehicle sales process. This concept has now started to gain a foothold on this side of the Atlantic.

How it Works

1 All new vehicles are priced for sale at the lowest price that the retailer will accept.
2 All trade-ins are bought in at their 'true value', the best price that vehicle would fetch for cash in its best marketplace today – trade, auction, what have you.
3 The salespeople stop selling and start helping the customers buy. They don't work on big commissions: they are paid a higher basic and usually share a percentage of a profit pool. Sometimes they are no longer called salespeople, but become customer advisers or managers.

The customer adviser's job is to meet and greet the customers and explain the system to them. He still qualifies customers, presents products and encourages test drives. What is different about 'Best Price' or 'no hassle no haggle' selling is that customers are encouraged to:

- Think it over
- Go and compare competitors' prices
- Shop around

However, both customer advisers and managers do go to great lengths to point out the other benefits of buying from their company. These can include:

- Best Price finance rates
- Best Price service rates
- Free loan vehicles
- Free collection and delivery
- Free power wash every Saturday
- Open and honest advice at all times

How it Does Not Work

The system breaks down the first time you give in to a customer and start to haggle.

As Greg Stewart of Westwood Buick said: *"The first time I give someone an extra fifty dollars for their trade-in, I make a fool out of all my other customers."* Greg has strong feelings about the type of customer who demands his last few dollars to do a deal. The kind of customers he refers to as 'two-dollar Charlies'.

"Who needs them anyway? These are the people who you bend over backwards to do business with and they then want more. Then, if you do manage to do a deal with them, they are the ones who give you all the hassle afterwards."

The Future of Best Price

At least one manufacturer and 10% of the dealer network are operating this system in the USA. At the time of writing, one UK manufacturer, one importer and three substantial dealer groups are heading down the Best Price route. Dudley Murfin, Managing Director of Greenhous Group, for instance, claimed that 'no haggle' pricing and a 'people first' programme had helped Greenhous new vehicle retail sales improve by 15% in the first eight months of 1995. Used vehicle sales were lifted by more than 20% over the same period.

The Best Price system and sons of the system are here to stay, but will *never* be the only route to follow.

3 The Controlled Sale

This style of retailing has not changed that much since its birth in America in the 1960s. Many dealerships and groups have in the past made money from this fairly hard and inflexible system. Salespeople are taught scripts to follow and tricks to find out information from customers that might help sell a vehicle. These include:

- *"You're a brave man buying a vehicle without your wife!"*
- *"How much are you expecting to get for your part-exchange?"* (This question is supposed to be asked when customers are turning right in heavy traffic when driving their own part-exchanges while the salesperson appraises them.)
- *"If I knew of a way to save you some money and I didn't tell you, you wouldn't 'think much of me' would you?"*

In its pure form, this system is hard both on the customers and on the salespeople.

One salesman who works for a company that operates this system told me that he had been told off by his controller one Sunday for letting a couple of customers go home to lunch without buying. He was instructed to follow them home and not come back without a signed order. As he had no choice, he did what he was asked and held up their Sunday lunch until his pleads and cajolery achieved the signed order that his controller expected. He got the order, and the customers cancelled on Monday morning.

The Role of the Controller in the Controlled Sale

The controller is a Sales Manager in the true sense of the word, a 'person who manages the sales'. Every deal is controlled by the controller, who instructs each salesperson on their every move during the sales process. The controller will often decide which vehicle the customer is to buy.

The Controlled Sales system has been around in the UK since the mid 1970s and, as stated, has enjoyed some success. Before controlled selling arrived so many salespeople were simply left to their own devices. What some Dealer Principals discovered was that any system is better than no system; customers were expected to buy, and many did.

4 The Management Led Sale

Somewhere between the Controlled Sale and the Flexible Sale (see below) is a new-born selling route which is beginning to show great promise. In this process the salesperson is in control and the Sales Manager is involved in part-exchange valuation and any negotiation as a third party. This could be considered as an Anglicised version of an American system. Traditionally, there has been one major buying difference between the two sides of the Atlantic: Americans like to be sold to and the British like to be convinced.

Convincing people to buy is far easier if the salesperson is in control of the sales process and is given a certain amount of flexibility. The Management Led Sale also allows for it to be 'someone else's fault' regarding any part-exchange valuation or offer. This allows the salesperson to preserve the 'good relationship' that in turn will increase the customer's conviction to buy.

The Management Led Sale is often the foundation for motor groups' selling methods: the Branch Managers remain very firmly in control of the gross profit, but expect the salesperson to take some responsibility for the volume of sales – they must convince more customers to buy through sales ability rather than by using an inflexible system.

5 **The Flexible Sale**

This system is formulated from the best practices of all sales systems and operated in a multitude of ways. Customers are treated as individuals, and there is more emphasis placed on the qualification process than on trying to close the sale.

Most companies who operate this system are inclined to show the salespeople how to do the job and then let them get on with it, with minimum management interference. If salespeople need help, they only have to ask. If the Sales Manager thinks that a salesperson needs help, praise or criticism, then they will get that too. The salespeople are individually targeted and their performance, related to sales objectives, is appraised on a regular basis.

This can be a very successful route to follow, as long as the salespeople remain motivated to get on with the job, and the Sales Manager really knows how to motivate and lead the sales team.

Which Route to Follow?

As a salesperson, the best route to follow is the one your company operates! As a Dealer Principal, you will probably have a much better idea which route to take once you have read this guide.

The main points again

1 Most changes in the sales process have happened very recently.

2 Western philosophy regarding change is based on *"If it ain't broke, don't fix it"*.

3 Eastern philosophy regarding change is based on *"If it ain't broke, make it better"*.

4 The five basic routes to follow in automotive retailing are:

- The Closed Sale
- The Best Price Sale
- The Controlled Sale
- The Management Led Sale
- The Flexible Sale

5 Irrespective of what system you operate, most of the ideas and techniques that are contained in this book will be applicable.

SECTION TWO

Preparing to Travel

"Nothing in the world was going to stop him."

CHAPTER 2
The Job of a Salesperson

"If you don't know what you are supposed to be doing, how will you know when you've done it?"

Almost 20 years ago I interviewed a young would-be salesperson who was virtually a perfect match for the 'picture' of the person we had decided we needed. This picture was based on the job description that detailed what we wanted our new recruit to do. But there was an extra quality about this person. When I asked him why he wanted to get out of his current non-selling career and move into vehicle sales he told me:

"I like cars and I think that I will be good at selling them. But apart from that, I have the desire to be 'number one'. That's something I could never maintain in my present job."

Not a bad ambition, I thought, as I made the job offer, which he accepted.

Our new recruit worked long and hard to achieve his ambition, but he had competition in our team of six: I was blessed with the two most awkward but brilliant salesmen I had ever met. Bill and Ben worked hard and played hard, but they could be disruptive.

- Like the time they set fire to another salesman's cardex system. *"We thought we would give him some hot prospects,"* they told me by way of an explanation.
- Like the time they heaped Cornish clotted cream into the ear-piece of the telephone of another of their sales colleagues and then rang his number.

They didn't mess with our newest recruit, though. Apart from being very physically fit, there was a quality about him that implied 'Mess about with me and you will be sorry'. There was one thing that Bill and Ben did do, though: they kept him in third place. They were just very good indeed at selling.

After a few months our new recruit came to my office and handed in his resignation.

The reason he gave for leaving was that he could not make the number one spot here and so he would go elsewhere. Nothing I could say would persuade him to stay, and I was very sorry to see him go. Even Bill and Ben were sad that he was going: "*Good bloke that. He's going to make it you know.*" This was praise indeed.

It was 15 years later that I discovered what had become of our would-be number one. I picked up the *Motor Trader* and there was his picture staring out at me, a little older but still instantly recognisable. The headline read: '*New Chief Executive for Major Motor Group*'.

I wrote to him and congratulated him for achieving his ambition and becoming number one. A short while afterwards I discussed what had happened with Bill and Ben, who I still keep in touch with. They were not surprised that he had made it. Bill said: "*Do you know, David, that bloke really made number one the day he joined us.*"

"*Yes,*" said Ben, "*he had decided that he was number one and nothing in the world was going to stop him.*"

...And it didn't.

Whether you think you can or can't, you're right!

You too can do anything that you want to if you want it badly enough. You have got to want it so much that you can SEE, HEAR and FEEL your ambition. If you can get to that level, there will not be much to stop you because your unconscious will organise your behaviour to achieve your goal. Just as certainly as if you really believe you can't do something, and your unconscious finds a way to make sure that you don't.

Put It This Way (because this is what you do)

You can programme yourself to be positive or negative. Both emotions are just as easy to programme into your unconscious, but the end results can be devastatingly different.

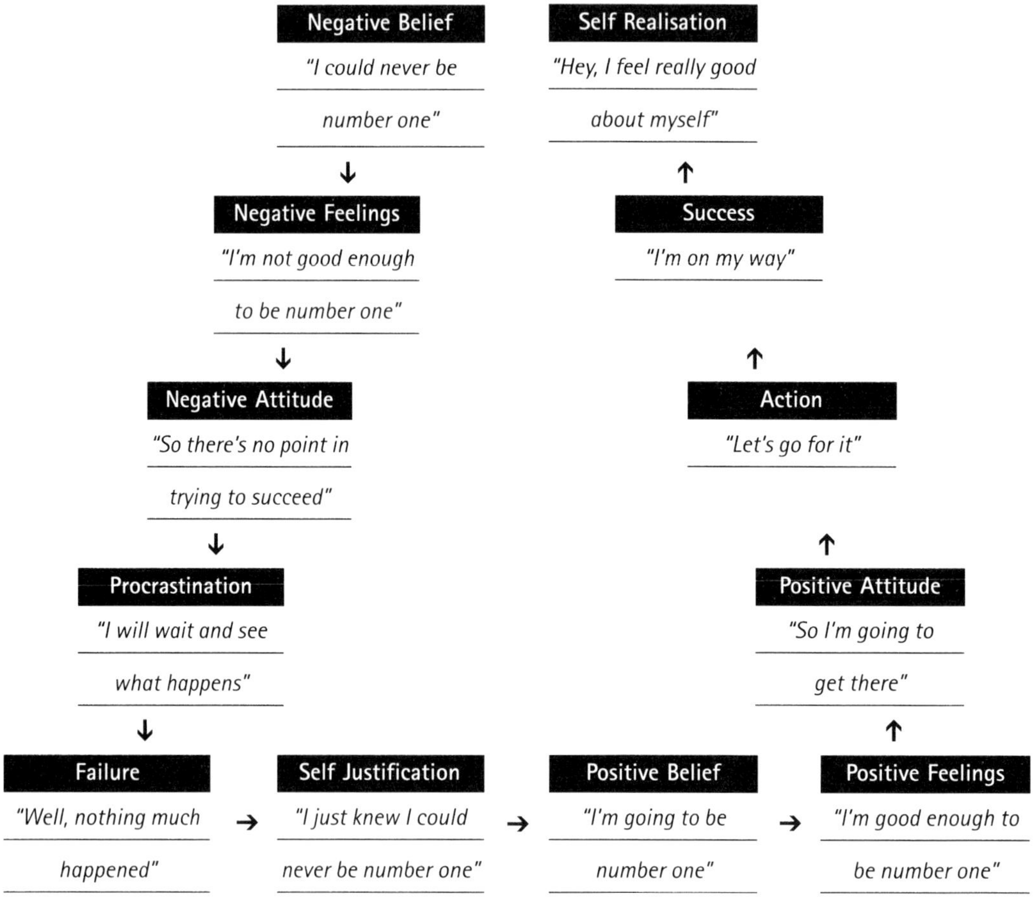

Salesperson's Job Description

Now then, what is the job of selling vehicles all about? What is it that needs to be achieved? Just how do I achieve what I want to achieve?

Let's start with the job description. It's much easier to do things when you know what you are supposed to be doing. A job description can guide you on your way.

Job Description (Example Only)

Company	Department	
Location	Job Title	Vehicle Sales Specialist
Date	Responsible To	Sales Manager/ General Sales Manager
	Existing Job Holder	

1 Main Purposes of Job

- To be directly responsible for selling a targeted number of new and pre-owned vehicles
- To achieve personal gross profit and volume standards
- To contribute towards long term profitability of entire dealership
- To retain customers and create new referrals through regular planned follow-ups
- To follow up all sales enquiries and generate new opportunities to do business through pro-active selling activities

2 Relationships

Directly responsible to	Sales Manager/General Sales Manager
Relationships Within Company	Other dealership sales staff General sales office Other departmental staff
Relationships Outside Company	Prime relationships with customers - past, present and future Franchise operations staff - regional and central

3 Limits of Authority

Capital Expenditure	As agreed with Managing Director
Operational	• Petty cash purchases limited to £_______ • Customer entertainment limited to £_______ • Raising orders on the manufacturer against written orders from the customer • Credit control limits within the company policy • Fuel requisitions for demonstrators and vehicle delivery drivers as required

4 Major Responsibilities and Duties for Results

- To have full knowledge of the specification of the products the company sells, the services it offers and the ability to discuss these specifications and services with customers and prospective customers.
- To be familiar with the pricing and products of competitive manufacturers.
- To be able to demonstrate the company's product range professionally.
- To provide the highest possible level of customer service.
- To provide regular information on customer history for input into the sales department's prospecting system.
- To assess the condition of part-exchange vehicles.
- To maintain a daily record of sales activities.
- To co-ordinate, through the Sales Administrator, customer service between all other departments.
- To negotiate personally with prospects and existing customers.
- To obtain profitable orders.
- To maintain regular contact, through telephone calls, direct mail and personal visits, with established customers and prospective customers.
- To increase the company's customer/prospect base.
- To attend sales meetings as and when required.
- To plan and co-ordinate new model launches as required.
- To complete all paperwork/returns as required by the Sales Manager/General Sales Manager.
- To participate in any promotions, cold canvassing and prospecting exercises as required by the Sales Manager.

5 Method of Measurement

- Achievement of volume targets as agreed.
- Achievement of targets for retained profits.
- Achievement of targets for volume of business opportunities and number of sales conversions.

Every Salesperson Should Have One

If you haven't got a job description, then you should get one that accurately reflects what you are supposed to be doing. The job description here is based on a real one in current use, and is shown as an example only, and not necessarily a recommendation.

If your company has given you a job description, then it should describe your job. If they haven't, then this example should give you a good idea what the job of a vehicle salesperson is all about. Let's expand our example a little to make it even clearer.

Job Title

Can be anything:

- Vehicle Sales Specialist
- Vehicle Salesperson
- Customer Information Assistant
- Sales Executive

And so on...

Many modern business cards don't give a title; they give the name of the person, with the words 'Sales Department' printed underneath.

Responsible To

Salespeople need to be responsible to somebody. In larger dealerships this is usually a Sales Manager. In smaller dealerships you could be directly responsible to the Dealer Principal.

1 Main Purpose of Job

- To sell vehicles
- To make profit
- To achieve targets
- To assist the whole dealership to be profitable
- To keep customers
- To find new customers
- To use your time effectively

2 Relationships

Having a good working relationship with your boss is a good idea. Keep your boss informed about what you are doing and if you have any problems or need help in any way.

Having a good working relationship with other people you work with is also very important if you are to achieve what you want to achieve. You are the person who should know how to open good relationships with customers. Consider the people you work with to be like customers, and use the same skills to work with them and not against them.

3 Limits of Authority

- Always stick to your agreed levels of authority, particularly regarding levels of expenditure
- If you do need to go beyond your limits, then get permission before, rather than after

4 Major Responsibilities and Duties

- Get to know your product well
- Get to know your competitors' products
- Work out the advantages of what you sell over your competition
- Become an ace demonstrator and demonstrate every chance you get
- Give all your customers the same very high level of attention and service
- Keep the prospecting system up to date
- Really get to know how to assess the condition of a part-exchange accurately
- Start to learn how to value a part-exchange if you have not already done so
- Keep a daily record of your activities. Not so much for the company's benefit, but for your own
- Co-operate with other departments to give customers a high level of service
- Strive to deal profitably with both new and existing customers
- Keep in touch with all selling opportunities using the most appropriate method, ie telephone, letter, face-to-face etc
- Try to bring more customers and potential customers in to your business to make up for the ones that move away or go elsewhere for some reason
- Be prepared to give your time to attend training and sales meetings – communicating and sharing ideas is one of the most successful ways of helping your business grow

- Get involved with activities such as new model launches, and be willing to invest some extra time when it's wanted. (If you do, then you will usually find that you can get some time back when you need it)
- Stay on top of that paperwork; if you get behind, it will really drag you down
- Co-operate with your Manager and participate in any activity that you are asked to do. It may not always be convenient, but people will notice your willingness and will be more inclined to help you when you need their help

Footnote on Focus

Don't do all this just for the benefit of the company you work for. Do it for yourself, for your benefit. Adopting this attitude means that you will do things because you want to do them rather than feeling that you have to.

5 Method of Measurement

- The best way to hit a target is to aim through it. If you are given a volume target to achieve, set your own higher target. You might miss that one, but it will help you hit the company one
- The same rule applies for profit targets: aim high
- Know your closing ratio. If you are converting one customer in four, then start to aim for one in three
- Set yourself a daily target for prospect and follow-up calls; then make sure that you do that number every day
- Do everything you can to hit your monthly targets. Put the effort in and the effectiveness should follow

Then What?

Most of us go to work for one thing in particular. To earn money to do what we want to do when we are not working. That does not mean to say that we should not enjoy going to work. By adopting the attitude that we are working for our own benefit as well as our company's, the work that we do becomes easier and far more rewarding.

The Complete Sales Guide will show you how to do all this and more. Read it and act on it and you too can be a Chief Executive one day.

The main points again

1 You can do anything that you want to if you want it badly enough.

2 If you really want something, then your unconscious will organise your behaviour to achieve your goal.

3 Your unconscious will also find a way to make sure that you don't achieve what you don't think you can achieve.

4 It's much easier to do things when you know what you are supposed to be doing.

5 A job description can guide you on your way.

6 If you don't have a job description, then get one that is an accurate reflection of what you are supposed to be doing.

7 You too can be a Chief Executive one day.

CHAPTER 3
Packing Your Bag

"Achieving success is an inside job"

One of the silly things that I used to do if I wasn't working on Saturday was to finish work on Friday night, go home and go straight to bed, get up at 2am on Saturday morning, drive to Cornwall through the dawn and catch the early morning waves off Fistrel beach in Newquay.

Throughout the summer months I did this once a fortnight, driving back to London late on Sunday night, Bilbo hot dog surfboard strapped firmly to the lid of my Fiat 500. I stayed at the White House Hotel on the Saturday night. It wasn't expensive, and it was clean and run by the very friendly Hosey family.

Late one August, my last trip of the summer surfing season, I asked Bill Hosey if he was open at Easter. The thought behind the question was the opportunity to take a four-day trip instead of a two-day one. Bill told me that it wasn't worth opening at Easter because the lack of customers meant that it would not be viable. "*Unless you can fill the hotel,*" he added.

"*How many is that?*" I asked.

"*Fifty-four,*" he replied.

"*Alright,*" I heard myself say, "*that won't be a problem.*" We worked out a cost per head and I left, reconfirming that I would be back at Easter on Good Friday morning with 53 other people for breakfast.

I drove my Fiat 500 back to London with mixed feelings. Half of me was telling the other half that I was stupid: the other half was asking the first half how we were going to do it. Two hundred and sixty-five minutes and miles later both halves had it sorted. Apart from inviting people that I knew, I would stick an ad in the *Times* announcing *'David Upsher's celebrated Easter house party to Cornwall will happen again this year. Please telephone for details'*.

Long before Easter I had organised a coach to take us and a place to meet – the Steering Wheel Club in Curzon Street, Mayfair. We would meet on the Thursday night,

have a party and load everybody on the coach at midnight. Then they could sleep for the eight hours that the coach would take to get to Fistral and breakfast at the White House. Six weeks before Easter the advertisement went in the *Times* and the phone went potty. I didn't take 54, I took 70, using extra vehicles and booking more accommodation down the road to take care of the overspill.

What a party we had. By day there were wetsuits, surfboards and crashing near-winter waves. There was riding, the horses frisky with the long winter solus behind them. There was the coach to take us places. By night there was dinner and disco, drinks and dancing (who was it who used to sing *'In the summer time when the weather is hot'?*). It wasn't summer and it wasn't hot, but it was incredible fun.

Not long after it was all over, by popular request I organised a May bank holiday to the Wye Valley. We went in a 1932 Renault Paris bus, but that's another story. Not long after that I asked Ernest, the Manager of the Steering Wheel Club, if I could hold a reunion party one Saturday for the people who had come on the trips. *"We are not very busy on Saturdays,"* he said. *"I was thinking of closing because of the lack of customers."*

"How many do you need to make it worth your while?" I asked.

"Oh, somewhere around sixty," came the reply.

"I can find them," I said.

"What every Saturday?" said Ernest.

Telling my two halves to shut up for a moment I said: *"Yes, every Saturday."*

And I did... for five years.

Before you can set out on your journey you will have to decide what to take with you. You need to travel as light as possible but take everything you need. Here's a checklist of the kinds of items that you should consider taking:

- ☐ **A Job Description**
  Got one – it's here in the book already.
- ☐ **A Destination**
  You will need a goal, something to aim for.
- ☐ **A Route to Follow**
  You will need to develop a plan of action and then work the plan.
- ☐ **Some Product Knowledge**
  To create confidence, enthusiasm and sales
- ☐ **A Positive Attitude**
  Attitudes are contagious, so what are you spreading around?
- ☐ **The Right Appearance**
  One of the secrets of being successful is to look successful.
- ☐ **Everything You Need to Hand**
  What do you need to have on or near you to do your job properly?
- ☐ **A 'Things To Do' List**
  Created every day first thing in the morning or last thing at night.
- ☐ **A Knowledge of Selling**
  A pattern to follow that is not rigid, but is flexible enough to blend in with each and every customer.
- ☐ **A Starting Time**
  Start a little earlier in the morning, every morning.
- ☐ **A Plan to Maximise Time Available**
  Journeys do take time, but once they are started, then the rest is inevitable.

That's the bag packed, so you're ready to start – or are you?

There are a couple of other things that might ease your path a little. For instance, you have probably decided that you need knowledge of your product and how to help customers buy it; but are you fully aware of all the resources that are available to help you on your way? Surprisingly, very few people take the trouble to notice what they already have going for them. If they don't notice, then they can't take advantage of it.

Here's a resource checklist for you covering:

- Franchise resources
- Company resources
- Personal resources

Franchise Resources

- Supplies of product
- Parts and accessory supplies
- Stocking plans
- Access to late low mileage vehicles
- Franchise staff
- Vehicle location system
- Supply of prospects
- Training
- Point-of-sale material
- Used vehicle plans
- Ability to dispose of unwanted stock
- Finance house links
- Goodwill available
- Quality of product
- National advertising
- Advertising support
- Marketing efforts
- Press releases and editorials
- Brochures and other sales aids

Company Resources

- The premises
- Trained staff
- Demonstrators
- New vehicle stock
- Used vehicle stock
- Working space
- Aftersales services
- Prospect and follow-up system
- Sales support staff
- Telephone receptionist
- Sales literature
- Link to finance house
- Telephone and fax equipment
- Parts and accessories stocks
- Loan vehicles
- Dealership reputation
- Location
- Parking space
- Local advertising
- Promotions
- Marketing efforts

Personal Resources

- Effective use of time
- Personality
- Flexibility
- Perseverance
- Appearance
- Inter-personal skills
- Motivation
- Decision-making ability
- Tenacity
- Self-confidence
- Professionalism
- Customer knowledge
- Product knowledge
- Knowledge of competitors
- Listening skills
- Empathy
- Open mindedness
- Time management skills
- Ability to handle telephone enquiries
- Ability to qualify
- Ability to create rapport
- Presentation skills
- Sensory acuity
- Ability to appraise and value part-exchanges
- Negotiation skills
- Objection handling skills
- Closing skills
- Keeping customers
- Obtaining referrals
- Finding new customers
- Follow-up skills
- Writing skills
- Mathematical skills

Resource Availability

It is quite feasible that not everybody has all these resources available, so you will have to make do with what you have. In reality you could probably find at least ten things that are wrong with the company you work for. Look at it another way and you will also find at least ten things that are right. As you take your own journey through sales time, you will notice that it is the salespeople who concentrate on what's right about the organisation that they work for that achieve the best results and the highest level of job satisfaction. Could this be a coincidence, do you think?

Personal Resources

Personal resources: now that's a different matter. If there are a few things on the personal resources list that you do not currently have, please feel free to develop those resources within yourself.

This is not as silly or as hard as it sounds; as Paracelsus wrote in the 15th century:

> *"As man imagines himself to be so shall he be*
> *And he is that which he imagines."*

If you are not into 15th century philosophers, then more recently Sir Walter Scott wrote:

> *"Success or failure is caused more by mental attitude*
> *than by mental capacity."*

Just the other day, Tad James, Founding Director of Advanced Neuro-Dynamics Inc, said:

> *"Imagine anything and you can master it."*
>
> So who are we to argue?

You will also need to be fully aware of the time it takes to sell one vehicle.

- All the things that you have to do
- The realisation that it takes on average ten hours work to sell one vehicle

You will benefit if you understand the steps in the structure of a sale.

- Traditional, showroom selling
- Proactive, away from the showroom selling
- How both structures are interchangeable

The Time Involved to Sell One Vehicle

To sell one vehicle, you will have to carry out most (if not all) of the following tasks:

- Handle an incoming telephone enquiry
- Get face-to-face with the caller
- Find out what the customer wants
- Present your products
- Have the right product knowledge
- Demonstrate the vehicle
- Appraise a part-exchange
- Help the customer to want to buy
- Sell the customer extras
- Sell the customer finance
- Handle all objections
- Ask for the order
- Follow up the enquiry
- Sign the customer up
- Collect the deposit
- Arrange the delivery
- Make sure the vehicle is ready
- Physically inspect the vehicle before delivery
- Deliver the vehicle to the customer
- Collect full payment
- Inspect the part-exchange
- Complete all paperwork
- Arrange first service
- Write a thank you letter
- Update company records
- Keep in touch with the customer

Now that is a fair chunk of work. You don't win every time, so you might have to start the process two, three, four or more times for one enquiry to get to delivery stage. That's why it takes, on average, ten hours to sell one vehicle.

Selling Structures

Salespeople should be flexible enough to handle each customer in an individual and personal way.

At the same time, you will benefit if you understand the steps in the structure of a sale.

The Structure of a Sale

Traditional, Showroom Selling

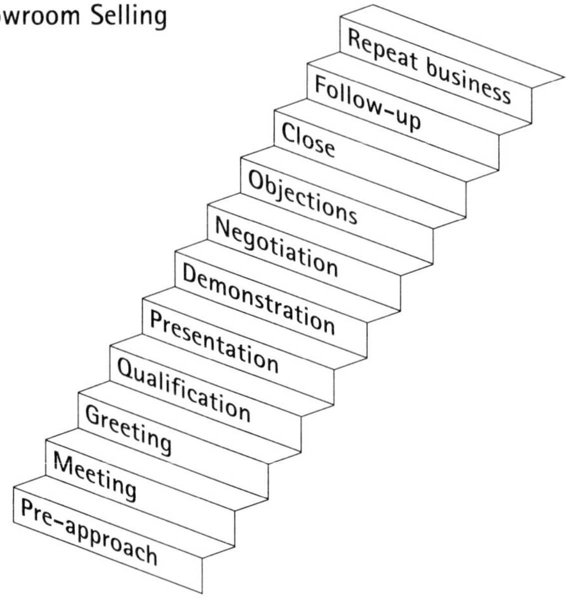

Traditional, Showroom Selling Steps

Pre-approach

- See everything, believe nothing
- Always acknowledge every caller
- Judge timing of approach

Meeting

- Visual contact before voice contact
- Go to where the customer is
- Match customer's style and state

Greeting

- Use non-standard greetings
- Offer full attention
- Find out name and reason for the call

Qualification

- Sitting down away from product
- Find out how to help customer buy
- Tell customer what you propose to do

Presentation

- Personalise presentation
- Concentrate on customer's interests
- Show product that matches customer's needs

Demonstration

- Use the right vehicle and the right route
- You drive first, then the customer
- Prove the product in action

Negotiation

- Negotiate only if you have to
- Never ask customer what he wants for part-exchange
- Sell 'value for money' rather than buy business

Objections

- Prevent objections where possible
- Avoid creating objections
- Turn objections into questions and answer the questions

Close

- Close only once, at the end
- Check for excuses by using *'Apart from that?'*
- Remember profit comes from deals you do not do

Follow-up

- Non buyers with a 'thank you for calling' letter
- Buyers with a letter confirming the order
- Progress of sold vehicles, and check over before delivery

Repeat Business

- Make a show out of delivery
- Ask for referral business after delivery
- Keep in touch by letter, telephone and face-to-face

Very much a stepped approach visualised as a flight of ascending steps; this sales structure has been around for years. Used properly and with consideration for the customer's needs, it is probably still the best way to convert showroom enquiries into sales.

Proactive, Away from the Showroom Selling

Proactive selling is based on non showroom activities. This is where you take the initiative and selling effort to the customers rather than waiting for the customers to come to you.

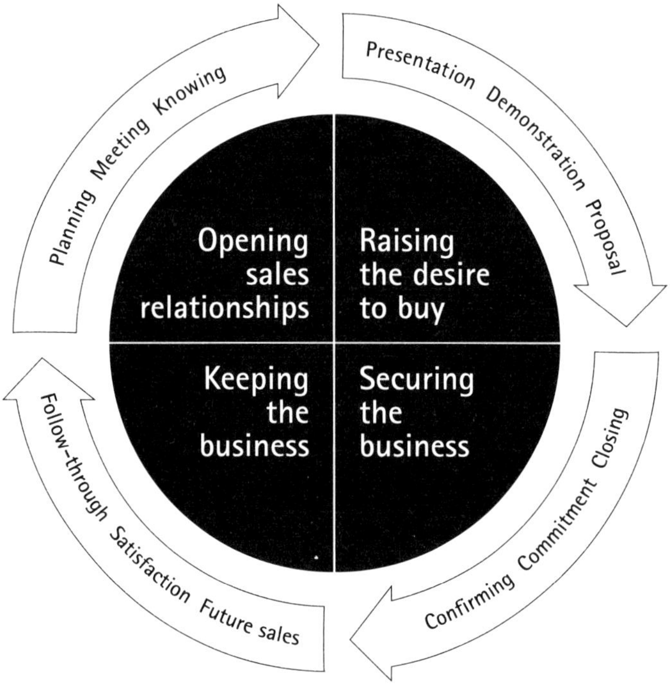

Opening Sales Relationships

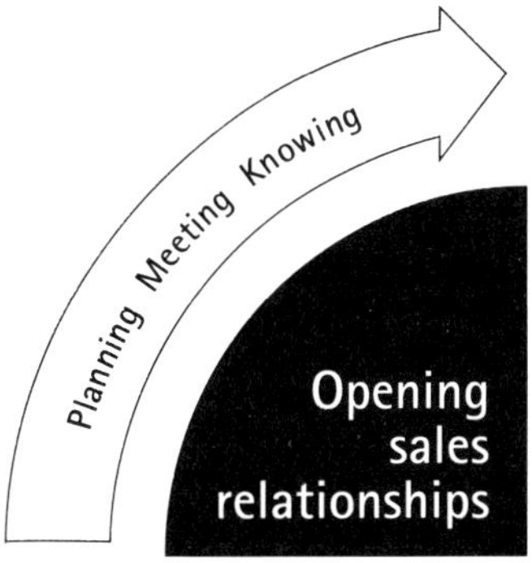

Planning

- Territory
- Time
- Account management
- Promotion
- Market identification
- Target analysis
- Prospect planning
- Call preparation

Meeting

- Establish rapport
- Open relationship
- Prove credibility
- Sincerity
- Trust
- Gather information

Knowing

- Prospect's personal style
- Business needs
- Objectives
- Financial status
- Build relationship
- Raising the desire to buy

Raising the Desire to Buy

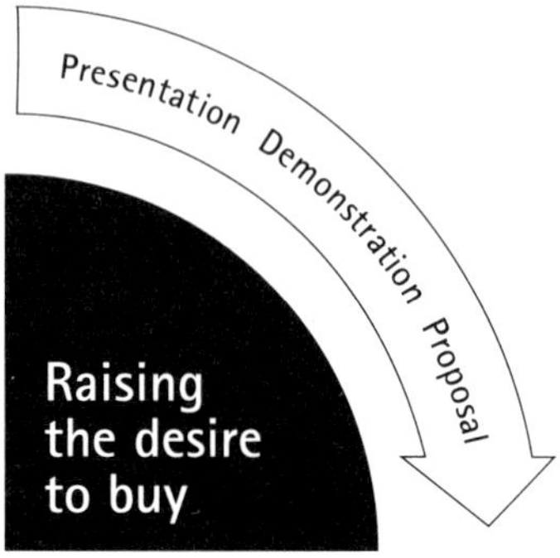

Presentation

- Solutions to problems
- Custom-tailored
- Personalised benefits
- Objection prevention

Demonstration

- Prove the product in action
- You drive to show how
- Customer drives to see how
- Route to suit the customer

Proposal

- Tailor-made for customer
- Written in presentation form
- The proposed vehicle(s)
- Methods of acquisition
- Benefits to the customer
- Substantiation of claims
- The investment
- Why customer should buy
- Why from your dealership
- Administration arrangements

Securing the Business

Confirming

- Take the proposal – never post it
- Take sufficient copies
- Page numbered and indexed
- Well typed and correctly presented
- Talk through with customer
- Listen to reactions
- Take notes for further use

Commitment

- Spend time
- Make sure everything is understood
- Agreement of proposal

Closing

- *'When'* and not *'If'*
- Complete paperwork
- Confirm in writing

Keeping the Business

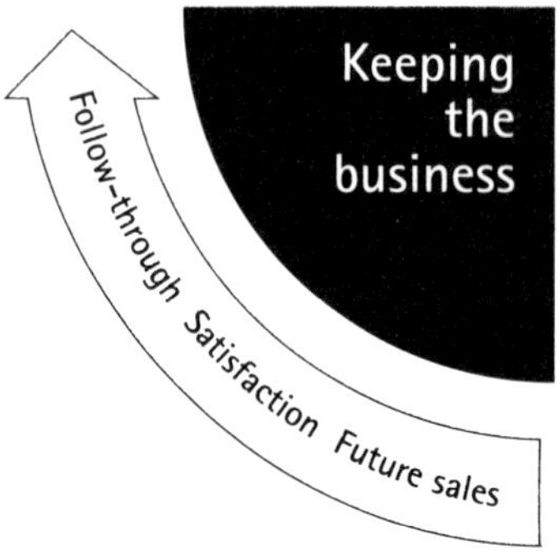

Follow Through

- Keep customer informed of progress
- Track sold vehicles
- Work with your colleagues
- Pre-inspect
- Be involved with deliveries
- Thank customer for business

Satisfaction

- Keep in regular contact
- The customer is king
- Build relationship
- Understand customer's business
- Offer suggestions and ideas
- Work hard to keep the business
- Open and honest communication
- Respond quickly to complaints or requests
- Anticipate future needs
- Think ahead of your customer

Future Sales

- Look for other business opportunities
- Ask for referral business
- Become a transport adviser to your customer
- Plan, meet, study
- Present, propose, confirm
- Commitment, follow through
- Satisfaction, future sales

...And so on!

Traditional, Showroom Selling vs Proactive, Away from the Showroom Selling

Both styles have their uses and both are interchangeable and can be adjusted to suit any customer. Selling vehicles successfully calls for a certain amount of flexibility particularly as most motor industry salespeople find that they spend time both in and away from the showroom.

The main points again

1 Before you can travel, you need to decide what to take with you, ie:

- A job description
- A destination
- A route to follow
- Some product knowledge
- A positive attitude
- The right appearance
- Everything you need to hand
- A 'Things To Do' list
- A knowledge of selling
- A starting time
- A plan to maximise time available

2 You also need to be fully aware of the resources that are available to help you:

- Franchise resources
- Company resources
- Personal resources

3 You will also benefit from having knowledge of different types of 'selling structures'.

Traditional Showroom Selling Steps

- Pre-approach
- Meeting
- Greeting
- Qualification
- Presentation
- Demonstration
- Negotiation
- Objections
- Close
- Follow-up
- Repeat business

Proactive, Away from the Showroom Selling

- Planning
- Meeting
- Knowing
- Presentation
- Demonstration
- Proposal
- Confirming
- Commitment
- Closing
- Follow through
- Satisfaction
- Future sales

CHAPTER 4
The Correct Use of Time

"Nobody has enough time

But everybody has all the time there is"

The first tangible object I ever remember selling was a conker; I must have been around ten at the time. When I went to bed the night before, one of those early autumn storms had begun. Heavy winds and driving rain were gusting and lashing at my bedroom window. The conkers will be down, I thought, as I fell into a deep sleep.

Where the idea of selling conkers came from that night is beyond my recollection. On awakening to a peaceful, storm-free morning, it was just there. Conkers were in short supply that year; late frosts had done much to decimate the early profusion of conker blossom candles. But I knew of one tree in a sheltered spot that was covered in conkers. It was tucked behind a large church in the corner of a graveyard halfway between home and school. So, books under one arm and an empty satchel over my shoulder, I set off early to gather the harvest that was mine for the picking.

Within a few minutes of arriving at the tree I had a satchel full of the largest and most beautiful conkers I had ever seen. I could hardly lift it, but determination helped me carry my shoulder-numbing booty on to the school. I sold my load with ease for ten a penny to my conker crazy class mates. That doesn't sound much in today's terms, but a Mars bar was less than two pence at the time, so that day I was rich! I made several trips to the tree and the sweet shop until the conker market and my stomach were both sated.

This was the start of my career in sales: I was hooked. As the son of a war widow on an RAF paid education, I did not have the spending power of the majority of my fellow students. During the spring I caught and sold pond life; anything from tadpoles to larger crested newts. During the long hot summers I sold marbles; I became an ace marble player and sold my winnings back to my losers.

I had a bike that my uncle and stepfather had made, mostly from scrap, but I wanted a 'real' one, and I wanted it badly. Badly enough to give up my summer holiday. When I was fifteen I took a summer job at the Cumberland Hotel at Marble Arch in London. Instead of doing all the things a fifteen-year-old boy would do during the long summer holidays, I spent my time serving food and drinks to hungry and thirsty tourists.

Towards the end of that summer holiday, I took all of the six weeks' wages to Arding and Hobbs in Clapham Junction and bought the best racing bike in the shop. It was blue and had a hand-dipped frame and continental quick-release hubs. It was every schoolboy's dream. I was so excited that I pushed it home the three miles to Wimbledon Park where I lived. I dared not ride it for fear of affecting its perfection in some way. It took a long time, but to me it was time well spent. I looked at it for days before I gingerly started to ride it.

When school started again, at first my friends did not believe it was mine; some thought that I had stolen it, others were just puzzled. I did not tell them that I had spent the entire summer holiday slaving away for it. I just enjoyed their envy and puzzlement.

Shortly after this I started to work on Saturdays and Sundays in a Lyons Corner House in London. Five days at school and two days at work was not the most fun combination for a schoolboy, but I earned the money most of my friends were given. I don't begrudge them their money, but I am grateful that I discovered early in life that you can do anything that you want to and have anything that you want to have. You just have to make the time and the effort to start your journey. The rest is inevitable.

Heading for Failure

This is how some salespeople spend their day:

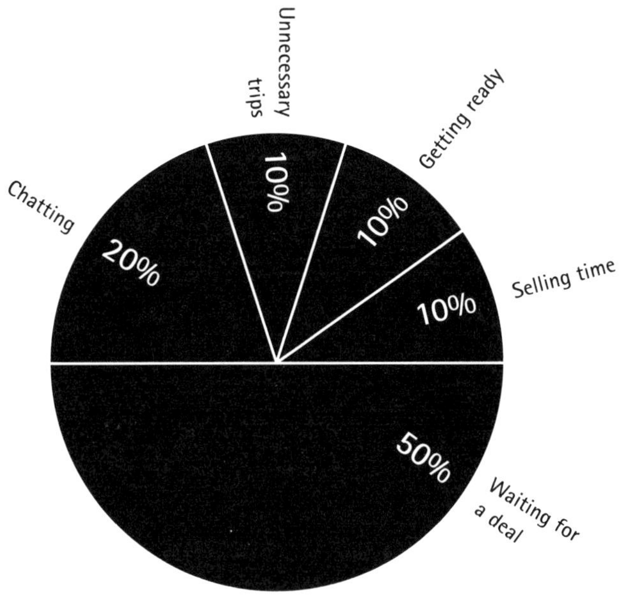

Waiting for a Deal

Up to 50% of a day can be spent waiting for something to happen. Some salespeople seem to think that this is part of their job.

Chatting

Another 20% can be spent in 'chatting'. This is not chatting to customers, this is time spent in talking to other salespeople, receptionists, service advisers or anybody else that is prepared to listen.

Getting Ready

With practice, 10% of a day can be spent 'getting ready': getting ready to start work, getting ready to stop work, to go to lunch, come back from lunch and so on.

Unnecessary Trips

When some salespeople get bored with waiting, chatting and getting ready, they get more creative and start to invent 'unnecessary trips'. Anything to relieve the pressure of a long boring day. These trips can vary from the simple *"I'll walk down the road and buy a KitKat for my coffee"* to the more complicated *"What a nice day. I'll invent a demo and hit the coast"*.

Selling Time

If a salesperson does hang around a showroom long enough, then sooner or later someone will walk in and buy something. This sales activity can occupy up to 10% of the selling day.

Now you can see why this kind of day is referred to as 'Heading for Failure'.

Heading for Success

This is how other salespeople spend the time of day:

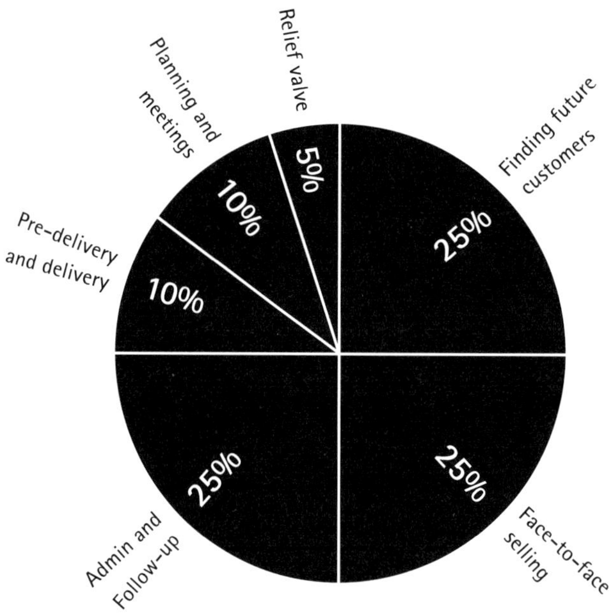

Finding Future Customers

25% of the day is spent looking for future business, seeking out people who could buy but haven't yet. These activities can include mailshots, telephone calls and face-to-face visits.

Face-to-face Selling

If you do spend 25% of your day trying to find future customers, then you will get face-to-face with more selling opportunities – up to 25% of your day instead of 10%.

Admin and Follow-up

A major part of a sales persons day can be taken up by administration and follow-up work, particularly if you are generating far more contacts than your 'Heading for Failure' colleagues.

Pre-delivery and Delivery

These activities become a larger part of the day because you will be selling more vehicles.

Planning and Meetings

This is internal work, mostly spent in a creative frame of mind; this is the time you spend planning where to find your future customers. Some time could also be spent attending sales meetings or getting involved in training activities.

Relief Valve

After all this there will still be the time to go down the road and buy a KitKat, chat to a receptionist or grab a light lunch. Relief valves are very necessary in a job that can be mentally taxing and sometimes disappointing or even frustrating. If you do try to work 100% for 100% of the time, then it is most likely to start to reflect on your physical or mental health. However, relief valve activities should never occupy more than 5% of your working day; the rest will be filled with activity, success and satisfaction.

The question is:

> "*Which of the two kinds of day most closely matches your own?*"

Why not take a salesperson's time test and find out for sure?

Salesperson's Time Test

Just tick the column that matches your behaviour and score yourself after you have answered all 21 questions.	Always	Usually	Sometimes	Rarely	Never
1 Do you prepare a daily plan and set priorities?	☐	☐	☐	☐	☐
2 Do you do things in priority order?	☐	☐	☐	☐	☐
3 Do you accomplish what needs to be done during the day?	☐	☐	☐	☐	☐
4 Do you tackle difficult or unpleasant tasks without procrastinating?	☐	☐	☐	☐	☐
5 Do you feel you are achieving your full potential?	☐	☐	☐	☐	☐
6 Do you get your paperwork done on time?	☐	☐	☐	☐	☐
7 Do you use your waiting and travelling time effectively?	☐	☐	☐	☐	☐
8 Do you spend enough time planning?	☐	☐	☐	☐	☐
9 Do you always check that you have everything you will need with you before you start to talk to customers?	☐	☐	☐	☐	☐
10 Do you keep something handy, to do or read if you are kept waiting for any reason?	☐	☐	☐	☐	☐
11 Do you have a specific purpose for each follow-up to a prospect or customer call (not a social purpose)?	☐	☐	☐	☐	☐
12 Do you keep a list of your customers?	☐	☐	☐	☐	☐
13 Do you keep a list of your best prospects?	☐	☐	☐	☐	☐
14 Do you update customer and prospect records as soon as possible after the meeting?	☐	☐	☐	☐	☐
15 Do you take enough time to prospect and develop new business?	☐	☐	☐	☐	☐
16 Do you always do what you promised to do for your customers?	☐	☐	☐	☐	☐
17 Do you avoid having 'Heading for Failure' days?	☐	☐	☐	☐	☐
18 Do you have 'Heading for Success' days every working day?	☐	☐	☐	☐	☐

	Always	Usually	Sometimes	Rarely	Never
19 Is your working area organised so that everything is accessible and useful?	☐	☐	☐	☐	☐
20 After each enquiry or call, do you schedule the date of the next contact?	☐	☐	☐	☐	☐
21 Do you review your 'Things To Do' list either last thing at night or first thing in the morning?	☐	☐	☐	☐	

Score yourself in the following manner:

Number of '*always*' answers	______	x 5 =	______
Number of '*usually*' answers	______	x 4 =	______
Number of '*sometimes*' answers	______	x 3 =	______
Number of '*rarely*' answers	______	x 2 =	______
Number of '*never*' answers	______	x 1 =	______
Total			______

20 – 49 – Good candidate for the 'greatest improvement award'.
50 – 74 – Could be heading for trouble. Time management needs serious attention.
75 – 89 – Good but could use some improvement.
90 – 100 – Superstar salesperson.

Time can be your worst enemy or it can be your greatest ally. With time on your side you will always be successful – eventually. The trick is to make sure that you are getting enough. Here are 40 ways to choose from to make sure you do.

40 Ways to Create More Time from the Same Days Available

Most salespeople suffer from a lack of time. Here are 40 ideas collected from successful salespeople, both inside and outside the motor industry.

Naturally, not all of them will apply to you personally: it will depend on the nature of the job that you do, eg showroom selling, proactive selling or perhaps a blend of the two.

Choose the ten ideas that would really make a difference by helping you find some extra time in your working day. Then make them your own way of working and make them work for you.

Creating More Time Through Planning Your Work

1 **Prepare**

- your daily plan and set priorities

2 **Develop**

- a system for tracking your daily activities, a 'Things To Do' list

3 **Buy**

- or obtain a wastepaper basket and use it frequently

4 **Consider**

- what would happen if you threw the piece of paper in your hand away. If the answer is nothing, then throw it away

5 **Never**

- get too organised

6 **Adopt**

- as your personal motto 'Do it now!'

7 **Set**

- yourself deadlines to complete tasks

8 **Be aware**

- of how the past teaches you and use that knowledge to improve your current plans and efforts for a more successful future

9 **Revise**

- your short and long term goals on a regular basis

10 **Review**

- your 'Things To Do' list last thing at night or first thing in the morning

Creating More Time Through Working Your Plan

11 **Before**

◆ you do anything, see what you can get someone else to do for you

12 **Organise**

◆ your working area so that everything is accessible and useful

13 **Keep**

◆ things in order, hours can be wasted every week looking for things that are misplaced, misfiled or mislabelled

14 **Break down**

◆ major tasks into smaller ones because the work will be more manageable in smaller pieces

15 **Remember**

◆ the old Chinese proverb '*A journey of a thousand miles starts with a single step*'

16 **Do**

◆ what you have to do first, not what is easiest or most pleasant

17 **Start**

◆ with the big tasks, not the small easy ones

18 **Never**

◆ try to do more than one major task at any one time

19 **Handle**

◆ a piece of paper once only whenever possible

20 **Save**

◆ a task that you enjoy doing for later in the day so that you have something to look forward to

Creating More Time Through Personal Working Habits

21 **Get up**

- earlier in the morning and get to work in a relaxed frame of mind

22 **Drive**

- to work earlier and miss the heavy traffic

23 **Use**

- the extra time to catch up on those time-consuming administration tasks and paperwork

24 **Eliminate**

- self-made interruptions and distractions

25 **Minimise**

- unnecessary interruptions imposed on you by others

26 **Learn**

- to say 'no' easily and graciously

27 **Don't**

- just 'be busy' – ensure that you are truly productive

28 **Visit**

- shops, restaurants, petrol stations and banks during non-peak hours

29 **Ask**

- yourself the question "*What is the best use of my time right now?*" often

30 **Leave**

- work behind you when you go home and home behind you when you go to work – wherever you are, be there!

Creating More Time Through Customers and Prospects

31 **Create**

- enough time to prospect and develop new business

32 **List**

- all upcoming commitments or reminders at one central source to help you plan better

33 **Always**

- check that you have everything you need with you before making sales calls

34 **Use**

- waiting time as a gift

35 **Keep**

- something handy in your briefcase to do or to read if you are kept waiting to see somebody

36 **Avoid**

- asking customers and prospects to call you back – call them later and stay in control

37 **Try to**

- return calls and correspondence on the same day

38 **Telephone**

- 'long-winded' customers just before lunch or the close of working hours

39 **Update**

- customer and prospect records as soon as possible, because time can erase memory

40 **Promise**

- less, but try to deliver more than you promised

30,000 Days

Nobody has enough time but we all have all the time there is. There are 86,400 seconds in a day and you have got around 30,000 days, the same as most people. Time can be very useful, if used wisely. It is the thing that stops everything from happening all at once. Time wasted or misused is gone forever, and you can never get it back.

A couple of door-to-door salespeople called the other day and offered to help me buy a religion. I explained that I was happy with the one I already had. This they accepted after a while, and as they left one of the two turned and said: "*Have a nice day.*" I told him that I had other plans. They both looked at me in total shock horror, so I thought I'd better explain what my plans were. I told them that I was planning to have a wonderful day; to have just a nice day seemed to be a total waste of time. They looked at each other with that look that told me that somebody had bought something after all, and their time and mine had not been wasted.

The main points again

1 You can have anything you want to have, you just have to make the time to start your journey. The rest is inevitable.

2 Salespeople who are 'Heading for Failure' spend their days:

- waiting for a deal
- chatting
- getting ready
- on unnecessary trips
- plus some sales time

3 Salespeople who are 'Heading for Success' spend their days:

- finding future customers
- face-to-face selling
- on administration and follow-up
- doing pre-delivery and delivery
- planning and attending meetings
- plus a little bit of 'relief valve'

4 Salespeople should:

- create more time through planning their work
- create more time through working their plan
- create more time through personal working habits
- create more time through customers and prospects

5 Nobody has enough time, but we all have all the time there is:

- time wasted or misused is gone forever and you can never get it back
- avoid having nice days – have wonderful days instead

SECTION THREE

Setting Out

"I walked up the longest front path I'd ever seen."

CHAPTER 5
The Telephone Enquiry

"In our business, selling is face-to-face"

The telephone call came close to the end of the day.

"Ah yes," the caller said, *"my name is Westlake and I want the brochure, price list and colour card relating to the BMW Seven Series range. Please can you get them in the post to me tonight."*

"No problem," I said, *"consider it done, and your address is... ?"*

I took down the full name and address (he wouldn't give me his telephone number). I then checked it back to make sure I had got it right. A rather posh address in Highgate, I noted. In the time it took to gather the information together, find a large envelope, a compliment slip and a business card, I knew that I wasn't going to post it. I had, in fact, totally convinced myself that Highgate, in north London, was on my way home to Wimbledon, south-west London, from my office in Park Lane W1.

He did seem keen to get the information as fast as possible, I justified to myself. I'll just nip in on the way home and drop it off, I thought. The idea was commendable and not well timed. The traffic meandering homewards towards Highgate was heavy, and so was the rain. It was a long slow journey north that night, but eventually I got there.

Finding the house wasn't difficult. It was massive and majestic, the wrought iron gates firmly locked in place to guard the long gravel drive that swept so graciously up to the house. So I parked in the road and used the side gate and walked up the longest front path I have ever seen and it was still raining. Eventually I reached the steps that staggered ever upwards to the heavy, wooden, highly polished front door.

It was dark by now, but a pair of porch lights guided my squelching feet up the steps and my hand to the bell-pull. I pulled the chain and listened for a sound. Nothing, just the patter of the falling rain. I pulled the bell again and thought I almost heard a distant tinkle, which could have been a bell. To make sure I gave the chain a hard tug downwards and noted with satisfaction that the chain and the tinkle were related to each other.

I extracted the envelope from under my jacket and examined it critically in the porch lights. It was slightly crumpled but at least it was dry. Not like me, I thought, as I waited for the door to be opened, rain transferring itself from my hair to the back of my neck to start to soak further and further under my shirt and downwards between my shoulder blades. Still silence. Just the rain and the sixth sense that there were people inside the house. It was a long wait, but then it could have been a long walk to the front door from inside that massive house, I rationalised, as I reached for the bell pull again.

The door sprung open just as my fingers closed around the handle for the fourth time. I literally jumped. I could not help it. There was no sound; suddenly the door just wasn't there any more. Instead there was a large fat, grumpy crumpled-looking man, with a round head and a flat nose, who looked like his body was two sizes too big for him. He was jacketless, wearing a white shirt, black bow tie, black trousers with shiny stripes down the sides and highly polished shoes.

"*When I am rich,*" I thought, "*I think I would prefer to employ a better-looking butler!*"

The man scowled at me "*What do you want?*" he said sourly.

"*Mr Westlake?*" I asked pleasantly.

"*Why?*" he said even more sourly.

"*I have some BMW brochures and other information for him that he has requested urgently,*" I said. "*Please inform him I am here.*"

"*How dare you knock on my door*" said the fat man. I looked behind me to see who he was talking to, there was nobody there. Suddenly it dawned on me this **was** Mr Westlake and he was talking to me.

"*I didn't knock on your door, I rang the bell,*" I offered.

"*Don't you get clever with me,*" said Mr Westlake, "*this is private property and would you please remove yourself at once.*" Then surprisingly he added: "*I'm trained to kill, you know.*"

It sounded to me like he wanted me to go.

"*But don't you want the brochures?*" I asked.

"*I told you to post them,*" he slobbered as he grabbed them from my hand. "*Now go away!*" The door sprung back into place as silently as it had opened.

With mixed emotions I trundled back down the steps and started the long, wet walk between the squads of rose bushes lining Mr Westlake's path. There were some loose bricks at the edge of his pathway, but I dismissed the idea before it had fully formed. "*I know,*" I thought, with some satisfaction, "*I won't sell him a car.*"

...And I didn't.

"The trouble is," said John, *"I'm not very good at dealing with enquiries over a telephone. Now put me face-to-face with the customer and I'll do a good job."*

The above situation is very common. Some salespeople, including very good ones, just don't like using the telephone. Let's get one thing straight here and now: the telephone is in the sales office to enable you, the seller, to get face-to-face with a buyer.

Selling in our business is usually face-to-face, the Johns of this world will be pleased to hear, although business can be done on the telephone, particularly with established company customers and the like. Leaving those exceptions to one side, the following scenarios, hints and ideas have been collected to help all salespeople get face-to-face with more selling opportunities in the future.

The Retail Telephone Enquiry – Case Study I

"Car sales, hello."

"Oh good morning. I see you have a second-hand Fiat Uno in red for sale. Have you still got the car?"

"The Fiat Uno – yes we have still got it."

"Can you tell me the mileage on that car please?"

"Ah – hang on a sec, I'll nip out the back and check it. Don't go away!"

(Two-minute wait.)

"Yes, we have still got that car and the mileage is... the mileage is... oh yeah, sorry, I forgot for a moment – 22,000 miles."

"I would like to pop in and see it. What time are you open to?"

"It's Friday today, so we will be here until seven."

"What about tomorrow?"

"Ah – nine 'till six."

"Right, I will pop in with my wife to see the car tomorrow morning. Will that be OK?"

"Yes, by all means. Ask for me, my name is Gavin and I will show you the car."

"Thank you, Gavin. I'll see you tomorrow then."

"Right – bye."

The Retail Telephone Enquiry – Case Study II

"Good morning, car sales, how can I help?"

"Oh good morning. I see you have a second-hand Fiat Uno in red for sale. Have you still got that car?"

"The Fiat Uno – yes we still have it at the moment. It's a lovely car, twenty-two thousand miles. It has a full service history and it has been looked after very well. What else can I tell you?"

"Well, you have told me what I needed to know most, and that was the mileage. I would like to see it – what time are you open to?"

"Well, we are open to seven this evening. Where are you phoning from?"

"I'm phoning from Bath."

"That's not far away. My name is Gavin Groves, and what's your name please?"

"David Upsher."

"That's U - P - S - H - E - R?"

"Yes."

"And what's your phone number there – 01225... ?"

"743894."

"743894?"

"Yes, that's right."

"And the address is... ?"

"Station House, Bath Road, Box."

"Fine, so when and where would you like to see the Uno, Mr Upsher?"

"Well, my wife and I could pop in tomorrow."

"Just approximately what time would you be thinking of calling?"

"Oh – around eleven."

"That's great. I'll pull it out and have it ready for you both to see and try. Is there anything else I can do to help you today, Mr Upsher?"

"No that's it – I will see you tomorrow at eleven."

"Thank you very much indeed. Oh, by the way, how did you hear of our company?"

"I read your advertisement in the Bath Weekly Chronicle."

"That's useful for us to know. I look forward to meeting you and Mrs Upsher tomorrow then, around eleven."

"Thank you, goodbye."

Based On Reality

Any similarity between these two calls and what actually happens when you try to buy a used vehicle today is purely intentional. Neither call is perfect, but which of Gavin's personas do you think sells the most vehicles? Let's model Case Study II, shall we? It will save us starting with a blank sheet of paper.

"Good morning, car sales, how can I help?"

- 'Good morning' – far more professional than 'hello'.
- Offer of help given.

"The Fiat Uno – yes we still have it at the moment."

- 'At the moment'. The unsaid message here is '*We don't expect to have it in stock for long*'.

"It's a lovely car, twenty-two thousand miles. It has a full service history..."

- Gavin has all the information to hand.
- 22,000 miles could cause an objection, so Gavin used a sandwich technique here to reduce the possible negative effect of the mileage.

  It's a lovely car.
  22,000 miles.
  It has a full service history.

"...and it has been looked after very well. What else can I tell you?"

- Yet another benefit, plus the offer of further assistance.

"Well, we are open to seven this evening. Where are you phoning from?"

- Straight answer to '*What time are you open to?*', plus open direct question to find out information.

"That's not far away. My name is Gavin Groves, and what's your name please?"

- Reminder for customer of short distance to travel.
- Gavin gives both first name and surname. The customer now has a choice of what to use.
- Gavin now asks customer for his name, having established good two-way communication.

"That's U-P-S-H-E-R?"

- Gavin spells out name:

1 To get it right.

2 To show that he is writing it down.

"And what's your phone number there – 01225… ?"

◆ Gavin has discovered that if you start off a telephone number, then the customer will finish it without thinking.

◆ He uses the code on this occasion; if he did not know it, then he would have said '*Bath?*' instead.

"743894?"

◆ Repeats number to make sure it's right and writes it down.

"And the address is… ?"

◆ Gavin gets the address without difficulty, as he usually does.

"Fine, so when and where would you like to see the Uno, Mr Upsher?"

◆ Unsaid messages. You would like to see the Uno, and you don't have to come here to see it.

"Just approximately what time would you be thinking of calling?"

◆ Gavin establishes the time to expect Mr and Mrs Upsher.

◆ Unsaid message: you will be calling.

"That's great. I'll put it out and have it ready for you both to see and try. Is there anything else I can do to help you today, Mr Upsher?"

◆ Unsaid message: you are going to drive it.

◆ Includes wife in the conversation.

◆ Gavin checks there is nothing else he needs to know or do.

"Thank you very much indeed."

◆ Even customers like to be thanked.

"Oh, by the way, how did you hear of our company?"

◆ Pure market research to establish customer source.

"That's useful for us to know. I look forward to meeting you and Mrs Upsher tomorrow then, around eleven."

◆ Gavin gives reason for marketing question.

◆ Confirms date and time.

◆ Lets the customer hang up first.

Face-to-Face with Telephone Enquiries

The question is often asked: *'How many telephone enquiries should I be able to convert into face-to face selling situations?'*

The truth is that our industry is pretty lousy at converting telephone enquiries into showroom visits or appointments to go and see. Test shopping and vehicle buyer surveys indicate that an insignificant 10% conversion rate would be an industry norm, and you would be wise not to model that. If you follow the recommended framework for converting telephone enquiries into face-to face selling situations, then a 50% conversion rate could be yours. But you will have to work at it.

Recommended Framework for Converting Telephone Enquiries into Face-to-Face Selling Situations

The Telephone Receptionist's Role

Not every company has one but as most have, let's start from there.

1 The receptionist takes the call

- Answers within four rings
- Gives the name of the company
- Establishes reason for the call
- Finds out name of caller
- Creates a good first impression by sounding business-like and friendly

2 The receptionist advises the person in sales who is going to deal with the enquiry

- Who the caller is
- What the caller wants
- Advises the caller of the name of the person who is going to deal with the call
- Puts the caller through

Note: If you do not have a telephone receptionist, then you will have to do most of the above that's applicable for yourself.

3 The person who takes the call should already be prepared

- New vehicle price list, specifications and colour options to hand
- Something to write on and to write with (two)
- Used vehicle stock list and current used vehicle advertisements
- Diary or forward planner
- Mentally pleased to take the call

4 The salesperson greets the caller: *"Good morning, Mr Morris, how can I help you?"*

- Do use 'Good morning' or 'Good afternoon' – it is so much better than 'Hello'
- Remember the importance of first impressions (just as important on the telephone as face-to-face) and sound warm and friendly, business-like but not stiff
- Put a smile in your voice: it's true that you can hear a smile on a telephone

5 Qualify the customer

- Who the customer is
- What do they want
- What have they got
- Get the follow-up information
- Source the enquiry
- Write down the information

6 Establish the next step

- How you propose to help them
- Preferably face-to-face
- They come to you or you go to them?
- If not, one of the above, what is going to happen next?
- Confirm arrangements
- Let the customer hang up first

7 Do what you have agreed to do

Tricks of the Trade

As already established, it is important to realise that although it is possible to sell and buy a vehicle over the telephone, in our business, it is normally face-to-face. What is even more important is to realise that your first contact with a potential customer is not a time to practise trickery or skulduggery, neither of which have any place in any part of good sales practices.

Things to Forget

Forget the 'I'll phone you back' technique

This – frankly, very ineffective and sales costing – technique is still being taught today. Customers expect instant attention and do not want to hear *'I'm not in my office at the moment, give me your number and I will call you back'* or any of the other variations designed to make it easier to get a customer's telephone number.

Forget 'high balls' and 'low balls'

These are refugees that landed here from across the Atlantic over 30 years ago and are still in use today.

- 'High ball' means to offer a telephone enquirer a very high price for a part-exchange over the telephone.
- 'Low ball' means to offer a low cost to change from a customer's existing vehicle into a new one or another used vehicle.

These techniques are used to tempt potential customers to come in and see you because they expect a better-than-possible deal.

Forget 'Hold it up to the phone'

And its dubious brothers perfected by GT Thomas, late of the Dallas Cowboys turned vehicle salesman. When a customer asked GT for a price for a trade-in over the telephone, GT would beam and say: *"Hold it up to the phone, so I can take a look at it."* In the same category you can put questions like:

- *"How much do you think this watch I am wearing is worth?"*

  or
- *"How much do you think the house I live in is worth?"*

These statements and questions have been, and still are, used as a kind of proof to show customers it's impossible to price things you haven't seen.

Forget 'Go and snap his hand off'

This is still used both on the telephone and in face-to-face situations if the customer tells you that an offer has been made for their vehicle that is more than you can match. Some 'think they are clever' salespeople will say: *"If they have offered you that much, I suggest you should go and snap their hands off."*

Or

"Take their offer before they sober up."

Or even

"Then there are two idiots, one for offering that much and one for not accepting the offer."

This technique is designed to let the customer know, at best, that someone has been pulling the customer's leg. At worst, you know that the customer has been pulling your leg.

The Problems

The problems with the 'I'll phone you back' technique

- People really do want instant attention
- Often they will say *'It's okay, I will telephone you back.'*
- If it does work, when you try and contact them, they will already be telephoning your competition

If the customer is answering your advertisement in the vehicles for sale section of the local paper, what do you think that the customer will be reading while waiting for you to return the call?

The problems with 'high balls' and 'low balls'

Yes, customers will come and see you, and the result is usually the same. Anger, frustration and a lack of trust. Not the best foundation upon which to build a good business relationship.

The problems with 'Hold it up to the phone'

Unfortunately, in today's marketplace, many customers are put off by such 'clever' remarks. Statements like this don't prove anything, apart from the salesperson's own lack of professionalism.

The problems with 'Go and snap his hand off' and the like

The trouble with this one is that some customers will overstate the amount they have been offered for their part-exchange. By using this type of remark, you make it impossible to do business with yourself without the customer proving that a 'lie' has been told. Who would want to be proved a liar?

The Alternatives

If you want to get a customer's follow-up information, *ask for it.* They will normally give it to you. The fear of giving it is in the seller's mind, not the buyer's. The only realistic alternative to 'high balls' and 'low balls', 'hold it up to the phone' and 'go and snap his hand off' is not to get drawn into pricing vehicles on the telephone.
What's wrong with being straight with customers?

"I can't price it over the telephone, but I would like to see it. Can you bring it here or would you prefer me to come and see you?"

The same rules apply to telephone discount enquiries. Be frank with customers and make the effort to meet them at your place or theirs. This will give you an opportunity to open a relationship before discussing the deal.

"If you are looking for value for money, Mr Austin, my company can certainly help you. Would you like to come here to discuss the details, or would you prefer me to come to you?"

If the customer is really insistent, try something like:

"We are not the sort of business to give you false information over the telephone, just to tempt you to come and see us. But please do come and talk to us, otherwise you could be leaving the best deal on the table."

Simon's Simple Method

Simon didn't have a lot to say on the course that he attended. He appeared to be more of a listener. He followed the conversation with bright eyes and an expressive face, showing interest even in the occasional odd idea that came from the floor during open discussion sessions. Simon's eyes practically danced when the topic turned to the best way to get face-to-face with the telephone enquiry, and he spoke for the first time since the introductions earlier that morning. (You know how it is when someone who is usually silent starts to say something – everybody stops talking and listens.) Simon said that he found that the best way to get face-to-face with telephone enquiries was to go round and knock on their door.

Do What?

The other delegates did not stay silent for long. "*What a silly idea!*" and "*People do not like to be disturbed at home or at their place of work without an appointment*", even "*If you did that to me I would throw you off the doorstep*".

Simon just smiled. "*All I'm saying is that what I do is I get the follow-up information from the caller, and that night I go round to the house (if they are local), knock on the door, explain who I am, apologise for disturbing them, and tell them the reason that I called was so that they could put a face to the name the next time we speak on the telephone or face-to-face.*"

"*And then they tell you to push off,*" said a delegate.

"*No – I offer to go or even turn around to go.*"

"*So what's the point?*" our cynical delegate said.

"*The point is,*" said Simon with a patient smile, "*that most of them won't let me go! They drag me into their homes and they thank me for calling, and at least half of them end up sooner or later as friends as well as customers.*"

"*But all this takes time, it means that you are always going to be late home,*" said a doubtful delegate.

"*I must admit that I don't do it every night, maybe twice a week, but even at that level it creates an extra fifty friendly profitable sales in a year, not to mention the extra money I earn from doing it.*"

"*I would never do that,*" said our doubtful friend.

"*Not many salespeople would,*" said Simon, "*and that is what makes it so worthwhile for me.*"

Deliver Brochures – Never Post Them

In 15 years of taking brochures to customers, Mr Westlake was the only real problem. One of the secrets to achieving sales excellence is to always hand-deliver brochures. It is the perfect opportunity to get face-to-face with a potential customer and have a good reason for doing so.

Patrick Stone is a very successful retailer of vehicles. In his newspaper advertisements he includes a brochure hotline number: '*Phone this number now for your free brochure pack*'. Many people do, and each pack is hand-delivered by a salesperson. Not a pushy person, a nice friendly one. An opportunity for the potential customer to feel the quality of Patrick's company and the people who work there before they do business. Patrick Stone is a very successful retailer of cars.

On reflection, all these years later, it was rather juvenile not to sell Mr Westlake a car. Very satisfying at the time, but you can't cash satisfaction! Apart from that, as salespeople, it is not for us to decide the people with whom we will or will not do business – that prerogative belongs to the people who pay our wages.

The main points again

1 Some salespeople believe that they are not very good at dealing with enquiries on the telephone. The good news is that the telephone is in the sales office to enable you, the seller, to get face-to-face with a buyer.

2 If you have a telephone receptionist, then that person should get the name of the caller and pass it on to the person who is going to take the enquiry.

3 Salespeople should have everything to hand that they might need before taking the enquiry.

4 Use 'Good morning/Good afternoon', sound warm and friendly – business-like but not stiff. Remember to smile on the telephone.

5 Qualify the caller – who they are, what they want, what they have got – and get follow-up information.

6 Establish the next step, which is preferably face-to-face, and then do what you have agreed to do.

7 First contacts with potential customers are not a time to practise trickery or skulduggery.

8 The best way to get a customer's follow-up information is to ask for it.

9 Tell the customer frankly that you are not prepared to price part-exchanges or discuss 'deals' over the telephone.

10 Deliver brochures – never post them. Never miss any opportunity to get face-to-face with a potential customer.

11 Be prepared to do business with all customers not just the 'nice' ones.

CHAPTER 6
Customer Expectations

"Customer expectations
are their concepts of reality"

It was one of those bleak, grey winter days, with a weak sun failing to show through the heavy cloud hovering over Hyde Park. Still, the Park Lane showroom downstairs offices were reasonably warm, and I had just made myself a large mug of hot coffee. Not one sip had passed my lips when the tannoy barked its demand: "*A retail salesman to the showroom please.*"

Potential customers are more important than coffee, so I dumped the mug, stubbed the Dunhill and hit the stairs fast. You had to be quick because there were four sales staff on shift at any one time. I didn't know where my three fellow shifters were, and I didn't stop to look either.

I leaped into the showroom, complete with customer greeting grin, appearing for all the world like a pantomime magician springing through a trap door in a puff of smoke. Only there was no smoke. That's why I could see instantly that my time was about to be wasted. Just my luck, I thought, grin fading fast, I am about to get stuck with a rather untidy looking youth with stars in his eyes and holes in his pockets while one of my colleagues will pick up the next real customer. Still, perhaps I could get rid of the youth fast.

He could not have been more than 18 years old. He had untidy hair and looked unshaven. He was wearing an old khaki jumper with patches on the elbows. His corduroy trousers looked like they had seen better days and his boots appeared to be too big for him and were not exactly clean. "*Good morning,*" I said, but with not too much welcome or enthusiasm showing in my voice.

The youth did not seem to notice my reluctance to communicate, and greeted me quite brightly. I almost recovered a bit of hope, but it was quickly extinguished when he pointed towards the most expensive BMW Coupe in the showroom. "*How much is that?*" he said, in a conversational tone. I told him the price (today's equivalent of a three-bedroom semi in Surbiton), thinking that this conversation was going to be most unrewarding.

"I'll take it," he said. *"You'll what?"* I said. *"I want to buy it,"* he said. *"Oh you do, do you? Then you will have to sign an order form and pay a deposit." "No problem,"* he said.

Quite frankly, I just did not believe him, and neither did the tone of my voice, but I had to go through the motions. I told him to sit down and I would go and get an order form. He sat down and I went down to find one. I took my time, the coffee was still hot and the youth could wait. Eventually I returned to the showroom, order form in one hand and pen in the other. He was still there.

I sat down opposite the youth. *"Right,"* I said, *"this is an order form and it is a legally binding document. I am going to fill it in and ask you to sign it."* He agreed that that was right so, wondering what the catch was, I took the lid off the pen and said: *"Okay, now your name is Mr... ?"* He said: *"Actually it is Earl."*

"Mr Earl," I repeated, to make sure of the name.

"No," said the youth, *"not Mr Earl, my name is Earl Grosvenor."* And it was. Fresh off all-night army manoeuvres on Salisbury Plain, as it turned out – which explained his appearance.

I am convinced that the current Duke of Westminster must have been aware of my acute embarrassment and my initial arrogance all those years ago, but he never batted an eyelid. We completed the paperwork, the deposit was delivered the same day and the Earl collected his Coupe the following week.

It was a vehicle and a customer that I will never forget. The Coupe was black and the registration number was LUC5K. I wrote to the then Earl Grosvenor several times. You know – the usual typed follow-up letter that gets sent out to everybody. The Earl Grosvenor always wrote back to say the vehicle was well and to thank me for my interest. The letters he sent to me were always in his own handwriting. He referred several other customers to me and part-exchanged LUC5K for a new one two years later.

Thank you, your Grace, for being such a gracious and generous customer. You taught me not one, but two, valuable lessons. They were and still are:

Never judge a book by its cover
and
Manners maketh man.

What a customer for a new or used vehicle expects and what a customer gets can be totally different. This is not to say that a person who sets out to buy a four-door family saloon ends up with a two-door sports car. It's the buying experience that can be so dramatically different. Fifteen years of taking part in and organising test shopping activities means some exposure to the bad and the ugly and, of course, the often quite good.

The ugly often revolves around food and drink and have included:

- A salesman who continued to eat a substantial pork pie when sitting talking to a customer.
- Another who ate his sandwiches from a Tupperware box from the back seat of a vehicle that a couple were test driving.
- Or even worse, the husband and wife who returned from a demonstration and complained to the manager that the salesman was deep in inebriated sleep on the back seat of the vehicle that they had just been out in.
- Or even crazy, like the salesman who produced a bottle of whisky from his desk drawer at 10am, poured some into his own coffee and offered to do the same for his lady customer. *"Purely for medicinal purposes,"* he said.

How's Your Visualisation?

Let's try a little experiment for a minute.

Put a picture of the inside of a Marks & Spencer store in your mind...
Got that? Great!
Now look for a cash desk...
Can you see the people who take the money?
Fine, there is nothing wrong with your imagination.
Now try and imagine one of those people eating a tomato sandwich.
That's more difficult, isn't it? That's hard to imagine because it would never happen.
So why does it happen in vehicle showrooms?

That's not fair, did someone say? M&S have staff canteens, whilst we poor salespeople don't get lunch breaks, let alone somewhere to eat it.

It is so fair. It should never happen, whatever the excuse. What to you is a simple tomato sandwich may to your customer often be a reason for not buying.

What is not fair is that customers should make their 'to buy' or 'not to buy' decisions in such fickle fashion, but they do.

Bad Experiences

Bad experiences from real life situations are those that make customers feel unimportant or unwelcome. They include:

- Looking at a row of used vehicles and being told by a pre-recorded tannoy voice: "*You are welcome to look at our used cars, but you are being videoed.*"
- Walking into a showroom and being totally ignored by salespeople.
- Probably the most ugly experience was the test shoppers who reported the case of two salespeople tossing a coin to see who would handle the enquiry – the one that lost was the one that had to deal with them.
- One of the more interesting comments relating to test shopping, recorded in a survey by the *Yorkshire Post*, was when they set out to discover how easy it was to buy a vehicle. The reporter said: "*We did not have to ask for the salesman's name, it was tattooed on his knuckles.*"

Good Experiences

Luckily, there is always the good to balance things out a little:

- Like the test shopper who was greeted most politely outside the showroom by the young vehicle cleaner, then taken into the showroom and introduced to a salesperson who dealt with the enquiry in a most professional manner.
- Like the saleslady who personally moved four vehicles so the customers could test drive the vehicle of their choice.
- Like the salesman who left the showroom and invited the couple to come in and take a closer look. They had been sitting in their vehicle outside, not too sure if the garage had what they wanted. The garage had, they bought it, the salesman sold it. Or did he help them buy?
- Like the salesman who approached a customer who was outside looking at the used vehicle display. "*Don't worry about me,*" said the customer, "*I'm not really a serious customer.*" "*That's fine,*" said the salesman with a smile, "*I'm not really a serious salesman.*" So they chatted, they looked, the customer bought and the salesman sold.

We can understand why there are good buying experiences. Salespeople normally get paid for selling. We can also understand why there are bad and ugly. Some customers are a waste of time. Sensible salespeople will always give all customers the benefit of the doubt – and the time of day.

What Do Customers Expect?

So what do potential customers expect when they call to a dealer's premises to look at and/or enquire about a vehicle? Many conversations with many customers and would-be customers indicate that the following concepts must be a close match to the customer's reality, as far as expectations go.

Customers Expect to Find Your Business Easily

That's fine for some, but not so good for others. If you do work in an off-the-beaten-track business, then consider what you personally and your company can do to make it easy for the customers to find you.

Adverts, including *Yellow Pages* and so on, should contain a location map. So should mailshots. 'How to find us' sheets should be included with requests for brochures. If the customers can't find your business, they will have to buy elsewhere.

Customers Expect to be able to Park Without Difficulty

This can be a difficult one. Some franchised dealers are really stuck for space. What is parked on your premises? Can your company make some space by relocating vehicles that don't really have to be there:

- Staff vehicles?
- Trade vehicles?
- Sold vehicles?
- Your vehicle?
- The boss's vehicle?
- Vehicles waiting for parts or service work?

Careful space management can usually create customer parking. This, combined with other space-saving activities such as 'just in time' collection and delivery services, can make many more selling opportunities become a reality.

Customers Expect to be able to Find the Part of Your Business or Person they Want to Talk to Easily

This means that good clear signs should be there to point people in the right direction. Staff – all staff – should take a leaf out of the latest supermarket training manuals:

- There was a time when, if you asked an employee of a supermarket where the cat food was, they would say: "*Try aisle six,*" or "*It's down there on the left*". Today it is different; "*The cat food, sir? Certainly, follow me and I will show you.*"
- The difference that this change has made to customer satisfaction and attitude is incredible – not to mention the sales of cat food!

Your customers are not there to buy moggy mash; they are there to buy motor vehicles. They are entitled to and will expect the same standard of service at the very least.

The Customer Expects that New and Used Cars Displayed For Sale Will Look Like New and Used Cars Displayed For Sale

In the hustle and bustle on a turbulent day, it is easy to take a used vehicle out of line, to demonstrate for instance, and put it back skew-whiff or even the wrong way round. You get caught up with some other pressing activity and, presto hey, you're all up jumbled.

The Customer Also Expects that Cars Will Be Priced For Sale

Long gone are the days of "*How much is that car?*" "*What do you want for yours?*" and similar routines. Would you even enter a restaurant that had an unpriced menu in the window? Would you take a book to the cash counter and say you'd take it without looking at the price first?

The Customer Expects that Your Premises Will Be Clean, Neat and Tidy

That there won't be crisp packets blowing in the wind, overflowing bins, weeds growing up showroom walls, flat tyres, seagull splats trailing down paintwork, lack of lustre bodywork or murky windows.

The Customer Expects the Door to the Showroom will be Easy to Locate and Easy to Open

How's your door? Not sure? Go on – give it a tug.

There is a franchised garage that I called at once – and only once. The problem was the door. I had genuinely called to see a model that had just been launched. Could I get the showroom door open? I could not! I tried everything, but it stuck firm. Then I noticed two things:

1 There was a salesman inside the showroom who was having hysterics because I could not open the door.
2 There was a little sign on the door that said '*Please use the side door during hours of business*'.

I didn't use the side door; I did not do business and neither did they with me that day – or any day. The nicest doors to do business with are those electric doors. Just as you walk up to them they glide open seductively and you find yourself inside the showroom. Then they quietly hiss together behind you. The doors don't have to be electric. They do have to be easy to enter. Otherwise you will lose the business.

Customers Expect to Walk into a Friendly and Non-Threatening Atmosphere

How's your atmosphere? Do you have some? Can you get some more? Particularly the friendly, non-threatening kind. What exactly is 'atmosphere' anyway? It's the feeling you get when you enter an area. It could be cold and threatening or it could be warm and welcoming. The kind of atmosphere that you want and the customer expects is a combination of the correct environment blended with the right people.

A little bit of space as the customer enters will help. A short window of time, for them to adjust to their new environment before anybody approaches them, will certainly make them feel more comfortable. Some form of order or plan should be evident. Corporate identity or careful use of colours, textures and lighting will all create a pleasing atmosphere even before the customer gets to talk to someone.

The people who inhabit the showroom should also be friendly and non-threatening, wearing smiles not scowls, sensible clothes, not extremes of fashion, talking in pleasant tones, not grumpy or impatient. Where is this paradise you say? Why, it should be your showroom.

Customers Expect to be Greeted Warmly in a Helpful Fashion

They do, they do! It makes such a wonderful difference, especially if they feel a bit down themselves.

Two days before I wrote the above words, I was in a supermarket at the delicatessen counter waiting for number 94 to be called.

"Ninety-four," one of the ladies called.
"That's me!" I answered with glee.
"What do you want?" she growled.
"Six ounces of your Milano Salami," I replied.
"Thick or thin?" she barked.
"Thin," I said with a pleasant smile.

She sliced the salami, weighed it and told me the price with a sour look on her face. I thanked her, took the salami and put in into my basket. When the lady had asked if there was anything else I wanted. I just smiled sweetly and said: *"No thank you."* I was tempted to say: *"I suppose a smile would be out of the question?"* That would not have helped her any and it would not have done too much for me either.

What the poor lady was probably suffering from was a 'negative thought virus'. It is more likely that you have heard of a computer virus and have a rough idea what that is. A 'negative thought virus' is a similar thing but it affects your built-in computer, your brain.

This is how you get them.

It normally starts with a 'negative emotional experience', such as somebody telling you off, or being rude to you, or even you telling someone else off. Feelings such as road rage, guilt, anger and fear can all cause negative emotional experiences which, in turn, will create thought viruses every time you remember the original incident, either consciously or unconsciously.

Say, for instance, that our supermarket salami lady once got food poisoning from eating Milano Salami. Just the name of the product would be enough to send her back into a negative emotional state. Perhaps she was once threatened with physical violence by a Milano Salami wielding shoplifter. That too would trigger a negative emotional state every time she saw the product or heard the name. It would not be necessary for her to remember the original incident consciously. Her unconscious is more than capable of doing that for her.

Thought viruses are deadly to customer-facing people. It is very difficult to greet customers in a warm and helpful fashion if you've got one going at the moment you meet them.

How to Eliminate a Negative Thought Virus

Try this simple technique if ever you are feeling a bit down:

Notice Your Body Posture

How you feel is reflected in the way you sit or stand. People who feel fed up hang their heads, look miserable, droop their shoulders and look downwards.

Now Change Your Body Posture

Raise your head. Look happy. Straighten your shoulders and look straight ahead or upwards.

Notice Your Feelings Now

How you sit or stand, how you hold your head, how you look, how you hold your shoulders and where you look effects the way you feel.

> You can't feel fed up and look happy
> You can't look happy and feel fed up
> ...And that's a fact.

Do not think that this is not a quick fix that can really work well for you, but if you constantly find yourself deep in negative feelings, then some other technique might be more beneficial.

A doctor friend, Andrea Kingston, told me about this patient who called to see her. This lady had such a strong negative thought virus that it was stopping her from sleeping at night. Andrea asked the patient what exactly caused the problem. After some discussion it was established that she was hearing her own voice inside her head, a cross kind of voice nagging at her.

The doctor asked: "*What would happen if you changed the voice into a kind, friendly voice?*" The patient said she didn't know, and tried it out there and then. She immediately fell into a deep and peaceful sleep in the surgery chair for 20 minutes.

Just Why is Matching Customer Expectations So Important?

There are several very good reasons and many plain good ones. Customers' expectations are their concepts of reality. This is not necessarily fair, but it is how customers make their judgements.

Tom Peters, the American business guru, once said: "*Coffee stains on flip-down trays in aircraft mean that you have not done your engine maintenance right.*" Of course, this is highly unlikely to be true, but that's how customers make their judgements.

More than a few vehicle customers have said: "*Grease smears on steering wheels mean that you have not serviced the car properly.*" This, again, is not fair, but that's how customers make their judgements.

After a few disappointments, most customers have realised that their expectations are not going to be realised. A recent survey indicated that 95% of companies deliver their product or service late, which means that customers:

- No longer expect the plumber to turn up on time
- No longer expect there won't be a queue at the post office
- No longer expect to be treated in a cheerful and helpful fashion

The trouble is that even though you no longer expect it, it does not make it any better when it happens. Oh, but when they don't expect it to happen and it does, then the giver of good service will shine out like a beacon on a dark night.

It is the providers of prompt attention, a ready smile and a genuine willingness to assist from the very start that get more than what would be their fair share of business in today's fickle marketplace.

The main points again

1 What customers expect and what customers get can be a totally different experience.

2 Customers expect:

- To be able to find your business easily.
- To be able to park without difficulty.
- To find the person they want to talk to easily.
- That new and used vehicle displays will look like displays of vehicles for sale.
- That all vehicles will be priced for sale.
- That your premises will be clean, neat and tidy.
- That the door to the showroom will be easy to locate and open.
- To walk into a friendly and non-threatening atmosphere.
- To be greeted warmly, in a helpful fashion.

3 Why matching customer expectations is important:

- Customers' expectations are their concepts of reality.
- This is not necessarily fair, but that's how customers make their judgements.
- Most customers have realised that their expectations are not going to be realised. This does not make it any better for the customer when it happens.
- When customers' expectations are met, the giver of good service will shine out like a beacon on a dark night.
- Striving to meet customers' expectations will win business in today's fickle marketplace.

CHAPTER 7

Rapport and Opening Sales Relationships

"Rapport happens when you meet
someone else in their model of the world,
or they meet you in yours,
or you both find the same model
of the world at the same time"

Rapport is the naturally occurring 'dance' that happens when two people meet. One of the leading experts regarding rapport skills is Dr Willie Monteiro, a brilliant teacher with whom I have had the privilege to work on several occasions. Not only does Willie teach rapport, he personifies rapport. He does this very easily and naturally. There are many stories about his extraordinary abilities. This is the one that illustrates his rapport skills best.

Dr Willie was caught up in the early evening rush-hour traffic that populates the lower end of Park Lane in London. He inched his way forward, gradually moving closer to Hyde Park Corner in his badly battered, elderly vehicle. When he finally reached the roundabout, he was on the inside lane behind a brand new, large shiny Ford.

The Ford was waiting for a gap in the traffic, and Willie waited behind with his usual patience. The Ford started to move, and Willie noticed that the gap they had been waiting for was about to happen. Willie started to move forward too, ready to roll out and follow the Ford. The Ford was moving quicker now as the gap approached. Willie, with one eye on the Ford and his other on the gap, stayed close-in behind. The Ford accelerated suddenly, and so did Willie. As Willie cast one last look to check the gap, the Ford braked suddenly and viciously.

It is so easy to do, and Willie did it. He hit the Ford with more than a gentle nudge but less than a heavy blow. The damage would be minor, Willie thought, as a very large and angry man leaped from the Ford and menacingly moved towards Willie who was still sitting in his vehicle.

*"Come out of there you little *?!&*, I am going to knock your *?*@!? head off your #?!@*$ shoulders."*

The Ford man was furious and his anger was all channelled directly at Willie. He was reaching with one hand to open Willie's door. His other hand was already clenched and held back in readiness to convert the threat into a promise.

Willie moved fast. Before the Ford man could open Willie's door, Willie did so and sprang through it. He faced his tormentor square on, matching his stance, with one hand forward the other held back. Willie's face was wearing the same anger as the Ford man's face, with slit eyes and flared nostrils. The only difference between them was the ten inches of height and the width of the Ford man's shoulders.

This all happened at incredible speed, and before the Ford man could take another breath, let alone carry on with his threat, Willie was talking. Well, not talking exactly. He was shouting at almost the same level that the Ford man had been doing.

Willie glared at the man as he bellowed: "*I've just got one thing to say to you, this is all my fault, and I will be paying for this damage.*" The Ford man's jaw dropped and his fist unclenched and he said: "*Well, that's all right then.*"

...And it was.

Rapport is Natural

Rapport is natural – people do it all the time. Look around you and start noticing what most people never see. Or, as Meg Ryan told Tom Hanks in the film *Joe versus the Volcano:*

"Only a few people are awake, and they live their lives in a state of constant amazement..."

Only a few salespeople are 'great'. Without exception, every great salesperson has the ability to create a high level of rapport with customers.

So, apart from being some kind of natural dance, what exactly is rapport? What will it do for you and how can you get it?

Rapport is...

What makes you feel comfortable with some people and not with others. You feel that you are in harmony in some way with someone else.

This harmony, in turn, creates a sense of acknowledgement, some form of mutual respect.

The reasons for the rapport that exists between people are normally outside of conscious awareness. In other words, you've got rapport, but you don't know why. For example:

A delegate on a sales training course once asked me: *"Why is it that when one person you don't know bumps into you in a pub and spills your beer your want to kill him yet some other bloke who you don't know does the same and you don't mind at all?"*

The answer is, of course, rapport. Now, this is the interesting bit.

You Can Create Rapport Consciously

There's a thought! If you get good at creating rapport with customers, you might get better at selling. That's what it will do for you. So that just leaves: '*How can I get it?*'

Getting Rapport

There are a number of levels and ways you can do this, normally by matching the other person – for instance:

- Body posture
- Arm movements
- Energy level
- Facial expressions
- Verbally
- Rate of breathing

Get to grips with these six and you will suddenly find that selling starts to be more fun, as well as more profitable. So let's explore them one at a time.

Body Posture

You can see unconscious examples of this all the time. People often do quite naturally adopt the body posture of the person that they are talking to. Couples in love in restaurants, for instance. There they sit, the mirror image of each other, oblivious to the world around them. Resting their heads on their hands, both leaning forward in deep conversation.

Or watch two elderly people sitting on a park bench having a conversation. They will quite often sit the same way, even though they are side by side. Heads nodding in agreement and harmony like two puppets on the same string.

Try it yourself sometime. The next time you are talking to someone, adopt their body posture.

- If you're sitting, sit as they sit
- If you're standing, stand as they stand

You will be very conscious of what you are doing, but the other person won't. Unless, of course, you match with too much enthusiasm!

Arm Movements

People often talk with gestures. Try matching arm movements using a mirror image. If the person you are talking to uses the right hand, then you should use your left. The reason for this is that the person opposite you will unconsciously see a reflection of themselves – and that's rapport. You don't have to match exaggerated movements, a gentle reflection will do quite nicely.

I was once talking to a customer, sitting across a desk enjoying the cup of coffee that he had offered me. This customer used very grand gestures. In an effort to match him in my newly acquired skill, I caught the cup of coffee square-on in mid-sweep and sent it soaring from his desk, clear over his shoulder where it smashed and splashed on the wall behind him. We both got a nasty shock, but I still managed to get the order!

Energy Level

We will explore more fully the possibilities of matching energy levels in the meeting and greeting chapter in the section *Getting Into Step*. It is a contributory factor in sales success. Great salespeople do this; most of them don't know that they are doing it.

Facial Expressions

Salespeople have used positive head nods for donkeys years. "*Would you like this?*" Nod, nod. "*Would you like that?*" nod, nod.

There are many ways to match at face level, apart from nodding your head. It's fine to raise eyebrows with a customer, share a smile or two. It's most acceptable to share expressions of interest or enthusiasm. The grave danger that faces salespeople is a mis-match situation, when the customer says something that the salesperson does not like. You see, your customer is already an unconscious expert in body language – we all are.

Sidney Rosen records a 'teaching tale' of Milton H Erickson in his book *My Voice Will Go With You.*

"When a six-month old baby who is being fed Pabulum looks at its mother's face and its mother is thinking 'that horrible stuff – it just stinks', the baby reads the headlines on the mother's face and spits it out."

Verbal Rapport

There are so many ways that you can verbally match your customers.

A great way to gain verbal rapport with customers is to match volume, speed of delivery and any key 'buzzwords'. This works very well unless it sounds like you are trying to mimic someone. Problems can also arise if you try to match regional accents. Rapport is all about being in harmony with your customer.

On one occasion, I was in Yorkshire with a colleague, talking to a couple of potential customers. We had dinner together to discuss the possibility of doing some business. The customer who did most of the talking was a large man with a big voice, my colleague who did most of the listening was a smaller man with a smaller voice.

By the time we had got on to the main course, my colleague had started to match the customer in most of the ways mentioned here. Suddenly the large customer turned to his quieter colleague and boomed: *"Do you know, Harold, this lad here speaks our language. Let's do some business"*.

...And we did.

Rate of Breathing

One of the least known and most powerful methods of creating rapport is to match the breathing of the person you are talking to. Richard Bandler and John Grinder, the founders of NLP, did much to develop these kinds of techniques over the past 20 years.

In their magical book *'Frogs into Princesses'* there is a report of a visit that one of them made to the Napu State Mental Hospital in California.

Apparently there was a catatonic who had been sitting on a couch in a day room for several years. A catatonic is a person who is in a type of coma where you cannot see, hear, feel, smell or taste. You are alive but do not move. You just stay in the same position that you are put in. But even a catatonic has to breathe. So Richard Bandler or John Grinder (the book does not say which one) decided to match the catatonic's breathing rate and body position. This was done for 40 minutes. When little variants in breathing where tried, the catatonic followed. This indicated that some level of rapport had been established. The catatonic could have been brought out of the condition by varying the breathing rate over a period of time. Instead the rapport was interupted as Richard (or John) shouted: *"Hey, do you have a cigarette?"*

The catatonic jumped off the couch and said: *"God, don't do that!"*

It is most unlikely that you will ever have to work to this level in relation to the sale of a vehicle. However, if you do match other people's breathing at the right time and in the right way, you too will be able to do magic.

For instance...

When you first meet, if your customer is breathing fast through 'fear of the unknown' or because they have been rushing, match their breathing for a while and then start to slow down. They will normally take your 'lead' and slow down with you.

Towards the end of the sales process, if your customer is trying to make the decision whether to go ahead or not, that too would be a good time to 'breathe in harmony' – it might just make the difference between a sale and a fail.

The main points again

1. Rapport is natural. People do it all the time.
2. Every great salesperson has the ability to create a high level of rapport.
3. Rapport is that feeling of being in harmony with someone else.
4. The reasons for rapport are usually unconscious.
5. However, you can create rapport consciously through:

- Body posture
- Arm movement
- Energy levels
- Facial expressions
- Verbally
- Rate of breathing

6. Good rapport is created by using the same language as our customers.
7. Matching a person's rate of breathing can be a powerful way of creating rapport.

SECTION FOUR

Getting Into Step

"Right in the middle of a full look they would feel a gentle pressure on their shoulder."

CHAPTER 8
Meeting and Greeting

"You will never get a second chance to make a good first impression"

The General was very tall and very smart. You would know the instant he approached you that he was a military man. The trouble was that you never saw him coming.

On his showroom duty days, the General could be found idling in one of the dimmer corners of the showroom. He had the chameleon-like ability to blend in with the background. You would never see him unless you knew he was there. The General would watch and wait, with one eye on the front door of the showroom and the other eye checking everything else – the vehicles on display, the desks, the tapestry on the wall, the flowers, people, plate glass windows and the marble floor. He did not miss much at all.

If a person walked through the showroom door, started to look at the stock and then settled on one particular vehicle, they would meet the General. Initially they would not see him and they would not hear him, but they would feel him. Right in the middle of full look they would feel a gentle pressure on their shoulder. They would start and spin round. Their eyes would re-focus up a foot to find the face of the person who had touched them.

I watched this technique on many occasions. What actually happened was this: when the door-checking eye spotted a person entering the showroom, the other roving eye stopped meandering and joined its companion gazing doorwards. The General would grow three inches and take a good look, doing a dead ringer of a plain prairie dog standing on hind legs. He would then shrink a foot or more as he adopted the slight crouching stance of a yesteryear Olympic athlete. He was now primed and ready to fire.

The General, as still as a statue, would wait for the person to settle. As soon as this happened he would glide forward as silently as a silver ghost. Part of the secret was the size eleven crepe soled suede boots the General always wore at work. In next to no time he would be directly behind his target. He never spoke. His hand would just reach forward and rest on the settler's shoulder.

The next part was always the same. The spinning settler would find the General's face and say: *"I was just looking at this Rolls!"* in a very hard-to-describe kind of voice. (Do you remember what it was like when you were just a kid and your mum caught you with your hand in the biscuit tin?) The General would just look for a moment and then he would say, quietly and authoritatively: *"Have you got the money?"*

If the person said yes, the General, without changing expression, volume or tone would say: *"You had better come to my office then."* If the person said no, the General would narrow his eyes, say: *"Humph"*, turn slowly away and ghost back into the shadows surrounding the showroom floor.

Dylan had a different approach: he looked different too. Originally he hailed from one of the Carolinas. This explained the stetson and the high stacked heels on his hand-tooled boots. I got to know Dylan on the island of Guam in the West Pacific when I was running a sales training programme for his company.

Dylan was extremely successful both at opening relationships and at getting the orders signed, even though some of his techniques were a little unorthodox. For instance, he told me that he had taken a saw to the two front legs of his desk and had shortened them by a good inch or more. This gave his desk a gravitational bias towards the customer facing side. When he decided that it was order-signing time, he would write out the order, turn it round, reconfirm the purchase price or the cost to change and ask the customer to go ahead and sign.

As Dylan did this he would place his pen down (on top of the order form) and it would immediately start to roll towards the customer. The customer would have to grab it to stop it falling to the floor. There was the customer, there was the order form and there was the pen in the customer's hand. And that made sense to Dylan.

I was carrying out some showroom follow-up visits after the sales courses had been completed. One such call was to the showroom where Dylan was based. I walked through the door and spotted Dylan sitting at the desk at the back. Boots up on the desk, stetson on the back of the head, can of coke in his hand. *"Hi Dave,"* he said, *"have a chair and a coke and come and visit me."* I gratefully accepted his offer: the West Pacific can be very humid, even in May.

Dylan reached behind him and fished a can of coke out of the icebox behind him and placed it on his desk on its side. It rolled towards me and I grabbed it, pen-like, before it hit the floor and popped the tab. We talked a little about the course, about the fishing and the state of the used vehicle stock. Just light conversation, really, both relaxed and enjoying each other's company. Then, very suddenly, without warning, Dylan's feet left the desk, the coke can hit the desk and the hat just vanished. He shot to his feet, his whole face smiled as he moved cat-like towards the showroom door, right hand extended.

"*Hi there folks. Now just how can I help you good people buy a vehicle today?*"

...And he did.

Lost Sales

More sales are lost at meeting and greeting time than at any other time in the sales process. Most of us have long realised that it can take many hours to sell one vehicle, or it could take a matter of moments. What many salespeople fail to grasp is that it takes less than five minutes to lose a sale. Consider again customer expectations. If customers do not get what they expect at meeting and greeting stage, the chances of doing business are dramatically reduced.

There are many reasons for this but here are five well worth considering.

1 The Vehicle Buying Process

By the time customers get face-to-face with you, they have already reached step five of the nine-step vehicle-buying process.

2 The Promise of Advertising

Both national manufacturer and local franchised dealer advertisements often illustrate or promise a good experience when buying a vehicle.

3 Need to be Taken Seriously

If the seller does not recognise the buyer as a genuine customer, then in turn the buyer will not take the seller as a genuine salesperson.

4 The Four-Minute Rule

Potential customers, the same as most people, make a decision to carry on or not with a conversation with someone they don't know within four minutes. This is just plain simple human nature.

5 Confused Customers

Some customers like instant attention – others like to have some time and space to get used to your premises. Confuse the two and you will confuse the customer.

Let us now consider all of these five sale-losing reasons to make sure that we don't lose sales that are, in reality, already won.

The Vehicle Buying Process

Logically broken down into nine separate but linked steps

Step 1 – Franchise Awareness

Many potential customers become aware of the make before the model, as in:

"Mavis has just got a Renault."
"I hear that Proton offer a lot of car for the money."

Step 2 – Model Awareness

Having become aware that there is a particular make of vehicle, potential customers start to identify with models in that franchise.

"That Suzuki I was talking about was a Vitara."
"It's the Rover 626 that really interests me."

Step 3 – Inclusion on 'Shopping List'

Most customers have a shortlist of vehicles that they will choose from. The millions that manufacturers spend on marketing are aimed primarily to get more customers to put their product on that 'shopping list'.

"What about the new Lantra?"
"I would like to look at the QX before we make up our minds."

Step 4 – Dealer Awareness

Having decided to look at a particular make of vehicle, the potential customer has to identify where to see it.

"George – you have a Citroen. Do you know where the local dealer is?"
"I think the Saab dealer's down by the main roundabout."

Step 5 – Dealer Enquiry

This is where you come in – get it wrong and sales can be lost even before they are founded. The customer has already been through:

- Franchised awareness
- Model awareness
- Inclusion on shopping list
- Dealer awareness

Sales can often be lost for quite infantile reasons: an off-hand greeting, a slow greeting or no greeting at all.

Step 6 – The Sales and Negotiation Process

Having got over the five preceding hurdles, the selling process can truly begin. This can be completed during one visit or it could involve several contacts between buyer and seller.

Step 7 – Sale or Fail

There are only two possible outcomes from the sales and negotiations process.

- Sale – the customer has bought
- Fail – the customer has not bought

Step 8 – Customer or Prospect Follow-up

Customers who buy have to take delivery of what they have bought. There should then be some form of follow-up after the sale. Prospects who don't buy should also be followed up, not necessarily 'until they buy or die', but each according to their needs and the chances of doing business at some time.

Step 9 – Repeat Business or Lost Customer

Customers who enjoy what they have bought and how they purchased it will be more likely to want to repeat the experience. Customers who did not buy and did not enjoy the purchase process are very unlikely to want to try the same experience again.

The Promise of Advertising

Advertisements often show a rosy side to the sales process. Most advertisements make the customer look forward to the vehicle-buying trip. If the reality does not match up to the dream at face-to-face-with-dealer time, then sales are lost. The closer you can live to the promise of advertising and other marketing efforts, the more customers' dreams you will convert into signed orders.

A Need to be Taken Seriously

Most people who walk through your showroom door are in fact serious. Very few are a total waste of time. Even the most experienced salesperson is prone to error when assessing the likelihood of the person approaching to be a genuine customer. There comes a point in some salespeople's selling careers when they become an expert at judging which customers to take seriously by just looking at them. This profound knowledge and wisdom normally happens at around three weeks into the job.

What these salespeople are relying on is what most of us refer to as a 'gut feeling', which is an unconscious recognition of something that they have seen, heard or felt before. Or it could be what they 'think' they remember. These gut feelings do have some good uses, in all kinds of situations. Assessing which customers are the ones to take seriously even before you speak to them is not one of them.

Take as an illustration the following example.

You are standing in the showroom looking at a new model that your franchise has just brought out. You hear the showroom door open and you turn to notice that a man has just entered. You also notice that he has parked his elderly and somewhat tired-looking car outside. What you hear consciously in your mind is a voice telling you: *"This customer is not a buyer"*.

What you see unconsciously in your mind is something similar to the following:

- The person that has just entered the showroom has a sour-looking face and will not establish eye contact with me.
- The car he is driving is elderly and tired.
- He is wearing dirty down-at-the-heel brown brogue shoes and tatty trousers with turn-ups.
- Now he has folded his arms as he turns towards me.

- Now I can see that he has cut himself whilst shaving this morning.
- Gosh – his tie is dreadful!

Plus many other feelings that cannot be expressed consciously in words or feelings.

Now that's the information that generates your gut feeling. Your eyes have analysed a whole mass of information without you even realising it. Most of the information is correct. Unfortunately, we can all interpret this information incorrectly.

This Man Is In Fact a Customer

- *"He has a sour look."*

Because he is suffering with a back pain.

- *"He will not establish eye contact."*

Because he has not seen you yet.

- *"The car he is driving is elderly and tired."*

Because it is not his car – it is his son's car.

- *"He is wearing dirty down-at-the-heel brown brogue shoes and tatty trousers with turn-ups."*

Because he has just finished planting a new rose-bed (hence the back pain).

- *"He has folded his arms as he turns towards you."*

Because he has unconsciously noticed the look of apprehension on your face.

You can guess the rest! The customer gets a sudden gut feeling that he is not going to take to you very much, let alone buy that new model from you.

What Have You Done?

You have created a non-buyer out of a serious customer because your unconscious has informed you that past experience indicates that customers:

Who have sour looking faces
Who will not establish eye contact with you
Who drive elderly and tired cars
Who wear dirty down-at-the-heel brown brogue shoes and tatty trousers with turn-ups
Who fold their arms when they turn towards you
Who wear dreadful ties!

– do not buy cars!

What You Should Do

There is only one thing you need to do to avoid the risk of not taking a serious customer seriously and that is:

To see everything and believe nothing until you have checked it out.

The Four-Minute Rule

It is an established fact that most of us decide another person is worth talking to within the first four minutes of conversation. This rule applies equally to business and social occasions. By 'worth talking to' we are considering 'what we are going to get from this dialogue'. In order not to fall foul of the four-minute rule in a showroom enquiry situation, certain things have to happen.

The salesperson must take the customer and the enquiry seriously:

- Approach and greet the customer
- Live up to the promise of advertising
- Match in some way each and every customer's expectation
- Give the customer full attention

The customer must take the salesperson seriously:

- Feel comfortable with the approach and greeting
- See some resemblances between the enquiry experience and the promise of advertising
- Recognise that the salesperson is giving the customer full attention

The achievement of all these outcomes is the responsibility of the salesperson – not the customer.

Confused Customers

To approach or not to approach, that is the confusion. When people go into a strange place for the very first time, most need a little time to adjust to the new environment. There are a few people who know what they want before they enter a showroom and would prefer to be dealt with immediately.

The salesperson should make the decision how quickly to approach by looking at the customer's eyes.

- A customer who shuffles in quietly with downcast eyes should be given time to adjust.
- A customer who marches in looking neither right or left, with total attention on a particular vehicle, should also be given some time.
- Customers who gaze around aimlessly probably also need some time to settle.
- Customers who look at or for the salesperson and not at the product – now they are the ones to approach quickly, and that's the clue.
- If they don't look at or for a salesperson, give them time and space.
- If they do look at or for a salesperson, give them full attention as soon as possible.

Back-up Needed

Sometimes showrooms get busy and there isn't anybody to approach a new customer. These customers have to be acknowledged at the very least. By:

- Eye contact
- A nod of the head
- Hand movement

Some form of back-up system is recommended to take care of this customer-confusing situation, irrespective of the size of your business. There should always be someone else capable of carrying out a meeting and greeting. Someone who can keep a customer 'warm' until a salesperson is available. Someone who will get follow-up information if a customer cannot wait to be seen.

The Approach

So what's the best way to approach a customer? Should you be enthusiastic? I saw that happen once. We had all been on a weekend sales course – an American style evangelist affair. *"Always be enthusiastic,"* our guru beamed at us with tremendous enthusiasm. *"Heaven help the customers on Monday,"* I thought.

Mike got the first one. He actually ran across the showroom to get to him. Hand held out and a great big welcoming smile. He grabbed the customer's hand with both of his and pumped it up and down like a village pump. *"Welcome to BMW,"* Mike enthused at the startled customer, continuing the pumping action. The customer leapt back as though he had been stung. *"What have I won?"* he asked with a surprised voice.

Let's face it, if you are with a customer who is a bit down in the dumps, the last thing that person wants is to have a conversation with a fireball. Conversely, if your customer is very enthusiastic and full of the joys of spring, you are not going to hit it off if you had a very heavy night last night!

Just notice the energy and mood of the customer and reflect it back in your own energy and mood – that's rapport.

- Match happy with happy
- Match fast with fast
- Match slow with slow
- Match peaceful with peaceful
- Match busy with busy… and so on
- An enthusiastic fast-moving customer should be approached quickly and enthusiastically, a sombre slow-moving customer should be approached sombrely and slowly. And, all the other shades in between. If you have never thought of it, let alone tried it, then you should. You could very well enjoy it. What's more important, so will your customers.

"Just a minute, I was once told that it was important to be yourself when dealing with customers…"

It's true, you should be yourself. However, there are occasions when matching a customer's mood and speed will certainly help you open a good relationship.

Greeting Customers

'Can I help you?' and its relation, *'How can I help you?'*, can quite often create the response *'Can I just have a look around?'*

It could be that the salesperson was a little too fast and the customer genuinely would appreciate a little more time to feel comfortable. It could be that that really is what the customer wants, just to look around. Tell the customer *"That's fine"* and *"Please feel free to look around"*. Also, give the customer a business card and offer to help the customer if there are any queries or questions at any stage.

Business Cards

Since the subject has come up, let's deal with it now.

A card with the previous salesperson's name crossed or tippexed out and the new salesperson's name added in ink is just not good enough because it destroys the promises of quality and continuity. The same applies to business cards that just have a space on the card for someone to add their name after 'presented by'.

So What Should I Say?

You can usually avoid 'Can I just have a look around?' answers if you stop using 'Can I help you?' and 'How can I help you?' A good opener is to make a positive comment about the vehicle the customer has arrived in. You get the customer's attention because you have shown interest.

Again, it is very much a matter of matching your customer. A quiet customer would find a gentle *'Good morning'* most acceptable. A jovial customer would be likely to find *'Now then, you look like a genuine customer to me!'* more interesting.

A purposeful-looking customer who obviously wants to talk rather than look would appreciate a more direct *'How can I help you buy a vehicle today?'* A person who looks like they want to look around would really appreciate *'Good morning, please feel free to look around. I will be over there when you need help.'*

In the last case, it is vital to re-approach the customer within a few minutes if he has not come to you first.

Dealing with Families

More and more families are coming out to buy a vehicle. Is your business geared up to cater for all the people? Seating areas with hot drinks for the adults, cold drinks and distractions for the kids? Some companies now have children's play areas or someone who is available to look after children. It depends on both the need and the size of your business.

One small business I called at had a compact seating area complete with television and video player and a selection of children's videos to choose from. This proved very successful and allowed the salesperson to get on with helping parents buy without them having to worry what little Cuthbert or Camilla was up to.

Names

- Do get your customer's name as soon as you start the conversation
- Do give your customer your business card with your name on it
- Do wear a quality name badge to save your customer the trouble of remembering your name (they normally don't anyway)
- Do take the trouble to remember your customer's name and use it from time to time.

The best way to remember a customer's name is to write it down if you can. It also helps if you can make a mental picture that represents the customer's name. The sillier or funnier the better. Examples that spring to mind from the selling past include:

Mr Foster	Turned into a mind picture of four stars
Mr Samways	A man called Sam sitting on some scales
Mr Thompson	Tom Tom – the piper's son
Mrs Massie-Blomfield	A great big 'E' blooming in a field like a flower

Silly? Yes but it makes remembering names so much easier.

What's in a Name?

Selling in different parts of the country can be different. This makes it difficult to give firm guidelines on how to address your customers.
Generally, when you ask a customer for his name:

If he replies *"It's Mr Rowlands"*, then call him Mr Rowlands.
If he replies *"It's Steve"*, then call him Steve.
If he replies *"It's Steve Rowlands"*, then take your choice. If in doubt, use the surname, Mr Rowlands.

The main points again

1 It takes less than five minutes to lose a sale.

2 If customers' expectations are not met, then the chances of doing business are dramatically reduced.

3 Customers who have decided to put your product on their 'shopping list' need to be taken seriously.

4 The closer you can live up to the promise of advertising, the more customer dreams you will convert into signed orders.

5 When you first meet a customer you would be well advised to see everything and believe nothing until you have checked it out.

6 Different customers need to be approached and greeted differently. Matching customers' moods and movement can assist a smooth beginning.

7 Help should be available in busy periods to keep customers 'warm' and/or get follow-up information.

8 Quality business cards will match up to the promise of quality and continuity.

9 Obtain, remember and use customers' names.

CHAPTER 9
Qualification

"The quality of your qualification of a customer's needs and wants is exactly equal to the quality of the qualification questions you ask"

There is the old story about the salesman who visited a Wiltshire farmer who was sitting quietly in his farmhouse kitchen in his chair by his fire with his pipe in his hand and his Border Collie at his feet. *"That's a nice dog you've got there,"* said the salesman. The old Wiltshire farmer took a long pull at his pipe, gave the salesman a quizzical look and said: *"Now tell me something I don't know."*

Have you ever told a customer something that he already knows and been a recipient of that quizzical look? Have you ever said: *"I'm afraid that your trade-in isn't a very desirable vehicle"* or *"They're very hard to get hold of at the moment"*? I experienced this frustrating phenomenon when first moving down to the West Country, some years ago. At that time there were more buyers for houses than there were houses to be bought. Everybody looking to buy a house at that time would know this.

I did the usual round of Bath city estate agents, At one I waited patiently and politely while the only person in the office finished his call fixing up a squash match. He eventually tore himself away and condescended to talk to me. *"How can I be of assistance to you?"* he sniffed at me. You know the type.

I told the nose lifter what I was looking for. Nothing that difficult – three bedrooms, space for two vehicles, an old or new property. I added the fact that, for the first time in my life, I would love to own a house that I could walk all the way round instead of a semi or something in a terrace. But getting a house was more important than something you could walk around.

"There aren't many of those on the market you know," he sniffed again. *"I only want*

one," I replied, trying not to let the edge of my voice curl ever so slightly to indicate my growing negative emotions towards this person and his company, while hoping he lost his squash game. *"Oh very well, I'll have a look then."* He had, in fact, five or six on his books that could have suited my needs.

Luckily I found something even more suitable with his competition down the road. A nice place, with nice people, who didn't tell me things I knew. *"I would like to do business with these people,"* I thought.

...And I did.

Believing in your product and company

Qualification is definitely the most neglected step in the sales process. The better you are at it, the more successful you will be. Subject to two conditions:

- You must believe in your product
- You must believe in the company you work for

If you do not believe in what you sell and the company you work for, your customer will know. You can sell products that you don't like for a company that you don't enjoy working for, but neither you nor your customers will get much enjoyment from the sales process. Sebastian was such a salesman. He had just sold enough to qualify to be a member of the manufacturer's Sales Guild. A special invitation was sent to him, direct to his home, inviting him to come as an honoured guest to the annual dinner.

When the training manager of the manufacturer asked Sebastian what had happened to prevent him from attending, Sebastian didn't even know what the training manager was talking about. As the story unfolded, it became apparent that Sebastian never opened any mail sent to his home with the manufacturer's logo on it. *"Never have, never will,"* he said. *"I have to put up with them all day most days,"* he added, *"I certainly don't have to put up with them when I get home, because that's my time and I can do what I want."*

To be fair to Sebastian, he did plenty of useful and interesting things in 'his time'. It's a shame that he did not find his full-time employment useful and interesting. You could see it in his eyes (even more so in the down-turned corners of his mouth) and so could his customers. In today's competitive marketplace, buyers want to buy from sellers they feel they can trust. Competent salespeople. Salespeople who believe in themselves and what they are doing. Congruent salespeople whose body language reflects that this is so.

Why People Buy

People do not buy products: they buy what the product will do for them. The whole point behind the qualification process is to find out exactly what benefits the customer is looking for. The benefit to you, the seller of the product, is that through correct and careful qualification, you will understand two things:

- What the customers want
- How you can help the customers get what they want

Selling today is both a science and an art. The science is to find out what the customers want. The art is to help them get it – preferably from you and your company.

The Reasons for Buying

Different customers have different reasons why they want or need a particular product. There could in fact be several reasons; normally there is one prime reason for buying. This is more than likely one of the following.

Prime Reason	Example of Customer Benefit
1 Ego/Status	*"I want to look important"*
2 Fear/Safety	*"I don't want to break down"*
3 Money	*"I want to save some money"*
4 Love	*"This is for my family"*
5 Imitation	*"I want one because he has one"*
6 Recreation	*"I just want to enjoy it"*
7 Dream Fulfilment	*"I have always wanted one"*

1 Ego/Status Customers

"I want to look important"

Ego/status buyers are not difficult to spot. They want the best they can afford, they want the 'right' extras, they want the 'right' colour. Ego/status buyers can be difficult to sell to. If you haven't got exactly what they want, they probably will not do business with you. Worse than that, if you have what they want but question why they want it, then you will certainly lose sales.

I once called in to a showroom to order a vehicle. I knew exactly what I wanted. A salesman approached me in the showroom and we started to talk about what I wanted. *"Oh, I'll tell you what I do want,"* I told him, *"I want a set of those wide alloy wheels – you know the ones – they have little bolts all around the rim."*

"Yes, we do those," he replied, *"but you don't want them."*

"What do you mean, I don't want them?" I asked with a puzzled voice. *"The vehicle runs much better on the standard rims,"* was his answer. I went off him at once, made an excuse and left the showroom.

I soon found another salesman in another showroom selling the same make of vehicle.

"I want a set of those wide alloy wheels with the little bolts all around the rim." (*"Here we go again,"* I thought.)

The salesman said: *"You obviously have a reason for wanting those particular wheels."*

"Yes," I said, *"I do. It's because they just make the vehicle look so good."*

"You're so right, Mr Upsher," he said with enthusiasm and considerable rapport. So I bought the wheels from him, complete with a vehicle to put them on.

Look, I know it's not fair, but this is how customers make their purchasing decisions – particularly the ego/status ones!

2 Fear/Safety Customers

"I don't want to break down"

People can be frightened that their present vehicle could let them down in some way. It could be that it already has, and the feeling develops: *"If it has let me down once, then it will probably do so again"*. Perhaps they have been involved in an accident and they are concerned that the vehicle will no longer perform in the same way. They could believe that the vehicle itself is unlucky. Fear and superstition can be very powerful motivations to buy or not to buy.

If you ever find yourself in Hong Kong, call into MD Motors on the Gloucester Road and notice the unusual clock behind the reception desk. Before the showroom could be opened, the Feng Shui man was called in to make sure that the place was free from bad spirits and to give it good fortune. He told the manager that this he could not do until a large wooden clock with a very loud tick was placed behind the reception desk.

The manager had no choice but to get one. If he didn't, nobody would want to work there. The clock was found, bought and positioned, and the Feng Shui man came back and gave his blessing. *"It is delightful now,"* he said. *"Everybody who comes here will have good luck."* As the manager was relating this story to me, the door of the showroom opened and a very good friend of mine who I had not met for nine years walked in. Neither of us knew that the other would be there in Hong Kong at that time. Perhaps it was just good luck.

Feng Shui (wind and water) is all about being in harmony with the physical and spiritual world. It is older than fortune cookies and is a very deep and strong belief indeed. When a large block of flats and offices was to be built by the side of a bay in Hong Kong, the Feng Shui man decreed that a large hole should be left in the middle of the structure. He explained that the new building would block the flight path of the dragons that liked to descend from the hills and visit the bay area in the evenings. The hole was left, as requested, and there has not been a single case of a dragon colliding with the building. Feng Shui is that powerful.

3 The Money Buyer

"I want to save some money"

Most money buyers want to save money. Sometimes they might want to spend some. Perhaps they have been told by their accountant to get rid of some. Much of today's dealer advertising is aimed at the money buyer.

- 0% finance over 24 months
- A minimum of £1,400 for your part-exchange
- Nothing to pay for six months
- Free insurance
- Free portable telephone

And so on...

You don't get much for nothing these days. Somebody has to pay for it. Normally the customer, one way or another. Special offers that give specific savings do attract all types of buyers to your showrooms. Having classified a customer as a 'money buyer', it would be sensible to find out during the qualification process what other reasons that customer has for buying. Saving money might just have been that extra motivation that 'massaged' another prime reason into action.

4 The Love Buyer

"This is for my family"

Love buyers are nice people to do business with. Often the prime reason is comfort and convenience for the family. They will often put their own desires second, to make sure that their vehicle is suitable for their family's needs. This can sometimes even include the dog *("If Toby likes it, then we will have it").*

If through your qualification you can identify a way for the love buyer to give the family what they need and at the same time give the love buyer some benefits, then you double your chances of making a sale.

5 The Imitation Buyer

"I want one because he has one"

Many makers of products endeavour to attract the imitation buyer through:

- The use of sporting personalities in advertisements for sports-related products.
- Top fashion models for beauty products.
- TV personalities for just about anything.

All are designed to appeal to the little bit of imitation buyer that lurks somewhere in most of us.

Another form of imitation buyer is the referral. *"George had a good experience when he bought his vehicle from you. Therefore, if I buy my vehicle from you, then I too will get a good experience."*

6 The Recreation Buyer

"I just want to enjoy it"

The vehicle, in fact, could be just an accessory to a pastime or hobby. A means to get the clubs and the clubbers from home to golf course. Motoring is not so joyful as it used to be. Even so, there are customers who do love driving. You can tell by the enthusiasm in their voice as they relate to you that they were stuck in a 70-mile traffic jam last bank holiday.

You can include people who tow things like caravans, boats and horse boxes in this category, but look for more than one prime reason why they want or need the vehicle.

7 Dream Fulfilment

"I have always wanted one"

There is a category of people who just decide that their total fulfilment in life will come from owning a desired object. It could be a Rolex watch, a suite of leather furniture or even a vehicle. This is very much an emotional purchase. If you find yourself face-to-face with a dream fulfiller, then it would pay you to find out – sooner rather than later – how the fulfilment will be funded!

Find Out the Reasons

All these are reasons why customers want or need a particular vehicle. Find out the reasons and you will know how to help people buy.

As qualification is such an important step on the sales ladder, let's take it apart and look at it piece by piece. Otherwise, when you get to the top, you could find that your sales ladder has been leaning away from the customers needs instead of towards them.

The Qualification Process – One Step at a Time

1. Qualify away from product
2. Sit down with the customer
3. Involve all the decision-makers
4. Ask open-ended questions to get information
5. Ask closed questions to clarify understanding
6. Make notes of what your customer tells you
7. Get the customer's name, address and telephone number
8. Summarise what the customer has told you
9. Tell the customer what you propose to do to help them buy

1 Qualify Away From Product

In the real world (wherever that is) you can't always qualify every customer away from the product. The point is, if you can, it will be more comfortable for both you and the customer. At this stage the product is a distraction and could create confusion. The danger is that before you know it, you are involved in presenting a product to customers when you don't know what they want.

Some salespeople try to blend qualification with presentation; sometimes you can get away with it, and no matter what you sell, sometimes you can't.

"So this is the vehicle, what do you like about it?"
"It's such a nice shape".
"You're right. That's because it's rear engined."
"Rear engined? Oh no, I would not want one of those."

"So, here's a picture of the style of windows I would recommend, Mrs Robinson."
"They're nice and they're double glazed, are they? I would want that."
"Absolutely. Apart from keeping your house warm as toast, they will cut out most external noise – you won't even hear the birds sing."
"Not hear the birds sing? I would not want that at all."

We really do need to get the customer away from the product to qualify needs and wants. Then and only then can we embark on the presentation stage.

2 Sit Down with the Customer

Like most things, there are right ways and wrong ways to do this. Let's start with the wrong.

Wrong Way 1 – Sitting down across a desk.

A desk is a barrier between two people. Unfortunately this style of layout is still prevalent in vehicle showrooms today. You don't need barriers between you and your customer during any stage of the sale.

Wrong Way 2 – Taking the customer to a sales office.

The poor customer has just had the experience of entering one strange door to come into your showroom. The very worst thing you can attempt to do is to expect them to go through another one.

Right Way 1 – Sitting by a desk on the same side.

A working surface is useful when qualifying customers. It's somewhere to rest whatever you are making notes on. There could be information that you need. Besides that, a desk gives the conversation a focal point (two or three chairs stuck out in the open will make you and your customer feel uncomfortable and exposed). But by a desk, on the same side or even across a corner will help relax all concerned and assist the conversation flow.

Right Way 2 – Special seating areas.

Often seen today in many a showroom, it could be a couple of couches and a coffee table. Sometimes it will be a purpose-built area recreating the relaxed style of seating that you would find in someone's home, complete with papers and magazines and the obligatory rubber plant! Some companies use round tables with mobile workstations that contain all the bits and pieces that a seller needs to help the buyers buy.

Customers will feel safe in such an environment, and a feeling of safety will enhance the flow of conversation.

3 Involve All the Decision-Makers

Establish early exactly who the customer is and try to involve all the decision-makers in the qualifying process. It is sensible to ask if anyone else who is not present is involved in the purchase, such as a company, partner or other family members. If all the decision-makers are not there, then bear in mind that there will normally be the necessity for a further meeting to confirm the order later.

4 Ask Open-Ended Questions to Get Information

Every salesperson must know about the six good serving men of Rudyard Kipling.

> *"I keep six honest serving men*
> *(they taught me all I knew)*
> *Their names are what and why and when*
> *and how and where and who"*

Start your early questions with one of the good serving men and you should get more than 'yes' or 'no' answers. Customers will tell you exactly what they want and their prime reasons for wanting it, but only if you ask. Why risk losing business by guessing?

Open-Ended Questions – Examples

FIND OUT THE PRIME REASON FOR WANTING OR NEEDING A VEHICLE

"You obviously have a reason for wanting a vehicle, what would that be?"

"Yes, I changed my job and I will have to drive to work in future." Prime reason: **Fear/Safety?**

"Well, the kids don't get any smaller, and young James has been complaining about the lack of room behind my seat." Prime reason: **Love?**

"We've bought a boat and I need more space to lug stuff back and forth at weekends." Prime reason: **Recreation?**

"The thing I've got at the moment just eats petrol. I must get something more economical." Prime reason: **Money?**

"Do you know, I've always wanted one of these ever since I was a boy." Prime reason: **Dream fulfilment?**

"My next door neighbour but one has just got one and swears by it – I would like to get something similar." Prime reason: **Imitation?**

"My next door neighbour but one has just got one and swears by it – I would like to get the GTi version with the rear spoiler and wider wheels." Prime reason: **Ego/Status?**

CHECK FOR A SECONDARY REASON

"Apart from that, what else is important to you about the vehicle that you drive?"

"I want something that's cheap to run." Secondary reason: **Money?**

"I still want good performance as well as space." Secondary reason: **Ego/Status?**

"Yes, I would want the ABS option." Secondary reason: **Fear/Safety?**

"I don't want anything that is going to cost a fortune to insure." Secondary reason: **Money?**

"It's got to be the bright red that you do, something really visual." Secondary reason: **Ego/Status?**

"Well, comfortable seats are important." Secondary reason: **Love?**

"Well, can you get me a personalised number plate?" Secondary reason: **Ego/Status?**

CHECK WHAT PRIME REASONS MEAN TO THE CUSTOMER

Once we establish the prime reason or reasons, the next step is to find out what that prime reason means to the customer in his model of the world, which could differ considerably from yours.

"What's important about driving to work?"
"How much space will James need to stop him complaining?"
"How much extra space will you need?"
"How would you judge that a vehicle was economical?"
"What would it be like if you didn't get one?"
"What would having a vehicle like your neighbour's do for you?"
"What would happen if your vehicle didn't have the rear spoiler and wider wheels?"

This style of questioning will eventually help you to personalise your presentation, concentrating on exactly what the customer wants rather than what you think their wants should be.

FIND OUT MORE ABOUT THE CUSTOMER

This is often a good place to start. Most people do love talking about themselves.

"How many are you in your family?"
"Who do you know that has one of these?"
"What do you do when you are not working?"
"Where do you live?"
"How long have you lived there?"
"When are you thinking of getting one?"
"When did you start to look?"
"When do you need a vehicle by?"
"What factory options do you want?"
"What accessories are you considering?"
"What made you think of us?"
"What do you know about our company?"
"What attracts you to our make of vehicle?"

FIND OUT MORE ABOUT THE PRESENT VEHICLE AND MOTORING NEEDS

"What do you like about your present vehicle?"
"What don't you like about your present vehicle?"
"What has your present vehicle got that you would want on your next vehicle?"
"What doesn't your present vehicle have that you would want on your next vehicle?"
"How else would you like your next vehicle to differ from the one you have now?"
"What is happening to your present vehicle?"
"How do you use your vehicle?"
"Who drives it apart from you?"
"What annual mileage will you be doing?"
"What other vehicles do you have in the family?"
"How many people do you normally take with you in the vehicle?"
"When did you get your last vehicle?"
"Where did you get it?"

FIND OUT MORE ABOUT FINANCIAL CIRCUMSTANCES

"What is the name of the finance company you normally use?"
"Who will own the vehicle, you or your company?"
"Who else is involved in the decision to buy?"
"How do you propose to fund your purchase?"
"What sort of monthly figure are you thinking of spending?" (Always follow this with a closed question: *"...up to what sort of figure?"*)
"What are your present monthly payments?"
"Where do you work?"
"How long have you been there?"
"What do you do there?"

Because some financial circumstances questions could be seen as rather personal, it is best to leave these types of question until later in the qualification time. If you feel that the customer you are with would feel uncomfortable being asked some of these questions, then go with that feeling and leave them out. Because of the personal nature of some questions and as an aid to a free flow of conversation, it is always best to ask qualification questions out of earshot of others.

5 Ask Closed-Ended Questions to Clarify Understanding

"I keep eight useful checking men,
(all good salesmen should),
their names are IS, DO, DID and DOES
and IF, CAN, WILL and WOULD"

These words were not part of Rudyard Kipling's poem. They should be part of your qualification process. Many salespeople try to stick only to open questions during qualification. Yet another accident of sales training history?

There was a time when asking only open-ended questions appeared to be the prime objective of the qualifying process. A conversation with a customer using only open questions can be successful in finding out exactly how you can help a customer buy. But it just does not flow very well and it can certainly break down or weaken any rapport that you have managed to build with the customer. This is because it can make the conversation feel disjointed and unnatural.

- Closed-ended questions improve the flow of the conversation and make it much more natural.
- Closed-ended questions clarify your understanding of the customer's wants and needs.
- Closed-ended questions confirm your interest in the customer and your interest in helping them get what they want.

Closed-Ended Questions – Examples

- *"Is delivery by the end of this month absolutely vital?"*
- *"Do you want to part-exchange your present vehicle?"*
- *"Did you see the one outside as you came in?"*
- *"Does your company mind where you buy your vehicle?"*
- *"If I can find one to this specification, would you be in a position to go ahead soon?"*
- *"Can I bring it to your home for your wife to see and try one evening?"*
- *"Will you want us to arrange the finance for you?"*
- *"Would the extended warranty be useful as you plan to keep the vehicle for some time?"*

There are obviously more than eight ways to start a closed question. It does not matter what word you use. It does matter that you should use both open and closed questions during qualification and any conversation with your customers, doesn't it?

6 Make Notes of What Your Customer Tells You

Wrong Way 1

Usually across a desk. A small buff-coloured printed card is produced which the salesperson shields from the customer's view with his hand as he writes the answers to the questions.

Wrong Way 2

The salesperson produces a four-page questionnaire which is filled in with much enthusiasm by the salesperson or sometimes the customer is expected to fill it in without much enthusiasm.

Right Way 1

When sitting down comfortably with the customer the salesperson will reach for a blank pad of A5 paper and say something like: *"Do you mind if I make a few notes, as we talk? This will help me fully understand how I can help you best."*

Right Way 2

If there is a part-exchange involved, then a part-exchange appraisal form could be produced near the start of the conversation to note down the details, plus other qualification information. Many of these forms are available – big chunky ones are best, not small secret ones that are designed to fit in *Glass's Guide* or a pocket book. If you are going to use such a form, then share it with the customer. Let the customer see what you are doing. It's less threatening that way.

7 Get the Customer's Name, Address and Telephone Number

Without follow-up information you will not be in a position to follow up a customer who does not place an order on the first visit – which is most of them. 'If they want it, they will call in again' is just not good enough and is downright unprofessional. It costs a fortune to get a customer to call in the first place. If you want to maximise sales, then it is vital that you follow up customers who haven't yet bought.

The very first thing that should happen if a customer leaves without placing an order on the very first visit is that the salesperson should write a 'thank you for calling' letter.

Example

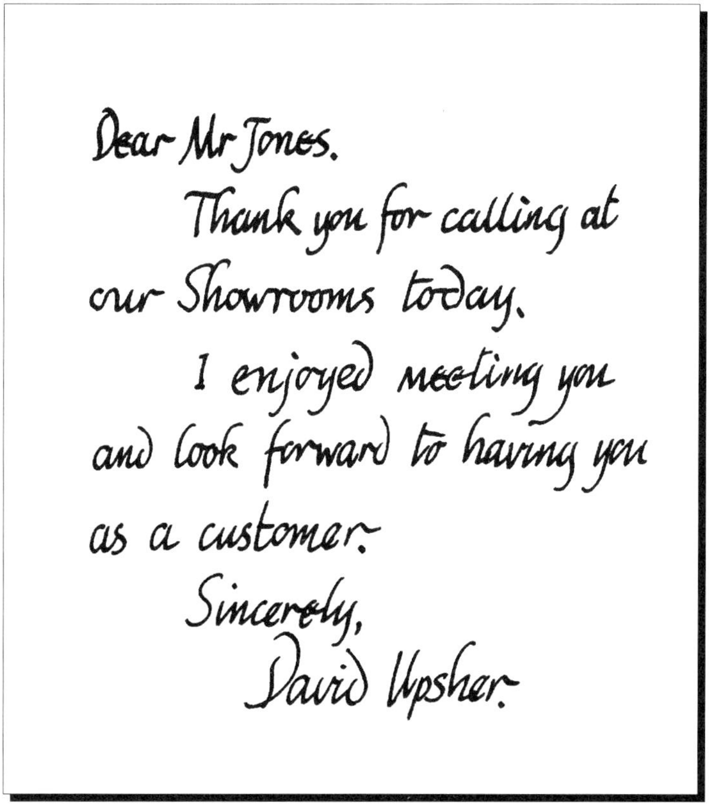

Dear Mr Jones.

Thank you for calling at our Showrooms today.

I enjoyed meeting you and look forward to having you as a customer.

Sincerely,

David Upsher.

Recommendations

- Hand-written
- Real pen
- Real ink
- Company notepaper
- White envelope
- Real first class stamp
- Sent as soon as the customer leaves without buying

How to Increase your Sales by 10%

In 1981 motorcycle sales in this country dropped by 23%. In the same year motorcycle sales rose by 70% at Station Garage, Taplow.

I asked Mark, the General Manager at the time, how much of the increase could be attributed to the sales training programme that we had been running for his company. "*Not a lot,*" was his dismal reply, "*most of the increase is due to our marketing activities and the fact that I am a brilliant manager.*" (This was true.) "*But,*" he went on, "*I will give you credit for 10% of the increase based on one thing alone – your follow-up letter. Absolutely brilliant.*"

"*For example,*" he said, "*after the course, when we discussed the idea, I went out and bought the pens and ink. I even got a book for one of my blokes on how to do joined-up handwriting. I gave them the paper, the envelopes and the real first class stamps. I then made it a condition of employment that nobody walks without getting a 'thank you for calling' letter the next day. If someone did not buy and did get the letter, all was forgiven. If someone did not buy and did not get the letter, then it was 'career adjustment' time!*

Just after we started this campaign, a very large 'rocker' shouldered his way sideways into the showroom. What worried the salespeople was not his size or his aggressive face and attitude – what really worried them were the words written in brass studs on the back of his black leather jacket. They simply said:

I KILL SKINHEADS

[across the top] and

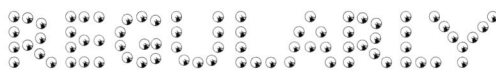

REGULARLY

[across the bottom]

When he decided to leave without buying, nobody was very much inclined to try and stop him! But he did get the follow-up letter.

The very next day, he was back – looking bigger and even more aggressive. He stormed into the showroom, the letter clenched in his fist, glared at the salesman who had dealt with him and said: 'You wrote to me. My dad read me this letter. I'm buying my bike from you 'cos you really care.'"

That was a long time ago. Today, the computer age has caught us up. Follow-up letters can be produced and sent with minimum effect and minimum effort BUT when was the last time you received a hand-written letter?

If you were to adopt this technique, then you too could increase your sales by 10%. The message that the customers will get will be far more than just the words on the paper. That message is **you really care.** That's a really powerful message to get in today's technological world.

8 Summarise what the Customer has Told You

Simply tell the customer what the customer has told you, to clarify understanding and show you have been listening and that you really do care.

"Right, Mr Riley, so what you are looking for is a Pelegra 1.8 GTX with ABS and an automatic gearbox. You would prefer the blue, but black would be your second choice. If you decide to go ahead you will want the vehicle by the end of next month and you need a price for your present vehicle. You would prefer to arrange your own finance. Both you and Mrs Riley drive your vehicle, so you would both like to try it before making up your mind. Have I missed anything?"

Such a vital step. Such a help in clarifying understanding, such a way of showing your interest and professionalism. Such a shame that not that many salespeople do it.

9 Tell the Customers What you Propose to Do to Help Them Buy

Simply tell the customer what happens next.

"Fine, Mr Riley. The first thing I suggest we do is to go out and take a look at your part-exchange. That will give me an idea of the condition of it. While my manager is working out a value for it, I will show you the 1.8 – take you for a short test-drive, just to get the feel of it. We can then fix a time for both you and your wife to try it. Before that happens, I will check delivery of the 1.8 GTX to your specification and colour choice."

Now the customer is happy. Mr Riley knows exactly what will happen. That knowledge will give him confidence.

- Confidence that he is dealing with a reliable company.
- Confidence that he is dealing with a professional and capable salesperson.
- Confidence that if he does decide to go ahead and place an order, he will actually enjoy the vehicle-buying experience.

Conversation Communication Skills

For most face-to-face conversations there are six conversation communication skills.

1 Reflecting

Mirroring what the other person has just expressed in both words and feelings. This behaviour shows that you really are listening to what the other person is saying.

2 Encouraging

Making encouraging sounds that invite the other person to continue talking – saying things like:

"Tell me more"
"Yes, do go on"

This shows that you are genuinely interested in what the other person is saying.

3 Asking

Asking your customer questions designed to extract further information, desires and opinions. These could be open-ended questions, in order to gather information, or closed-ended questions, to clarify understanding.

4 Summarising

This behaviour will prove to your customer that not only are you listening, but you also understand what has been said. You will also help keep the discussion on track, pull together everything that has been talked about so far and set the scene on how you propose to help them buy a vehicle.

5 Giving Information

Stating points which are facts, or which are genuinely thought to be facts. This is where you start supplying your customer with information about the product or service that he may be interested in, or that you may wish to draw attention to.

6 Giving Opinions

Expressing views or opinions, feelings or emotions.

A Closed Mouth Gathers No Foot

When using conversational communication skills during the qualification process, the very best salespeople will normally restrict their behaviour to the first four only.

1 Reflecting

2 Encouraging

3 Asking

4 Summarising

Having fully qualified the customer, the salesperson will then start:

5 Giving Information
Particularly during the presentation and demonstration phases of the sale. The danger area, the graveyard for unsuccessful salespeople, is:

6 Giving Opinions
They will not help you sell, and they might even damage your chances. You will be best advised to think before giving your opinions to your customers.

The main points again

1 Try to avoid telling customers about possible problems they already know, such as:

- They are very hard to get hold of
- Your part-exchange will not be worth much

2 At best only 20% of potential customers are properly qualified.

3 If you do not believe in the product you sell, or the company you work for, the customer will probably know by unconsciously reading the message in your body language and your face.

4 Correct qualification will help you understand what the customers want and how you can help them get what they want.

5 The prime reasons for buying anything are:

- Ego/Status
- Fear/Safety
- Money
- Love
- Imitation
- Recreation
- Dream Fulfilment

6 The qualification process is:

- Qualify away from product
- Sit down with the customer
- Ask open-ended questions to get information
- Ask closed-ended questions to clarify understanding
- Make notes of what your customer tells you
- Get the customer's name, address and telephone number
- Summarise what the customer has told you
- Tell the customer what you propose to do to help them buy

7 The qualification conversation communication skills are:

- Reflecting
- Encouraging
- Asking
- Summarising
- Giving information
- Giving opinions

8 When you have fully qualified the customer, by all means start giving the customer information.

9 The danger area, the graveyard for unsuccessful salespeople, is: giving opinions.

CHAPTER 10
Sensory Acuity and the Sales Process

"If you can feel how your customers feel,
their buying motives you will reveal.
If you can hear through your customer's ear,
how to help them becomes more clear.
If you can see through your customer's eye,
you will see what your customers buy"

Lestrade, lean and ferret-like as ever, was standing by the doorway and greeted my companion and myself.

"This case will make a stir, sir," he remarked. *"It beats anything I have seen, and I am no chicken."*

"There is no clue," said Gregson.

"None at all," chimed Lestrade.

Sherlock Holmes approached the body and, kneeling down, examined it intently... Gregson and Lestrade had watched the manoeuvres of their amateur companion with considerable curiosity and some contempt. They evidently failed to appreciate the fact, which I had begun to realise, that Sherlock Holmes' smallest actions were all directed towards some definite and practical end.

"What do you think of it, sir?" they both asked.

"It would be robbing you of the credit of the case if I was to presume to help you," remarked my friend. *"You are doing so well now that it would be a pity for anyone to interfere."* There was a world of sarcasm in his voice as he spoke.

"...I'll tell you one thing which may help you in the case," he continued, turning to

the two detectives, *"there has been murder done, and the murderer was a man. He was more than six feet high, was in the prime of life, had small feet for his height, wore coarse, square-toe boots and smoked a trichinopoly cigar. He came here with his victim in a four-wheeled cab, which was drawn by a horse with three old shoes and one new one on his off foreleg. In all probability, the murderer has a florid face, and the finger-nails of his right hand were remarkably long. These are only a few indications – but they may assist you."*

Lestrade and Gregson glanced at each other with an incredulous smile.

"If this man was murdered, how was it done?" asked the former.

"Poison," said Sherlock Holmes curtly, and strode off.

Extracts from *A Study in Scarlet* by Sir Arthur Conan Doyle, first published in 1887.

What is Sensory Acuity?

Sensory acuity is the ability to 'read' what other people are thinking and feeling. All good salespeople have got this ability naturally and unconsciously. There is nothing new about sensory acuity; it has been around as long as life itself. The trouble is that most of us have forgotten how to use it. If, as salespeople, we can re-learn or remember how to use sensory acuity, this ability will have a very dramatic effect on our awareness of other people and our ability to communicate with them.

So How Do We Communicate?

- 7% of communication is through the use of words
- 38% of communication is the way we say these words
- 55% of communication is in fact 'non-verbal'

Non-verbal communication includes:

- Facial expressions and skin colour changes
- The way we stand or sit
- Breathing and pulse rates
- The way we move our arms, legs and hands

Non-verbal communication will always tell us much more than words will about other people and their wants and needs. It is also a more accurate reflection of their thoughts and feelings than what they say will ever be.

So How Will Sensory Acuity Help Me?

If rapport is all about how to meet other people in their model of the world, then sensory acuity is all about finding out what and where their model of the world is. This ability, together with rapport, will be of great assistance to you throughout the sales process and in all your other communication with other people. It will be of particular benefit during the 'presentation' and 'demonstration' steps, because if you are able to understand what people really want, you will really be able to help them get what they want.

The Five Senses

We use our senses to make sense of the world around us. Most of us have five, a few have less, and some think they have more. For the sake of clarity and common sense, let us stick to the five senses that are common to most of us. These are:

- Seeing (visual)
- Hearing (auditory)
- Feeling (kinesthetic)
- Smelling (olfactory)
- Tasting (gustatory)

Just as most of us prefer to write with one hand rather than the other, we also prefer to use some senses more than others. Luckily, you can usually tell what another person's preferred sense is by the words that they use. For instance:

Visual people will say:

- You look bright today
- Look at the view, isn't it colourful?
- I see myself as a bit dull at the moment
- Oh yes, I see what you mean
- Let's look at it this way

Auditory people will say:

- You sound well today
- Listen to the wind, isn't it loud?
- Do I sound a bit out of harmony at the moment?
- Oh yes, I hear what you say
- Let's try saying it this way

Kinesthetic people will say:

- It feels like you are in touch today
- Do you grasp how I feel?
- I feel a little under pressure at the moment
- Oh yes, I understand how you feel
- Let's grab the chance while it's there

It is expected that some of the time the seeing, hearing and feeling words that people use are chosen because they fit a particular situation. But most of the time, they will indicate a visual, auditory or kinesthetic preference.

- Do you see where this is leading?
- Are you in tune with this concept?
- Can you grasp the significance of this?

This is the exciting bit. The sense that people prefer to use will indicate how they are processing information into their brain.

- Visual people predominantly think, store and retrieve information as pictures
- Auditory people predominantly think, store and retrieve information as sounds
- Kinesthetic people predominantly think, store and retrieve information as feelings

Naturally, your brain gets information from all your senses most of the time. But you, just like everybody else, will have a preferred sense that you use both for processing information internally and communicating with others externally.

How About You?

Don't take my word for this, see it for yourself, by grabbing a pen and completing the quiz that follows. Indicate your preferred answer or answers by sharing a total of five points between A, B and C for each of the twenty questions.

You can allocate all five points to just one answer. For example:

A	B	C
5	0	0

or

A	B	C
0	5	0

Or you may want to share the five points between two or all three answers:

A	B	C
3	2	0

A	B	C
2	2	1

1 A job description covering the duties of a salesperson should:

A Tell me what I have to do

B Show me the right way to do things

C Make me feel that I know what to do

A	B	C

2 It is important to have a good relationship with all the people you work with because:

A A business works more smoothly that way

B It reflects the promise of good service

C Harmonious relationships mean happy customers

A	B	C

3 In reality, you could probably find at least ten things wrong with the company you work for. Then again:

A You could probably picture ten things that are right

B You could probably describe ten things that are right

C You could probably feel that there are ten things right

A	B	C

4 Salespeople should be flexible enough to:

A Handle each customer differently

B Tune in to the differences that each customer has

C Focus on each individual customer

A	B	C

5 During the qualification process I like to:

A Ask customers lots of questions about their needs and wants

B Get a good feel of what customers want

C Get a full picture of customers' requirements

A	B	C

6 Presentation of the product is a great way to:

A Describe in detail the features and benefits

B Paint the picture of the product's advantages

C Get the customer to grasp the benefits of the product

A	B	C

7 The customer should always drive the car during the demonstration because:

A The feeling of ownership is generated

B The customer can tune in to the idea of ownership

C It will give the customer the vision of ownership

A	B	C

8 The very best salespeople:

A Seldom see a need to negotiate

B Are in tune with their customers at negotiation time

C Will handle most sales without the need to negotiate

A	B	C

9 When it comes to selling vehicles:

A I like to sell vehicles that look good

B I prefer to sell the customers what I feel will be right for them

C I am happier if the customers tell me exactly what they want

A	B	C

10 When it comes to closing sales:

A I just know when it is time for the customer to place an order

B I look for the visual signs that tell me a customer is ready to buy

C I like to ask the customer if they would like to go ahead

A	B	C

11 When it comes to the customer picking up a new vehicle:

A I like to make a show of delivery

B I like to hear the excitement in the customer's voice

C I want the customer to feel satisfied

A	B	C

12 When the customer has taken delivery:

A I would prefer to keep in touch when I feel it is right to do so

B I like to have a visual plan so I can see who to follow-up when

C I would prefer to do as much follow-up as possible by telephone

A	B	C

13 Good salespeople can expect repeat business because:

A They have kept in touch with their customers

B They have developed a harmonious relationship

C They have shown their customers that they are interested in them

A	B	C

14 Most salespeople would be far more interested in prospecting if they:

A Could see the benefit to them personally

B Felt that they would get a benefit

C Were told of the personal benefits

A	B	C

15 The reason behind finding your own customers is to make sure that you:

A Speak to the right people at the right time

B Get face-to-face the day someone wants to place an order or to see a vehicle

C Handle people at the time they would be interested in a firm commitment

A	B	C

16 A complaining customer is a customer:

A Who sees you deserve a second chance

B Wants to talk about problems to someone who is prepared to listen

C Who will become doubly loyal if handled smoothly

A	B	C

17 When it comes to finding out about something:

A I would understand much better if I could see it

B I want to try it before I can fully understand it

C I would prefer to have someone explain it to me

A	B	C

18 When it comes to finding my way:

A It's no problem if I have a map

B I need someone to tell me the way

C I just know if I have got it right

A	B	C

19 When I have a problem to solve:

A I often talk it over with myself

B I can visualise the answer

C I think it through until I can feel the right answer

A	B	C

20 Contented customers are:

A What we all want to see at the end of the day

B What everybody wants to hear about

C The way to a smooth future

A	B	C

How did you do?

To find out your own preferred sense, simply fill in the scores that you allocated to each of the three alternative answers to the twenty questions, then add up the scores to identify your own preference.

	Visual		Auditory		Kinesthetic	
1	B		A		C	
2	B		C		A	
3	A		B		C	
4	C		B		A	
5	C		A		B	
6	B		A		C	
7	C		B		A	
8	A		B		C	
9	A		C		B	
10	B		C		A	
11	A		B		C	
12	B		C		A	
13	C		B		A	
14	A		C		B	
15	B		A		C	
16	A		B		C	
17	A		C		B	
18	A		B		C	
19	B		A		C	
20	A		B		C	
Totals						

It is most unlikely that you have scored all the points in the same column. The largest of your three totals indicates the sense that you prefer to use to communicate and to input information into your brain.

The Verbal Clues to People's Preferred Senses

Just listen, really listen, to the words that other people use. They will tell you how the person you are talking to is processing information. Words like:

VISUAL Seeing Words	AUDITORY Hearing Words	KINESTHETIC Feeling Words
Sight	Sound	Feel
Clean	Harmonious	Firm
Hazy	Soft	Touch
Bright	Loud	Impact
Expose	Tune in	Connect
Murky	Discordant	Sticky
Colourful	Rhythm	Tap
Sparkle	Resonate	Smooth
Flash	Splash	Smash
Reveal	Clash	Crash
Show	Low	Throw
See	Hear	Stir
Spectacle	Noisy	Heavy
Scan	Note	Move
View	Listen	Stroke
Glimpse	Growl	Grab
Screen	Screech	Strike
Reflect	Tell	Handle
Vision	Describe	Blended
Preview	Say	Stir
Insight	Rings a bell	Uptight
Paint	Music	Texture
Illustrate	Amplify	Intense
Outlook	Tone	Pressure
Picture	Rattle	Solid
Perspective	Call	Grasp
Draw	Voice	Rub
Focus	Shout	Hit
Look	Alarm	Shock
Dull	Word	Feeling

Other Clues to Preferred Senses

You can also establish other people's processing preferences through body type, breathing and tonality.

Visual people:

- Can be thin and tense
- Breathe high and shallow
- Speak high and quickly

Auditory people:

- Can be less thin and less tense
- Breathe lower and deeper
- Speak clearly and melodically

Kinesthetic people:

- Can be overweight and relaxed
- Breathe low and slow
- Speak deeply and slowly

Hand gestures and arm movements also tell much about people:

- Visual people often gesture at face level
- Auditory people often gesture at chest level
- Kinesthetic people often gesture at stomach level

Establishing People's Preferences Through Eye Movements

People's eye movements will often give away much non-verbal information, including their preference in processing information.

- Visual people are inclined to look upwards
- Auditory people are inclined to stay level
- Kinesthetic people are inclined to look downwards

The eyes give away so much of what is going on inside the other person's mind. Good spellers, for instance, 'remember visually' how to spell a word. If you want to check this out, ask someone who you know can spell to spell, say, 'necessary', and just watch that person's eyes shoot up to your right. There is a small percentage of the population that go the other way, mostly left-handed people.

The eyes are but pictures of your thoughts

People's eyes will always tell you whether at that moment they are seeing, hearing or feeling internally.

If you start watching people more closely, you will very soon discover that people's eyes DO move as they think. As you are watching them, if their eyes go:

- Up to your right = They are remembering things seen
- Up to your left = They are constructing visual pictures
- Across to your right = They are remembering things heard
- Across to your left = They are constructing sounds
- Down to your right = They are talking to themselves
- Down to your left = They are experiencing internal feelings

For example:

◆ *"Where did I put those keys?"*	Visual remember
◆ *"What would the display look like if... ?"*	Visual construct
◆ *"What did she say when we met?"*	Auditory remember
◆ *"What should I say when we meet?"*	Auditory construct
◆ *"What should I do about... ?"*	Talking to self
◆ *"I really feel upset about that."*	Internal feelings

It will pay you well to remember this, because if you know whether someone is using pictures, sounds or feelings, you can then tailor your words to fit the thought process they are using at that moment.

For example:

- *"Yes, I do see exactly what you mean."*
- *"Yes, I can hear and understand what you are saying."*
- *"Yes, I know exactly how you feel about this."*

Speaking the Customer's Language

Speaking the customer's language is important if you want to maximise your chances of maintaining rapport. The very best salespeople do this automatically. This is one of the reasons why they are the best. Another way to speak the customer's language is to deliberately match people's thought processing patterns.

Visual

If your customer is inputting information into his brain by using pictures, use visual words to make it easier for him to see what you are saying:

- *"Let me show you this."*
- *"Can you see the advantage of that?"*
- *"Is this what you are looking for?"*
- *"Doesn't this look good?"*

Auditory

Some customers process information using mainly sound. This is made much easier for them if you are talking on the same wavelength.

- *"Let me tell you about this."*
- *"Did you say that you need more room?"*
- *"Just wait until you hear how quiet the engine is."*
- *"The styling of this is most harmonious."*

Kinesthetic

A few people that you meet will process by feelings. Around 15% of the population do this. It is important to make them feel at home with your words.

- *"Just feel the material on the seats."*
- *"The engine is as smooth as silk."*
- *"Just a gentle pressure releases the catch."*
- *"How does this grab you?"*

Start to Look More and See More

Milton Erickson tells the story about a patient of his whose perception of colour was phenomenal. He was sitting in the sun on the lawn outside Milton's home. After about an hour and a half the patient came dashing into the house and said to Milton: *"Do you realise that every blade of grass is a different shade of green?"* He had arranged a selection from very light to very dark. He was so surprised! (The amount of chlorophyll in each blade differs and that will affect the colour.)

Start to Listen More and Hear More

Ernest Vent had a remarkable sense of hearing. You could toss a coin and slap it on the bar in the club that he worked in and he could always tell you whether it was heads or tails. Ernest had taught himself to notice the difference in 'sound' between a head and a tail side. If it was sharp, then it would be heads down and tails up. If it had a hollow ring, then it would be tails down and heads up.

Start to Feel More and Experience More

Sean Murphy lost his whip years ago. He runs an Irish jaunting car, carrying passengers through the Gap of Dunlow by the lakes of Killarny. If he wants the horse to go faster, he just slackens the reins slightly. As soon as the horse feels the rains go slack, he thinks that Sean is reaching for his whip and speeds up to avoid a 'negative kinesthetic experience'.

Start to Smell More and Experience New Smells

My daughter Katherine was walking towards school the other day with her friend Evergreen when it started to rain. Evergreen turned to Katherine and said: *"Doesn't the pavement smell wonderful when it rains?"* Katherine was slightly amazed, took a good sniff and realised for the first time in her life that pavements really do smell wonderful when it starts to rain!

Start to Taste More and Experience New Tastes!

Oriental Lobster

Cut the onion and the ginger into small strips. Cut the lobster into 3-inch pieces and the spring onions into 2-inch pieces. When the oil is hot in the wok, add the onion, ginger and lobster. Stir fry over a high heat for no more than 4 minutes. Then take out the lobster and add some minced pork and a little salt. Stir fry again over a high heat for less than 2 minutes. Add a mixture of rich stock, soy sauce and rice wine, and stir until it boils. Put back the lobster with the spring onion pieces, mix together well, close the lid and cook for another 3 minutes. Open the lid and serve immediately with a chilled bottle of rich, buttery Puligny-Montrachet 1986 – or would you prefer a McDonald's and coke?

The main points again

1 Sensory acuity is simply the ability to 'read' what other people are thinking and feeling.

2 Most of us have forgotten how to use it.

3 If we can remember, it will have a very dramatic effect on our ability to communicate.

4 Only:

- 7% of communication is through the use of words
- 38% of communication is the way we say these words
- 55% of communication is in fact 'non-verbal'

5 Non-verbal communication includes:

- Facial expressions and skin colour changes
- The way we stand or sit
- Breathing and pulse rates
- The way we move our arms, legs and hands

6 Non-verbal communication is a more accurate reflection of people's true thoughts and feelings than what they say will ever be.

7 Redeveloping your own sensory acuity ability will be of particular benefit during the 'presentation' and 'demonstration' steps in the sales process.

8 Most of us have five senses and all of us prefer to use some senses more than others.

9 Really listen to the words that other people use. They will tell you how the person you are talking to is processing information.

10 You can also establish other people's processing preferences through body type, breathing and tonality.

11 Hand gestures and arm movements also tell much about people.

12 People's eye movements will often give away much non-verbal information: you can always tell whether people are seeing, hearing or feeling internally.

13 Another way to speak the customer's language is to match their thought processing patterns deliberately.

14 Develop your own sensory acuity:

- Start to look more and see more
- Start to listen more and hear more
- Start to feel more and experience more
- Start to smell more and experience new smells
- Start to taste more and experience new tastes

SECTION FIVE

Moving Forward

"Perhaps the time has come to forget about six-step walk-arounds."

CHAPTER 11
Personalising Presentations

"You can't know too much about the product,
but you can talk too much about it"

Once you have fully established and understood exactly what the customer wants, your next step will be to show and present your product to the customer. Presentation simply means 'physically showing the goods you have for sale to the potential purchaser'. Sounds easy, doesn't it? So how come so many salespeople don't do it so well?

I went into a specialised camera shop knowing exactly what I wanted to buy – a camera as a Christmas present for my wife. I even knew how much I wanted to spend. The assistant greeted me with a cheerful and quite acceptable "*Can I help?*"

"*You certainly can,*" I replied. "*I want to buy a camera for my wife for Christmas. My wife likes taking photos but does not like fiddling around with lots of buttons. Have you got something for around about £100 that she can just point and press a button?*"

"*Yes, there are several of those on the market,*" said the assistant, "*very easy to use – you just pick them up, point them and with one click the camera does everything else for you totally automatically.*"

"*Just what I want,*" I said. "*Can I see one?*"

"*They are over there on that display. Have a look and see what you think.*"

I did take a look and became totally confused. I went back to the assistant to ask for further help, but he had got caught up with another customer.

As there was no-one else to help me, I left the shop to call in at Boots around the corner to purchase the other bits and pieces that make up safe and acceptable Christmas gifts. At the back of Boots there was a film processing department. They also had a display of cameras. I asked the assistant if they had what I wanted. "*Yes, no problem. I know exactly what you are looking for. Take a look at this,*" he said, handing me a camera. The camera looked neat and felt good to touch – shiny and solid, but at the same time light and purposeful.

"Let me show you how it works," said the assistant. *"You press this to switch it on, you point it and press this red button. Simple as that,"* he enthused.

"To load it you just pull this catch and the film goes in here. Just pull out the end of the film and click the door shut. The camera loads itself and even adjusts to take into account the type of film you are using."

He put the camera up to his eye, pointed it and pressed the button.

"When you do this," he said, *"the camera focuses itself and adjusts to the light available. If it's too dark, then the flash will automatically pop up, which means that it is very difficult to take a bad picture."*

"Wow!" I said. *"How much is it?"*

"It's only £115," he said. *"Would you like me to put in a suitable film for your Christmas snaps?"*

"Yes!" I said. *"Oh, and would you give me a spare one as well. I think my wife will like using this."*

...And she did.

Somewhere in there was a presentation. It may not have been the best presentation in the world, but it had the desired effect and turned a prospect into a delighted customer. Turning prospects into delighted customers is such a pleasure for both buyers and sellers.

How Not to Present

Today's customers appear to know much more about vehicles than they used to. They will often come into your showroom with a very good idea of what they want, when they want it and how much they expect to pay for it. All this customer knowledge does not do away with the importance of the presentation step.

Presentation is, or should be, the smooth step that moves you and your customer from qualification (what do you want?) to demonstration (this is what you want). Traditionally, salespeople have been taught 'walk-around' techniques to be used when presenting vehicles. Unless you have a brand new model and/or the customer wants to know 'absolutely everything' – perhaps the time has come to forget about five, six or seven step walk-arounds.

Considerable research into selling methods in the mid-1980s was carried out by BMW North America. Indications were that customers were not interested in being shown a 'laundry list' of features any more. They were certainly 'switched off' by well meaning but misguided vehicle circling salespeople who appeared to be out to prove how brilliant they were at absorbing and recalling product knowledge information.

Selling used to be like a battlefield:

"Let's throw every feature we've got at them. Something is bound to get through the defence by sheer weight of numbers. Quick – they are beginning to crumble. Throw in the SIBS, that will finish them off!"

How to Present

The presentation approach of today and tomorrow is one of total flexibility. Presentations should be joyful and meaningful occasions, concentrating on what the customer wants rather than what the product has. Which means that each presentation has to be different because no two customers want exactly the same thing.

The seven 'reasons for buying' (see chapter 9, *Qualification*) give us clear direction on what to present to whom.

Ego/Status Presentation

- Show the best features
- Talk about ergonomics
- Emphasise design concepts and image

Fear/Safety Presentation

- Talk about reliability
- Trouble-free mechanics
- Safety body construction

Money Presentation

- Talk about low drag coefficiency
- Low cost servicing and running costs
- High residual values

Love Presentation

- Talk about space and reliability
- Active and passive safety features
- Child-proof locks and comfort for all

Imitation Presentation

- Talk about the many satisfied customers
- How they enjoy what they have bought
- How they appreciate your aftersales backup and services

Recreation Presentation

- Paint the mental pictures of how the customer will enjoy using the vehicle
- Talk about using the vehicle in conjunction with a hobby or pastime
- Present the vehicle as an accessory to a sport or pastime, emphasising space and load capacity

Dream Fulfilment

- Let the customer do the talking
- You concentrate on being a good listener
- Share the customer's dream with the customer

Again, it would be sensible to emphasise the vital importance of a full customer qualification before you even start to consider your presentation.

What to Present

Remember those recommended qualification questions? For instance:

- *"What do you like about your present vehicle?"*
- *"What don't you like about your present vehicle?"*
- *"What has your present vehicle got that you would want on your next vehicle?"*
- *"What doesn't your present vehicle have that you would want on your next vehicle?"*
- *"How else would you like your next vehicle to differ from the one you have now?"*

These five questions alone should give you a fair idea of what you should be presenting.

Part of your qualification process was to establish the main reason or reasons why the potential purchaser wanted to buy.

Your question

- *"You obviously have a reason for wanting to change. May I ask what that is?"*

Their possible answer

- *"I've always wanted one."*
- *"My kids are growing up, and we need more space in the back."*
- *"I really think this vehicle looks the business."*
- *"Someone at my office has bought one and is very pleased with it."*
- *"I've got to get a new one. My present vehicle keeps letting me down."*
- *"Your special finance offer appeals to me."*

The same question can elicit a multitude of different answers. These different answers will have a knock-on effect on how you should present your product, based on the classification of buyers.

The *"I've always wanted one"* will need a **dream fulfilment** presentation. *'This is the vehicle you have always wanted, which means it will fulfil your dreams.'*

The *"My kids are growing up..."* will need a **love** presentation. *'This has plenty or room in the back which means that your family will have all the space they need.'*

The *"I really think this vehicle looks the business"* will need an **ego/status** presentation. *'This vehicle has been styled by Giacosa Fratelli, the famous Italian designer, which means that it really does look the business.'*

The *"Someone at my office..."* will need an **imitation** presentation. *'Everyone who has bought one of these has been delighted with their decision to buy, which means that you will be delighted too.'*

The *"I've got to get a new one..."* will need a **fear** presentation. *'This model has a very good record of reliability, which means that it is most unlikely to let you down.'*

The *"Your special finance offer..."* will need a **money** presentation. *'Apart from our special finance offer, this model is particularly good on fuel consumption, which means that not only will you be saving money up front, you will continue to save money every time you use your vehicle.'*

Different presentations to different potential purchasers. All interested in buying the same vehicle.

Which means that:

People buy things, not for what they are (features), but for what those things will do for them (benefits). There are several ways to link features to benefits. 'Which means that' is as good as any and better than most.

Feature		Benefit
'The vehicle you always wanted'	Which means that	*'Your dreams are fulfilled'*
'Plenty of room in the back'	Which means that	*'All the space your family will need'*
'Styled by Fratelli'	Which means that	*'It looks the business'*
'Others have been delighted'	Which means that	*'You will be delighted too'*
'Good reliability'	Which means that	*'It will not let you down'*
'Good fuel consumption'	Which means that	*'You will save money every time you use the vehicle'*

Speak the Customer's Language

Literally! Use the words that your customer uses. Not all the time and not heavily emphasised. If the customer tells you *"we need more space in the back"* during qualification, repeat the same words during presentation. Not *"there is plenty of room"* or *"this is quite big"*. Use the customer phraseology and you will be talking his language – literally. *"This has more space in the back."*

Successful salespeople use the same words as their customers. They have the ability to talk at any level using similar words as the person they are talking to. If your customer is using what is called 'digital language', it would make sense to do the same, even if this is not your normal speech pattern. This means that the answer to *"Could you tell me about your acquisition alternatives"* would be different to the answer you give to *"Can I have it on the strap?"*. It is recommended that you steer clear of digital language unless your customer is using it. If in doubt, always use plain, simple language that anybody will be able to understand.

Motor Industry Sales Jargon

Why do sales staff talk in riddles to each other and, worst of all, to customers? Once someone has been selling vehicles for around three weeks, they will still have problems with appraising part-exchanges, let alone valuing a customer's current vehicle. They will still be less than knowledgeable regarding product knowledge. They won't know much about methods of finance and they would not recognise a cam shaft even if they fell down one.

But there is one area that they have totally mastered and that is the art of '*Motortradespeak*'. That's the problem – that's the bit than can confuse, and even lose, your customers. Remove from your conversation forever the silly jargon that has polluted everyday conversations with customers.

Here are some of the things that are said, together with more suitable alternatives.

Don't Say	Say Instead
"Can I help you?"	*"How can I help you buy a vehicle today?"*
"What do you smoke at the moment?"	*"What vehicle do you drive currently?"*
"What's it got on it?"	*"What extras and options does it have?"*
"What's on the clock?"	*"How many miles has the vehicle done?"*
"Is it on the strap?"	*"Is there a balance outstanding to a finance company?"*
"Any dings or biffs?"	*"Is there any damage to the bodywork?"*
"How experienced are the boots?"	*"How many miles have you done on the current set of tyres?"*
"Do you want it – or what?"	*"Would you like to place an order?"*
"It's worth about a gorilla and three daughters."	*"Its approximate value would be in the region of seventeen hundred and fifty pounds."*
"Does your wife drive or did it come like that when you bought it?"	*"It's a very nice vehicle but the paintwork will need a little attention."*
"That's the wedge all up, including the bidet."	*"That's the total cost, including the rear wash wipe option."*

"Do you want it on the drip?"	*"Would you like to put the vehicle on finance?"*
"This is Stan Stan the chucky man."	*"May I introduce you to our Business Manager, Stan Baker?"*
"If you've been offered that, then go and snap his hand off."	*"That is a very good offer for your vehicle."*
"Are you a punter or a rucker?"	*"Are you just looking around, or is there a vehicle that you have particularly called to see?"*
"That one over there. Now that's the reproductive organs of a canine."	*"That model is the top of the range and comes fully equipped with just about everything."*
"This one comes with the wheels."	*"The Executive model is fitted with cross-spoke alloy wheels."*

◆ ◆ ◆

Getting Into Step with Customers

The Visual Customer

- Will notice the gleaming bodywork
- Will notice the sleek lines of the vehicle
- Will notice the beautiful alloy wheels
- Will notice the colour co-ordinated bumpers and wing mirrors
- Will notice the careful match of both interior and exterior colours
- Will notice the subtle hint of brown tint in the windows
- Will see themselves driving the vehicle
- Will see the admiring glances of the people on the pavement as they pass by

The Auditory Customer

- Will appreciate the clunk as the door shuts
- Will appreciate the whirr of the electric motor that raises the driver's window
- Will appreciate the swish from the seat-belt as it is pulled across and fastened
- Will appreciate the sound of the engine bursting into life as he starts the vehicle
- Will hear the sound travelling from under the bonnet through the exhaust system to emerge from the rear of the vehicle
- Will enjoy driving the vehicle, appreciating the harmony of subtle engine notes blending with the sound of the CD playing through the powerful six-speaker system

The Kinesthetic Customer

- Will notice the luxurious feel of the seats that can be adjusted to fit his body
- Will touch the upholstery and feel the quality of the internal fittings
- Will enjoy the feel of the wheel under his hands
- When he starts the vehicle he will feel the surge of power from the engine
- Will feel the pressure on his back as the vehicle accelerates
- As he turns, he will sense the wheels working together with the suspension to lock the vehicle to the road
- Will feel that he and the vehicle are but one: machine and man blended together

Three Customers, One Vehicle

You've guessed it, each of the customers is experiencing the same vehicle.

If you really want to carry out meaningful presentations and demonstrations for the customer, then step into your customer's world. Share his vision, get into harmony and understand how your customer feels through the use of rapport and sensory acuity. You will be amazed at the difference it makes to your volume of sales. You will also be amazed at how interesting and mind-developing it is to experience all the information processing worlds instead of just your usual preference.

Present the Package

Some salespeople think that presentation is all about showing a customer a vehicle. It is much more than that. There are so many other things to show and explain. Today's customers are very influenced by your company's reputation.

- Tell them about your company – the people that work there and the satisfied customers who buy vehicles and use your other services.

Today's customers like to buy from a person they feel they can trust.

- Take the time to tell them a little about yourself. More importantly, make sure you take the time to continue to find out more about your customers, who they are, what they want and what they need.

As Dale Carnegy said:

"You can make more friends in two weeks by being interested in other people than you could in two years by trying to get other people interested in you."

Perfect Personalised Presentations

So there is far more to presentations than meets the eye, rings the bell or grabs the spot. Perfect, personalised presentations are all about understanding what customers want and showing them that you can provide it (or something close to it). Perfect, personalised presentations include multi-level pacing and communication of which the customer will never be aware.

Get it right and the end result will be a customer who is well on the way to buying what you sell. More importantly, the customer by this stage will be keen to buy from you and your company. So let's to the demo. Or, if your customer prefers, let us now proceed with emphasising the vehicle's pertinent advantages through vehicular activity!

The main points again

1 Before you 'present' you have to have an exact understanding of what the customer wants.

2 Presentation is the smooth step that moves you and your customer from 'qualification' to 'demonstration'.

3 Perhaps the time has come to stop using traditional 'walk-around' techniques.

4 Each 'presentation' needs to be custom-tailored to each customer's specific needs.

5 The seven 'reasons for buying' give us clear direction in what to present to who:

- Ego/Status
- Fear/Safety
- Money
- Love
- Imitation
- Recreation
- Dream Fulfilment

6 Personalise each presentation based on the knowledge you gained from your qualification questions.

7 People buy things not for what they are (features) but for what those things will do for them (benefits).

8 There are several ways to link features to benefits – 'which means that' is as good as any and better than most.

9 Speak the customer's language. Use the same key words and phrases that your customer does.

10 Use more of your customer's language and less of the motor industry sales jargon.

11 Present the package. Sell the product, sell your company, all your services and, above all, sell yourself.

12 Get the presentation step right and the end result will be a customer who is well on the way to buying what you sell.

CHAPTER 12
Demonstrating Your Product

"The best salespeople in the world
just do the basic things brilliantly"

There are for and against lobbyists on the value of demonstrating the product in action. Surveys carried out by manufacturers and others can indicate that 'the customer' puts less importance on having a demonstration than the sales training manual does. Then again, some salespeople who avoid demonstrations like a trip to the tax office still sell plenty of vehicles; sometimes more than their more demo-minded colleagues.

In spite of all this controversy, demonstrations have long been accepted as a major force in convincing customers to buy. Perhaps the reason for customers to put less emphasis on the need to try before they buy is because so few customers are actually offered the opportunity. Perhaps the reason why some salespeople who avoid demonstrations are still good at selling is that they are selling the deal and not the vehicle. It could be, of course, that they are just brilliant salespeople!

Years ago, I was a fairly new recruit to a sales team. My sales performance could be described as 'average'. You know, the best of the worst or the worst of the best. I was very keen to do better. "*Why not be the best while I'm about it,*" I thought. The one thing that most of my sales colleagues avoided, if they could, was giving demonstrations. There were, however, some reasons for this.

- There was no on-site parking, so the demonstration vehicles were in a car park down the road.
- There were yellow lines outside, which added to the difficulty.
- The company had a less than supportive petrol allowance policy. That meant that if you used your 'demonstration petrol' allowance to do demonstrations, then you would have to pay for petrol to get you home!

- The demonstration vehicles reflected vehicles that had reached the end of their free stocking period – rather than the more popular models.
- The roads were pretty busy and the location was not the best area to carry out meaningful demonstrations.

Get the picture? Demonstrations were easier to do without.

However, I was totally convinced that there was a strong link between order rate and demonstration rate – it just made sense to believe that the more you exposed your product to the customer, the more product you would sell. Unless of course you were selling total utter rubbish, which we were not. So I decided to demonstrate every chance that I could. This was the difference that would make the difference, I was convinced. I put my demonstration plan into immediate action.

Rule 1	Offer everybody a chance to try the vehicle.
Rule 2	Use the walk or the drive to the car park to continue to qualify and build the relationship.
Rule 3	Pay for the petrol home out of increased commissions.
Rule 4	If we hadn't got the model that the customer was interested in, then take the customer out in anything with the badge on and demonstrate the quality of the product.

Other salespeople took the Michael out of my efforts but I pressed on regardless. By the end of that year I had hit the number one spot. This was achieved in spite of being less selling accomplished than some of my colleagues.

This story is told not to establish how clever I was, but to emphasise the vital need and the incredible benefits in demonstrating the product in action on every possible occasion to anyone you can.

Six 'Good Reasons' not to Demonstrate

1 *"I can't do a demonstration because I haven't got the right vehicle."*

2 *"There is no point in demonstrating. They are bound to want too much for the vehicle they are driving at the moment."*

3 *"The boss does not like us to use his company vehicle for demonstrations."*

4 *"We will give a demonstration, but only if the customer signs the order first."*

5 *"We don't like demonstrating the vehicle because it puts mileage on which will affect what we will get for it when we sell it."*

6 *"I would do a demonstration but the vehicle is only here from nine to six."*

The real problem is that these good reasons not to demonstrate are all actual statements made by sellers to buyers, or the justification made to colleagues and managers for not demonstrating. Demonstrations do and always will take time and effort. However, there is nothing like the power of influence that a good demonstration will bring to bear on a borderline customer.

Let's Take Another Look at These Six Reasons

Reason 1	Recommendation
"I can't do a demonstration because I haven't got the right vehicle."	Do a demonstration in the wrong vehicle. *"This isn't the model that you are interested in, Mr Grant, but it does have the right badge on the front. As you are here, come out with me now and just feel the quality of the product. I will tell you about the differences and then arrange for you to see the right vehicle later this week."*

Having carried out many 'feel the quality' demonstrations, the conclusion is that it really does not matter if you demonstrate up or down your product range. The fact that you took the interest and trouble has a very positive effect on most potential customers.

Reason 2	Recommendation
"There is no point in demonstrating. They are bound to want too much for the vehicle they are driving at the moment."	A demonstration can often solve that problem. If you raise the desire to buy your vehicle, then you will reduce part-exchange price resistance.

This would be a marvellous opportunity to practise some of your new-found sales skills – particularly rapport and sensory acuity. Some customers you spend time with will not, or cannot, buy from you. That is the nature of our business and has to be expected and accepted.

Reason 3	Recommendation
"The boss does not like us to use his company vehicle for demonstrations."	Find out why your boss doesn't like his vehicle being used, and try to overcome the objection.

"Good morning, boss. You obviously have a good reason for not liking your vehicle to be used for demonstration – may I ask what it is?"

"Yes, it comes back filthy, empty of petrol and often late – I feel it's just not worth it."

"I know exactly how you 'feel'. If you 'felt' it would come back clean, with the same amount of petrol and on time, then you would probably 'feel' that it was worth it, don't you?"

It's worth a try. If it does not work, then you will have to find another vehicle (or in extreme cases, another job), or carry out a 'feel the quality of the product' demonstration instead.

Reason 4	Recommendation
"We will give a demonstration, but only if the customer signs the order first."	Make it easy for your customers to buy from you.

This is an odd one. This conversation was witnessed in a showroom in Birmingham. A customer came through the door, marched up to the saleslady and asked: *"Do you do demonstrations without me having to sign an order first?"* She replied: *"Yes, of course."*

The customer relaxed and said: "*That's great – because they won't down the road.*"
"*Well, we will,*" the saleslady told him. "*You have the demonstration first here, and then you sign the order.*" And that is exactly what the customer did.

The logic behind this rather odd and very sales stopping policy is that some showrooms can get callers in who want to try a vehicle and then their company sources the vehicle from another supplier. Proper qualification can take care of this type of problem.

"*Who else is involved in the decision on what you buy and where you buy it?*"

If you do have a customer who wants a demonstration and can buy from you, then don't play games. If you do have a customer who wants a demonstration and his company will then source the vehicle elsewhere, then you have but two choices:

- Refuse to do the demonstration.
- Do the demonstration, find out about the company, the name of the person responsible for the acquisition of vehicles, who the customer is, where he lives, what other vehicles are in his family and who else he knows who might be interested in buying a new or used vehicle from a nice friendly helpful person like yourself.

See... the choice is yours!

Reason 5	Recommendation
"We don't like demonstrating the vehicle because it puts mileage on which will affect what we will get for it when we sell it."	Do the demonstration. You will make more sales and more profits in the long run.

This rather pathetic excuse was given to a customer in a rather up-market showroom by a rather superior salesman.
Yes – demonstrations put mileage on demonstrators.
Yes – that will affect the retail sales value.
Yes – demonstrations do take time and trouble.
Yes – demonstrations use petrol and make vehicles dirty.
Yes – you will still make more sales and more profits overall, if you have a vigorous "*we love to demonstrate and it's no trouble at all*" policy, irrespective of what makes of vehicle you sell.

Reason 6	Recommendation
"I would do a demonstration, but the vehicle is only here from nine to six."	In a true customer-caring dealership, the salesperson would have found out when the husband and wife who he said this to could make it, talked to the Fleet Sales Manager, come to some agreement, carried out the demonstration, asked for the business and expected to get it.

The reason given was that the vehicle was used by the Fleet Sales Manager for his own purposes outside those times.

It cost the company a sale because the husband and wife that wanted to try the vehicle could not make it between those times. They were not offered any alternative so they tried and bought elsewhere. The question is, how many other potential sales were lost for the same reason? The customer-caring salesperson deserves the business. The *"only here from nine to six"* salesperson has not earned the right to deserve anything.

Why we Demonstrate

There are a multitude of good reasons that will easily outweigh the bad. Here are the main ones:

- It gives the customers the 'real experience' of driving your product.
- It shows the customers you are taking them seriously, and this makes them feel important.
- It has the effect of removing or reducing objections.
- It gives the customers a very strong and positive feeling of ownership.
- It will always show your product off in its best light.
- The more demonstrations you do, the better at doing them you become.
- It can turn 'time-wasters' into customers.
- No amount of presentation skill will ever replace the experience of actually driving the vehicle.
- There is a definite link between demonstration rate and order rate. The more demonstrations you carry out, the more orders you will take.

How to Demonstrate

A demonstration should be made as simple as possible, but not simpler! Here are some simple guidelines to help you accomplish this. All you need to carry out this exercise is a vehicle and a customer. When you mix these ingredients together correctly, you instantly expose yourself to the risk of selling something. The more you expose yourself to this risk, the more vehicles you will sell. It's as simple as that.

Instantly, with Enthusiasm

Demonstrations should be so easy to obtain. Nothing can sell the vehicle as well as the vehicle can sell itself.

> *"A demonstration? Sure – no trouble at all."*

Let's face it: a demonstration could very well be trouble, sometimes impossible right at that moment. If you have fully qualified the customer and presented your product and yourself in the best light, then most customers will give you the time to sort something out for them in the very near future, if you really cannot manage it instantly. In fact, if you have a customer who is very determined to buy your product from your company and from you personally, then you will have a very hard time trying to stop him.

Perfect Vehicles for Perfect Demonstrations

A demonstration vehicle is a demonstration vehicle. Who uses it to do what outside office hours is irrelevant. Demonstrators should be:

- Neat, clean and tidy inside and out, including seats, carpets and especially glass
- Free from damage and accessories that don't work
- Bare of all personal effects, including the boot space
- Accessible and have sufficient fuel in them
- Free from smells, including tobacco smoke
- Free from squeaks, rattles and other funny noises
- The latest models, representing a good cross-section of your range
- There! Not out on loan or having the day off!

Your Place or Theirs

It will be easy to remember the deals that you did not do when you demonstrated from your customer's home. That is because there will be so few of those situations to recall. There is something magical about calling at a customer's house or office to do the demonstration. The customer is on 'home ground' and is far more relaxed than in the showroom situation.

The family get to see the vehicle and share the excitement. If you're lucky, so will the neighbours! You get invited in and share tea or coffee and a little idle conversation. Everybody is relaxed and happy. If you can demonstrate a vehicle from your customer's house, you will double the chances of getting a signature on the order form.

Demonstrations by Appointment

Do you know, you have to have an appointment to be ill these days!

> *"Is that the surgery? I'm ill – can I see the doctor?"*
> *"Yes, there is a space at 9.17am on Thursday."*
> *"But it's Monday and I'm ill today. I might not be ill on Thursday."*

Get the picture?

It is not always possible to work to appointments. In fact, it is highly undesirable that you should when face-to-face with a qualified, presentation-primed customer. There are times when an appointment could be of benefit to buyer and seller alike. For instance:

- Existing customers that you have followed up by telephone who express an interest in seeing and trying a new model.
- Incoming telephone enquiries can be converted into face-to-face selling situations through the offer of a demonstration by appointment, but without obligation.

This is where demonstrating the vehicle from the customer's home becomes such a worthwhile idea. A customer can tell you that he will call at 10.30am on Friday and just not turn up. The demonstration is much more likely to happen if you arrange to call at the customer's home or place of business at 10.30am on Friday, because you will be there as arranged!

What Vehicle to Demonstrate

Preferably the 'right' vehicle – an example of the vehicle that the customer is thinking of buying. If you have not got that, then demonstrate whatever is closest. If all else fails, then it has to be a 'quality of the product' demonstration.

Who Will Drive?

You will drive – initially. This is to warm the vehicle up and prove that it can be driven without difficulty. Before you leave your premises, it would be sensible to find out who will be driving, when dealing with partners, husbands and wives.

Talking about husbands and wives, let's kill an old motor trade tale here and now. It does not matter where the salesperson sits in the vehicle during the demonstration. The number of times the 'we are not covered if we sit in the back' statement comes up would indicate some errors of understanding by the salespeople or their bosses.

This type of restrictive clause is never written into your insurance policy unless you deal with a very odd insurance company or there is a specific reason that relates to the type of product that you sell. The whole point is that after you have driven, let Mr and Mrs Morris sit where they normally sit. They will be more comfortable that way and that feeling of comfort will help you make a sale.

How Will You Drive?

You will treat your product like diamonds, that is what you will do. When you do this, so will your customers. Drive considerately, showing respect for your product. Customers are never impressed by salespeople's ability to do four-wheel drifts and hand-brake turns! They will be more concerned about survival than about the qualities of the vehicle.

Where Will You Drive?

Set, planned routes are a reasonable idea – different driving experiences that will match the customer's own requirements are even more reasonable.

Uphill or up-gradients while you are driving and down-hill gradients when your customer is driving will make a difference to the way a vehicle feels. Also, there is sense in the old idea of having a route without right turns. The reason for this is that turning right in traffic is the most potentially dangerous manoeuvre you can attempt. This danger must be increased if your customer is driving a vehicle that he is not familiar with. The other consideration, of course, is – where are you situated when the customer carries out this manoeuvre?

Talking about the Customer Driving

The customer should drive. If they don't, then they will not get the 'ownership' experience that has converted many an *"I'll think it over"* to a *"Wow – when can I have it?"* The reasons why a customer is reluctant to drive is usually based on one factor alone. *"I don't want to make a fool of myself in front of this stranger."* You, of course, being the stranger.

It all begins to fit together, doesn't it? If you have spent time with your customer, particularly during the qualification process, and have managed to develop the right level of rapport, then you will no longer be a stranger. When the customer's 'friend' (you, of course, being the friend) says *"It's your turn to drive now"*, the customer is far more likely to respond positively.

Take It From Here

It's as simple as that. You do not ask the customer if they would like to drive. At a safe and convenient spot, you pull over and say: *"It's your turn now"*.

Take a little time at this point. Talk about the vehicle. Clarify any grey areas.

"I'm still not sure about front wheel drive."

"That's understandable, Mr Morris. After all, you have had rear wheel drive for a long time now. So what you need for me to clarify is what are the advantages to you personally of front wheel drive?"

Re-present the vehicle if you feel the need. Re-qualify the customer if you feel that there is anything else you need to know about the customer or the customer's needs and wants.

I Will Come with You!

It is a well established practice to switch the engine off and take the key out of the ignition at changeover time. There are two good reasons for this:

1 There is less likelihood of the customer knocking you down and killing you as you cross the front of the vehicle and he tries to slide across into the driver's seat, knocking the vehicle into gear as he goes.
2 It eliminates 'the long walk home' syndrome that can and has happened as the 'customer' drives away with a cheerful wave and leaves you standing there, open-mouthed at the roadside, vehicle and 'customer' never to be seen again.

Be warned – the crooks have gone one stage further on this technique now. Quite recently, a saleslady was demonstrating an up-market vehicle to an up-market customer. Sensibly, she kept the keys with her at changeover time. As the customer was driving the vehicle, they approached a T-junction. As the vehicle came to a stop, the vehicle behind collided with the rear of the demonstrator. Naturally, the saleslady got out to sort it out. As she approached the other driver, both vehicles accelerated away. Do bear this in mind if this kind of situation ever happens to you.

Make it Easy for the Customer

- Take the keys with you
- Slide the driver's seat back
- Go round and open the door for the customer
- Get the customer settled in the driver's seat
- Help adjust the seat and anything else that is adjustable to suit the customer
- Go around and sit in the front passenger's seat
- Talk the customer through the controls
- Make sure that he is happy and comfortable
- Hand over the keys
- Sit back and relax

Keep out of the Customer's Way

The customer cannot listen to you and concentrate on driving a strange vehicle at the same time. In the interests of safety and lower repair bills, this is a very good time for you to rest your mouth. Sit quietly and observe the customer and the way he drives. Answer questions by all means, but apart from that just keep out of the customer's way and let him get used to the vehicle for a while and a mile or two.

Encourage and Eliminate Objections

Some well meaning and misguided sales trainer gave me some very unsound advice a few years ago. It was this:

> *"Never answer an objection until it has been raised at least three times."*

I took that advice and lost a few sales in the process of learning the incorrectness of the technique.

> ***"I can't get used to the pedals."***
> *"Turn left here."*
> ***"I said I can't get used to the pedals."***
> *"Now straight on to the roundabout."*
> ***"What about these pedals?"***
> *"Oh, the pedals. Don't worry – you will get used to them – they are different."*

Then the customer makes an excuse and goes away. Then you diligently follow up by telephone the next day.

"Thank you for phoning, but I bought something else."
"Oh, why was that then?"
"I told you – I couldn't get used to the pedals."

If what you are doing is not working, do something different.

There are some deals that you do that you will never forget! There are also a few deals that you didn't do that return to haunt you from time to time. That's fine as long as you can learn from the negative experience.

"I can't get used to the pedals."
"Turn left here. In what way can't you get used to the pedals?"
"They seem to be all set to the left."
"Now, straight on to the roundabout. Set to the left? Oh, I see what you mean, so what is worrying you is, will you get used to them?"
"Yes, that's what is worrying me – I see it as a problem."
"Well, look at it this way, Mr Morris, you have had your present vehicle for forty thousand miles. That's about twice around the world. It is not surprising that you have adjusted to the controls of your present vehicle.
When you have this vehicle and have driven it for forty miles, you will have already adjusted to these controls. By four hundred miles, this will be the norm for you. Do you see that?"
"Well, yes I suppose so."
"I tell you what, Mr Morris, if at that point you were to get back in to your present vehicle, it would look to you like the pedals were set to the right."
"Oh, I see what you mean."

Deal with Objections Straight Away

The message is to deal with the objections there and then, remembering to talk in the customer's preferred method of processing information (visual, auditory or kinesthetic). Don't even wait for the customer to raise the objection. As you are observing, if you feel the customer is finding something a little uncomfortable or difficult, check it out after that initial period at silence.

"Is that seat belt okay for you?"

"Do you find the seat comfortable?"

"How about that steering wheel, is that okay for you?"

If this type of checking question is used as you observe the customer's driving experience, then most potential problems in driving the vehicle can be dealt with before the development into sales-stopping objections. This is a great time for salespeople to practice the forgotten art of sensory acuity.

Dangerous Driving

Selling vehicles for a living should never be considered a terminal or life-threatening occupation. If you do have a customer who is driving at all dangerously, then you will have to do something about it.

"Pull over here, Mr Jones, I will take it back from here."

The vehicle, your safety and the safety of your customer are all your responsibility. If the customer objects to you taking over, explain what the problem is and exactly how you feel about it. You could very well lose the order – but you will be around in order to find another one tomorrow! Salespeople have been seriously injured and even killed, so never hesitate if you feel that the customer is putting your life at risk.

Fortunately, this demonstration dilemma will not happen that often, whatever make of vehicle you sell. Maybe once a year, twice if you are very unlucky. If it is happening much more than that, then it could be that you are the problem by being a more than average nervous passenger. If you drive the vehicle with respect, then the chances are your customers will too.

Now is the Time Not to Close

This used to be taught. Perhaps it still is. "*As soon as you get back from the demonstration, close the sale while the customer is most enthusiastic.*" It could work. Experience has shown that if you ask for the order as the customer's parking the vehicle, then most of that enthusiasm appears to evaporate.

Talk it Over Afterwards

Old demonstration tricks no longer seem to have their place in today's new selling world.

"Just park the vehicle right behind yours, Mr Jones. My, I can see why you are keen to change!"

"If you don't want to buy this vehicle, Mr Jones, take it to the back of the used vehicle display. If you do want it, then can you park it by the service department."

You can use them if you want. They are taught, but not that many salespeople ever feel it is necessary to use them. What is necessary is to talk it over afterwards. This is often best done sitting in the demonstration vehicle with the customer in the driving seat.

"Well – what do you think, Mr Morris?"

"It's a nice vehicle. It runs well, really smooth."

"How does it compare with your present vehicle?"

"It doesn't! This is a totally different driving experience."

"In what way, Mr Morris?"

"I feel far more in control of this vehicle. It seems to have more grip on corners and the brakes seem much firmer."

"You're obviously enjoying that feeling of safety. Let's go in and work out some figures."

It does not have to be a long chat – just long enough to get the feel of the customer's reactions to the vehicle. If they are positive, then it would make sense to go back to the showroom and talk about the price, the monthly payment or the cost to change.

Give Partners a Little Space

This is the golden opportunity for partners or husband and wife teams to have a private chat without you around.

"Why don't you two sit in the vehicle, while I go and organise some coffee? This will give you the opportunity to have a chat about the vehicle without me being in the way."

"Oh, you won't be in the way, will he, dear?"

Yes you will – get out of it – let them get on with it!

Unaccompanied Demonstrations

"Grab the keys and help yourself."

There can only be two reasons for allowing customers to take vehicles out without a salesperson in attendance:

- The salesperson is too busy.
- The salesperson is too lazy.

Either way, unaccompanied demonstrations are not a particularly good idea if you want to maximise selling opportunities.

Customers will often find reasons not to buy, which could be based on misunderstandings, wrong information or lack of knowledge. It is the salesperson's job to be there and deal with these sales-preventing, limiting beliefs. Surely the demonstration is the golden opportunity to get to know your customers better and give them the opportunity to get to know you.

There is also the question of your company's insurance cover. You may or may not be covered; policies can and do differ. Even if your customers are driving your vehicle covered by their own insurance, you could still have a problem. So check exactly what your insurance policy covers you for.

In all cases it is your responsibility to make sure that an unaccompanied driver has a current driving licence. Unless the person is well known to you, it would be more than sensible to make sure that they leave something of value with you. This could be a driving licence or the customer's present vehicle.

If you are covered for unaccompanied test drives, then the Mr and Mrs Morrises of the world might just appreciate the opportunity to take the vehicle out by themselves after you have carried out the normal demonstration. Overnight or weekend loans can also be most effective in converting a borderline case into a signed order.

A Final Word about 'Time Wasters'

Ask any salesperson about the importance of demonstrations and the response will include respectful recognition of their importance, countered with a few cautionary tales of when it's wise to make exceptions. A system of elimination exists in some salespeople's minds, a process each potential customer has unwittingly to go through before the salesperson deems the customer suitable for a demonstration. Some people are classed normally as a 'waste of time' and can be sub-grouped as follows:

Category 1 – 'The shopper'

Those who appear to be shopping around with a very long list of 'possibles' may not be suitable since an immediate order is so unlikely. On the other hand, since shopping around produces barely one demonstration in ten, why not make your dealership the one that offers the test drive and raises the customer's desire to buy.

Sales success rate, say 25%.

Category 2 – 'Got one already!'

Some salespeople believe that customers who already have last year's model need not have a demonstration since they will see no difference between the vehicles and therefore there is no point in trying this year's model. Conversely, depending on the manufacturer in question, somewhere between 30% and 90% of owners buy from the same 'stable' within three years. So raise desire by demonstration, by reminding him again how wonderful a new vehicle can be.

Sales success rate, say 30%.

Category 3 – 'Doesn't look genuine to me'

Those that don't look right, smell right or say the right things can easily be identified as flippant enquiries, not deserving too much valuable effort and therefore are classed as a waste of time by many salespeople. Simply because your customer has just been gardening or 'mucking out' the pigs does not mean he will not buy from you. Similarly, his abrupt manner or defensive attitude may be due to the difficulty he has experienced in trying to obtain demonstrations. Surprise him, and raise his desire to purchase by offering a test drive.

Sales success rate, say 50%.

Category 4 – 'He always buys the rival make'

Some salespeople believe that those who have been loyal to another franchise for 25 years and have only come in to announce how marvellous their present vehicle is will obviously never change franchise anyway. Sensible salespeople consider the real reason for his visit. He may be thinking of changing his franchise for any number of reasons. Make it possible by means of demonstration.

Sales success rate, say 40%.

Category 5 – 'He doesn't look like he can afford one'

Let's face it, we have all been caught out by this one! Those for whom the cost to change can be seen to be too large by the simple process of 'my vehicle minus his equals a lot and he doesn't look like he's got much money' can still be converted into customers in large enough numbers to make it worth the effort. Remember: the desire to purchase is governed more by emotion than price, and whether a person can 'afford' something has more to do with their credit rating than their bank balance. Raise desire with a demonstration, remembering it's not the price that dictates the decision to buy, it's desire for ownership.

Sales success rate, say 35%.

Category 6 – Manufacturers' prize draws

The people that make the vehicles have known for a long time that the best way to sell them is to get the potential customers to drive them. Manufacturers have often tried to help by sending out 'test drive invitations' combined with a prize draw. Upon producing the slip in the showroom, the customer will quite often meet with a strange response: *"Oh, that's OK, you don't have to have a test drive, we'll put your number in the prize draw anyway."* Surprisingly, people who have test drives in order to 'win something' can still be impressed by vehicles and will often be converted to buy a vehicle that they would never normally consider. Always insist that people that want to be in the prize draw must drive the vehicles.

Sales success rate, say 8%.

Category 7 – Manufacturer-originated enquiries

And then, of course, there are the slips of paper that arrive at the dealership with obscure names and addresses on them. Sometimes spelt wrong, just another waste of time that is allocated fairly quickly to a wastepaper basket somewhere. If that is the case, then these enquiries are, of course, a waste of time. Conversely, it is fairly simple to eliminate the 'schoolboys' and the 'real' time wasters that do exist (but in smaller numbers than is commonly thought) by writing the following letter:

Mr C Jones
14 The Close
Bath
Avon

Dear Mr Jones
Thank you very much indeed for your recent enquiry regarding the Pelegra LX model. By now you will have received the information pack direct from the concessionaire and you probably cannot wait to try out this superb vehicle for yourself.
In order to assist you, I have arranged a demonstration from the showroom above at 10.15am on Saturday. If this time and date is inconvenient to you, or if you would prefer to test drive the vehicle from your own home or office, please contact me. Otherwise, I look forward to meeting you at 10.15am on Saturday.
Yours sincerely

David Upsher

This will produce one of the following results:

- A demonstration – good news
- A cancellation – nothing ventured...
- An apology from the parents, since the addressee is a small child. Not really a problem: some parents actually drive vehicles!
- No response. Well, you can't win them all

Much better than throwing them in the bin, surely?

Sales success rate, say 18%.

The result of offering a demonstration to 100 time wasters of all the above categories could be:

- 29 sales

That can't be bad!

The main points again

1 Not everyone believes that there is a definite link between demonstration rate and order rate.

2 Some salespeople go out of their way to avoid carrying out demonstrations.

3 Demonstrations do take time and effort. However, a well planned and carried out demonstration will have a positive effect on borderline customers.

4 If the right vehicle is not available, it is perfectly reasonable to carry out a 'quality of the product' demonstration.

5 Demonstrations will raise the desire to buy your vehicle and reduce part-exchange price resistance.

6 Make it easy for the customer to have a demonstration instantly, wherever possible.

7 A demonstration vehicle should be perfect in every way and be ready to go.

8 Demonstrating a vehicle from a customer's home or office increases your chances of doing business.

9 You drive first to warm the vehicle up and prove that it can be driven without difficulty.

10 At all times, treat your product like diamonds and drive sensibly.

11 Use a route to suit the customer.

12 Make sure that the customer also drives.

13 Adjust the vehicle for the customer and go over the controls.

14 Keep quiet initially, but observe how your customer is driving and reacting to the vehicle and controls.

15 Encourage and eliminate objections.

16 Discourage and terminate dangerous demonstrations.

17 Talk it over afterwards.

18 Check out your company's insurance policy regarding unaccompanied demonstrations.

19 Make it your policy always to accompany a customer initially, even if there is going to be an unaccompanied test drive or overnight loan afterwards.

20 Demonstrations are so convincing that even 'time wasters' can become customers.

CHAPTER 13

Meta* Programs and Sales Excellence

"People don't come with handbooks,

... until now that is"

Some time ago it was reported in the motor industry press that the managing director of one franchise had left to join another. My company did work for the franchise he was leaving but not for the one he was going to. I had met this managing director on several occasions. It could not be said that I knew him well, but I knew him well enough to know that he would be a hard man to approach, particularly if you were going to try and sell him something. As I was keen to cash in my slight acquaintance and try to get some training and consultancy work with the new company, I decided that I would write to him. Because that letter was meant to get an appointment, I would have to take care to ensure it was personally appealing.

In spite of my limited knowledge of the person that I was about to write to, I knew that he:

1 'Moved away' from things – rather than 'towards'
2 Concentrated on 'possibilities' – rather than 'necessities'
3 Was 'self focused' (What's in it for me) – rather than 'focused on others'
4 Noticed what was 'different' or missing – rather than what was 'similar' or the same
5 Was interested in 'details' instead of 'big pictures'
6 Preferred to 'make judgements himself' – rather than asking for 'other people's opinions'
7 Was very much 'conscious of time' and liked things to happen straight away – rather than at 'some time in the future'

*Meta – from the Greek *'above'* or *'beyond'*

Bearing all this in mind, I sent him the following letter (the numbers in brackets refer to his behavioural tendencies, as already highlighted.

Dear Mr Jones

Congratulations on your recent appointment as Managing Director of ________. When, or if, you have decided what you want to do (6), there could very well be the possibility (2) that my company could be of assistance to you.

If you do have some missing pieces (4) in your overall plan, we could be available immediately (7) to discuss your needs and any specific requirements that you may have (5). The opportunity to work with you again would be appreciated.

If you feel that an exploratory meeting would be of benefit to you (3) and your company, please do let me know.

Yours sincerely

David J Upsher

Six out of seven can't be bad, I thought, as I signed the letter. Seven, if you counted the fact that I had (most unusually) not finished with the usual 'I will contact you by telephone shortly to make an appointment...'. There was no point in doing this because of the danger that he would 'move away' from such a direct approach. I had never written to anybody using their own Meta Programs to structure the letter before. As I popped it in the post tray, I wondered if it would work.

...And it did.

There's an area of sales excellence that is above or beyond the reach and understanding of all but the most fully awake salespeople. If you would care to consider joining these people, then this chapter is for you. Read on if you would like to become fully awake and totally amazed.

Every day you, like most everybody else, are constantly barraged with a deluge of information. Far more information than your brain can possibly cope with, let alone categorise. Your brain has to do something with all this stuff. So, quite frankly, it cheats!

It does this is one of three ways. Your brain will:

◆ Delete	Incoming information
◆ Distort	Incoming information
◆ Generalise	Incoming information

In other words, your brain will be selective in what it programmes in. Four people having a conversation about the same thing could end up contributing the following to the conversation:

◆ *"Did you see that big black cat?"*	Statement
◆ *"What big black cat?"*	Delete
◆ *"I thought it was a squirrel."*	Distort
◆ *"Once you've seen one, you've seen them all."*	Generalise

Yet they were all looking at the same cat.

In order to help the brain decide what to do with information, certain 'filters' are used, to help you select what you should pay attention to – what information to keep and what information to discard. There are many of these filters: they are called Meta Programs. For the sake of clarity, interest and understanding, let us consider seven generally recognised ones that have the most influence on your day-to-day thinking and that of your customers.

Seven Common Information Filters

Moving Away		Moving Towards
◆ Avoid	or	◆ What I like
◆ Get rid of		◆ What I want
◆ Stay clear of		◆ What I need

Necessity		Possibility
◆ Need	or	◆ Choices
◆ Obligation		◆ Possibilities
◆ Responsibility		◆ Opportunities

Self Focused		Focused on Others
◆ What's in it for me?	or	◆ What can I do for others?
◆ How will I benefit?		◆ How will they benefit?
◆ This is no help to me		◆ This will help others

What's Similar?		What's Different?
◆ Sameness	or	◆ What's missing?
◆ Similarity		◆ What doesn't match?
◆ What's there?		◆ What's changed?

Chunking Down		Chunking Up
◆ Smaller	or	◆ Larger
◆ Specific		◆ Overall concepts
◆ Definite steps		◆ The big picture

Internally Referenced		Externally Referenced
◆ Own criteria	or	◆ Other people's views
◆ Own evaluations		◆ Outside evaluation
◆ Own judgements		◆ External approval

In Time		Through Time
◆ Now	or	◆ Linear
◆ Today		◆ Continuous
◆ At this moment		◆ Uninterrupted

The Seven Common Information Filters With Examples

Moving Away		Moving Towards
"I would not want a green one."	or	*"I am particularly drawn to the metallic blue."*

Necessity		Possibility
"I must have it by Thursday."	or	*"Do you think I could have it by Thursday?"*

Self Focused		Focused on Others
"I am mostly interested in what I am going to get out of owning this vehicle."	or	*"I am mostly interested in getting a vehicle that will meet all the needs of my family."*

What's Similar?		What's Different?
"This is just like the one I had before."	or	*"Oh I see, they have changed the windscreen wiper knob."*

Chunking Down		Chunking Up
"What's the input valve clearance at 6000 revs?"	or	*"How many cylinders has it got?"*

Internally Referenced		Externally Referenced
"I make the decision on what vehicle I drive."	or	*"I would want to seek advice from a friend of mine before making up my mind."*

In Time		Through Time
"I would like to do something about this now."	or	*"I really can't make a decision today – I need to sleep on it."*

Just a minute – I recognise all this!

Of course you do, you have been using the information filters for as long as you have existed. They are old friends of yours that help you make sense of the world as you see it. There is nothing mystical or difficult about that. These information filters can be sales-losing enemies too. Particularly when you are working on opposite filters to that of the customer you are talking to. If this happens, then you get the following conversations.

Moving Away		Moving Towards
"I would not want a green one."	or	*"I am particularly drawn to the metallic blue."*
↓		↓
"Why on earth not? It's a lovely colour."		*"Well – frankly, the metallic colours can be difficult to match if you ever need bodywork."*

Necessity		Possibility
"I must have it by Thursday."	or	*"Do you think I could have it by Thursday?"*
↓		↓
"That might just be possible – you could be lucky."		*"We have an obligation to people who have already placed orders – it is necessary to progress these first."*

Self Focused		Focused on Others
"I am mostly interested in what I am going to get out of owning this vehicle."	or	*"I am mostly interested in getting a vehicle that will meet all the needs of my family."*
↓		↓
"Aren't your family's needs just as important?"		*"Yes – but aren't your own interests more important? After all, you're the one who is paying for it?"*

What's Similar?		What's Different?
"This is just like the one I had before."	or	*"Oh I see, they have changed the windscreen wiper knob."*
↓		↓
"Well, not really, they have totally changed the engine and suspension."		*"Yes – but it is the same vehicle."*

Chunking Down		Chunking Up
"What's the input valve clearance at 6000 revs?"	or	*"How many cylinders has it got?"*
↓		↓
"I haven't the foggiest – but it's got six cylinders."		*"Six in line enhanced by hemispherical twin action combustion chambers and sodium filled valves."*

Internally Referenced		Externally Referenced
"I make the decision on what vehicle I drive."	or	*"I would want to seek advice from a friend of mine before making up my mind."*
↓		↓
"Isn't that dangerous, you could end up with the wrong vehicle."		*"What would you want to do that for. Why don't you decide?"*

In Time		Through Time
"I would like to do something about this now."	or	*"I really can't make a decision today – I need to sleep on it."*
↓		↓
"What's the rush? What difference will a couple of days make?"		*"That's no good – I need to know today."*

In all the above examples, the seller is using the opposite Meta Program to the buyer. Deals can still be done that way, but they can be very hard work. Unfortunately, if you get totally out of 'Meta Step' with your customer, the chances are that the customer will feel so uncomfortable that he will walk away without buying.

Information Filters and the Sales Process

Moving away – moving towards

People who mainly 'move away':

- Talk about what they don't want
- Will tell you what they want to avoid
- Have a tendency to stay away from things they don't fully understand
- Like to get rid of things that they no longer need

When dealing with customers who are inclined to 'move away':

- Find out what they want to avoid
- Ask them what they don't want
- Reassure them that any problems can be sorted out
- Always be aware that these people can often find it difficult to communicate what they do want

Moving Away	
"I would not want a green one."	*"Oh, that won't be a problem – what other colours do you want to avoid? Let's just cross them off this colour chart and see what we are left with."*

A pal of mine got so fed up with his partner's tendency to move away from things that he put a glass of water and two aspirins on her bedside table one night. As she got into bed she said: "*What's this for? I haven't got a headache.*" So he said: "*That's all right then.*"

People I know who 'move away':

People who mainly 'move towards':

- Are attracted to what they want and what they like
- Will often find it difficult to recognise what they should avoid
- Dismiss or minimise possible problems
- Are often attracted to special offers and incentives

When dealing with customers who are inclined to 'move towards':

- Find out what they want
- Get them to talk about what they will gain through purchasing a vehicle
- Talk about how they will use the vehicle
- Discuss the extras and options they want to include
- Emphasise that you are going to help them get what they want

Moving Towards

"I am particularly drawn to the metallic blue."	*"If that is what you want, then I will help you get it. What else do you want?"*

People I know who 'move towards':

Necessity – possibility

People who mainly focus on 'necessity':

- Tend to be fatalistic:

  "This is the way it has to be done."
  "I do not have any choice."
  "It is necessary for me to do this."

- Give the impression that they have to do what they have to do
- May well feel uncomfortable if they do not know how to proceed
- Feel more comfortable if they know what's going on – or what will happen next

When dealing with customers who mainly focus on 'necessity':

- Tell them what you propose to do in order to help them
- Explain that this is the way the system operates
- Tell them what you expect them to do
- Use key phrases like:

  "These are the procedures."
  "This is what will happen."
  "This is the right way."
  "This is the correct way of doing things."

Focused on Necessity	
"I must have it by Thursday."	*"Well the correct way would be to check with our workshop to find out exactly when your vehicle would be ready. I will check and tell you precisely when we can deliver."*

People I know who focus on 'necessity':

People who mainly focus on 'possibility'

- Always look for other ways to do things
- Will often do things differently, to see what will happen
- Look for new opportunities and challenges
- Have the desire to learn new things and expand their options

When dealing with customers who mainly focus on 'possibility':

- Follow a loose and flexible procedure
- Tell them about the possibilities and options open to them
- Let them know that you are interested in helping them expand their options
- Use key words like 'new ways', 'optional choices', 'possibilities' and 'choices'

Focused on Possibility	
"Do you think I could have it by Thursday?"	*"That could very well be possible. If it's not, then you would always have the option of collecting it at the weekend."*

People I know who focus on 'possibility':

Self focused – focused on others

People who are self focused:

- In extreme cases, can be very selfish and can suffer from narcissism *
- Are inclined to start from the perspective/position '*What's in it for me?*'
- Often find it difficult to listen to other people
- Judge the success of communication by what they think, rather than the responses they get

When dealing with people who are 'self focused':

- Explain what's in it for them
- Handle with care
- Ask lots of open questions to encourage their participation in the conversation
- Emphasise key points and repeat as necessary, to make sure that they get the message

Focused on Sell	
"I'm mostly interested in what I am going to get out of owning this vehicle."	*"This vehicle is built for the driver. It's a vehicle that you will really enjoy driving and owning."*

People I know who are 'focused on self':

* Narcissism: morbid self love or self admiration – like the cat in the BBC television series *Red Dwarf*.

People who are 'focused on others':

- Can, in extreme cases, be too interested in trying to please other people
- Think: *"what can I do for somebody else?"*
- Judge the success of communication by the responses they get from others
- Try and 'fit in' with other people's wants and needs

When dealing with people who are 'focused on others':

- Explain what benefits there are for other people
- Handle with friendliness and openness
- Take the time to make sure that you understand what they want to achieve
- Reflect your interest and encourage them to talk further by showing that you are listening to them

Focused on Others	
"I am mostly interested in getting a vehicle that will meet all the needs of my family."	*"Yes, I understand. Please do tell me all about your family and what needs they have."*

People I know who are 'focused on others':

What's similar – what's different

People who are sorting by 'what's similar':

- Look for things that are the same
- Tend to notice what matches, rather than what doesn't
- Are more comfortable with familiar things and situations
- Like to keep to what they know

When dealing with customers who are sorting by 'what's similar':

- Give them time to get comfortable in what could be strange surroundings
- Point out what is the same rather than what is different
- Find out areas of mutual interest
- Use 'similar' language such as 'same as', 'just like', 'similar to', 'has this in common' and 'keep the same'

Sorting by 'what's similar'	
"This is just like the one I had before."	*"You're right – it's very similar to the vehicle you had. You will be very comfortable with it."*

People I know who sort by 'what's similar':

People who are sorting by 'what's different':

- Look for things that are different
- Tend to notice what doesn't match, rather than what does
- Are inclined to look for what's missing
- Are attracted by anything new or revolutionary

When dealing with customers who are sorting by 'what's different':

- Point out the differences, rather than what is similar
- Emphasise the difference between the customer's present vehicle and your current model
- Present the differences as 'new' or 'revolutionary'
- Use different words such as 'new', 'changed', 'different', 'unique', 'leading edge', 'up to the minute' and 'radical'

Sorting by 'what's different'

"Oh, I see, they have changed the windscreen wiper knob."	*"Yes they have. There have been many changes made. These together with the use of leading-edge technology make this model very up-to-date indeed."*

People I know who focus on 'what's different':

Chunking up – chunking down

People who tend to 'chunk down' information:

- Are more interested in specifics than generalities
- Break down tasks and activities into small specific steps
- Will want all the details before they make up their minds
- Once they have all the facts, only then will they consider the 'big picture'

When dealing with customers who tend to 'chunk down' information:

- Think of them as using a microscopic lens
- Break things down for them into small pieces of information
- Use precise specific language – vagueness and generalities will only confuse them
- Use 'chunking down' language – 'precisely', 'specifically', 'exactly', 'organised', 'structure' and 'fine detail'

Chunking Down	
"What's the input valve clearance 6,000 revs?"	*"Rather than me guessing, let me look up at the exact measurement for you, plus any other fine detail that you want to know."*

People I know who 'chunk down':

People who tend to 'chunk up' information:

- Tend to concentrate on generalities, preferring to look at overall objectives
- Need to get the 'big picture' first before they can consider smaller definite steps
- Have difficulty in understanding step-by-step procedures
- Don't want to get bogged down with the details

When dealing with customers who tend to 'chunk up' information:

- Think about them as using a 'wide angle lens'
- Give them the 'big picture' first, without too much detail – concentrate on generalities
- Talk them through the key points so they don't fill in the details incorrectly
- Use 'chunking up' language – 'framework', 'overview', 'concept', 'generally' and 'overall'

Chunking Up	
"How many cylinders has it got?"	*"Six, which generally gives good performance with good fuel consumption overall."*

People I know who 'chunk up':

Internally referenced – externally referenced

People who use an 'internal reference':

- Rely mostly on what they think rather than what you tell them
- Resist being 'sold' things before they have had a chance to make their own judgement
- Are inclined to tell you what they want and what they have decided to do
- Will relate to you positively when you agree with what they have already decided is right

When dealing with customers who use an 'internal reference':

- Emphasise that only they will know what is right for them – *'It's for you to decide.'*
- Give them facts by all means, but they will not be very interested in your opinions
- Try to help them clarify their own thinking – *'What is it that you want?'*
- Confirm that in the end it is their decision regarding what they should do

Internally Referenced	
"I make the decision on what drive."	*"Absolutely, only you will know what vehicle is right for you."*

People I know who are 'internally referenced':

People who use an 'external reference':

- Rely mostly on what other people think and decide
- Enjoy being sold to and having help to make their minds up
- Will ask other people what they should do
- Are very influenced by other people's opinions and suggestions

When dealing with customers who use an 'external reference':

- Emphasise what other people think about your product and services
- Produce plenty of third party references such as road test reports, letters from satisfied customers or newspaper editorials
- Give them plenty of positive feedback about their decision to consider changing their vehicle
- Talk about the services you offer your customers and how many satisfied customers you have

Externally Referenced	
"I would want to seek advice from a friend of mine before making my mind up."	*"Sure, would you like to talk to one or two customers of ours as well? I could arrange that for you."*

People I know who are 'externally referenced':

In time – through time

People who are 'in time':

- Make decisions more quickly
- Are inclined to think of time as now, today and at this moment
- Tend to be less aware of the duration of time and can get caught up in what they are doing
- Can often be late or miss appointments

When dealing with people who are 'in time':

- Expect to do business with them the first time you meet them
- Avoid making any promises that you might not be able to keep
- Allow plenty of time to help them buy
- Be prepared to do some 'running around' to finalise delivery, as they are inclined to get 'in time' with other activities or priorities

In Time	
"I would like to do something about this now."	*"Okay, so what do you need from me to help you do that?"*

People I know who are 'in time':

People who are 'through time':

- Make decisions much more slowly
- Are inclined to think of time as uninterrupted and continuous
- Are very much aware of the duration of time
- Have the tendency to be on time

When dealing with people who are 'through time':

- Expect to do business with them, but in a matter of time
- Help them go through their long and laborious process to make the decision
- Always be on time if you have arranged to meet them

Through Time	
"I really can't make a decision today – I need to sleep on it."	*"That's fine. Might I suggest that I telephone you tomorrow at eleven fifteen to see what you have decided?"*

People I know who are 'through time':

Just think about it

If the greatest sales aid or ability is the art of being able to get into step with your customers, the greatest aid to getting into step has got to be Meta Programs.

Listen to your customers. Are they:

Moving away?	or	Moving towards?
Driven by necessity?	or	Driven by possibility?
Self focused?	or	Focused on others?
Looking for what's similar?	or	Looking for what's different?
Chunking down information?	or	Chunking up information?
Internally referenced?	or	Externally referenced?
In time?	or	Through time?

Why just listen to customers? Listen to everybody – friends, family, the people you work with and the people you come into contact with. Practise on these people and learn all you can about Meta Programs. Then stop just listening and start hearing and understanding. It will give you an edge by honing your sales ability into something far beyond normal sales techniques.

Have you got it?

This is probably the heaviest chapter in the book. It's probably the most valuable in helping you create more sales opportunities for yourself and your company. Take the time to read it again. Then try it over a period of seven weeks, concentrating on one Meta Program at a time. Take a whole week identifying if the people you are talking to are 'moving away' or 'moving towards', then communicate using each person's own Meta Program preference and not yours.

Start to use the space available to note down the Meta Program away/towards preference of each person you meet or know, and the following week, try adding necessity/possibility. In less than two months you will be able to identify and use all seven examples without difficulty. Here is a simple exercise that will show you how much you have remembered about information filters (Meta Programs) so far.

Question: What are the seven filters that this person is using?

"I want to buy a new vehicle, but I have to have it quickly. It's got to be big enough for all my family's needs. I want something different from what I have had before. Something really new. For instance, it must have an ABS braking system and twin air bags, and it's got to be Iron Silver metallic with a blue cloth trim. I can make the decision to go ahead, and if I like what you show me, I would like to sort out the paperwork and delivery while I am here."

You've got it!

Use it. It makes good sales sense and makes good selling more fun.

Oh, it will also have a dramatic effect on your volume and profit levels.

The main points again

1 The brain has so much incoming information coming its way day-to-day that in order to make sense of the information, it cheats. It:

- Deletes
- Distorts
- Generalises

2 The brain also uses filters when processing incoming information:

- Moving away from or Moving towards
- Necessity or Possibility
- Self focused or Focused on others
- What's similar or What's different
- Chunking down or Chunking up
- Internally referenced or Externally referenced
- In time or Through time

3 If you understand and use this, it will be most valuable in helping you create more sales opportunities and achieving the highest level of sales excellence.

SECTION SIX

Gathering Momentum

"I broke out into a cold sweat with the realisation that this was the car I had come to collect"

CHAPTER 14
The Part-Exchange Appraisal

"Part-exchange appraisals which take place behind the customer's back are a breeding ground for suspicion and distrust"

In our business, the part of the sales journey where you need the most specialised knowledge (or to know someone who has) is dealing with the part-exchange. Making mistakes in this area can cost a fortune. It's best not to make any, but if you do, only make them once.

At one company I worked for, each salesperson was personally responsible for appraising and valuing each part-exchange they dealt with. Most part-exchanges were sold to the trade. We were supplied with a list of approved traders who we could approach to get the part-exchanges underwritten ('underwritten' simply means *'I will pay you this much for the car subject to it matching your description'*).

If a vehicle did not realise the underwriter's value, then the salesperson was responsible for making up any shortfall IN FULL! We got very good at underwriting vehicles, but still got it wrong from time to time. Like Mr MacBride, for instance. Just to recall his name sends a shiver of negative emotions down my central spinal cortex.

It all started so innocently, with a telephone call. Mr MacBride wanted to buy a new car and part-exchange his present one.

"*When can you bring it in?*" I asked.

"*That will be difficult,*" he told me. "*I'm phoning from my home in Scotland.*"

"*What's the car like?*" I asked him, reaching for an appraisal form. He described the car. It was perfect. Plenty of extras and the right colour.

"*Only about 20,000 miles,*" he added. "*I have it hand-washed twice a week.*"

"*What's the biggest dent on it?*" I asked him.

"It hasn't got any dents," he told me with a slightly incredulous edge to his voice, indicating his displeasure of the question.

"Okay," I said, *"I will talk to our buyer and come back to you with an offer."* And that's what I did. The car sounded so desirable that I knew that the best place to get the best price would be from Ron Stratton in Manchester.

I rang Ron and gave him the description. He was pleased to offer top money for such a delightful car. I rang Mr MacBride, who found the price I offered him acceptable and the deal was done there and then over the telephone. When the new car was ready, I loaded it and me on the overnight sleeper from Kings Cross to Edinburgh and we both set off on our long journey.

The next morning the car and I looked fresh and bright as we drove up Mr MacBride's drive on the Edinburgh outskirts. Parked outside his house was a heap. I had no idea that there were so many shades of one paint colour. I can only imagine that the car had been regularly driven down hawthorn-edged, bolder-strewn footpaths. This would have accounted for the long lines of scratches down both sides and the badly battered wheel rims. What a shed, I thought. I wouldn't like to have that underwritten. Then it dawned on me – this dog was Mr MacBride's part-exchange. I broke out in a cold sweat with the realisation that the number plates matched the car I had come to collect.

Leaping from the car, still half hoping that it was all a ghastly mistake, I started to check the heap out. The more I looked, the worse it seemed. Hope rose for a micro-second when I noticed that the mileage on the car was 28,000 miles; the one I had underwritten was 20,000 miles. Then I remembered that Mr MacBride had said *"about 20,000 miles"*. This was the car all right, and I had bought it. In fact, Mr MacBride was most indignant when I had the audacity to suggest that he had misdescribed his part-exchange.

"If that's the way you feel," he said, *"just forget the whole thing and take the new one away."* It did cross my mind. The only real advantage would have been in stopping Mr MacBride getting away with it. Because I had felt certain that everything was what it seemed to be (genuine part-exchange and genuine customer), the new car had been fully paid for and registered in his name before I left London. The only thing I could do was to swallow both the bile and the pride and drive the dog to Manchester.

My face must have been a picture when I first saw the part-exchange. But it was nothing compared to Ron Stratton's.

"But this can't be it," Ron said. *"You are pulling my dipstick, aren't you?"* I told Ron the story – from the very first telephone call. *"What have you learned from this experience?"* he asked me. I went through the list of lessons.

- Never agree a price on a part-exchange without someone seeing and driving it
- Customers tell lies or bend the truth a little – they call it negotiation
- Taking shortcuts or chances in motor vehicle transactions can be very costly
- Selling is normally face-to-face and not over a telephone
  and so on...

"Right," said Ron, *"It'll be a long time before you make that mistake again. I think you have learned your lesson. Now,"* he added, *"I will tell you what it is going to cost you."*
...And he did.

The Part-Exchange Appraisal

Most customers already have a vehicle. Most of these vehicles will be offered to you as part-payment for the new or used vehicles that they are thinking of buying.

This is the bit that makes selling vehicles different from most other selling jobs. This is also the bit where it can go expensively wrong. There is no substitute for experience. Here are some guidelines that will help you gain that experience in as short a time as possible if you are relatively new to the job. For those who have had part-exchange appraisal experience, please do study these pages. They will form a useful reminder of how to maximise sales and profitability and minimise those occasions where most salespeople talk themselves into a deal that they should never have done. The very experienced will have discovered by now that 'profit comes from the deals we do not do!'

There are three steps to dealing with the customer's part-exchange:

- APPRAISAL – estimating the condition of
- VALUATION – estimating the worth of
- NEGOTIATION – a price to do business at

Part-Exchange Appraisal

The most important step is the first one, appraisal. Get the appraisal wrong and the deal will go from bad to worse. During the qualification process, you will have established if there is going to be a part-exchange involved. The very best time to appraise a part-exchange is directly after you have qualified the customer.

Recommended Structure

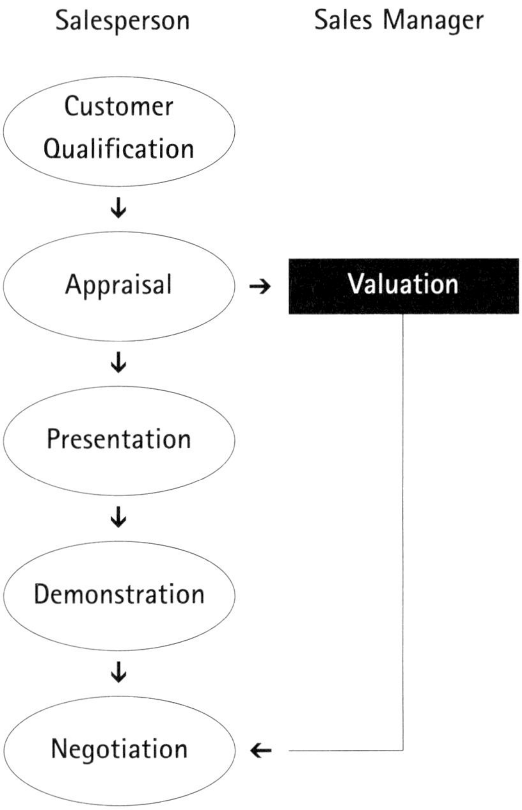

- First you qualify the customer and the fact that there is a part-exchange.
- Then you appraise (estimate the condition of) the part-exchange.
- Next you present and demonstrate, while a third party establishes the value
- Finally you tell the customer what the value of the part-exchange is and negotiate or not, according to need and company policy.

Reasons for Recommendation

Having qualified the customer, why not appraise the part-exchange straight away? There are many good reasons for doing it this way.

- You can continue to qualify the customer as you 'qualify' the customer's vehicle.
- It gets the appraisal out of the way and it will give someone else plenty of time to establish the true value of the part-exchange while you get on with the presentation and demonstration.
- It gives the customer time to see and drive the vehicle that they are interested in while the valuation is being carried out.
- There is no wasting time after the demonstration. The price has been established, 'while you were out'.
- The price can then be discussed with the customer at exactly the right time – shortly after the demonstration, on your return to the showroom.

How to Appraise the Part-Exchange

The kind of expertise needed to carry out a thorough and accurate appraisal cannot be learnt by reading a chapter in a book. Recognising professionally repaired body damage or those little tell-tale noises that indicate that all is not well is a skill that is acquired over time, with practice, with help and through a certain amount of trial and (let's face it) error.

The easiest and least costly way to gain this knowledge is to 'role model' those who have it, such as:

People Inside Your Business

You could be working both with salespeople and managers who have the skill and would be prepared to share it. Perhaps you have someone in the service department who would be prepared to show you how to detect mechanical faults and potential problems. It could be that you have your own body shop, where in a very short space of time you could gain the necessary skills to spot past problems as well as present needs to put the vehicle into retail condition.

People Outside Your Business

Spending time at a car auction is time very well spent (don't go if you have an itchy nose!). If your company uses auctions, then they will probably have contacts inside the auction who would be prepared to guide you through what's going on and how to make best use of your time. If your company does not use auctions, then you will find that a telephone call to the manager to explain who you are, who you work for and what you want to do will give you an instant invitation to 'come on down' and you will receive help when you get there. Most auctions are keen to make contacts in the retail motor industry at any level, whether you currently do business or not. It makes good future business sense to them as well as being a great way for you to find out what used vehicles are really worth.

Used car traders and retailers are a good short cut to appraisal expertise. If your company disposes of unwanted stock through these channels, then a day spent with a good used car buyer will pay handsomely for itself time and time again.

If you do not have your own body shop, then who does your repairs? Find out, contact them and ask if you could spend some time with someone who knows how to appraise bodywork.

All these activities can only help you, and they should be done with your management knowing about them. Conversely, if you are the management, these ideas will not only make your job easier, they will also add a significant contribution to your departmental bottom line.

Customer requirements

DATE	SALESMAN
NEW/USED	CUSTOMER NAME
EXTRAS	CONTACT ADDRESS
TRANSACTION TYPE	TEL PRIVATE BUSINESS
PAYMENT SOURCE	SOURCE OF ENQUIRY
SPECIAL REQUIREMENTS	REFERRAL BY
	BEST METHOD & TIME OF CONTACT
COMPETITION	

CAR	MODEL	REG. NO.	1ST REG.
COLOUR	UPHOLSTERY	TAXED	M.O.T.
OWNERS	MILEAGE	CHASSIS NO.	H.P.I.

GENERAL APPEARANCE	
EXCELLENT	
GOOD	
AVERAGE	
FAIR	
POOR	

o CHIPS ETC.

RUST

X DENT

— SCRATCH

EXTENSIVE DAMAGE

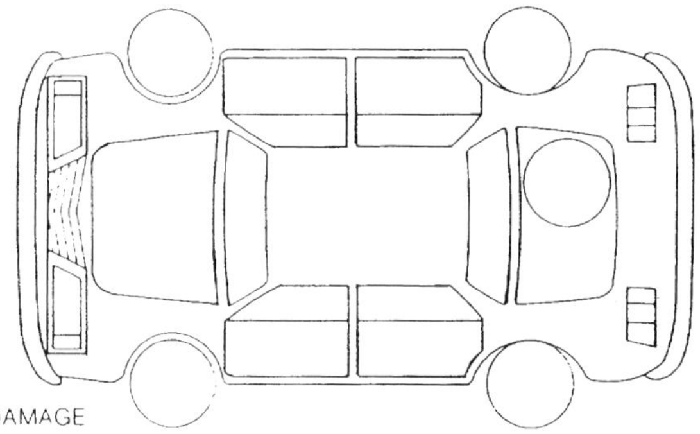

BODY DAMAGE	RECON COSTS	MECHANICS	RECON COSTS		RECON. COSTS
1		Engine		Dampers	
2		Gearbox		Brakes	
3		Rear axle		Steering	
4		Drive shafts		Battery	
5		Exhaust		Lights	
6		Tyres		Others	
£		Clutch		£	

INTERIOR	A	B	C	ACCESSORIES				RECON. COSTS	
Carpets				Automatic		P.A.S.		Body	
Roof lining				5 speed		Tinted windows		Mechanics	
Seats				Electric windows		Sunroof		Interior	
Door trims				Radio/Stereo		Alloy wheels		Others	
Fascia				Spot lamps		Metallic paint			
	Good	Ave	Bad	Leather		Cloth seats		Total £	

TRADE (GG)		RETAIL (GG)		BUYING	TOTAL	MARGIN
TRADE VALUE		ESTIMATED RETAIL		CAR		
ADD		LESS		EXTRAS		
OVER ALLOWANCE		PROFIT TARGET		FINANCE	—	
MAX ALLOWANCE		RECON. COSTS		BONUS	—	
TRADE BID BY		STAND-IN PRICE		OTHERS		
PHONE/SEEN		ADD				
		OVER ALLOWANCE				
		MAX ALLOWANCE		DISCOUNT/DEAL WANTED		

DATE OF RECONTACT	PHONE	LETTER	FACE TO FACE	DEAL DONE ☐ FOLLOW-UP ☐	REVIEW DATE	S/M APPRO
1st FOLLOW UP				SEND THANKYOU FOR CALLING LETTER (NOW)		
2nd FOLLOW UP				PROSPECT RECONTACTS OR CONTACT PROSPECT BY PHONE OR FACE TO FACE (WITHIN 48 HOURS OF ENQUIRY)		
3rd FOLLOW UP				PROSPECT RECONTACTS OR CONTACT BY SALES MANAGER TELEPHONE OR FACE TO FACE		
4th FOLLOW UP						
5th FOLLOW UP						

NO FURTHER ACTION	
OWNER CARD RAISED	
LONG TERM PROSPECT CARD RAISED	

Used Vehicle Appraisal Forms

There are those who think it is 'sissy' to use an appraisal form to appraise a part-exchange. They much prefer to wander around the vehicle, price guide in hand, and then state their price. Using an appraisal form is not a recommendation: it is an absolute must. Here are some very good reasons for doing so:

- It looks, and is, professional
- It involves the customer in the sales process
- It helps you obtain follow-up information
- It creates the basis of a 'hot prospect' file
- You will not miss anything
- It's a management guide to the condition of the part-exchange
- It's an excellent guide to the reconditioning needed
- It helps make the trade or retail decision
- You can describe the vehicle accurately to a third party over the telephone
- It sets the scene for a sensible sales structure
- It helps a third party to price the vehicle
- Other people can see the full situation if you are out
- It's a record of the condition of the vehicle when you first saw it

Oh, and don't forget, a fully completed appraisal form will help you price the vehicle accurately. What is even more important is that the customer will believe that price because it is written down.

The Appraisal Structure

After you have fully qualified the customer and explained what you propose to do to help him, this is the time to appraise the part-exchange.

Take the appraisal form (preferably on a clipboard) and invite the customer to go to the part-exchange with you because:

- Appraisal forms look smarter on a clipboard
- You can continue to qualify and build a relationship
- You want the customer to know that you know exactly the condition of his part-exchange
- Appraisals that take place in secret, behind a customer's back, are a breeding ground for suspicion and mistrust

Only appraise part-exchanges when it's not raining, when it's daylight and when you and your customer have the time to do it properly because:

- Vehicles covered in rain can hide a multitude of faults and blemishes
- You need the daylight to see the vehicle properly
- Rushed appraisals are inaccurate appraisals
- You can always take the vehicle out of the rain, wait for the daylight and for the time to do the job properly

Check the vehicle over externally. Look for signs of damage, past and present, and get the overall impression. At the same time make a note of all key information – make, model, series, mileage, registration number, date of expiry of MoT and road fund licence etc. – because:

- It's that first impression of the part-exchange that will give you a good indication of the condition of the vehicle
- The key information is needed to help your Sales Manager (or other third party) price the vehicle later

Now take a closer look at the external components and surfaces. This should include tyres, light clusters, bumpers and windows because:

- It's the visual defects that can really detract from its value
- Vehicles that look 'well loved' externally are usually well looked after internally too
- Items like cracked or broken light clusters can cost a fair amount of money to replace

Note down on the appraisal form any damage, past damage and discrepancies as you go because:

- It looks, and is, professional
- You will not forget anything (you are bound to if you fill in the form later)
- The customer will know that you know exactly what the condition of the vehicle is

Be kind about the condition of customers' vehicles. Make notes of defects but without verbal comments or facial displeasure because:

- Quite often customers are attached to the vehicles they currently drive
- If they feel you do not like their vehicle, they lose enthusiasm for you personally
- They will lose the desire to do business with your company
- Negative emotions are contagious. If you feel unhappy about doing business, then so will your customer

Look under the bonnet and in the boot, open all doors, check for missing items, signs of rust, and oil or water leaks, because:

- Anything that can be opened by you will probably be opened by the next person who is thinking of buying it
- It will give you an accurate idea of how the vehicle has really been looked after

Check through all interior items and fittings, from the roof lining to underneath the carpets, because:

- Missed interior rectification needs can be very costly
- Tidy and well maintained interiors will be a great help to sell the part-exchange on again

When you have completed your static checks, ask the customer for his keys, explaining that you would now like to check the transmission:

- All part-exchanges, without exception, must be driven
- Retail customers sometimes 'get rid' of vehicles when they are going wrong
- Some company car customers treat their cars with less respect. That could cause premature wear and the need for early repair and replacement of parts
- It will help the customer 'believe' the price you place on the vehicle, because you have driven it

Take the customer with you when you drive the part-exchange because:

- What will the customer be doing if you don't? Probably standing around in the showroom getting bored and apprehensive
- It helps you continue to build a good relationship
- The customer will know that you know what the vehicle is like mechanically
- Remember to leave the family with something to do while you are both away

Drive the vehicle with respect, listening for any unusual noises, while you get a general feel of the vehicle, because:

- Gone are the days when you had to 'thrash' vehicles to bring out the defects
- If modern vehicles have faults, they are much easier to detect than they used to be
- The customer will not appreciate you throwing his vehicle all over the road

Continue to qualify and find out more about the customer as you drive because:

- It will relax both you and your customer as you do your job (ever had your hair cut by a silent hairdresser?)
- The better you get to know your customer, the better your chances of doing business

When you have a good overall impression of the vehicle's mechanical condition, return to the showroom, stay in the vehicle and make your notes, because:

- It will give you and your customer a little breathing space before moving onto presentation
- If you do not note things down straight away, they can easily be forgotten

At the same time make a note of all extras and options. Ask the customer if anything is going to be removed, including the road fund licence, because:

- Extras and options add value to the part-exchange
- Removed items, including the road fund licence, will detract from the value

If you feel confident that the appraisal form represents a true description of the part-exchange, hand the keys back to the customer, because:

- This will indicate to your manager or the person who will be valuing the vehicle your confidence in the appraisal that you have carried out

If you do not feel confident or are unhappy in any way with your appraisal, clip the keys to the clipboard that the appraisal is on because:

- This will indicate to the 'valuer' that you need help or that you are not sure about the appraisal
- Irrespective of your experience, there is always the unusual
- Asking for help when you need it is sign of personal strength, not weakness

Take the customer and the appraisal form (with or without the keys) back into the showroom because:

- The next step will be to 'present' the vehicle that the customer is interested in
- This will normally be carried out in or near the showroom area

Leave the customer briefly in the showroom. Take the appraisal form to the person who will be valuing it, normally the Sales Manager, because:

- If you are not very experienced, then you will need all the help you can get to price part-exchanges accurately
- Even if you are qualified to value the part-exchange yourself, you will keep far more credibility with your customer if someone else is responsible for pricing the part-exchange
- If it is your 'opinion' what the vehicle is worth and the customer does not like it, then the customer will hold you responsible
- If it is someone else's 'opinion' what the customer's vehicle is worth, then your good relationship will remain intact

Leave the forms with the manager to deal with and go back to the customer to start the presentation and demonstration process.

"Right, Mr Wolsey, while my manager is getting on with working out the current value of your car, let's take a look at the car you are interested in." Because:

- This gives the manager plenty of time to value the part-exchange
- This gives you the time and the customer the inclination to take a look at the vehicle being considered – and to try it
- This removes that disastrous situation where the customer starts drumming his fingers with impatience in the showroom while you are drumming your fingers with impatience in the manager's office

While you are waiting for the price, get on with the presentation and demonstration. Use the information that you obtained during the qualification and appraisal to personalise both steps to match your customers needs because:

- The part-exchange price is being dealt with by someone else
- You can concentrate on each individual customer's likes and dislikes, needs and wants
- Everything that you have done so far will show the customer that you are interested in helping him to get what he wants, rather than selling what you want

Appraisal form example pages 208/209

The example shown is both sides of the one I put together in 1976. If you ever wondered where that flattened car came from, you now know.

The main points again

1 Appraisal means 'to estimate the condition of a part-exchange'.

2 Always see and drive a part-exchange before agreeing a price.

3 Customers can tell lies; they call it negotiation.

4 Dealing with part-exchanges is what makes selling vehicles different to most other selling jobs.

5 Appraising part-exchanges is a skill that has to be learnt.

6 The very best time to appraise is directly after 'qualification' and before 'presentation' and 'demonstration'.

7 This gives someone else plenty of time to establish the true value of the part-exchange.

8 This gives you and your customer the time to get on with the presentation and demonstration.

9 The best way to learn how to appraise is to 'role model' people who have the skill inside and outside your business.

10 Using an appraisal form is not a recommendation – it is an absolute must.

11 Take the customers with you when you appraise the part-exchange.

12 Check everything, and always drive the vehicle.

13 Check the equipment, and ask if anything is to be removed.

14 Give the appraisal form to the manager to price.

15 Always let it be a third party's opinion what a customer's vehicle is worth.

16 While the manager is working out the price, you get on with the job of presenting and demonstrating.

CHAPTER 15
The Part-Exchange Valuation

"Be smart enough to be dumb"

I first met Bob when I first got involved in training – around 1980. Bob had just been given his first opportunity to run his own show. The established company that he worked for had just been awarded the Honda franchise. A small showroom and workshop had been purchased to handle the relatively small allocation of new vehicles that would be forthcoming. Bob was going to be the general manager. He was also going to be the Sales Manager. He was also going to be the salesman as well. In his spare time, Bob would act as service receptionist, help out on the parts counter and clean the odd car or two.

About three months after this was set up and running, I called in to see how Bob was doing. He was doing very well, in spite of the many hats he had to wear.

"*Do you have any problems?*" I asked him, pleased to see him so cheerful and coping so well.

"*Not really,*" he said. "*When I first got going, I found your appraisal system a bit difficult. It was hard to third party the valuation when there is only me here. But I've solved this now.*"

"*How did you manage that?*" I asked, more than a little intrigued.

"*Come with me and I will show you,*" he said and he led me to a staircase that went up to what had been the general manager's office in the previous business. He opened the door. There sitting on the floor of the bare office was a very large but (if tail wagging is anything to go by) friendly dog.

"*Meet the boss,*" said Bob. "*I appraise all the part-exchanges; the boss does the valuations,*" he told me with total sincerity.

Oh dear, I thought, this is a serious head case caused by pressure of wearing too many hats and all at once. Humour him for he might get violent and so might his dog.

"*How does this work?*" I asked Bob, as gently as possible, trying to keep sadness from my voice.

"*It's very simple,*" he said. "*The customer calls in and is interested in part-exchanging his present car for a new Honda. I sit him down as you showed us. I qualify him. Then I take the customer with me and go and appraise the part-exchange using the appraisal form and clipboard, as recommended. Then I bring the customer back to the showroom. I tell him I won't be long as I need to see the boss about a price for it. I run up the stairs, leave the appraisal form with the boss to sort out and get on with the presentation and demonstration steps, just as you taught us.*"

"*Yes, I can see that,*" I said, "*but what happens next?*"

"*Well give me a chance and I will tell you,*" said Bob. "*When we get back from the demonstration, I bring the customer back from the showroom, and ask how he would like his coffee, black or white? Then I sit him down and tell him that I will get the value for the part-exchange from the boss. Then it's just a simple case of sticking the kettle on. While that's coming to a boil I run back up the stairs and ask the boss what he thinks about the car.*"

"*Bob,*" I said, "*a dog would have no idea.*"

"*I know that,*" he said. "*The stupid dog thinks every car I give him to sort out is 'rough', or at least that's what he says when I ask him. So I take no notice and look in the book, make the phone call or use my own trade knowledge to price the car. I write the price on the appraisal form, thank the boss, run down the stairs, complete the coffee, give it to the customer and tell him what the boss thinks his car is worth.*"

I still wasn't totally convinced about his sanity. Then he added: "*Do you know, I've been dying for a customer to run up the stairs to have a row with the boss about the value of his car, but it hasn't happened yet. The boss only wags his tail when I am about and at other times he thinks he's a tiger!*"

Fifteen years or so later I still see Bob from time to time. He has his own multi-franchise group now and is a very successful businessman. Most of the ideas and methods that helped him achieve that success can be found in these pages. All you need to add is what Bob did. Sheer hard work and a little determination mixed together with a large dollop of imagination plus a pinch of creativity.

Valuation: Estimation of the Worth of

Every vehicle you will ever be offered will have a value – several in fact.

1 The Asking Value

The first value will be what the customer will ask you to pay for it *("I would expect to get £10,000 for it").*

The price is normally based on what the customer has seen similar vehicles being advertised for in papers or on forecourts. It could be the price 'a friend in the pub' told him to ask for it. Asking value is sometimes based on retail price guides that can be bought at newsagents. It could even be a percentage of what the customer paid for it two years ago.

The most important thing to remember, is that 'asking value' in today's enlightened marketplace has no relationship at all to what the vehicle will actually be worth.

There was a time, in the dim and distant past, when the golden rule in 'buying the part-exchange at the best price' was always to ask customers what they wanted for their part-exchange. Sales Managers would correctly tell their salespeople: *"Don't talk to me until you find out what the customer wants for his part-exchange – then we will work out the deal."*

This era started early in the century and ended around the mid-1960s as customers started to realise what their part-exchanges were really worth. This was compounded by the tendency to over-value for the part-exchange, in an effort to 'buy the business' from a new breed of customer who appeared to consider it a sign of personal virility to screw as much as possible out of a new car dealer for their part-exchange, in return for the privilege of supplying a new vehicle.

The Sales Managers were right to ask the question *"How much does he want for it"* in the period spanning 1924 to 1964. There was a time when you could do very profitable business indeed because of the tendency for some customers to 'undervalue' their part-exchanges. Those days have long gone, but unfortunately there are those who still ask the *"How much does he want for it?"* question today and today that question will usually cost you money.

2 Liking Value

The second value will be what the customer would really like to get for it *("I would really like to get £9,000 for it").*

This price is based on a lesser value than the asking value. It is quite often the first price the customer establishes in his mind. Then he will inflate this value to create an 'asking value', in the belief that whatever price he asks, someone will expect him to take less. Rather like selling a house, really – *"We would like to get £100,000 for it, so we will ask for £115,000. Someone is bound to want to negotiate."*

3 Taking Value

The third value will be what the customer will really be prepared to take for it *("I would not take a penny less than £8,000 for it").*

This is often a somewhat vague value, one that lurks between the conscious and the unconscious, often slipping in and out of focus.

This price is always the lowest of the three customer values, and certainly the most interesting and rewarding to establish before you start to negotiate with the customer.

4 Guide Value

Usually based on *Glass's Guide* or CAP monthly trade value figures and can be fairly accurate. It is important to bear in mind that trade vehicle value guides are put together weeks before they are published and are not regionalised. A guide is exactly what it says it is. It is a guide; not an offer to buy the vehicle at the price quoted.

5 True Value

The fifth and final value is the 'true value'. What the vehicle will fetch in its best marketplace for cash 'today'. Salespeople who have 'insight' will never tell the customers that their part-exchange will be sold to the trade. They might just be in love with their vehicle and imagine that it will be going to a good home, so why spoil their day?

This price will normally be based on a firm offer from a third party, a trade purchaser or another used car retailer who has underwritten to buy that vehicle, subject to it being available by the agreed date and remaining in the condition as seen. Vehicles can be underwritten over the telephone without too much problem, subject to them being in the condition and specification as described when seen.

Many companies prefer to establish what they think the value is, rather than let a third party 'run their business' for them. It is a good point, as long as the person in the company has the ability and knowledge to forecast accurately what a sensible 'true value' or trade price is.

'True value' can also be based on what your own company will 'stand it in at', when the decision is made to retail the vehicle through your own used vehicle facility. Sensible companies will never stand a used vehicle in at more than its true 'true value'.

As already mentioned, true values can be based on the salesperson's, the Sales Manager's, or, if you have one, a used car manager's expertise, which means that they do not have to be underwritten by a third party before coming into stock. This is usually the case when your company uses auctions for disposing of unwanted part-exchanges.

Help taking guesswork out of this is normally available direct from the auctioneer in advance. Most are prepared to share their own expertise and provide a 'quoted value', which will normally be safe to base a 'true value' on.

The Values Involved in Negotiation

Customer's Asking Value	*£10,000*
Customer's Liking Value	*£9,000*
Customer's Taking Value	*£8,000*
Guide Value	*£7,750*
Your Established True Value	*£7,500*

It has already been said that asking customers what they want for their part-exchanges is no longer a sensible policy today; in fact, asking the question will usually cost you money – and this is why.

Scenario One

If the salesperson says to the customer: "*What are you hoping to get from your part-exchange?*", the customer will say something like one of the following:

- *"As much as possible"*
- *"How should I know – you're the expert"*
- *"You tell me"*
- *"Well something in the order of £10,000"*
- *"I've been offered £10,000 for it"*
- *"If you want me to buy a car from you then you will have to give me £10,000 for it"*

So what do you get?

- Sometimes a fatuous answer
- Sometimes the asking price (£10,000)

Either way, you haven't gained much. At best a bit of antagonism; at worst the thought that if you want to do business with this customer, then you will have to pay around £10,000 for his part-exchange.

Scenario Two

If the salesperson has carried out all the steps laid out here, the point will be reached where the salesperson is now sitting down with the customer, sharing tea or coffee, and holding a fully completed appraisal form on which the Sales Manager has written the true value (£7,500) and which he turns towards the customer.

The salesperson says to the customer: *"As you can see, Mr Riley, my manager has put a true value on your car of £7,500."*

The customer will say something like one of the following:

- *"How much?"*
- *"Is that all?"*
- *"That isn't enough"*
- *"I wanted more than that"*
- *"No no, I would like to get £9,000 for it"*
- *"I wouldn't take a penny less than £8,000 for it"*

So what do you get this time?

- Sometimes a customer does not think much of your manager's price
- Sometimes a customer wants more than the true value
- Sometimes the 'liking value'
- Sometimes the 'taking value'

What is most important at this point is that you and your customer are both thinking about the true value (£7,500) and not the asking value (£10,000).

This means that the negotiation that is about to happen will start at your price of £7,500 and work upwards. Not at your customer's price of £10,000 and work downwards.

"Just a minute," did someone say? *"If I tell my customer that his car is worth £7,500 and he is expecting to get, or has even been offered, £10,000, then he will simply stand up and walk away."*

Well, the good news is that there are many salespeople who have been using the method outlined here for many years and it hasn't happened yet.

As Long As (and this is important)

The salesperson has:

- Opened the relationship well
- Qualified the customer properly
- Established and maintained rapport
- Appraised the part-exchange
- Given the appraisal form to the Sales Manager to price
- Personalised a presentation
- Raised desire with demonstration
- Got the part-exchange price from the Sales Manager
- Sat down with the customer, sipping tea or coffee, and saying something like *"As you can see, Mr Riley, my manager has put a true value on your car of £7,500."*

Customers just do not walk away because you have earned the right for them to stay. Those that do will usually negotiate upwards, from your price. Most of the business you do in this way will carry far higher profit margins than deals negotiated downwards from customers' asking prices.

For example, I was standing in the Sales Manager's office of a Saab dealership with Andrew, the Dealer Principal who also doubled up as Sales Manager. My company had just installed this system of handling part-exchanges in his company. All the salespeople had just been taught how to use it. Not all were totally in favour of it. Lloyd, a doubting salesman, entered with a newly installed appraisal card attached to a newly acquired clipboard. *"He wants £1,000 for his old dog,"* he said without feeling, and added: *"I didn't ask him, he told me"* in order to ward off the question 'Why did you ask him?'.

Andrew got quite excited. *"Great,"* he said, *"that's on, for ages I've been dying to get shot of that estate car he is interested in. Do it Lloyd, before he changes his mind."*

I got quite indignant. *"Just a minute,"* I said to both of them. *"This is not the way the system works. You are supposed to tell the customer the true value and negotiate up from there."* Both their faces fell and they looked doubtful.

"We can't do that," said Andrew. *"It's only worth £500. Why risk upsetting the customer and losing him when I can afford to do the deal that he wants?"*

"He will go bananas," added Lloyd, *"if I start talking about £500."*

"But," I reasoned, *"you are paying me a lot of money to show you how to do it another way. You should at least give it a try."*

They still looked doubtful.

"Go on, give it a go," I urged.

Andrew struggled and said: *"Why not?"* Lloyd's doubtful expression turned to fear as Andrew wrote £500 on the appraisal form in the bottom left-hand corner.

"Go on," said Andrew, rather like a father sending his son off to certain death, *"go and tell him it's worth £500"*. Lloyd did it wrong, totally wrong. He crept across the showroom floor, appraisal form clutched tightly to his chest and a look of total anguish on his face. He stopped about eight feet from the customer, who was standing in the showroom, and emotionally blurted out: *"I'm ever so sorry but your car is only worth £500."*

Lloyd was right. The customer did go bananas, and he shouted at the cringing Lloyd. *"Don't be so ridiculous,"* he blared, *"I wouldn't take a penny less than £700 for it."*

And that's the figure they did business at.

The Steps in the Valuation Procedure

The Sales Manager or other authorised person should be responsible for valuing all part-exchanges because:

- The manager is responsible for the overall profitability of his department
- It allows the salesperson to get on with the job of presenting and demonstrating
- Rapport will stay intact between salesperson and customer if it is a third party's opinion of what the part-exchange is worth
- Qualified salespeople can still value part-exchanges but they should have someone else to take the responsibility of the price
- The whole sales process flows so much more smoothly when carried out this way

If the Sales Manager has been given the keys with the appraisal form, then it becomes his responsibility to drive the vehicle before valuation and check the appraisal for accuracy because:

- The keys attached to the clipboard indicate that you need help with that particular part-exchange

- There is something about that part-exchange that you don't like or don't understand
- If it is a particular worry that you have, then time can be found to discuss this with the Sales Manager. Ideally, before you go out on the demonstration

If the Sales Manager does not see the keys to the part-exchange, then he does not have to see the vehicle, because:

- It is your way of telling the Sales Manager that you are confident that the appraisal form shows a true reflection of the condition of the part-exchange
- It will let your manager know when the time has come, through practice, that you have the confidence to appraise part-exchanges without help

Having established the 'true value' of the part-exchange, the Sales Manager will write this amount down in a prominent place on the appraisal form, because:

- When you get back from the demonstration, the priced appraisal will be ready and waiting
- When you show the form to the customer, the price will be clearly seen
- The customer can also see that a third party, expert opinion has been used to establish the price
- All this will make the price shown be far more believable to the customer as being a true and accurate figure, which it should be

The main points again

1 Every vehicle you will ever be offered will have a value – several in fact.

- The Asking Value
- The Liking Value
- The Taking Value
- The Guide Value
- The True Value

2 The last thing you want to do is to ask customers what they want for their part-exchanges.

3 The Sales Manager or other authorised person should be responsible for valuing all part-exchanges.

4 This 'true value' should be written down in a prominent place on the fully completed appraisal form.

5 The salesperson should tell and show the customer the true value.

6 This means that the negotiation that is about to happen will start at your price and work upwards, and not at your customer's price and work downwards.

CHAPTER 16
Negotiation

"The person who has the most
power in the negotiation process
is the person who thinks he has"

The trouble with discount is that for every ten pounds you give away, one of those pounds is yours (if you are on a 10% commission). This is the reason why I did not automatically give Marks and Spencer a discount. I had been in contact with them for some time and had put a car in for demonstration purposes. Nothing positive had come from this until one morning when my telephone rang to announce Mr Carpenter, the Marks and Spencer transport buyer.

"Pop in and see me, would you, I want to order a couple of Seven Series." That sounded like a buying signal to me, so I zipped up my fitting kit and nipped up to Baker Street fairly fast. I was ushered into Mr Carpenter's office and he told me what he wanted. I wrote out the two order forms, complete with specifications required and a breakdown of the total price for each of the two cars.

"If you would just like to authorise these orders, Mr Carpenter, I will set the whole thing in motion and arrange delivery as soon as possible," I told him calmly and formally, but seething with internal excitement. As I turned both the order forms round to face him, he took my proffered pen. Instead of signing the orders though, he started to check each one line by line using my pen as a marker. When he had finished he looked up and looked puzzled. *"Something wrong, Mr Carpenter?"* I said. *"Have I made an error?"*

"Well, yes you have actually. I can't see the discount," he said.

"Ah yes, the discount," I said. *"Do you know, we get so few of these, we cannot afford to discount them,"* I remarked in conversational tone. He looked at me closely. His look told me that he did not believe what I was saying. But he turned his gaze back to the order forms and signed each one.

"All right," he said, as he did so, *"I hear what you say. You sort out the delivery and I*

will sort out the discount." He did not say this in a threatening way. It was in more of an inevitable, it will come to pass, type of way. I must admit I was slightly puzzled, if not uncomfortable. He seemed so sure of himself. But I had the signed orders.

Back at Park Lane I started to process the two orders. The cars were in short supply, but delivery was not urgent. My telephone rang again. "*I have Jonathan Sieff for you,*" she said. "*Who?*" I said. "*I just told you, a Jonathan Sieff, whoever he is.*" I knew very well who Jonathan Sieff was. He was the chairman of the whole BMW shebang. In the British BMW world at that time, you could not get more important than Mr Jonathan Sieff. There are telephone calls that you stand up for and this was one of them. "*Put him through,*" I said at the third attempt. It is most difficult to talk properly with your heart in your throat.

I had never met Jonathan Sieff. I had seen him once, when he came to inspect the Park Lane premises. I had read about him on several occasions, in the like of Nigel Dempster's society columns. And now I was about to speak to him for the very first time. As I waited for his secretary to find him, I wondered why he was calling me, a mere Park Lane salesman. The penny hadn't dropped yet. And there he was, his voice actually talking to me. "*Look here, Upsher, whilst I can appreciate your efforts to retain profitability, I would be awfully grateful if you could offer my uncle's company some sort of discount.*" The penny positively clanged.

Marks and Spencer's chairman at that time was Marcus Sieff, who was my chairman's uncle. Why didn't I know that I knew that? I mumbled something. Probably "*Yes of course, Mr Sieff,*" but I can't really remember the words, only the emotion of the moment. Taking the two orders, I wandered into the General Sales Manager's office: "*Hi there, Boris, how are you doing?*" I said in a nonchalant way. It didn't work. "*What do you want, David, what have you done now?*" A bright lad, Boris, so I came straight to the point.

"*I've just had a telephone call from Jonathan Sieff,*" I said.

"*You mean his office,*" he said.

"*No, I mean from Jonathan Sieff himself.*"

There are face-to-face conversations that you stand up for. Boris jumped to his feet, his chair hitting the floor behind him, a look of total terror on his face. "*Why, why, why?*" he hammered the whys in quick succession, as if one would not be enough.

"*Oh, I have just taken an order from Marks and Spencer for two Seven Series, and Jonathan Sieff thinks that there should be a discount.*"

"You idiot!" Boris didn't mix his words. *"You flaming idiot,"* he added. *"For goodness sake, sort this out fast. What on earth were you thinking of not giving them a discount in the first place?"*

"I was thinking of profit, Boris."

"Well stop thinking of profit and start thinking of 'will you be with this company tomorrow?'"

"That's unfair," I said, *"you wouldn't sack someone for selling cars at full profit."*

"I won't," said Boris. *"Mr Sieff can, and will if you don't clear this up in the next five minutes. Go back to them now and offer them twelve and a half per cent."*

"But Boris," I started to say.

"You're still here, David – no buts, just action – and fast! Do it!" he said in ever-rising volume. I did it. I telephoned Mr Carpenter and apologised profusely for not giving him a discount. *"I thought you would be on the phone,"* he said, in a most matter of fact way.

"I have spoken to our General Sales Manager and he has asked me to give you a discount of seven and a half per cent," I said.

"That's better," Mr Carpenter said. *"Please thank your boss for me."*

"I certainly will, Mr Carpenter, and thank you for being such a patient and understanding customer," I added rather unnecessarily, but it seemed to go down well.

Back to Boris's office. *"Okay Boris,"* I said, *"that's all sorted, and Marks and Spencer are happy."*

"What did you offer them?" he said. I told you before he was clever. *"They have accepted our offer of seven and a half per cent,"* I told him.

"What's wrong with you, you unmitigated moron, I said twelve and a half per cent," he bellowed towards me.

"Okay, okay, I will go back to Mr Carpenter and tell him that his acceptance of seven and a half is not on and he has got to agree to take twelve and a half or forget the whole thing." (Do you know, if I was a Sales Manager again, I would hate to have the kind of salesman that I was at that time working for me.)

"You're a clever little git, aren't you," he said, without expecting an answer.

"All right," he said, *"leave it at seven and a half per cent, but if Jonathan Sieff comes back on the phone about this, it is you that will be taking full responsibility."*

"That's fully understood, Boris." As I left his office I added: *"but I don't think he will."*

...And he didn't!

To Negotiate or Not to Negotiate

If you went to your local supermarket, selected a trolley-load of goods, what chance do you think there would be of having a deal on the price you pay? Or would it go something like this:

- You select your goods
- Take them to the checkout
- The checkout person prices, as you pack
- The total to pay comes to £112.42
- You offer a hundred pounds for cash
- The checkout person laughs and thinks you are joking
- You insist that you want a discount
- The checkout person calls the supervisor
- The people in the queue behind you start questioning your parenthood
- The supervisor says pay up or push off
- You insist that you expect a discount
- The supervisor calls the manager
- The people in the queue behind you have decided you're off your rocker
- The manager says pay up or push off
- You continue to insist that you want a discount
- The manager calls security
- Security escorts you off the premises and kindly advises you to seek medical assistance

It might not happen this way. Someone might take the trouble to explain that the goods for sale are already competitively priced. What would happen is that you would not get a discount. So why has the motor industry been discount mad for so long? There are a myriad of reasons. Here are some of the key ones:

- After World War Two, vehicles were in short supply and customers paid full price
- Then production got going and more vehicles were produced than there were customers
- Dealers started to 'buy' business by offering discounts
- Discounting became the established norm
- Customers were educated by the dealers that the price you see is not the one that you pay

- Until very recent times, dealers had far larger margins, which allowed them to discount or offer inflated part-exchange prices

The big dealer margins have mostly disappeared now. Which means that the haggler's way of doing business should surely disappear if you want to stay in business. But many dealers still continue to negotiate. Maybe it is the degree of negotiating that has changed.

Today's customers look for things such as:

- Funding options on offer
- Aftersales service
- Company reputation and location
- Friendly, caring salespeople

Don't, whatever you do, forget that last one.

As long as there are vehicles to sell and people to buy them, someone somewhere will be getting a discount. Nevertheless, to be successful in selling vehicles in the future, both the companies and the individual sellers must always keep firmly in mind that discounting is optional. Look for other ways of securing the business than buying it.

The Part-Exchange Negotiation

It's common sense that if someone is getting a new vehicle, then something must be happening to the one they drive at present. It could be passed on to a member of the family in retail cases, it could be placed with someone who works in the same company in business cases, or it could come to you as a part-exchange.

Why are so many salespeople worried about part-exchanges? Every vehicle has a value, a price you could afford to give for it. Surely the best place to start when taking a part-exchange against another vehicle is to establish exactly what it is worth, the 'true value'.

One of the best kept secrets in the motoring world is that customers who have 'difficult' part-exchanges actually know. By the time they get to you, the chances are that someone else will probably have told them (some of them actually manage to work it out for themselves). Bearing this in mind, if there is a part-exchange, start the negotiation process by telling the customer what the true value is.

The Part-Exchange Negotiation – Recommended Structure

In most businesses, the only thing that is not negotiable is the 'true value' of the part-exchange. This is the price established by the Sales Manager or other person responsible and relates to what the vehicle will fetch in its best marketplace for cash, today, because:

- The 'true value' would normally be the same as the 'stand-in value' if the vehicle was going to be taken into stock
- It would be the price that a trader or used vehicle retailer would pay for it
- It would be the Sales Manager's 'guesstimate' or auctioneer's 'quoted value' if the vehicle was to be disposed of at auction

Having completed the 'selling' phase of the process, after the demonstration, the salesperson should take the customer back into the showroom, sit him down, organise coffee and explain that he is going to get the 'true value' of the part-exchange from the Sales Manager, because:

- It will remind the customer of what is happening and what is going to happen
- The customer will remember that it is someone else who will be responsible for pricing the part-exchange
- It sets the scene for the negotiation steps of the sale.

The salesperson should then go to the Sales Manager's office, collect the priced-up appraisal form and take it back to where the customer is with the coffee, because:

- This gives the salesperson a chance to talk briefly with the Sales Manager regarding any room to negotiate
- It gives the Sales Manager a chance to find out what's happening and offer assistance if necessary
- It gives the customer a little breathing and thinking space. After all, who is comfortable when being rushed to spend a few pounds, let alone many thousands?

It is important to share tea or coffee with the customer at this point, even if you don't particularly want one, because:

- This action will emphasise rapport and that you are on the same side as your customer – you want to help him buy a vehicle
- If the customer is going to spend some money, it would be preferable for the customer that the experience was an enjoyable one, conducted in a friendly and relaxed manner

When sitting down with the customer, show the appraisal form so that the 'true value' can be read. At the same time tell the customer what the 'true value' is with confidence, because:

- It is important for the customer to realise what the 'true value' is
- It is important that the customer feels that you have confidence that the 'true value' quoted is a fair and reasonable price

Having told and shown the customer the 'true value', pause for a moment to let this information sink in. Then expect the customer to query the price, particularly if the customer has been shopping around, because:

- You should be expecting some form of reaction, so give your customer time to react
- Half of vehicle buyers today are looking for a 'deal' as opposed to buying a vehicle
- Customers who have been 'shopping around' can often be given some very misleading prices

A customer's perception of what their part-exchange is worth will often bear little or no resemblance to the part-exchange's true value because:

- Many customers have been led to believe that their part-exchanges are worth much more than 'true value'
- Much of this misleading information comes from misleading advertisements and prices quoted over the telephone, or face-to-face 'subject to' prices that are sometimes given out to get customers to come back after they have shopped around

Customers will normally be disappointed when you show and tell them the 'true value' of the part-exchange. They will also normally believe that the value you give is correct, because:

- You saw and drove the vehicle
- You fully completed an appraisal form
- You sought expert advice to establish the price
- And the price is written down

It is likely, at this point, that you will have to explain to the customer what exactly a 'true value' is, because:

- A 'true value' is not normally a part-exchange offer
- The customer could get more for his vehicle than the true value, which would depend on what vehicle was being considered.

Explain to the customer that the 'true value' is what the vehicle would be worth if you were buying it for stock or in its best cash marketplace, today. Then ask the customer how much more than the 'true price' he would be looking for, because:

- You are now starting the negotiation process properly, from the right place, the 'true value'
- When you ask the question *'How much more?'*, the customer realises that there is every chance that he will get more than the 'true value'

It is most likely that a customer will tell you what he wants over and above the 'true value' of his part-exchange because:

- Most people want more for their part-exchanges, irrespective of what price you start with
- Some people will have already been offered more for their vehicle by another dealer
- Most customers think that you have to 'haggle' to make sure that you are getting the best deal

Listen carefully to the words that the customer uses during the negotiation process because:

- Customers who say *'I would like to get... '* are giving you their 'liking value'
- Customers who say *'I would not take less than... '* are giving you their 'taking value'

It is going to be a great help to all concerned if you can establish a price (any price) at which a customer would be prepared to do business with your company, preferably today, because:

- That means that your customer has said that he will buy a vehicle from you and your company today
- That is the position you have to be in if you want the customer to buy from you

You should be able to start to negotiate from the position of 'friend' of the customer; help him to buy a vehicle from your company at some price between the 'true value' and the customer's 'taking price' (eg £7,500 and £8,000) because:

- The role that you are now playing in the transaction is rather like an estate agent
- It is your responsibility to negotiate the 'deal' between the customer and your company
- What you are hoping to achieve is the classic 'win win' negotiation outcome: a good deal at an acceptable price for both customer and company
- You can now say: *'If we can agree the figures, Mr Riley, would you be in a position to place your order today?'*

Having a committed customer means that you can now negotiate within the guidelines that will be set by your own company, because:

- Every company is different
- Some salespeople are given a margin to negotiate with
- Some salespeople have to refer to management
- This system for appraising, valuing and negotiating the part-exchange is flexible to allow for this

The final negotiation is often switched to a 'cost to change' or a 'monthly payment', and a degree of bargaining can continue to take place:

- *"If you could have this car for £164 per month, would you be prepared to go ahead?"*
- *"So if the cost to change figure was a couple of hundred pounds less, you would be tempted, would you?"*

The Part-Exchange Non Negotiation

Some companies use the outline structure explained here but with one major difference: instead of quoting a 'true value', a part-exchange allowance price is established, and the customer is given this price. Normally speaking, there is no further negotiation – the company relies on the other benefits of buying from them to secure the business.

As before, the price given is often shown as:

- A cost to change
- A monthly payment

But this system has less flexibility than the negotiation system and is more in line with 'best price' retailing practice. It does and will work, but only as long as the other benefits from buying offer the necessary incentives to buy.

What If No Part-Exchange?

You still have the same two choices:

- To negotiate
- Not to negotiate

The choice is your company's.

Customer's Question or Statement	Negotiate	Non Negotiate
'How much off?'	*'What deal do you want?'*	*'This is the deal, and these are the benefits.'*
'Can you give me 10%?'	*'If I can, will you buy?'*	*'This is the price, and this is why you should pay it.'*
'I would not pay that for it.'	*'What would you pay for it?'*	*'This is what makes it worth paying.'*
'Can you get the payments down to £150 per month?'	*'If I can, can I have your business?'*	*'Yes, however it will be over 42 months instead of 36 months.'*
'It has not got a radio.'	*'If I throw one in will you buy?'*	*'Which of these would you like to buy?'*

It should be difficult to mix the two systems, if not confusing for both buyers and sellers. People do and stay in business. Yet another proof of the golden rule in selling:

'THERE ARE NO RULES'

If what you are doing:

- Does not work for you and your company
- Loses or fails to keep customers
- Does not achieve volume and profit objectives

Then you are probably doing most of it wrong and should consider doing it differently.

If what you are doing:

- Works for you and your company
- Gains and retains customers
- Achieves volume and profit objectives

Then you are probably doing most of it right – for the moment.

The main points again

1 The motor industry has a history of discounting. This started when more vehicles were produced than there were customers and dealers started to buy business. Until recently, dealer margins were far higher which allowed them to do this.

2 Whatever we do, discounting is optional, and we should be looking at other ways to secure business.

3 Every vehicle that you are offered in part-exchange has a value.

4 The 'true value' is the price that the vehicle would fetch in its best marketplace for cash that day, irrespective of whether you are going to stock the vehicle or move it on.

5 The first price that the salesperson should give to the customer regarding the part-exchange is the 'true value'.

6 The salesperson should then ask the customer how much more would be needed to do business today. Then negotiate between 'true value' and the price the customer would like.

7 The alternative is not to negotiate, by giving a customer a fixed price to change or as a monthly payment.

8 This can be successful if the company can offer the customer other reasons to buy apart from price.

9 If there is no part-exchange involved, then you still have the choice:

- To negotiate
- Not to negotiate

10 It should be difficult to mix these two approaches, but some companies do and stay in business.

11 Yet another proof of the golden rule in selling:

'THERE ARE NO RULES'

12 If what you are doing is not working, then consider doing it differently.

13 If what you are doing is working, then you are probably doing most of it right – for the moment.

SECTION SEVEN

The Downhill Run

"*I won't ask him to sign this,*" I thought.

CHAPTER 17
Handling Objections

"We are all continually faced with
a series of great opportunities brilliantly
disguised as unsolvable problems"

Mr Bell had bought the car. We had just finished the demonstration and were driving back to his office in the East End of London. Mr Bell was pleased, I was pleased, as I mentally spent the commission as we sped along. Even the car seemed pleased. What a lovely day, I thought, as we got out of the car and climbed the long flight of stairs to Mr Bell's office.

Mr Bell was a partner in a fashion wholesaling business. His office, which was situated above his warehouse, was a fascinating jumble of old fashioned office desks, equipment and new fashioned garments in multi colours hanging meekly in rows or draped elegantly over high backed wooden chairs. Mr Bell invited me to sit down on an undraped chair, which I did. I opened up my folder and took out an order form. As I filled the form in, we both relaxed into irrelevant small talk. The pressure was off. He had finished his buying, I had finished my selling, the deal was done. All I needed was a signature on the order form and a deposit.

The form was almost complete when the door opened behind me to admit a dapper little man, his slicked back hair and bulging waistline indicating that he was a fan of both Brylcreem and big business lunches. He curtly acknowledged my presence, but had obviously come to converse with Mr Bell. I continued to concentrate on completing the order form and was hardly aware of the distant burble of conversation that was none of my business. My business was to get Mr Bell's signature on the line that is dotted, and I was just about ready to do that when I noticed that Mr Bell's partner, (for that was who he was) had been glancing at the order form on the desk in front of me as he spoke. I was not surprised to hear him say *"Oh, you are ordering a new car then?"* He now had my attention. Perhaps he might like to buy one as well? Partners in business often do, particularly if the partner's car being purchased is better than the one that the other partner is currently driving.

"Yes," said Mr Bell, *"I have decided to go for the new BMW."*

There was absolute silence and stillness for what appeared to be a long time. Then, suddenly and explosively, Mr Bell's partner changed from a waxwork impersonator into a raging demon, arms and legs going everywhere, head swivelling and spittle dribbling. I was too shocked to be amazed. I just couldn't believe my eyes; it was some kind of unexplainable nightmare. The apparition that was Mr Bell's partner was now speaking, well, shouting, ranting and raving. I could not understand a word he was saying at first, but as his frantic body movements started to eat adrenalin, his voice slowed and lowered to a comprehensible level.

"There is enough German shmutter in this country without you bringing more in," I heard him say. Mr Bell was shouting too by now. *"It's my decision to make. I can drive what I like,"* was his reply.

And then, as Mr Bell's partner got his second wind, they were off, hammer and tongs, broadswords and bayonets, and there was me stuck in the middle, feeling a bit like a chicken leg on a beach between two hungry seagulls. I won't ask Mr Bell to sign this, I thought. It didn't seem to be the right moment. I was embarrassed. I just wanted to get away from that place as fast as I could. So I stood up suddenly and shut my folder with a significant thud. They both stopped talking.

"I can see you wish to discuss this," I said, still feeling acutely embarrassed, *"so I will go now and leave you in peace."* With that, I started to head for the door, head in shoulders, folder in hand, heart in mouth.

Just as I reached the door, the silence was broken by Mr Bell's partner: *"This has nothing to do with you personally. We are all entitled to our own opinions,"* he said, finger waving in my direction.

You know what it's like sometimes when somebody makes a remark to you that you don't like. The reply is just there ready to roll out. Mine was there at that moment and on that day. *"Yes, we are all entitled to our own opinions. It's when we start ramming them down other people's throats that the troubles in this world start to happen."*

I thought it – it was there on the tip of my tongue – but I did not say it. I just wished them both a good day and left the room quietly, shutting the door on the recommencing row, which then rolled and rumbled on behind me. When I got back to my office there was a message waiting for me. It was from Mr Bell. "*Could I ring him?*" the message said. So I rang him.

"I am so sorry about all that, David (it had been Mr Upsher until now). My partner, Mr Leavy, has asked me to apologise on his behalf. That should never have happened in front of you. We are both truly sorry."

"That's kind of you, Mr Bell."

"*Call me Tony,*" he said.

"That's kind of you, Tony. It's a shame about the BMW though, you really did fancy that, didn't you?"

"*Oh, I still want the car,*" he said.

"*You want it?*" was my shocked reply. "*But what about your partner, Mr Leavy?*"

"*Yes, you're right,*" said Tony. "*What time are you there until tonight?*"

"*Six thirty,*" I said.

"*Fine,*" said he. "*I will call in and complete the details just after six.*"

...And he did.

Less objections make more orders

It appears to be an unjust world. As soon as you start to observe the kind and the frequency of objections that are raised by customers, you cannot fail to notice a very strange phenomenon. That is, if two salespeople sell the same product to the same types of customers from the same showroom, one will often get far more objections than the other. The one who gets less than a fair share of objections will always take more orders – and that's not fair.

Careful observation of many salespeople selling many products from many showrooms has helped to identify why this is so. Perhaps you would like to know the reason. Actually, there are ten reasons. Salespeople who handle fewer objections always:

1 Spend more time on the qualification process.

2 Very quickly gain rapport with customers.

3 Have the ability to 'read' their customers through sensory activity.

4 Make it easy for the customer by explaining how they propose to help them buy a vehicle.

5 Present 'known' objections as benefits during presentation and demonstration.

6 Avoid raising objections themselves to stop people buying from them.

7 Refrain from offering customers personal opinions.

8 Prevent themselves from emphasising the customers' objections.

9 Turn customers' objections into questions, then answer the questions.

10 Expect the customer to buy.

Let us take each one of these apart for you. However, before we do so, let us look at the objections themselves.

Categories of Objections

There are only three categories of objections:

1 Time
2 Price
3 Competition

1 Time

Normally, if a customer is interested enough in something, then he will find the time to deal with it. However, time objections can be created by impossible deadlines. A customer could spend a whole year making up his mind what to buy, and then expect to get delivery the very next day. Other time objections will be set to delay the purchase decision as in:

- *"I will not get one till next year"*
- *"I will get one when the new registration letter comes out"*
- *"I will wait till I have paid the finance off on this one"*

2 Price

It is hard sometimes to split price and competition objections.

- *"I just can't afford to buy it"*
- *"You are asking far too much for it"*
- *"I can't raise that much deposit"*
- *"If that's what my part-exchange is worth, then I will not have enough to go ahead"*
- *"That monthly payment is beyond me"*

Or even:

- *"That's too cheap – I want to spend a lot more than that"*

3 Competition

Everybody who retails vehicles appears to have this 'man down the road' who offers the most incredible deals. Has it ever crossed your mind that the man down the road thinks that you are the man down the road! Customers can get hooked on to a particular make of vehicle: a fair proportion of buyers like to 'stick to what they know'. It could be a feature of a vehicle, such as front wheel drive or six-cylinder engine, that becomes a necessity on the customer's shopping list, but that could cover several makes of vehicles. It could be the service that they get both from sales and aftersales that will create a competition objection to switching allegiance to you.

Types of Objections

Time, price and competition objections will all be one of four types of objection:

1. False
2. Perceived
3. Misunderstanding
4. Real

Time

The time objection, *"I will wait till I have paid the finance off on this one"*:

- Could be a deliberate lie to get away from you – FALSE
- Could be because the customer thinks it would cost him more money per month if he were to change now, which is not necessarily so. – PERCEIVED
- A mistake – it's his wife's vehicle that he is still paying for, not his – MISUNDERSTANDING
- Could be the absolute truth. This is exactly what the customer has it in mind to do. – REAL

Price

The price objection, "*That monthly payment is beyond me*":

- Could be said just to get rid of you – FALSE
- It could be that the customer could make those monthly payments but does not realise it – PERCEIVED
- Perhaps the customer has not realised that the payment period could be extended to match his monthly preferred payment – MISUNDERSTANDING
- The payment really could be beyond the customer's means – REAL

Competition

That old chestnut of a competition objection, "*The man down the road offers the most incredible deals*":

- Could be a 'wind up' – FALSE
- Could be a misconception based on what friends have told him – PERCEIVED
- Could be based on the man down the road's advertising, which has been misunderstood – MISUNDERSTANDING
- Perhaps the man down the road has, on this occasion, offered an incredible deal – REAL

It would certainly be of great help to you if you could remember:

The Three Categories

Time

Price

Competition

The Four Types

False

Perceived

Misunderstanding

Real

This understanding will form 'the root' of clearer thinking when dealing with objections.

The Objection Root

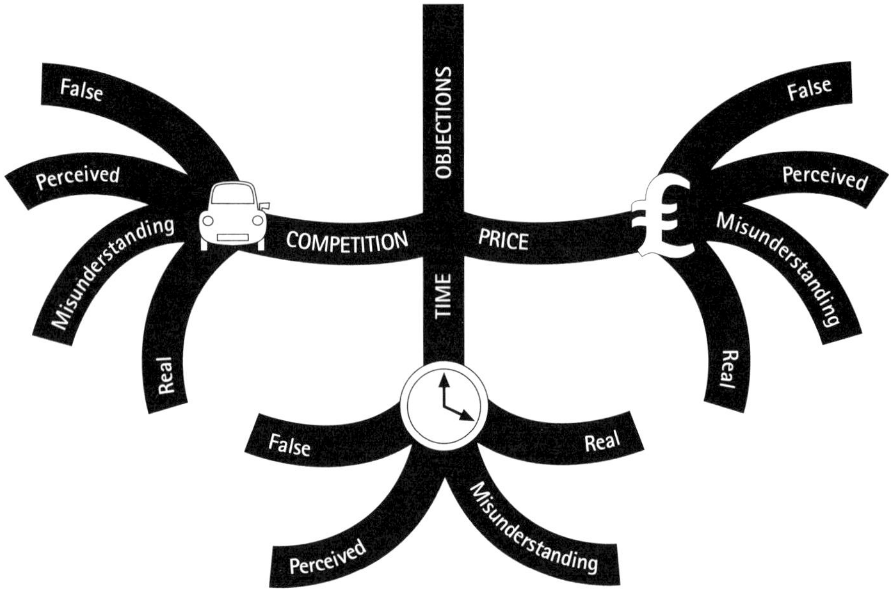

Let us take another, harder, look at what successful salespeople do to eliminate, reduce or answer objections from customers.

1 **Successful salespeople spend more time on the qualification process**

The longer you spend correctly qualifying your customers, the less time you will spend in answering objections. The more you find out about the customer's needs and wants, the more good reasons you will be able to present to the customer that will outweigh possible product disadvantages, such as price, for instance.

Look at the sale this way:

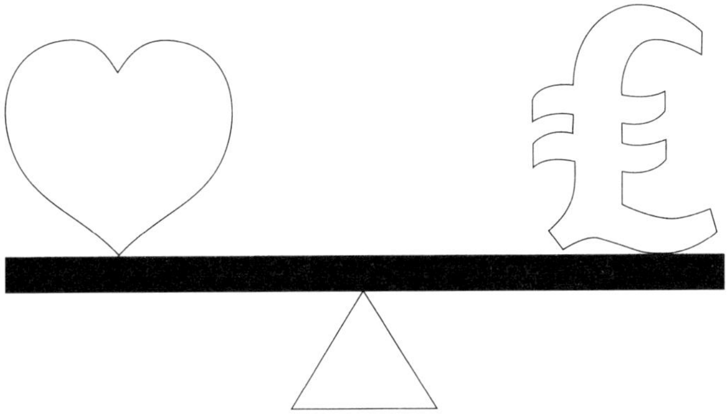

In the diagram:

- Desire is represented by a heart on the left hand side
- Price is represented by a pound sign on the right hand side
- The desire and price representations both rest on a thick, solid, unbendable bar
- The bar balances on a pivot

If by fully understanding what the customer wants you manage to raise the desire to buy, then you will automatically reduce price objections.

This means that the diagram will now look like this:

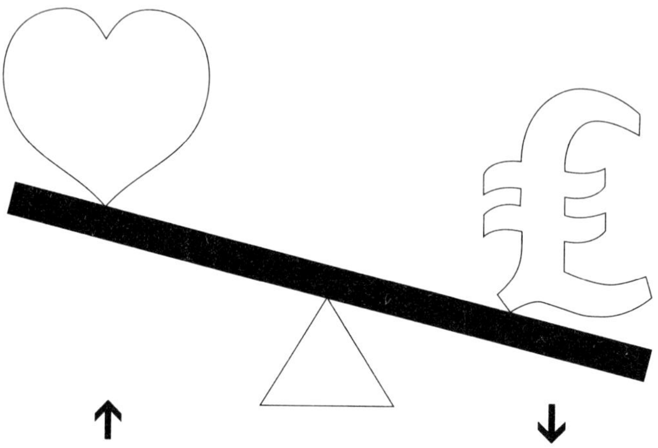

You can blame Newton for this. He stated it as his third law of motion:

"To every action there is an equal and opposite reaction"

This means that a force acting in one direction is always accompanied by an equal force acting in the opposite direction. This explains how jet and rocket propulsion works, why guns recoil after firing and, more importantly, why salespeople who take the trouble to qualify manage to raise desire, which reduces objections. If Newton was around today working as a vehicle salesman, his third law could very well have been:

"Desire dictates the decision to buy, not the price"

2 Successful salespeople very quickly gain rapport with customers

Good salespeople do this automatically and unconsciously. To improve your own rapport skills, you will have to be conscious of what you are doing until you manage to achieve the level of rapport that you need to reduce objection levels. You will find this consciousness a strange feeling at first. As you study the notes on rapport and start to use the techniques, you will be pleased to find that in a very short while, both the strange feeling and the objections will fade away together.

3 **Successful salespeople have the ability to 'read' their customers through sensory acuity**

All good salespeople have highly developed sensory acuity. There is nothing to stop you developing or refining your own skills. It is often a case of noticing what most people do not notice.

A high level of sensory acuity will help you eliminate and reduce objections if you:

- Start to pay attention to how people say words rather than the words they say
- Become more aware of how different people process information. Start to use the same 'channel' when you talk to them, ie VISUAL, AUDITORY AND KINESTHETIC
- Be more like your customers, by matching behaviour like posture, breathing rate and general demeanour
- Learn to read people's thoughts through eye movements and their body language
- Re-read the chapter on sensory acuity, practise techniques during your own time as well as work time – it is a skill that is well worth working for

4 **Successful salespeople make it easy for the customers by explaining how they propose to help them buy a vehicle**

Often the most forgotten step in selling. People, and that includes customers, do like to know what is going on and what is going to happen. Sensible salespeople always confirm what they have found out through qualification. Then they tell the customers what will happen next. If the confirmation is correct, then the customer will say so. If it is not quite right, the customer will normally say so too:

"No, that's not quite right, my wife does not drive the car herself, but she does like to pick the colour and interior trim."

Bang goes another potential misunderstanding objection that was primed to be fired further down the sales line. If the customer is happy about what the salesperson proposes to do next, then that will happen. If not, the customer will bring it up:

"No, no – I'm sorry, I just don't have enough time to do all that today. I've just remembered that I have to be at my flower arranging class by 3.30."

Bang goes another potential time objection that was primed to be fired at 3.15 just as you were in full swing. If you find this out at 2.15, then you can do something different that will maximise both use of available time and the chances of concluding a sale tomorrow.

5 Successful salespeople present known objections as benefits during presentation and demonstration

Every product has them; the same old objections come up time and time again. Good salespeople do not wait for them to arise like sales-killing phoenixes. They catch them in embryo form, when they can be eliminated without too much difficulty. Before the customer says "*The seats are too hard*", you say something like:

"*You will notice that the seats are fairly firm, Mr Jones. This is because the suspension is firm too, which means that the car has very good road holding characteristics. Matching the spring rate in seats and suspension gives you the maximum amount of comfort, since the car and you will move together, rather like an expert rider on a fine horse.*"

Before the customer tells you that it costs too much, you tell her:

"*Notice the fine detail and high quality finish, Mrs Meadows. Every car is built to a very high standard. You can see this in the way the door shuts and how the gaps around the door frame are all the same. Quality like this is well worth paying a little extra for.*"

Before the customer says he can't possibly wait for delivery, you say:

"*Yes, we could get you a blue one. We would want to order the car from the factory for you which means that you will have your car built to your exact specifications and requirements. In fact, Mr Williams, when that car comes down the production line in three months' time, all factory fresh and gleaming, it WON'T be just a car, it will be Mr Williams' car.*"

Make a list of time, price and competition objections that come up regularly, and work out how you can present these objections as benefits. It will not always work for you, but it will work enough to make presenting known objections as benefits during presentation and demonstration a very worthwhile activity.

6 Successful salespeople avoid raising objections themselves to people buying from them

This is something that excellent salespeople never do. Dealership research, however, seems to indicate that the most common sale-killing objections can be created by the salespeople themselves:

- "*Ah yes, that model is a bit scarce at the moment, and I'm not sure we can get hold of one for you*"

- *"If they have offered you that much in part-exchange, then I suggest you go and take it"*
- *"I know you want the manual model, but I can do you a special deal on the automatic at the moment"*
- *"That's my best price – take it or leave it"*
- *"A demonstration? Yes, but not right now"*
- *"You don't seem to understand: we are making you an extremely generous offer"*
- *"There's no reason for it – it's company policy"*
- *"OK, try the other dealer first and then come back to me"*
- *"Ah yes, you need to speak to Mr Hargreaves, but he's not in today"*
- *"It would be foolish to fit that as an extra – it's just not necessary"*
- *"I know it's not much, but it's the best I can manage at present"*
- *"I've got to sell these two before the new model arrives"*
- *"With all due respect, that's nonsense"*
- *"Well, here's the brochure. Call back if you need more help"*
- *"Why don't you try selling privately first?"*
- *"They're so popular we're always running out"*
- *"No, you don't want the special wheels – it runs better on the standard rims"*
- *"If you want to try one, then I can't help you because we haven't got one"*
- *"Sure I'll give you a price – hold it up to the phone and I'll have a look at it"*
- *"How much are you expecting to get for your present car?"*
- *"Yes, we could take your present car in part-exchange, but I hope you're not expecting much for it"*
- *"Getting one of those for you would be extremely difficult"*
- *"I don't think we could deliver it by Friday – getting a car out of our service department is like getting gold out of Fort Knox"*
- *"I can't take your enquiry right now because I'm with a customer – give me your name and telephone number and I will call you right back"*

These kinds of statements should be eliminated completely if you really do want to maximise your chances of doing business.

7 **Successful salespeople refrain from offering customers personal opinions**

Good salespeople, the very best, do not have personal opinions. In fact, the more opinions you have, the less successful in selling you become. That is not an opinion, it's a fact. You must have met people with lots of opinions. How do you feel about them? Would you want to buy a vehicle from them? Years ago there was an old film on television about a battleship. In one scene the captain turned to his first officer and said: *"You have no enemies, Number One, why is that?"* The first officer replied: *"I have no opinions, sir."*

"But customers ask my opinion all the time! What can I tell them?"

Here are some ideas that just might help you:

Method 1 – Throw it back at the customer

Customer	Your Answer
"It's a choice between the red and the blue – which do you prefer?"	*"I don't know, what do you think?"*

If you say *"I don't know, what do you think?"* naturally and fast enough after your customer has asked for your opinion, they will never notice that you threw it back. Most of the time, the customer will know which colour they prefer at some level of consciousness. So when you say *"I think the blue is better"*, you will quite often get *"so what is wrong with the red, then?"* thrown back at you for your trouble.

Method 2 – Talk to the customer's unconscious

Customer	Your Answer
"What do you think I should do, because I am not too sure?"	*"If you were sure, what would you do?*

If you have never tried this, you really will be surprised how well it works and the extra business you will do. You have to say *"If you were sure, what would you do?"* naturally and seriously. Then you have to give the customer time to process both the slightly unusual question and the information on what he should do that you have just unlocked from his unconscious mind.

Other examples of technique:

Customer	Your Answer
"I don't know what to do"	*"If you did know, what would you do?"*
"I don't know what I want"	*"If you did know, what would you want?"*
"I don't know if I should go ahead"	*"If you did know, would you go ahead?"*

Method 3 – 'Third party' the opinion

Customer	Your Answer
"What will I get to the gallon from this?"	*"Our service manager is currently using the same car and has been getting close to 40 mpg, he was telling me."*

Third parties are safe: they are not your opinions, they are someone else's:

> *"My manager says that the 'true value' of your part-exchange is £7,500"*

Remember? You have third partied the opinion.

These are just three ways of avoiding giving opinions to your customers. Your opinions could cost you business or create aftersales dissatisfaction. Have opinions, by all means, but keep them to yourself. Be smart enough to be dumb, and always remember that a closed mouth gathers no foot!

8 Successful salespeople prevent themselves from empathising the customer objections

Or to put it more simply, if the customer tells you that he can't afford it and you can't afford it too, then there is a tendency for salespeople to agree with the customer:

> *"I hate that green" – "Oh, so do I"*
> *"I would never want an automatic" – "Neither would I"*
> *"I have to talk to my wife" – "So would I"*

Do you see the problem? If you just happen to share the same feelings as your customer, then you might be in 'rapport', but you could be out of a sale. Leave your problems out of a sales situation, particularly when they parallel the customer's.

9 Successful salespeople turn customer objections into questions, then answer the question and not the objection

This technique is **not** often used by the very best salespeople. They will have eliminated or reduced most objections before they surface, fully grown, towards the end of the sale process. Some objections will come up whatever you do. It will certainly pay you well if you can master the following techniques for handling and dealing with objections.

A Technique for Handling Objections

1 Handle Fewer Objections

Just a reminder: many objections can be eliminated by spending more time on qualification, presentation and demonstration. There was a time when most sales manuals used to say *"Always welcome and encourage objections... they are often a sign of interest and will help you close the sale"*. What a load of poppy cock (that's an opinion). Who needs objections when all you want to do is to get down to business. Objections do not help you to sell and they will not help you close sales (that's a fact).

2 Listen to the Objection Carefully

Don't just listen: really hear! As with seeing, many adults have a routine way of listening. Hear the words, hear the tone, and understand the meaning. Make sure that the customer is finished before you jump in.

3 Avoid Arguing or Defending

It's best not to argue with customers; even if you win the argument, you will usually lose any chance of doing business. If you really do feel that you have to disagree with a customer, then try this diplomatic face-saving approach:

"I'm not saying you're wrong, I just happen to disagree with you."

It is hard to be offended by such a tactful attitude.

"Your cars don't have very good resale values."
"I'm not saying you're wrong, I just happen to disagree with you."

Incidentally, what do you think would have happened if I had stopped in the doorway and delivered my ready-to-roll-out statement to Mr Bell's partner in the opening story of this chapter?

4 Refine the Objection if Necessary

Some objections are far too generalised to be handled. Try to refine them down to something more specific and manageable:

Objection	Refining Question
"It's too big"	*"How is it too big?"*
"It's too much money"	*"In what way do you mean it's too much money?"*
"I don't think this is the right time to change my car"	*"What would happen if you did?"*
"I'll talk it over with my partner"	*"What would happen if you didn't?"*
"It's not really me"	*"How in particular is it not really you?"*
"My wife might find it difficult to drive"	*"How exactly might your wife find it difficult to drive?"*

If you use these refining questions, then you will start to get some very useful information that will often help you deal with the original generalised objection. The problem here is that your customer is using a 'chunking up' Meta Program. On this occasion, you will gain much by 'chunking down' to find the exact objection, as illustrated by the refining questions.

Original	Objection Can Become
"It's too big"	*"I am used to something smaller"*
"It's too much money"	*"I've been offered a better deal elsewhere"*
"I don't think this is the right time to change my car"	*"I would be out of step with my fellow directors if I changed now"*
"I'll talk it over with my partner"	*"My partner likes to be involved in deciding what car we drive"*
"It's not really me"	*"I don't like this colour"*
"My wife might find it difficult to drive"	*"I can't see the front of the bonnet from the driver's seat"*

Now Restate the Objection as a Question:

By using phrases such as:

- What you want to know is...
- What you are asking me is...
- So what's worrying you is...
- So what concerns you is...

Then answer the question, not the objection.

OBJECTIONS ARE NASTY JAGGED THINGS TO HANDLE

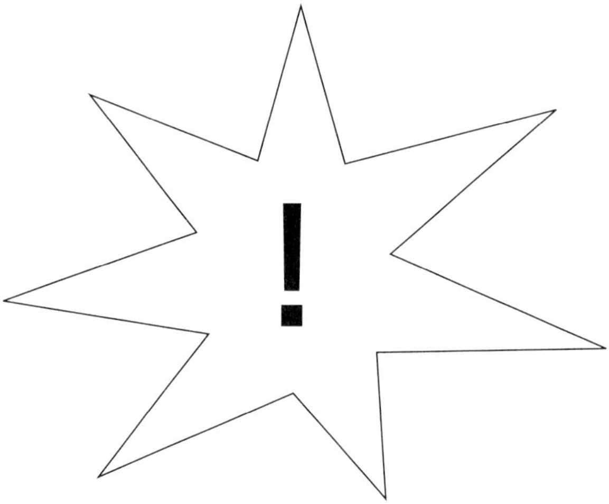

QUESTIONS ARE USUALLY SMOOTH AND ROUND

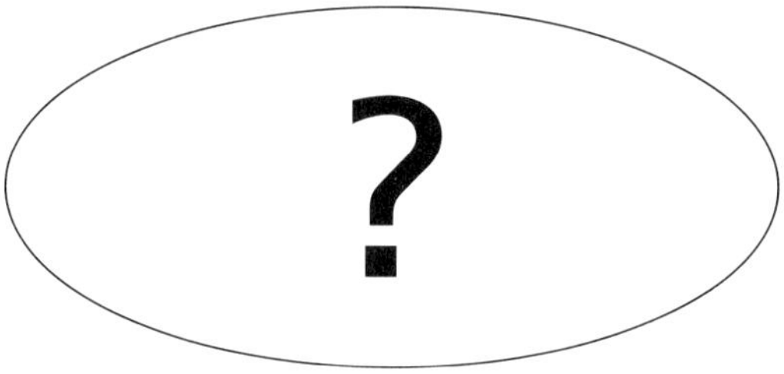

Keep turning objections into questions and answer the questions. It's far safer, more friendly and a far more satisfying way of doing business for both buyer and seller.

Objection	Turn Into Question	Answer the Question
"I am used to something smaller"	*"So what concerns you is, are you going to find it harder to drive?"*	By explaining: The benefits of power steering. Just as easy to drive as a smaller vehicle plus the bonus of extra space when needed. Plus more relaxing to drive over distance.
"I've been offered a better deal elsewhere"	*"So what you want to know is, what are the benefits of dealing with my company that will make up that price difference?"*	By explaining: All the other benefits apart from price that your company offers. Plus your company's reputation and the fact that you will always be there to offer help when needed before, during and after the sale.
"I would be out of step with my fellow directors if I changed now"	*"So what you need to find out are the benefits of changing your car now for both you and your company?"*	By explaining: Higher trade-in allowance now than next year. How much more the company will have to pay with new vehicle prices going up and part-exchange prices going down.
"My partner likes to be involved in deciding what car we drive"	*"So what's worrying you is how can you buy a car by yourself without upsetting your partner?"*	By explaining: That it is initially your fault that the customer now finds himself in this situation. You should have asked if anybody else was involved in the buying decision when finding out how you could help the customer. Then offer to make amends by bringing the vehicle for the partner to see at the very first opportunity.

Objection	Turn Into Question	Answer the Question
"I don't like this colour"	*"So what you want to know is, how long would it take to get the colour you want?"*	By explaining: That you might be able to do a swap to get the right colour or, if not, talk about a factory order and emphasise the benefits of waiting.
"I can't see the front of the bonnet from the driver's seat"	*"So what you want to know is, will it be difficult to park the car?"*	By explaining: How many of this particular model are on the road, virtually all of which drive around and park without difficulty. This is because when you have driven the vehicle for a very short period, you no longer need to see the front to know where it is. Example: Typists don't have to look at the keys to type.

10 Successful Salespeople Expect the Customer to Buy

There are some objections that you just can't get over. Sometimes the vehicle really is too big or too small. Then who said selling was easy? The more you expose yourself to the risk of selling something, the more 'impossible to overcome' objections you will come across.

Conversely, the more you study the techniques of salespeople who never seem to get their fair share of objections, the more vehicles you will sell, in spite of the odd 'stonewall' (an objection you just can't get over).

Probably the most powerful sales-producing aid ever thought of is the thought that the customer you are with is going to buy the vehicle. Salespeople who adopt this attitude always get fewer objections and always sell more vehicles.

Who was it that said:

"We are all continually faced with a series of great opportunities brilliantly disguised as unsolvable problems"?

The main points again

1 If two salespeople are selling the same product to the same type of customer from the same showroom, one will often get far more objections than the other.

2 Salespeople who handle fewer objections always:

- Spend more time on qualification
- Very quickly gain rapport with customers
- Have the ability to 'read' their customers
- Explain to customers how they propose to help them
- Present known objections as benefits
- Avoid raising objections themselves to stop people buying
- Refrain from offering customers personal opinions
- Prevent themselves from empathising with the customer's objection
- Turn objections into questions and answer the questions
- Expect the customer to buy

3 There are only three categories of objections:

- Time
- Price
- Competition

4 There are only four types of objection:

- False
- Perceived
- Misunderstanding
- Real

5 Objections don't help you close sales. When they do arise:

- Listen to the objections carefully
- Refine vague objections into something easier to handle
- Then restate the objections as questions
- Answer the questions and not the objections

6 Salespeople who believe that the customer they are with is going to buy the vehicle, always get fewer objections and always sell more vehicles.

CHAPTER 18
Securing the Business

"Your customers should have the absolute freedom to do exactly what you suggest in any way that they want"

When it came to getting the order signed, Joe Moggs was no slouch. Joe is a fascinating character. He looks a little like an English version of a River Kwai prison commandant – small beard, big glasses, the lot. The only difference is that the prison commandant had trouble with 'R's, Joe had trouble with 'H's. One morning Joe was frantically phoning a particular number, time after time: *"I'll get 'im,"* he said, *"I know 'e's there."*

"Who are you trying to get, Joe?" I'd asked, being nosy. *"Oh, some Arab prince 'oose not being very co-operative,"* he told me, *"'e was supposed to pop in and sign an order for a new coupe and didn't come, and then 'e was going to come again and didn't come and then 'e... "*

"Okay, Joe, got the picture, so what are you going to do?" I was about to find out because Joe had got through: *"There you are, your 'ighness, I've been 'ere, this car's been 'ere but you 'aven't, what's going on?"* Joe listened intently, narrowing his eyes more than usual (which added to the prison commandant analogy).

"That's not the issue," he said, *"You 'ave already given me your verbal order and I 'ave accepted it on be'alf of my company."* He listened again, head down now, shoulders hunched over the telephone. *"Right,"* he said after some more intense listening, *"I will tell you what I am going to do. I am going to get in my car, come round now, stick the order under your nose and get you to sign it, so don't go out"*. Joe put the phone down and picked up his briefcase.

"You can't talk to people like that, Joe," I said, *"particularly an Arab prince."*

"You mean, **you** *can't,"* he replied. *"Well* **I** *can and will, and I will come back with the order."*

...And he did.

"Good morning, sir. Welcome to Nightmare Motors."

"Oh, good morning. This model here, does it come in a light metallic blue?"

"If I can get you this car in that colour, will you buy it?"

"Well, not just on colour alone. What's your finance rate?"

"If I can get you the colour you want and the finance rate you want, can I have your business?"

"Now, just a minute, slow down. I also need to find out what I will be getting for my present car in part-exchange."

"If I can get you the car you want, at the finance rate you want and give you a good price for your present car, then you would want to do business with me, wouldn't you?"

"No, I wouldn't actually."

"What do you mean 'no' and where are you going? Oh, he's gone. Some people, you could give them the earth and they still wouldn't take it."

Closing the Sale

There has been so much claptrap about closing techniques for so long, it's about time we put the whole closing matter straight. The best way to close the sale and the best time to do it is at the end. Simply ask for the business and expect to get it. For decades salespeople have been led down the wrong closing path by wellmeaning but misinformed sales trainers. Like many other so-called sales techniques, 'closing' drifted across the Atlantic from America.

Originally the techniques were taught to help salespeople sell relatively inexpensive goods and services, low cost items sold door to door. Insurance, clothing and household necessities paid for by small weekly payments. Closing 'early and often' worked well in its low cost marketplace. It was easier to say 'Yes, I'll take it' than face the embarrassment of 'No, I don't want it'. Problems arose when the same techniques were taught to sell higher priced products and services. Any form of closing puts pressure on the potential buyer. That pressure is multiplied by the cost of the item being sold. The bigger the potential price, the greater the pressure.

What Have We Been Taught?

Here are just some examples of closing philosophy that frankly doesn't have any place in today's sophisticated selling environment.

The ABC of selling

'Always be closing'. The idea is that you should start to close the sale as soon as you start talking to your customer.

Close five times before giving up

Salespeople were told to keep five coins in their trouser pocket and transfer one coin to the other pocket every time they tried to close the sale.

Know and use many closes

Salespeople were told (and still are) that they have to know and be able to use at least ten different closes. So if one does not work, they can go on to the next and then the next until one does work.

Close early and often

Salespeople are still taught this today. Close as soon as you can and as often as necessary. The pressure that that puts on customers is horrendous. Not the pressure to buy what you sell, but the pressure to get away from the salesperson as quickly and as far as possible.

Close as soon as the customer gives 'buying signals'

'Buying signals' are supposed to indicate that a customer is now ready to buy and should be 'closed' immediately.

Typical examples would be:

Kinesthetic signals	–	If the customer starts touching the goods for sale
Visual signals	–	If the customer's pupils expand when they look at the goods
Auditory signals	–	If they say things like 'This is a good idea' or 'I like this' or 'How much is it?'

Some of these ideas have their uses; others are downright dangerous to success in selling. Close too soon and you can close the door to helping that customer buy from you.

If you can't close the first time you meet then you never will

That's dangerous – and also very expensive.

My next door neighbour wanted a patio door and bay window for the back of his house. He contacted a company that specialised in supplying and fitting these types of goods, and their representative called by appointment one evening. The representative quickly established exactly what was wanted and completed an estimate there and then for the work to be carried out. The price was reasonable – £975 – and my neighbour thanked the representative and told him that he would let him know if they wanted to go ahead.

The representative was quite put out by this idea, and asked my neighbour what the problem was and why couldn't he authorise the go-ahead there and then? My neighbour explained that he was happy with the estimate, but was in the habit of taking a little time to mull over any decision that involved spending more than a little money. He went on to reassure the representative that he was sure that he would be going ahead, but was not prepared to commit himself that night.

The representative explained that 'call-backs' were costly, and that if he could see his way clear to a commitment tonight, then the price would be lowered to £885. My neighbour politely declined and told the representative that he appreciated the generous offer, but that he would really like to sleep on it. The representative, in a fit of desperation, asked where he was going to sleep. My neighbour told him to go home and sleep. The representative asked to use the phone to ring his manager to explain the situation. My neighbour, who is a very nice man, readily agreed.

After a fairly heated conversation with his manager on the phone, the representative, who was now perspiring profusely, told my neighbour that his manager had agreed to let him offer 'Show Home Status' discount. He went on to explain that if my neighbour would agree to let his company show other potential customers the work that they would carry out for him, then the price could be reduced to £755. But, he added, the agreement must be signed tonight.

My neighbour, who is a very, very nice and very patient man, said that he was going to sleep on it. The representative still kept reducing the price still further. When the price got to £545, my neighbour signed the agreement and paid the deposit. He went to bed, more than satisfied, and the representative went home in the same state of satisfaction.

It would be easy to say 'Well, that's okay then, isn't it? A happy buyer, a happy seller.' What more could you want? When my next door neighbour was telling me this saga the next day, he uncovered a flaw in the system. As he said to me: "*You know, David, the bit I really don't understand, and don't get me wrong, I am grateful for the discount, is that if the representative had gone home after giving me the first price, I would have telephoned him today and agreed to go ahead at £985.*"

Perhaps all the customers are not as nice as my neighbour, perhaps direct salespeople have to sell that way to be successful. Mind you, I did hear of a time share company in Tenerife that actually encourages their potential customers to go away and sleep on it before committing themselves. Apparently, they are making a fortune!

Why have out-of-date closing techniques been used for so long?

Because:

- They used to work
- Salespeople have liked them
- We stick to what we know
- We are frightened of change
- Even bad techniques will work, some of the time

We have to close the sales to get the orders

So how can we do this? Let us look at some of the closing techniques that have been well established in the past and are still in use today. You can then decide for yourself which you should continue to use and when.

Closing Techniques

Good, bad and positively ugly

Close	Also known as	Rating
Direct Close	*'Ask for the order'*	GOOD
Alternative Close	*'Either or'*	GOOD
Sharp Angle Close	*'Half nelson'*	GOOD
Assumptive Close	*'Order form'*	NOT BAD
Fear Close	*'Cautionary tale'*	NOT GOOD
Process of Elimination Close	*'What's not clear?'*	ALMOST GOOD
Balance Sheet Close	*'Duke of Wellington'*	ALMOST GOOD
Think it Over Close	*'Is it this, is it that?'*	GOOD AND BAD
Don't Waste My Time Close	*'You owe me the deal'*	BAD
Bid Me Fair or Bid me Farewell Close	*'The alternative – alternative'*	GOOD FOR SID, AND UGLY FOR MOST
Gobbledegook Close	*'Enthusiastic desperation'*	BAD TO UGLY
Trance Inducer Close	*'The hypnotist'*	UGLY
You Can't Afford It Close	*'Oh yes, I can'*	MOSTLY BAD
Final Objection Close	*'What's stopping you?'*	NOT TOO BAD
The Plea Close	*'Lost sale'*	PATHETIC
The Sooty Close	*'Third party reference'*	LEAVE IT TO GEORGE

Let us look at these examples one at a time.

The Direct Close

- *"Would you like to go ahead?"*
- *"When do you want it?"*

The more you are experienced at selling, the more you would use this close. It is simplest of all. When you use it, expect to get a positive answer. The best way to realise your expectations is to spend all the necessary time building the relationship and raising the customer's desire to buy before you ask for the order.

Recommendation – the perfect close

The Alternative Close (The either/or)

- *"Would you like metallic blue or the metallic silver?"*
- *"When do you want it, Thursday or Friday?"*

For people who are new to selling or really do find asking for the order difficult, the alternative has no real alternatives. It's easier and softer to use than a direct close, but again, only use it after all your finding out and selling is done.

Recommendation – the alternative perfect close

The Sharp Angle Close (Half-nelson)

- *"If you thought that you could get thirty miles to a gallon of petrol, would you want to own one?"*
- *"If we could agree the figures today, would you be in a position to place an order?"*

This is used when something is stopping the customer from going ahead. It could be a misunderstanding about cost or specification, or a doubt about aftersales efficiency or product performance. Avoid using the words *"If I can show you..."* or *"If I can prove to you..."*. This type of phraseology is a killer when it comes to rapport.

Recommendation – the sharp angle is a useful technique but only if used after all the other selling steps have been completed.

The Assumptive Close (Order form)

- *"Let's see what it looks like on paper, Mr Jones."*

Said as you reach for a blank order form and start filling it in. If Mr Jones does not object, you have probably got an order. You probably had an order anyway. There comes a point when you just know that the customer wants to go ahead. More customers will want to go ahead if you practise the full art of finding out what people want, and showing them that you can help them get what they want.

Recommendation – use this close if you want to

Only use the remaining closes described here if you really fancy a little fun with a 'test shopper'. At least you might get points for trying!

If you find yourself using these closes on a regular basis, then look again at the importance of opening good relationships before closing sales.

The Fear Close

Or, as they call it in America, '*Back the hearse up to the door and let them smell the flowers*'.

◆ *"It's the only one we have got. If you don't buy it today, then someone else probably will."*

What you really are saying is '*I'm sorry, Mr Customer, I have failed to raise your desire to agree to buy this here and now*'. More people will want to buy here and now if you become more proficient at raising their desire to buy.

Recommendation – spend more time on raising desire

◆ ◆ ◆

The Process of Elimination Close (What's not clear?)

This close was originally designed to be used with the more silent type of customer. You know, the ones that say nothing and show little emotion. It has been said, quite unfairly, that a typical example of this type of customer would be male pipe smoker with a beard who is a member of the civil service motoring association. This is how the process of elimination goes:

"I feel there is something that I have made unclear to you, Mr Morris, is it the delivery time?"
"No, you explained that."
"Is it the servicing intervals then?"
"No, I'm happy about that."
"Is it the boot space that is the problem?"
"No, that's more than adequate."

And so on... and so on... until Mr Morris tells you that he is happy with everything. That's when you ask for the order.

"So when do you want it then?"

It sounds good, doesn't it? The flaw is that if salespeople really did concentrate more effort into the opening parts of the sale, particularly qualification and presentation, then they could save themselves and their customers much time and trouble at closing time.

Recommendation – encourage 'silent' customers to talk, by asking more open ended questions

The Balance Sheet Close (Duke of Wellington)

Sometimes called the 'Benjamin Franklin' or the 'Winston Churchill' as well. This is for the 'more verbal, but less than decided what to do' customer.

"It is very difficult to know what to do really. You see my present car is perfectly roadworthy at the moment. Oh, and there is that new model coming out next year... " and so on, and so on...

You are supposed to say:

"Do you know what the great Duke of Wellington did when he was faced with a similar situation where he did not know the correct course of action?"

The customer is supposed to reply:

"No, what?"

Then you say and show:

"He used to get a piece of paper like this and draw a vertical line straight down the middle of the page. Put all the reasons for going ahead down the left-hand side and all the reasons for not going ahead down the right-hand side. Why don't we have a go?"

The customer is supposed to say:

"Why not?"

So you sit the customer down and help him fill in the left hand side.

"Don't forget you liked this and don't forget you liked that... " and so on and so on.

When you have come up with about 20 reasons between you for going ahead, you are then supposed to leave the now positive-charged customer trying to think of negatives by himself. Then, after the customer has failed to find more than three, you say:

"So how did we do? Ah! Twenty reasons for going ahead and three for not proceeding. That just about settles it then, Mr Austin. When do you want to collect your new car?"

It sounds so good, doesn't it? That's the problem – it is much more difficult to do than write it down and read about it. For a start, you have to find a customer thick enough to fall for it. For a middle, the three reasons for not going ahead could be:

"Haven't got time"
"Haven't got the money"
"Haven't got the inclination"

For a finish, more customers will be less inclined to dither if you have put enough effort into the opening relationship start of the sale process.

Recommendation – spend more time on presentation and demonstration

The Think it Over Close (Is it this, or is it that?)

I worked with a salesman once who got this one all wrong. He used to say to customers: *"Before you make up your mind, why don't you go away and think it over."* How times and timeshares change.

The close is supposed to be used when a customer utters these chilling words:

"I'll think it over."

You are supposed to say:

"I'm delighted, Mrs Singer, that means that you will give it very careful consideration. Just to clarify my own thinking, what exactly are you going to think about?"
"Is it the delivery time?"
"Is it the servicing interval?"
"Is it the boot space?"

And so on and so on. You've got it, it's our old friend, the process of elimination.

The next time a customer utters the chilling words *'I'll think it over'*, you will know that it is time to spend more time on opening sales relationships and raising desire to buy. The danger for even the best of salespeople is the natural unconscious inclination to shorten the sales process. So check yourself consciously from time to time.

"I'll think it over" is a common excuse not to buy, as well as a genuine reason for not going ahead there and then. It would make sense to find out which of the two alternatives it is. The simplest way to do this is to say with a smile: *"Apart from that?"*

"I'll think it over."
"Apart from that?"
"I'm a little concerned about the boot space."

And there you have it, the real reason – boot space. This will give you a further opportunity to re-qualify and present, which could eliminate the problem.

"I'll think it over."
"Apart from that?"
"Apart from what?"

And there you have it, a real desire to think it over.

Recommendation – what you do with a genuine *'I'll think it over'* is down to you. You could be like my neighbour's salesman and throw money at the *'I'll think it over'* till the problem goes away

The Don't Waste my Time Close (You owe me a deal)

Another similar way to destroy any chance of doing business is the superior attitude that is sometimes adopted by supercilious salespeople.

"Look, I have spent hours with you, trying very hard to help you buy this car. It would be very unfair of you not to place your order with me after all I have done for you."

All selling worlds have a sprinkling of this type of salesperson. Time spent together does equal commitment. But to ram this fact down someone's throat will have the direct opposite effect to the one intended – you will lose the business.

Recommendation – forget it

The Bid me Fair or Bid me Farewell Close (The alternative alternative)

There was a very nice man call Sid who sold second-hand commercials in the Old Kent Road who used to use this style of close with great success.

"Will you take an offer for that tipper?"
"Why certainly, there are two bids you can make. Bid me fair, or bid me farewell and push off."

(Come to think of it, it wasn't 'push'.) It has to be said that Sid was very successful. He had the right stock and the right charisma to get away with it. He was also the boss. His business lives on after him, and Sid more than likely still does business in that great used truck lot in the sky. 'Pay the price or go away' type statements will normally only antagonise the average customer and are best avoided.

Recommendation – leave this one to Sid

The Gobbledegook Close (Enthusiastic desperation)

These are often spur-of-the-moment statements from over enthusiastic salespeople in a last ditch effort to save a sale that is beyond recovery.

"Now you strike me as that type of wonderful human being that would enjoy the challenge of owning a car that is not quite suitable for your needs."

All this is said with the utmost sincerity, conviction and a beaming smile. But the customer still walks away without buying. People do buy vehicles that are not quite suitable for their needs, when the advantages of owning the product far outweigh the disadvantages. It's the salesperson's job to find out what the customer wants and then match those wants and needs to the product's features and benefits during presentation and demonstration. Then, based on your information, the customer will make the decision to buy or not to buy.

Recommendation – give the customer plenty of good reasons to buy your product, from you, from your company and you won't ever have to be desperate enough to use this

The Trance-Inducer Close (The hypnotist)

This is where the salesperson makes a statement or asks a question that tends to make the customer 'go inside' themselves to try to understand the true meaning of the words.

"I would not want you to think that this is not the car for you is this one – wasn't it?"

or

"Only you will know if this is the car for you, and you will want to go ahead and place your order – don't you?"

This is where the psychology of selling has got out of touch with the real selling world. The average customer will certainly pause if you use such phraseology, but only long enough to realise that you are using some kind of kiddology on them. Confused customers don't have all the pieces of the sales decision jigsaw – so they can't complete the sale, did they?

Recommendation – don't get clever enough to lose the business by using this one

The You Can't Afford it Close (Oh yes, I can)

Another highly dangerous close in the wrong salesperson's hands. It can work, and it has worked.

"It strikes me, Mr Abbot, that as you seem to be so concerned about discount and free-of-charge items and all, you probably can't really afford to buy this car."

The customer is supposed to pull out his cheque book and pay the full price with an "*Oh yes, I can*" to prove you wrong. For it to work successfully, you have to have the 'right' type of arrogant customer and the 'right' type of aggressive salesperson; anything else will usually fail. Like all the other manipulative closes, this should best be buried in the graveyard of broken sales and bad ideas.

Recommendation – sell the benefits apart from the price

The Final Objection Close (What's stopping you?)

This normally happens towards the end of a sale if the customer can come up with a real or perceived reason for not going ahead.

"I cannot buy this car because there is not enough boot space for my needs."

This could be absolutely factual, although it can be an excuse as well.

"Apart from the boot space, Mr Wolsey, are there any other areas of concern?"
"No, it's just the boot. It's a shame really."
"So, if you thought the boot was big enough, Mr Wolsey, you would be buying this car?"
"Oh yes, everything else is just fine."

Recognise it? You are, back at 'The Sharp Angle'.

Re-qualification and presentation could solve your customer's problem (wrong vehicle) and your problem (no sale). It could be necessary to switch the customer to a different model. It might be necessary to go for the refined sharp angle of *"If you can get what you want in the boot to fit in the boot, will you go ahead?"*

Recommendation – become the world's best salesperson at qualification, presentation and demonstration, far fewer people will have final objections and you will have more sales

The Plea Close (Lost sale)

This one is usually done down on one knee.

"Please help me, I don't want to let my next customer down. Where did I go wrong? How did I fail to satisfy you?"

A little tear in the corner of one eye is recommended at this point, but laughing is definitely out. The customer is supposed to say something like:

"You failed to satisfy me about the boot space."

And there you have it. The way home to the sale is via final objection and sharp angle.

Recommendation – not for serious salespeople

The Sooty Close (Third party reference)

I've only ever known one salesperson to use this close, but I must admit it worked for him. If he got into a final objection, say, *"That's not enough for my part-exchange"*, George used to say to the customer: *"Hang on, I'll just do a final check with my manager."* He would then stick his hand in the desk drawer and bring it out stuck inside a Sooty hand puppet. He would then say to Sooty: *"Sooty, this man says that his part-exchange is worth more than £3,000."* Sooty would then collapse over backwards and lie prone on the desk, then look up and shake his head at the customer in disbelief.

George did this very well and had the knack of picking the right customers to pull it on. After the laughter, and maybe a little more negotiation, deals were done.

Recommendation – better leave this one to George

So How Should we Close?

Only once – at the end. When is 'the end'? After, and only after, you have:

- Opened the relationship
- Fully qualified your customer
- Given a personalised presentation
- Raised desire through demonstration
- Overcome objections
- Summarised the benefits to buy

Then, and only then, should you:

- Ask for the order and expect to get it

The importance of summarising before you ask for the order

Please do remember to summarise what has happened, what has been agreed so far and the benefits of going ahead with the purchase. It pulls everything together, reminds both you and your customer of all the good reasons for buying and prepares the way to close and be closed.

Example:

"So, Mr Austin, when we first met today, you told me that you particularly wanted a car with more room in the back. This was to cater for your growing family's needs. At the same time, though, you were keen not to lose performance and drivability. Is that right so far?"

"Great. The car that meets both those requirements in our range is, as we both know, the Pelegra 1.8, which matches your requirements exactly. It also has the added advantage of extra boot space, which you thought would be very useful. You have seen the car and checked the space which, as you say, is much better than what you currently have. You have had the chance to drive the car and have experienced the responsive engine and road holding."

"The delivery would be no longer than three weeks, and here are the figures as discussed for both Hire Purchase as well as the personal leasing plan. Is there anything else you need to know about the car, the methods of payment or aftersales service?"

The whole point about closing is that these fancy closes can take more time and effort than getting it right in the first place. It is not the closing that causes sales to happen. It is all the careful uncovering of customers' wants and needs. It is the way you develop your relationship with your customers. It is your ability to engender confidence in your customers regarding you, your company and your product. Above all else, it's the first steps in the sales process that will secure a firm footing for you in the end.

Exception to the Rule

If a customer approaches you and tells you: "*I want one of those and here is the money*", raise your eyes to heaven and say "*Thank you, God, I do believe in miracles*", and take the money. Then, and only then, should you short circuit the system. You are best advised to remember this, and the old sales story that follows.

There once was a young stable lad who fell madly in love with a rich and very beautiful girl who came every Saturday to the stable where he worked. She parked her sports car and walked across to the stable as he led out her Arabian stallion for her to ride. She never noticed him or even acknowledged his presence. For her, he simply did not exist. Every Saturday it was the same, but instead of his love diminishing, his whole life was centred around those few precious moments when he could see her for such a brief time. "*There must be a way to get her to notice me,*" he started to think, "*but what?*"

You know what it's like when you have a problem that you think about a lot. Sooner or later your unconscious mind will come up with a solution. This was no exception. It came to the stable boy in a flash of inspiration, exceeding all his expectations. It was so sensible, it was so wonderful and it could not fail to work. "*What would happen,*" his unconscious mind said one day to his conscious mind, "*If you painted her horse's legs green?*" Then added: "*She would have to say something – she would have to notice you.*"

Yes, yes, yes, thought the stable boy. If I painted her horse's legs green, then she would notice me. She would have to say something like: "*Who painted my horse's legs green?*" and then I would say "*I did, I am the chief stable boy around here and I also ride*". She would say "*Fine, get your horse and come riding with me*". So I would get my horse and we would go riding together.

After a while she will say that she is getting hungry. I will say "*That's okay because I have brought some lunch*". We will then sit down under the big oak tree by the lake and have our lunch together. Then she will say "*It's getting cold*" so I will put my arm around her shoulders to keep her warm. She will say "*Gosh, your arms are strong, hold me tighter*", and I will.

It's around this time that we will start to make long, slow but passionate love.

The stable boy examined his plan in fine detail to try to detect any flaws. It appeared to be perfect. He went over his plan time and time again, until he knew every step, every word and every movement with total clarity.

She parks her sports car. I lead out the horse.

She comes over and says "*Who painted my horse's legs green?*"

I will say that I did it. And that I am the chief stable boy. And also I ride.

She will say fine, come ride with me. We will ride off together.

She will get hungry. I will have brought the lunch.

We will have lunch under the oak tree. She will start to feel cold.

I will put my arm around her to keep her warm. She will say "*Gosh your arms are strong, hold me tighter.*"

I will hold her tighter. Then we will make love.

Yes, yes, yes. Absolutely flawless. It's going to work.

And the following Saturday was the day he decided upon.

When the next Saturday came around, the girl drove into the stable yard, parked her sports car and walked over to where the young stable boy was leading out her horse. And sure enough, he had done it, he had painted her horse's legs green. She looked at her horse in horror, and for the very first time she looked directly at the young stable boy. He noticed for the very first time that her eyes were as blue as the cornflowers that were a perfect match for her corn coloured hair which framed her angelic face.

"*Who painted my horse's legs green?*" she said.

The very words of his plan, he thought. He got so excited that his plan was working that he said:

"*I did, let's make love.*"

Sensory Acuity and Closing

Good salespeople instinctively know when the best time to ask for the order is; they automatically 'read' the outward signals that confirm the customers thoughts and attitudes. Here are a few non verbal clues that will help you before you ask for the order and after the other selling steps have been completed.

Folded Arms

If a customer to whom you are talking suddenly folds their arms just as you say something, it is quite possible that the customer did not agree with what you were saying. This is a typical defensive action and would indicate that this would not be the best moment to say 'do you want one?'

Rubbing Nose

It could be that the customer has an itchy nose. Alternatively, it is possible that the customer does not believe what you are saying is true.

Tapping or Drumming Fingers

Usually a sign of impatience. You could be talking too much. Perhaps the customer wants to get away or to get on with the paperwork.

Steepling Fingers

An unconscious habit of people who think that they are smarter than you; the customer knows something that you don't know. You would be well advised to check this out before asking for the order.

Rubbing Back of Neck

The true meaning of many of these responses to certain situations is lost in the dawn of time – but not this one. One Saturday I was in the back of a police car being driven through the streets of London as a guest of two Class One police drivers. They spotted a Lotus being driven erratically.

They were using their equipment to check if it had been stolen, when one turned to the other and said: "*He has spotted us.*" I piped up at this: "*How do you know?*" "*Oh, it's easy,*" said one of my police officer friends, "*he just rubbed the back of his neck, they all do that.*"

If the customer is not agreeing with what he sees or what you are saying, then they will rub the back of their neck. It's a negative sign and now is not the time to close the sale.

Patting or Fondling Hair

As long as it is not on the back of the neck, it is a very positive sign. It's a sign of interest in what the customer is hearing, seeing or feeling. If you have completed your selling steps, now is the time to ask for the order.

Pulling or Tugging at Ear

Customers might do this because that is what they like to do. If however, you ask a customer for the order and they start pulling or tugging at their ear, they are probably trying to make a decision, they are on the borderline, give them some time and space to make up their minds.

Customer Lighting a Cigarette

People who smoke do not light up during a dilemma. They smoke after they have made a decision. Smokers are a dying breed, but not quite yet. As long as a proportion of your customers do smoke, you would be best advised to take down the 'No Smoking' signs in your showroom.

The reason is simple: you are sitting at your desk with a customer who has just seen and driven a vehicle. the customer suddenly produces a packet of cigarettes and lights one. It is virtually a 100% certainty that that customer has decided to buy as he turns to you and says those classic lines: *"So what's it going to cost me then?"* By all means have 'No Smoking' showrooms but don't put the signs up and keep an ashtray handy to close the smokers.

Resting Head on Hand

Usually a positive sign – the customer is relaxed and in agreement to what you are saying. Now is the time to ask for an order. If everything else has been done.

Tilted Head

Another positive sign. It is a sign of interest in what you are saying, what you are proposing.

Stroking Chin

The customer will do this while trying to make a decision; keep quiet and give the customer the time he needs.

Hands or Fingers Over Mouth While Speaking

Normally a negative sign, often indicating that a customer is probably lying. You know how it is when a three-year-old comes into the kitchen covered in mud and mother says: "*What have you been up to?*" The child's hand flies to its mouth in a desperate effort to stop the lie "*Nothing*" from leaving its mouth. The same involuntary reaction to lying continues to happen throughout life.

Hands in Pocket

Another form of body cross, it's a defensive gesture similar to folded arms. It could be that the person who you are talking to just finds it comfortable; but if it is done suddenly, as you are talking, then what you said has more than likely triggered this response in the customer.

Hands in Pocket Jingling Change

Defensive action mingled with concern about money. The customer might just have a couple of coins in his pocket and you could be discussing many thousands. It is amazing how strong the desire is to touch money when you are thinking or talking about it.

Pinching Bridge of Nose

This is the deep one. Usually, the customer will shut his eyes and close his ears in an effort to cut out external influences and so concentrate on inner thoughts.

This is the time to keep quiet and let the customer process internally without your outside interference.

Rubbing Eye

A negative sign. The customer is just not buying what you are saying unless of course the customer has an itch in the eye area. If in doubt, leave closing out.

Expanded Pupils

If people like what they see, their pupils dilate (expand). If the customer likes what you are saying, the same effect can be observed if you watch closely.

Contracted Pupils

It is even possible to notice that steely eyed look that contracted pupils give the face. It is a negative sign. The customer is not in harmony internally with what you are saying externally.

Looking Down

Indicates internal dialogue or feelings, which could be a negative sign. The customer does not want to be there and is not interested in your proposal or what you are saying. Give the customer some thinking time and then check it out.

Partner Looking Down – Face Turned Away

You will recognise this. A typical example of this happening is just after you have asked a closing question. The customer will turn to his wife (or husband) and say: "*What do you think, dear?*" 'Dear' is an expert on the partner's body language. 'Dear' immediately knows that the true meaning of the words is: *'Can I have your permission to buy it?'* 'Dear' will always say the same thing: *"It's up to you."*

If 'Dear' says this while maintaining eye contact and turned towards partner, then reach for your order form because the partner has just received permission to buy it. But, if 'Dear' says this while breaking eye contact, turning away from partner and looking down, the partner has just received the message 'You buy this and you're in trouble'. Such is the power of non-verbal communication. The moral of the story is for you to make yourself scarce as soon as you hear the words "*What do you think, dear?*".

With a little bit of practice, you will anticipate the question by 'reading' its imminent arrival. That is the moment to say to 'Dear' and partner:

"*While you have a chat about this, I'll just get some more coffee*" or "*Look, you don't need me around when you discuss this, do you mind if I just make a telephone call to confirm the delivery position?*" Then they can discuss whether to buy or not without the embarrassment of having you listening to:

"*Are you sure it's the right car for us? And what about the money, it's far more than we thought of spending. Don't forget we will need a new boiler shortly and, what is happening about the summer holiday? You can't rely on winning the lottery you know...*" And so on and so on.

The moral is, if you don't make yourself scarce at this point, then your customers will.

Eyes Looking Up To Your Right (or, if you prefer, to their left)

The customer is visually remembering something, for instance: *"I did like the look of that new French car we saw yesterday."* Check by asking the question *"So how does it look to you?"*

Eyes Looking Up To Your Left

The customer is visually constructing a picture, for instance: *"Will there be enough space for all of us when we go on holiday?"* Check by asking the question: *"Do you see this car as an answer to your motoring needs?"*

Eyes Looking Across To Your Right

The customer is remembering something heard, for instance: *"My friend told me that my car should be worth more that that."* Check by asking the question: *"Are you happy with what you have heard so far?"*

Eyes Looking Across To Your Left

The customer is constructing sound, for instance: *"What will John say when I tell him about this."* Check by asking the question: *"Is there anybody that you need to talk to about this before you make your decision?"*

Eyes Looking Down To Your Right

The customer is talking to themselves, for instance: *"I suppose it makes sense, I've got to change the car sooner rather than later and I feel like a change."* Give the customer time to finish the internal conversation before you check, by saying something like: *"Mr Johnston, do you have any further questions you feel you would like me to help you with?"*

Eyes Looking Down To Your Left

The customer is feeling some emotion, for instance, anything from *"I am excited about this"* to *"I feel terrified!"* Look at the customer's face and gauge the internal feeling by reading the expression. You don't have to be an expert on body language to do this – internal feelings are always to be found visually on the person's face. Give the customer time to experience the feeling and check by saying something like: *"So how do you feel?"*

With any of these eye accessing cues, you will normally know if you are on the right track because the customer will visibly **start** if your question matches their internal thought process. They will feel that you have just read their mind. You would be wise not to tell them that you did!

Second Chances

Salespeople do have to close sales. Sometimes customers will close themselves; others need a little push, but without too much pressure. Selling vehicles today has become very much more 'helping people buy'. Not everybody will buy from you the first time you meet them. Keep off the pressure and keep on the helpfulness and you will find that they will come back to buy from:

- A salesperson they like
- Who is selling a vehicle that they want
- From a company they trust

The main points again

1 Some salespeople can get away with much more than others at closing time.

2 The best way to close the sale and the best time to do it is at the end.

3 Any form of closing puts pressure on the customer.

4 The recommended ways to close the sale are:

- The Direct Close
- The Alternative Close
- The Sharp Angle
- The Assumptive Close

5 All the manipulative closes should best be buried in the graveyard of broken sales and bad ideas.

6 It is not closing that causes sales to happen, it is all the careful uncovering of customers' wants and needs.

7 It is essential that you practise the full art of finding out what people want. Then show them that you can help them get what they want, before asking for the order.

8 It is the first steps in the sales process that will secure a firm footing for you in the end.

9 Unless the customer comes in and says *"I want one of those and here is the money"*, never try to shorten the sales process.

10 Before you ask for the order, always summarise what has been agreed so far and the benefits of going ahead.

11 Good salespeople instinctively know when is the best time to ask for the order.

12 All salespeople can improve their own ability to do this by developing their own sensory acuity.

13 Selling vehicles today has become very much more 'helping people buy'.

14 Customers do come back and buy from:

- A salesperson they like
- Who is selling a vehicle that they want
- From a company they trust.

CHAPTER 19
Free of Charge

"I'd rather apologise once for our price than forever for our quality and service"

We all do it, well most of us anyway, give away things 'free of charge' when there is no real need to do so. You have made a sale, both you and your customer are happy – *"Oh I almost forgot, can I get a centripetal clasp on this model?"*

"Yes of course," you say, *"they are only £43 including fitting."*

A look of slight pain crosses your client's face, and that's when it happens. *"Don't worry – I will have it fitted for you free of charge, as a thank you for the business."* You want to keep the mutual feeling of contentment intact and you have enjoyed the mutual feeling of rapport for so long that you wipe a totally unnecessary £43 off your company's bottom line profit. All because you failed to qualify your customer properly in the first place, or because it is so easy to be generous with other people's money. I got cured of 'free of charge' years ago, and I owe it all to Mr Gold. It was my very first Rolls Royce sale.

I bumped into a friend of mine at the Steering Wheel Club in Curzon Street. He sold oil and he was entertaining a Greek called Lucki, a client of his who had just started to work in London. I joined them for a drink and when Lucki discovered that I sold cars he said that he needed a car. As we parted company, I invited Lucki to call in and said I would fix him up, *"As long as it is a Rolls Royce you want."* I said, with a not too expectant laugh.

One week later Lucki walked through the door and greeted me like a long lost friend. *"I've called to buy a car,"* he announced.

"Which one would you like?" I said, nonchalantly waving at today's equivalent of one millIon pounds worth of showroom stock.

"The maroon one, that looks nice. I'll have that." Lucki said, indicating a year-old Silver Shadow in the corner. We sat down at my desk and, desperately trying to stop my hand from shaking too much, I took an order form from my drawer and started to fill in

the details. When the form was completed, I turned it round for Lucki to sign. He checked it through while I waited in suspense still not quite believing that this was happening. Lucki looked up thoughtfully. "*What about the road fund licence? Is it taxed?*" he asked.

"*Don't worry about that Lucki,*" I said. "*I will tax it for you for six months as a thank you for your business.*"

Lucki beamed and signed the order. "*Our normal deposit is ten per cent but you can pay more if you wish,*" I said, starting to come back down to the reality of a closed sale. "*Why don't I pay the whole amount now, because I would like to take the car as soon as possible?*" said Lucki. With that, he took out his cheque book and wrote out a cheque that was equivalent to my next five years' wages. He then handed it to me with the signed order.

"*Thank you,*" I said feebly, thinking that the words were rather inadequate. "*I will just get the Financial Director to sign this on the company's behalf and then we can talk to our preparation people regarding an early delivery.*"

I shot up the stairs and, in a state of great excitement, entered Mr Gold's office. "*What do you want, dear boy?*" he said, not bothering to look up from his desk. "*I have just sold the maroon pre-owned Shadow in the showroom,*" I blurted out. "*Have you now?*" he said suddenly looking up, eyes focused on me, pen poised, face expressionless.

I went on more calmly, "*Here is the order form signed by the customer and here is a cheque for the full payment.*" Mr Gold took them from my hand in silence, put them on his desk side by side and started to examine both, just like a diamond dealer looking for a flaw. It seemed like ages before he said anything – but it couldn't have been. I didn't breathe until he spoke again. His pen had halted halfway down the order form. He looked up suddenly again, face totally without expression, "*What does this mean, dear boy?*" I looked to where his pen pointed.

"*It says six months road fund licence free of charge,*" I told him.

"*I can read that quite well for myself, dear boy. But the question is, again, what does it mean?*"

"*It means, Mr Gold, that I have told the customer that we will tax the car for six months free of charge.*"

"*Have you now,*" he said, waiting for me to go on, but I couldn't think of anything else to add, so he continued. "*Let me tell you this, dear boy, there are but two alternatives. Either your customer pays for the road fund licence – or you do.*"

"*But Mr Gold,*" I protested, "*how can I possibly go back to the customer and tell him that he will have to pay after I have told him that it would be free of charge?"*

"Now we have but one alternative," he said, still with his face devoid of expression.

"Are you saying that you expect me to pay for the road fund licence, Mr Gold?"

"Got it in one, dear boy! Have you got your cheque book on you?" His voice was ice cold. Still no facial expression.

"It's in my briefcase," I said.

"Go and get it," he said flatly. So I did, for there was nothing else I could do.

Mr Gold countersigned the order after I had given him my cheque for the road fund licence. He took his copy of the order and both the cheques and put them in his tray. *"You had better go and see your customer, dear boy. He will begin to wonder what has happened to you."* With this dismissal, Mr Gold dropped his gaze back to his desk and carried on with his paperwork. Our conversation was now closed so I left. I looked back at Mr Gold as I closed his door. His full attention was still on the papers on his desk and he was smiling.

I met Mr Gold several years after I had left the company. He looked very surprised when I greeted him warmly and shook his hand and thanked him for eradicating the 'free of charge' habit from me as a rookie salesman.

...That was the second time I ever saw him smile.

Qualification is the Key

Another advantage of full and complete qualification is that you remove the necessity to dole out dollops of your company's profits and your commission in no-advantage-to-you free of charge items at point of sale time. *"You did tell me that you were very interested in getting a centripetal clasp on your next car. This one has not got one, but it can be fitted as an extra for only £43 – that's including the cost of fitting it."*

If you have qualified that your customer wants a centripetal clasp, then the above conversation can happen in the correct place during presentation or demonstration.

Luck Money

There are parts of the United Kingdom that operate a 'luck money' system. When you are expected to give the customer some money back, as a thank you for the business. The 'luck money' system works normally North of Watford Gap and ends about Hadrians Wall. It is very important that you respond to the request '*Where's me luck money?*'. If you don't, it will not be one customer you lose, but possibly several villages full at the very least.

Thank You for Your Business

There is an old customer service saying: '*Promise your customer less but always deliver more.*' There is a very strong case for giving your customers a small gift at delivery time. The classic case of this has to be a bouquet of flowers.

It was a very disgruntled lady that stormed up to my desk in the showroom one Saturday. Apparently, the new car her local agents had promised had not materialised. The lady had come to us because she thought we were 'head office'. I explained that we were just another franchised outlet but that we would be happy to supply her with a new car. This was fairly simple since we had what she wanted in stock.

The lady placed the order and, somewhat more calmly, asked if the car could be delivered to her London address the following Saturday. Because the lady had been so upset, I placed a box of fresh flowers on the back seat of her car before I delivered it. I talked the lady through the controls, completed the paperwork and handed her the keys. Then I took my leave to head for Sloane Square and the tube train home. "*You have forgotten your box,*" she called after me.

"*That's not my box – it's your box,*" I replied to her over my shoulder. "*Thank you for your business. I am so sorry you were kept waiting,*" and then I left. When I got home half an hour later, my mother told me that 'some lady' had been trying to get hold of me and would ring me back.

The lady soon did, and told me that, not knowing my address or telephone number, she had been through all the Upshers in the London telephone directory until she had traced me (not that many, but still some effort required). The whole point was that she felt that she had to thank me, not for delivering her car but for the beautiful flowers. "*No problem,*" I said, "*thank you for the business.*"

"*I will find you some more,*" the lady said cheerfully.

...And she did!

It does not have to be flowers. If anything, flowers could be a little odd if only a man had been involved in the transaction! Like the Arab Prince who called to see Joe Moggs two weeks after he had taken delivery and asked: "*What are all those dead flowers doing in my boot?*"

Gifts at delivery time vary enormously. Here are just some of the multitude available:

- Golfing umbrellas
- Road maps
- Bottles of wine and spirits
- Floor mats
- Travel kits
- Car rugs
- Rally jackets
- Pen sets
- Notebooks
- Diaries
- Alarm clocks
- Watches
- Boxes of tissues

These gifts do not have to be expensive. One of the most effective ever was a box of king size tissues that had been personalised to the franchised garage's name. Every new and used vehicle sold went out with one. This was replaced or exchanged for a new full box at service time without charge. Once, when the company failed to do this, all hell broke loose as an angry customer stormed into the manager's office demanding: "*Where are my tissues? How do you expect me to drive without them?*" The best gifts are the ones that are personalised to your company and your franchise. Irrespective of cost, they should be of good quality.

The whole point about giving gifts is nothing to do with altruism, but to cash in on one of the basic rules of life: '*If you give, you get back*'. You will be truly amazed how much referral business can be generated by a £7 bunch of flowers. Far, far more than a last-minute free £43 centripetal clasp ever will!

The main points again

1 There is a temptation in most salespeople to give away 'free of charge items' at closing time, when there is no real need to do so.

2 This temptation can be eliminated through full and complete qualification of all customer requirements.

3 Items can then be presented and priced at presentation and demonstration time.

4 There are parts of the United Kingdom where customers will expect 'luck money' when an order is completed.

5 Not to respond positively to 'where's me luck money?' will cost you future business and referral business.

6 There is a very strong case for giving your customers a small gift at delivery time.

7 These gifts do not have to be expensive, but they should be of good quality.

8 It is truly amazing how much referral business can be generated by a £7 bunch of flowers or similar gift.

SECTION EIGHT

That Extra Mile

"I have spoken to Mr Sellers," she said. *"He suggests that you go and throw the thing in the ?*@!$* river!"*

CHAPTER 20
From Order to Delivery

"Failure and success both
need plenty of planning"

I sensed rather than felt a presence just an instant before I felt the slight pressure on my right shoulder. *"Good morning, General, how are you today?"* I asked, without turning in my seat or bothering to look up from my desk.

"What are you doing, dear boy?" he said quietly.

"I thought I would have a go at some fashion people," I said. *"They seem to be making money at the moment, so I was just checking to see who we don't do business with."*

"A good idea, dear boy. If they have a file, then leave them be," the General added – unnecessarily, because I was well aware of the rules. The prime directive was that any customer or potential customer who was already on file was the sole preserve of the salesman whose name was on the front of that file.

The files were kept downstairs in a massive room full of large filing cabinets. Anybody who was anybody had a file. The trick was to look for new money, people who had only comparatively recently become 'anybody'. The General had thousands of files and did not have to look for new business. *"I have something for you, dear boy. Would you look after a customer for me? You can keep the commission,"* he added. There had to be a catch. The General did not give anything away usually. *"Yes, Peter Sellers will be calling in shortly to order a car. I have to go out so deal with it will you?"*

"Sure," I said in pleasant surprise. I had been a long-time fan of Peter Sellers and would really enjoy meeting a man who had given me so much pleasure over so many years.

"Good," he said, and added: *"Don't forget to collect the money before delivery, will you?"*

There he was telling me the rules again. The second directive was 'get all the money in the bank before handing over the vehicle'. This rule applied to finance house cheques as well as company or personal cheques, all of which had to be cleared before handover.

Once, Mr Gold, the financial director, sent a couple of chauffeurs to the bank with a carrier bag of cash which represented full payment for a brand new silver shadow. The money was checked, counted and banked before the new car was handed over to its somewhat impatient and incredulous owner.

Peter Sellers came in just after the General had marched out. I offered him a seat and asked him what car was he interested in. He explained that his son Michael had his fourteenth birthday coming up shortly. As they had considerable grounds at their home outside London, he thought it would be a good idea to get him a Fiat 500 to drive around the garden in. "*No problem,*" I said, repressing my disappointment; after all it would be nice to deal with Peter Sellers.

The deal was done and the delivery was arranged. I was to deliver the car personally on trade plates, since the car would not be registered for use on the road. Friday week was the date set, so I asked Peter Sellers to let me have the cheque for full payment by the following Monday. I did not find this difficult to ask. After all, I was following company procedure. Peter Sellers did not find this difficult to accept: he had been buying cars from the General for years.

Monday came around and no money materialised, Tuesday brought the same situation. It was getting a bit tight for a Friday delivery, so I decided to telephone his London address. "*Good morning, may I speak to Mr Sellers, please?*"

"*Who's calling?*" she asked, sounding for all the world like a person capable of giving Joanna Lumley elocution lessons. I gave her my name and the company's name. "*Why do you want to speak to him?*" she asked. I explained the reason for my call, that Peter Sellers was expecting his son Michael's car to be delivered on Friday. The promised cheque had not arrived, which could delay delivery unless it was sent out fairly fast.

"*Oh don't worry about that,*" she plumbed, "*Mr Sellers pays for everything at the end of the month.*"

"*I do worry about that,*" I replied. "*I have to have the car paid in full before I can deliver it.*"

"*You are not asking Mr Sellers to pay for the car now?*" she asked in astonishment.

"*Yes I am,*" I said. There was silence for a moment, apart from her sharp intake of breath and air slowly expelling through, what I could imagine to be, well-manicured teeth.

"Very well then," she said, *"I will go and ask him. Be it on your own head – don't go away."*

I waited for a while and then she came back on.

"I have spoken to Mr Sellers," she said. *"He suggests that you go and throw the thing in the ?*@!$* river!"*

I can honestly say I have never heard the *'F'* word said with such style and eloquence.

The next day there was a letter to the General from Peter Sellers which started on the lines of *"Who is that upstart Upsher?"* and finished with *"As far as money is concerned, I could buy and sell your company tomorrow"*.

The General told me not to worry about it. After all, rules were rules, and he would write back and explain the situation. *"Perhaps he will still take the car, dear boy,"* he concluded.

...But he didn't.

Collecting the Money

It's a different world isn't it? Just reading the Sellers story through again brings home the difference between selling posh motors in the West End of London 25 years ago and selling Japanese imports in Doncaster today. One thing hasn't changed though, and that is the importance of getting the money before you deliver the vehicle. If anything, it is probably more important today than it was then. Profit margins are usually smaller today, and the chances of being 'conned' appear to be greater.

Let us take the whole business of what happens from order time to delivery day apart and examine each part step by step. Study this chapter and make the bits that you don't currently do the bits that you always do in the future. This will ensure that you enjoy handing over vehicles and your customers enjoy receiving them even more.

Make Out the Order

Order forms should be fully completed there and then, while the customer is still with you. Some salespeople try and short circuit this task in a rush to complete the transaction before the customer has a change of heart. Having made the decision to go ahead, most customers will wait, and be happy to do so.

Have you Helped Your Customer to Buy Everything?

"Harold, are you sure that I will like this?" said Amanda. *"You'll love it,"* said Harold.

"But you know I don't like curry. What's wrong with McDonald's?"

"We can't take Gaylord and Gwendoline to McDonald's now, can we? They like Indian food, I like Indian food. You don't like it, you say, but in the fifteen years that I have been married to you, you have never even tried it".

"But Harold..."

"Can I take your order, sir?" the waiter said. *"Yes,"* said Harold, *"you certainly can. We would like as starters two Chicken Tikkas and two Onion Bhajias."*

"Certainly, sir," said the waiter, ***"and for your main course?"***

"Right," said Harold with a gleam in his eye, *"can we have two Chicken Masalas, one King Prawn Madras for me and a Chicken Bangalor Phall for my good lady with a side order of chilli pickle and fresh chilli chutney."*

"Your good lady is a wondrous lady," said the waiter, eyes wide with admiration. ***"Would she also be wanting a bucket full of iced water?"***

"What would I want that for, Harold?" asked Amanda suspiciously.

"To stick the wine in, darling, that I'm about to order for you. Yes please, complete with a bottle of your house white," Harold told the waiter.

"Ah sir, may I now take a liberty and recommend the 1978 Puligny-Montrachet from the Pucellos vineyard?"

(Harold tried desperately to price it on the wine list.)

"Oh no, sir," the waiter said. ***"It is not on the wine list that you will be finding this wine. It is kept in reserve for only our most deserving of customers."***

"Yes," said Harold reluctantly, *"All right."*

"Now," said the waiter, ***"what rice do you want?"***

"Oh, two pilau and two plain," said Harold.

"What nan bread do you want?"

"Just a couple," said Harold.

"Shall I make it two plain and two peshwari?" said the waiter, with a slight nodding of the head.

"Yes, all right," Harold said.

"And vegetables?" said the waiter.

Harold looked uncertain and reached for the menu.

"May I be recommending the Saag Bhajee, some Bombay Aloo and complemented with a portion of Cauliflower Korma?" said the waiter. ***"Then your meal will be truly completed."***

Gaylord and Gwendoline looked impressed; Amanda looked terrified as Harold confirmed: ***"That will be fine."***

The waiter turned to move away and Harold started to relax in relief. He almost jumped out of his chair as the waiter spun around suddenly and said: ***"Oh sir! Calamity! We have forgotten the Papadams. I am truly sorry. Shall I give you four plain and four spiced?"***

"Yes, that sounds okay," said Harold, giving in.

"One more request if I may, sir. Would you accept with our compliments and gratitude for your custom our house speciality, curried cream creme brulee to finish your meal and sweeten your palate?"

Harold looked relaxed again, soothed by the words 'our compliments and gratitude': something for nothing would certainly sweeten the meal for him, as he was paying the bill.

The waiter continued: ***"It is most fortunate indeed that I can offer you a bottle of '67 Chateau d'Yquem to enjoy with your dessert, at a price that will truly astonish you."***

If a waiter from the back end of Bangladesh can do it in a Balti House in Sparkbrook, Birmingham, then what excuse have you got for not selling all your products and services?

Sell All Your Products and Services

Look, I know you can sell payment protection plans, accessories and the like at delivery time, or even after delivery. People do it all the time. Finance companies make a fortune out of selling payment protection after the vehicle has been delivered. All they do is ring up the customer to whom you sold the finance and say: *"Hey, you haven't got payment protection. Would you like me to add it on for you?"* Some finance companies sell more payment protection plans than motor retailers in this way, and guess who doesn't get the commission? That's right – you don't.

Why not make it easy for yourself and your customer. At 'making out the order time' check and make sure that you have given your customer the opportunity to buy all your products and services. Keep a checklist handy, and run through each item available with your customer. Once a customer has bought something, that is the best time to ask them to buy something else.

Sign the Order

For years now salespeople have been in the habit of avoiding the word 'SIGN'. Now is the time to bring it back into its rightful place in the English language. Today, it is perfectly in order to say to your customer: *"As you can see here, Mr Jones, the total cost to change comes to £8,734.00. If you would like to sign here, you have bought yourself a new motor car."*

The whole point is that the customer should leave your premises 'knowing' that a commitment has been made between the customer and the company. Throw out of your business vocabulary *"Just approve this"*, *"Would you authorise that"* or *"Stick your name down here where I have put the X for no publicity"*.

Use a Proper Pen

Irrespective of what vehicles you sell, be they new or used, use a quality pen to fill out orders and other paperwork. Feelings of euphoria can be severely shaken when you hand your customer a tatty, well chewed, cheap ball point with which to sign the order.

Collect the Deposit

Once the customer has signed the order form, that is the time to ask for a deposit. *"Our normal deposit is ten per cent, Mr Jones, but you can pay more if you wish."*

Part Company Politely

Once all the paperwork has been completed to both the legal and your company's requirements, and the deposit has been paid, it is time to part company temporarily. Thank your customer for the business and see him off the premises.

Try to imagine that the customer is a guest in your own home: the same rules should apply. Show the customer to the door, open it for him, escort him to his vehicle and stand and wave him goodbye as he drives off down the road for as long as you can see him.

There are three reasons for this:

- Your customer will enjoy receiving this level of attention
- You will enjoy giving it
- The chances of 'buyer's remorse' will be severely diminished

Sometimes when people buy things they start to doubt if they have made the right decision. This is perfectly normal. You are probably remembering an example of your own experience of 'buyer's remorse' right now. Let your customers leave you with a cheerful smile on their faces and feeling very comfortable with their buying decision and you will banish 'buyer's remorse' in most all of them.

Processing the Paperwork

Salespeople and paperwork do not normally go together like eggs and bacon. It has often been said that the better you are at selling, the worse you are at administration. In fact, as in most things, whatever you believe to be true is true for you. Many good salespeople seem to get behind with their paperwork. Usually about three days. Have you ever stopped to consider why it is always three days? Never less, never more?

It's rather like watching a cycle race or a marathon. There are the leaders and there are the followers, and they always seem to stay at the same distance from each other. That means everybody is working just as hard and at the same pace, but some are just constantly behind. Catch up with that paperwork and believe you can stay up, it just might make the difference between winning and being an also-ran.

Progressing the Order

Different companies have different methods of processing orders. This depends on the size of the company and the level of sales support it has. What should be clear to you is what exactly your own responsibilities are regarding processing orders.

There are two things which should always be your responsibility. The first is to write to your customer:

- Thanking him for his business
- Confirming delivery date, time and place
- Confirming the balance payable and how and when it should be settled
- Providing any other administration details and confirmation of any other special requests
- Giving a checklist of all dealer-fitted options and tasks as agreed

Example of a 'Thank you for your order' letter

Dear Mr Jones

Thank you for your order today. It was a pleasure to meet you again and my company is most grateful for the trust that you have placed in us by becoming a customer.

Thank you also for confirming that you will collect your vehicle from our showrooms at 5pm on Thursday and at the same time bring your present vehicle that we have taken as part-payment. The balance payable, as shown on the enclosed invoice, is £8,000 exactly.

We have noted that the balance payable will be in the form of a banker's draft at the time of delivery, and that you will be bringing in the registration documents and service history of your present vehicle. The notification of change has been passed on to your insurance company as requested.

The trust that you have placed in us will not be taken lightly, since we believe that no customer is truly satisfied until they have bought their second vehicle from us. It is our aim to make sure that you receive every satisfaction from your decision to buy and from the model that you have bought from us.

Before your vehicle is handed over to you we will make sure that everything is as you have requested, as follows:

- Full tank of petrol
- Full set of floor mats
- Mud flaps to rear wheel arches
- Road fund licence for full 12 months
- Return of insurance certificate

Looking forward to meeting you again on Thursday at 5pm.

Yours sincerely

Pre-delivery Inspection

The second task that should always be your responsibility is always to carry out your own personal pre-delivery inspection. In some companies, the relationship that exists between sales department and service department is less than harmonious. Having been on both sides of the potential brick wall, here are two reasons that can cause this totally unnecessary rift.

Some salespeople get into the habit of always calling everything up early. *"Look,"* they say, *"Mr Jones will be in on Wednesday night for his vehicle; I must have it by Wednesday 4pm at the latest."* Someone, somewhere in the service department, puts himself out to meet your deadline. The same person (or persons) sees that vehicle still undelivered on Thursday morning and all day Thursday. Which means that the next time you set a deadline, the line will be dead!

The second method of unhinging good relationships between sales and service regarding delivery is what has been christened the 'Nottingham tut, tut, around' after a notorious Nottingham salesperson who is no longer in the industry. This 'quite nice person really' would approach every vehicle that he was about to deliver with the utmost suspicion, usually with cloth in one hand and can of lighter fluid in the other. He would pounce on every blemish, wax deposit, mark, however small, with a loud *"tut, tut"*, a vigorous polish and a grumpy glare at the offending service department. There has to come a point when you wouldn't want to help this person in any way ever again.

The best way to carry out this final check before delivery is to imagine that you have spent your own money on the vehicle. *"If I had spent this much money on this vehicle, would I be truly satisfied?"* If the answer is no, for any reason, then tell somebody, remembering all that you know about rapport, sensory acuity and empathy. Why use these skills with customers alone when they can do wonders for interdepartmental relationships? If the answer is yes, you would be truly satisfied, then tell that to the same person that you would have complained to. People do like to hear good news as well – don't they? – particularly when coupled with a little praise and recognition.

Whatever else happens, having established exactly when the customer is coming to collect, or when you are going to deliver, make sure that everything is ready:

- The vehicle is as it should be
- The right documentation is with the vehicle

To help you do this, it is recommended that you give a copy of the 'Thank you for your order' letter sent to your customer to the person who will be responsible for carrying out or arranging the pre-delivery inspection. This should be part of the system that companies have in place to ensure the customers get what they want, when they expect it.

The Delivery

One problem about working in vehicle sales is that it is easy to forget how people feel about picking up their new vehicle. Most of us just get one from time to time and it's no big deal any more. Not so the customer. This day only happens every few years. The customer is excited, nay, even ecstatic as the special day arrives – the day that the new vehicle is to be collected. Help the customer fully enjoy the delivery experience, and make a show out of delivery.

- Always make a personalised delivery of the vehicle
- You sold it, you should hand it over

It is the golden opportunity to cement a long-term relationship that will lead to future business.

Set the vehicle off to its best advantage

- Try to arrange for the vehicle to be parked in a suitable and easy-to-get-out-of place
- Or have a special 'handover' bay to celebrate the occasion

Have all the paperwork to hand

- Any other documentation that needs to be signed by the customer
- Any paperwork that you have to hand over with the vehicle
- Handbook, dealer book and service record
- Invoice, insurance certificate
- Copy of part-exchange appraisal form

Check the part-exchange with the customer

- Do this diplomatically
- Is it the same vehicle you saw when you appraised it?
- Does it have the same equipment?
- Has the customer left any personal possessions in the vehicle?
- Is it in the same condition as it was when you saw it?

Check the new vehicle with the customer

- Have the list of extras and options required
- Check these off with the customer
- Go over the controls
- Explain warranty and running-in requirements
- Always take a test drive with the customer and make sure that the customer can drive comfortably knowing where everything is.
- Make sure the customer is fully satisfied before you complete the paperwork

Complete the transaction

- Go through the paperwork with the customer
- Get any signatures needed
- Collect any outstanding payments
- Explain anything that needs to be explained
- Book in the first service and/or introduce the customer to the service department

Delivery Enhancers

Asking for referrals

Most salespeople have been taught to ask for referrals at delivery time or even order time. There are, however, better times to do this – later when the customer has had a chance to get to know the new vehicle and for other people to have seen it.

Recommendation: avoid asking for referrals at delivery time.

How much fuel?

Some companies throw in a couple of gallons, others always put ten pounds' worth in. This means that soon after taking delivery of the new vehicle, the customer must stop and put petrol in it, often on the way home or back to the office. This is a psychological 'downer'. Customers do not get any enjoyment from this. Most, in fact, find the experience quite annoying. Why not fill the tank with fuel and charge the customer for it? If you are currently giving fuel away with every delivery you will save a small fortune. Why not say at order time:

"Now the on-the-road charges, including a full tank of fuel and a full year's road licence, are... "

It is highly unlikely that the customer will bat an eyelid, let alone object.

Recommendation: always deliver the vehicle with a full tank of fuel (which the customer has paid for).

Avoiding potential disappointments

If, for any reason, the vehicle is not going to be exactly as the customer expects it to be, then the customer should be informed before delivery and not at handover time. Say, for instance, you cannot get the mud flaps that were wanted. Telephone the customer before delivery, explain the situation and give the customer an indication of when they will be available to be fitted. This will not normally be a problem.

However, if you do leave it to delivery time, it is amazing how important mud flaps (or whatever) can become.

"Wow, what a cracking looking car it really is ... Where are the mud flaps?"
"Ah yes, Mr Jones, I was just going to explain that to you. We had run out of stock and we could not get any more by today. Don't worry, we will fit them on the first service."

Irrespective of how the customer responds to this, he will worry. By the time he has got home, it will be all out of proportion:

"Darling, your new car looks wonderful, but why so glum?"
Darling will reply with much head-hanging and sighing: *"They forgot the mud flaps."*

All this very human behaviour just does not make sense. Mr Jones could have spent thousands of pounds on a new car and has totally overreacted to a lack of tens of pounds worth of mud flaps. It might not make sense, but this is how Mr Jones makes his judgement not to buy from you ever again, or to recommend you to anyone else.

Recommendation: by pre-warning the customers of potential problems, the problems can often fade away into insignificance.

Say 'Hello' and not 'Goodbye' at delivery time

Having done everything that needs to be done, it really is just a case of waving your customer on his way. This should not be goodbye, more of a hello really. You will be keeping in touch with your new customer to make sure that everything is as it should be, to seek referral and repeat business. If your handovers follow anything like the recommendations laid out here, then you will certainly have earned the right to both.

The main points again

1 Collect full payment before you deliver the vehicle.

2 Fully complete order forms in front of the customer.

3 It's okay to use the word 'sign' today.

4 Get yourself a quality pen to complete and sign orders.

5 Collect deposits as soon as the order form is signed.

6 Reduce the chances of buyer's remorse by parting politely.

7 Catch up on your paperwork instead of always being three days behind.

8 Make sure that you know exactly what your responsibilities are regarding processing orders.

9 Always write and thank customers for orders, confirming all the details.

10 Always carry out your own personal pre-delivery inspection.

11 Ask yourself the question: 'If I had spent this much money on this vehicle, would I be truly satisfied?'

12 Always make a personal delivery of the vehicle.

13 Set the vehicle off to its best advantage.

14 Have all the paperwork to hand.

15 Check the part-exchange with the customer.

16 Check the new vehicle with the customer.

17 Complete the transaction.

18 Avoid asking for referrals at delivery time.

19 Always deliver the vehicle with a full tank of fuel which the customer has paid for.

20 Pre-warn customers of potential problems.

21 Say 'Hello' and not 'Goodbye' at delivery time.

22 Ensure that you earn the right to referral and repeat business through thorough handover.

CHAPTER 21
From Delivery to Repeat Business

"If you don't look after
your existing customers,
then somebody else will"

Steven, a friend of mine, had built up an incredible estate agency business, with branches in key upmarket areas in the suburbs of London. He and his partner had accomplished this over a 15-year period. As property values grew, so did Steven's business. Steven sold his business in 1989 to a vast estate agency group for mega money, just before property values crashed through the foundations.

"*What are you going to do now?*" I asked him.

"*Well not a lot,*" he told me, "*what I have done is bought a large chunk of a Palladian mansion just off the M25. I am also negotiating to buy this rather superior villa near the Marbella Club in Spain. Then what I fancy doing is living here in the summer months and then moving to Spain for the winter, and just enjoy life for a while.*"

"*Wow,*" I said, trying not to be envious, "*it sounds like you have got everything that you want.*"

"*Well almost,*" came the reply: "*The villa comes complete with a white convertible Mercedes-Benz and I have my Jaguar here. But what I have always fancied is a Rolls Royce. Not a new one – something a bit decent that I can use when the fancy takes me but without tying up too much equity, if you know what I mean.*"

"*Yes, I do,*" I told him. "*In fact I still have quite a few contacts in the business that supply that type of car.*"

"*I thought you might,*" he said, "*that's why I mentioned it. Could you possibly help by putting me in touch with the right person or company to buy the car from?*"

"*No trouble at all,*" I told Steven. "*I will get somebody reliable to contact you and fix you up with a car.*"

And that's exactly what I did.

A month or so later I was in Steven's neck of the woods and popped in to say hello and take a look at his chunk of stately home. It was incredible, from the chandelier-festooned seventy-foot-long drawing room to the similar sized swimming pool that was built into the basement next to the personal discotheque.

"It's all magnificent," I told him truthfully. *"You worked hard for it and you deserve it."*

"Well, to be honest, I did have some luck as well," he told me. *"Talking of luck,"* he added, *"there is something else I must show you. Let's take a walk outside."*

As we approached the garage block, he pressed a button on a handset and up rolled a large garage door. Inside the garage was the most hideous Rolls Royce Silver Shadow I have ever seen. It was the colour you get when you stir strawberry jam into rice. It had white leather seats piped in the same external colour; worst of all, it had a gold-plated flying lady mascot desecrating the simplicity of the famous parthenon grill.

"It's lovely, Steven." I said less than truthfully. *"How very nice, where did you get it?"*

"From your friend," he told me, *"Didn't you know?"*

I did not know. The person that I gave the referral to had never told me. It would have been nice if he had. He could have telephoned and said something like 'I sorted your friend out with a vehicle, thank you for the introduction'. He might have even gone on to say 'The next time you're in town, let's do lunch'. But this would not have been necessary. All I wanted was to hear the words *'Thank you for the introduction'*. The same as most other people would.

This was a while ago. At the time I decided that I would not give this person any more referrals.

...And I haven't.

Manufacturer's Survey

A few years ago, a manufacturer of vehicles decided to carry out a follow-up survey on a selection of customers who had recently taken delivery of one of their new vehicles. The objective was to measure the level of customer satisfaction with the product and with the supplying dealers. This was carried out by telephone, the selected customers first being advised by letter that the survey was going to take place and the reasons why it was being done. All the usual questions were asked – 'Are you happy with your purchase?' and 'Was the vehicle handed over to you in an acceptable condition?' But there were one or two more unusual questions:

- 'Would you have any objection to being followed up by the person who sold you the vehicle?'
- 'Has the person who sold you the vehicle followed you up?'

The answers to these questions were incredible. Virtually 100% of the customers said that they would be pleased to hear from the person who sold them their vehicle. Virtually 100% of the customers said that they had not been followed up by the person who sold them their vehicle... and this was six weeks after delivery.

I've bought a fair few vehicles in the last 15 years since starting in training and consultancy work. Apart from the odd circular letter, I can't remember any meaningful follow-up, certainly not by telephone or face-to-face, although this is something we recommend to delegates on our sales courses.

There was that bed company in Bath that followed us up though. This was some years ago. We had popped into Bath on Saturday to buy a bed for our son James. We found what we wanted at a price we could afford and, as customers, I suppose we were a pushover. The bed was delivered the following Tuesday, as promised, and that was that, or so I thought. On Friday night, I got a telephone call. It was from the bed shop.

"*Good evening, Mr Upsher. This is the Bath Bed Company here; you bought a bed from us last weekend.*"

"*Yes,*" I said and asked what the problem was.

"*There is no problem,*" the voice assured me pleasantly, "*I am ringing to make sure that James is happy with his new bed.*" James was, I told him, and so was I. It was only after I had put the telephone down that I realised that an incredible thing had happened.

More recently, I booked myself in for one night at the Hyatt hotel in Birmingham, a very smart and busy hotel. All I had in mind was to sleep for the night and then move on the next day. I ordered some sandwiches and wine from room service, and settled down to catch up on some paperwork. The sandwiches and wine duly arrived. The former looked and tasted delightful, the latter was chilled just right and hit the spot after a busy day on the road. Then, a short time later, this incredible thing again. The telephone rang.

"Hi, this is Daniel in room service."

"Yes," I said, *"what's the problem?"*

"There is no problem," said Daniel. *"I was just checking to make sure that you were happy with your sandwiches and the wine we selected for you."*

I told Daniel that I was more than happy.

...And I was.

From Delivery to Repeat Business

Now that the customer has taken delivery of the vehicle, you can really start to get down to business. The business of keeping in touch with that customer to maximise your referral and repeat business opportunities. There are some reasons given by salespeople for not doing this; and there are some reasons why salespeople should follow up and keep in touch. Let us consider both sides of the situation.

Reasons Against	Reasons For
Most salespeople don't	You will sell more vehicles
I see them when they come in for a service	You will sell more vehicles
It's a bit of a cheek	You will sell more vehicles
I haven't got the time	You will sell more vehicles
They might have a problem	You will sell more vehicles
Customers don't like being pestered	You will sell more vehicles
I don't like pestering customers	You will sell more vehicles
It does not work	You will sell more vehicles

To be scrupulously fair about this, let's take each 'reason against' apart to test its validity.

Most People Don't

That's the truth, but then if you think about it, that could be a very good reason to follow up. The following letter, written over 20 years ago, says it all:

Dear Salesman

I was surprised when you didn't see me a week or two after you delivered my new vehicle that morning not so many years ago, for I liked you and your company. I was planning on introducing you to some of my friends. I confess that I was a little disappointed when you didn't come. A good many times in the past years, especially those first two when it was hard to make the payments on the vehicle that you sold me, I wished that you would come and tell me again about the value of it, and make me as enthusiastic about it as I was on the day when I bought it... *but you didn't come back.*

I was a little flattered when you persisted in seeing me before I bought. It made me feel worthwhile. I thought perhaps you liked me for my own sake as well as for the sake of my business. I thought you judged me to be an interesting fellow. But I guess I was mistaken for *you never came back.*

Every year I think, well, perhaps I should trade in for a new vehicle, but then I spend more money on the old one and keep driving it. I have often wondered why you didn't come back and see me and save me that money... *but you never came back.*

The man who sold me my first insurance policy likes me enough to come and see me, even though he knows I don't need more insurance. The result is that I have been buying insurance from him all my life. I have spent lots of money with your company - more than I have in buying insurance... *but you never came back.*

Of course, I have bought lots and lots of vehicles from many different salesmen, each time thinking 'I like this man and I will let him be my vehicle salesman', but my life has been a continuous procession of strange salesmen... *because you never came back.*

Yours sincerely

New Vehicle Buyer

I See Them When They Come In for Service

The truth is that vehicles come in less and less for service. Apart from that, the customer might be in a hurry when he calls. You might be busy. You might just miss him. There are too many 'might be's' here for comfort. There must be a better way.

It's a Bit of a Cheek

Funnily enough, the total reverse is true. Most customers will be delighted to hear from you. Bear in mind that it does not happen that often. If you work as hard to keep your customers as you did to make them customers, then you will do very well indeed.

I Haven't Got The Time

If some salespeople spent less time worrying about how little time they have got, then they would have enough time to follow up every customer properly.

They Might Have a Problem

True, and if you don't keep in touch, you will not have to know or worry about it. Rather like the old saying 'Out of sight, out of mind'. Do you realise that in the Japanese language, the closest you can get to that saying is the translation 'blind idiot'? Salespeople who follow up customers are never blind and never idiots. They know what's going on. If a customer has a problem, then through follow-up they can nip that problem in the bud – before it blooms into something totally out of proportion to the original problem.

Customers Don't Like Being Pestered

It depends what you mean by 'being pestered'. It is most unlikely that a customer would appreciate a follow-up call every week asking for referral business. Fortnightly mailshots would have the same negative effect. Some form of contact by telephone, letter or face-to-face, say three times a year, would be enough to remind the customer of you, and for you to remind the customer that you are always there to help him – along with anybody he knows who might be in the market for a new or used vehicle at that time.

I Don't Like Pestering Customers

Just what do these words mean? What does making such a statement say about the person who makes it? The salesperson who makes such statements as *'I don't like pestering customers'* has got some work to do on themselves if they truly want to succeed. Change has to happen to remove such negative and sales-costing attitudes. If you do know anybody who needs to make those changes regarding this or any other similar negative statements, you will find all the tools you need in section nine, *Walking Beyond Your Limits.*

It Does Not Work

Joe Maguire used to tell the story about the time when his job was to install prospecting and follow-up systems in franchised vehicle showrooms. This was pre computer days, and was based on printed cards and follow-up sheets. Joe would install the system, instruct the Sales Manager and staff how to use it and then call back a month later to make his first follow-up call (practising what he preached!). On one such occasion, Joe entered the Sales Manager's office to find all the paperwork still neatly piled up on top of the filing cabinet. When Joe asked why they had not started to use the system, the manager said: *"Oh that, it doesn't work."*

Joe looked crestfallen for an instant, and then said: *"Doesn't work, eh? Give me all that stuff here. We will soon see about that."* The manager handed him the stack of cards and follow-up sheets, which formed quite a pile. Joe weighed them thoughtfully in his hands for a moment and then with a sudden movement, threw everything up in the air.

The office was full of flying paper, which soon settled like a white and pink patchwork covering the startled Sales Manager and his office. As it settled, Joe could see the wide-eyed look on the Sales Manager's face, mouth hanging open in amazement. Joe looked down at the paperwork and with both hands he beckoned to it: *"Come here,"* he said. *"Come here."* The paper did not move. He tried again and still the paper would not budge. Joe looked at it with disappointment and looked back up at the Sales Manager, who by now was looking absolutely terrified. *"You're right,"* said Joe quietly, *"It does not work. Perhaps you have to work... IT!"*

Joe is right. Systems don't work; you have to work them. When the systems start running you, everything goes haywire. Mind you, there are a few funny systems about.

The Computer Spewer System

Many of you will be familiar with this one. Somewhere there is a computer that keeps churning out computerised follow-up sheets day after day, week after week, year after year. If the salesperson gets behind, has a day off or goes on holiday, the sheets still arrive and the backlog jam goes from worse to terrible. This can all be avoided by sensible planning – so much a day, day-by-day, what can sensibly be achieved, without turning the average salesperson into a frustrated paper shuffler with no time to do anything, let alone selling.

The Impossible Volume System

Some companies make it a rule that every salesperson has to make, say, 25 contacts every day. This would be in addition to dealing with showroom and telephone enquiries, demonstrations and deliveries.

If a salesperson was to talk to:

- Twenty-five people on Monday
- Twenty-five people on Tuesday
- Twenty-five people on Wednesday
- Twenty-five people on Thursday

Then it is obvious what that salesperson will not be doing on Friday. That's right. If you do talk to a hundred people, prospects old and new, plus existing customers from Monday to Thursday, then you will not have time to talk to any additional people on Friday. You will be too busy dealing with enquiries and queries generated by the hundred contacts that you have already made that week. All sales department staff, including management, should sit down and sensibly work out what is a reasonable level of follow-up. Work out the plan and then work the plan.

Making Follow-up Work for You

Having delivered the vehicle to the customer, the very first thing that you should do is to write and thank that customer for taking delivery. This token of continued interest and attention can only help you in the future.

Example of 'Thank you for taking delivery' letter

Dear Mr Jones

Thank you for taking delivery of your new vehicle today. By now, you will have had the opportunity to try the vehicle, get a little more used to it and appreciate its many fine qualities.

Alan Thompson, our Service Adviser, is looking forward to meeting you again when you bring your vehicle in for its first service on Thursday 16th, as agreed. If you do want a lift to the station, I would be happy to arrange this for you.

I will keep in touch with you to make sure that you are totally satisfied with your new vehicle, but if in the meantime there is any way I can be of further assistance to you, please do not hesitate to get in touch with me.

Thank you again for both your trust and your business. Both are very much appreciated.

Best wishes.

You don't have to use these exact words: use your own. Just remember to:

- Keep the letter short and to the point
- Make it a friendly letter
- Say 'thank you' at least twice
- Continue to 'sell' the vehicle a little
- Tell the customer you will keep in touch
- Ask the customer to get in touch with you if your help is needed

The Personal Visit

Whenever possible and practical, make it your habit to visit the new owner personally within a month of delivery. Sometimes this is not possible because of the distance involved or the difficulty of getting face-to-face with some customers.

The personal visit will be of enormous benefit if you personally:

- Go to be of service to the customer
- Go to where the vehicle is available
- Make sure that the customer is still happy
- Help sort out any problem if the customer is less than satisfied
- Ask for referrals if (and only if) the customer is satisfied

"Mr Jones, as you may realise, much of our business is referred to us by satisfied customers such as yourself. Do you happen to know anybody that you feel I may be able to help, through your recommendation, of course?"

- Don't expect masses of referrals there and then – reminding the customer is the important part
- Thank the customer for the business and the time
- Part company politely

Keep In Touch Regularly

There are three good ways to keep in touch:

- Telephone
- Face-to-face
- In writing

The natural laws relating to rapport indicate that:

- Auditory people prefer the telephone
- Kinesthetic people enjoy face-to-face
- Visual people appreciate the written word

Most customers would probably prefer a blend, since everybody uses all of their senses some of the time. This is the occasion for a little variety. Every year:

- Speak to your customers once on the telephone
- Get face-to-face once with them

- Write to them once (with a specific reason to do so)

Then your customers will be more than happy, and you will be more than pleased with the level of referral business that you generate.

Dealing with Referral Business

The first rule of referral business is always to ask for it. The second rule is to remind the customer of your request for referrals from time to time. Just enough to plant the seeds of the thought. Never enough for the weeds of 'Oh no, not referrals again' to spread and choke the bloom of desire to help you find a few customers.

When you do get a referral:

- Thank your customer and make sure that you have all the information that is available about the referred customer and about the vehicle wanted
- Contact the referred customer, normally by telephone, to confirm their interest in buying and your interest in helping him buy
- Some referrals will make the first approach to you by telephone or by calling in to see you. IN ALL CASES the next step applies
- Get face-to-face: "*Your place or mine?*" and start the sales process
- Remember that the referred customers have an extra need or want. They have some level of commitment to buy from you because of some obligation to the person that referred you
- You too have an obligation to live up to the promise of professionalism that your existing customer has told the referral to expect
- Bearing all these points and obligations in mind, help the referred customer buy the vehicle
- Always let your customer know the outcome of any contact with a referral, whether successful or not. This should usually be in writing as it carries more weight than a telephone call and is a record of what happened

Dear Mr Jones

It was most kind of you to recommend your friend, Mr Hargreaves, to our company. I have been in touch with him and now have an exact idea of the vehicle and specification that he requires.

Naturally, we will take his present vehicle in part-exchange, and feel sure that we will be able to offer him an acceptable price.

There is a particular vehicle which might suit Mr Hargreaves. This will be available within the next ten days and I will check it over first before presenting it to him.

Thank you one again for the trust you have placed in us. I will let you know what happens.

Yours sincerely

Why we Follow Up Customers for Referrals

Most people know at least 100, if not 200, other people fairly well. These contacts will include family, business and social contacts. By giving your customer extraordinary service and by keeping in touch and asking for referral business, your customer will **want** to help you and to help the people they know by recommending you. If each satisfied customer was to give you just two successful referrals every year, the following would happen at the end of a three-year period:

In year one you sold the original vehicle plus two more vehicles to referrals	Total 3
In year two you sold two more vehicles to referrals from each of the three 'year one' sales	Total 6

In year three you sold two more vehicles to referrals from each of the nine sales in years one and two	Total 18
In year three the original customer also buys another vehicle from you	Total 1
Grand Total	**28 Sales**

If the mathematics above are true, then from one sale you will have produced a total of 28 sales over a three-year period. The bad news is that this is just theory. These figures have yet to be accomplished. The good news is that I knew a salesperson called Henry who managed to get it to 14. Fives and sixes are not uncommon. Perhaps the *good* news is that it does not entirely work. For if you sold 100 vehicles this year, you would have to face the prospect of delivering 2,800 vehicles in three years' time!

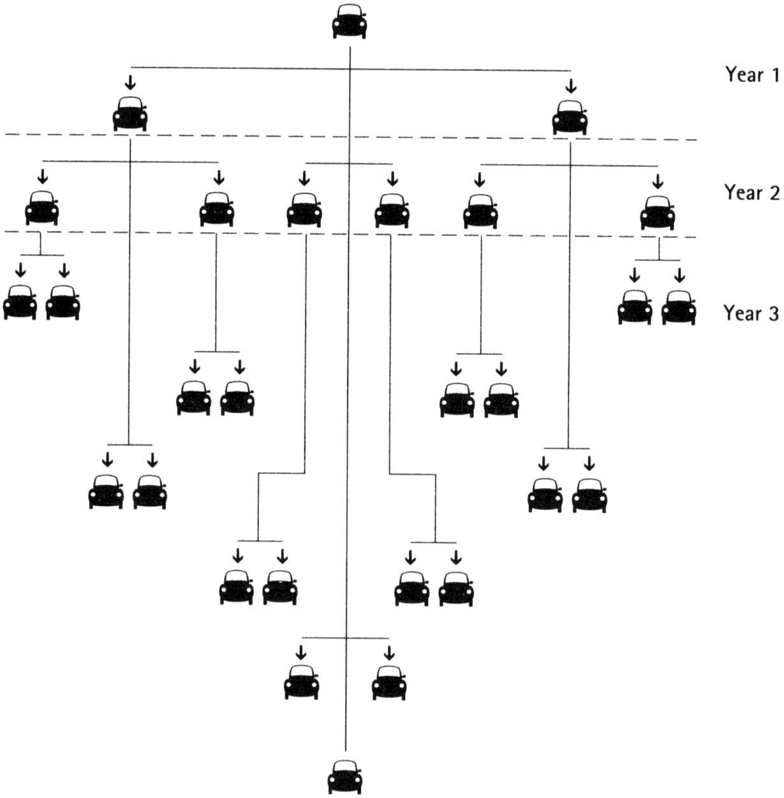

Rewarding Owners for Successful Referrals

There are two types of customers that will give you referral business, for two totally different reasons:

- Customers who do it for reward
- Customers who do it because they appreciate the way you looked after them

Some companies offer all their customers a cheque book system. *"Give us a successful referral and we will give you fifty quid."* This type of system has its place and can be successful, but it will only motivate a certain kind of customer. Other customers who give you referrals could be offended by offers of financial compensation for what they consider to be a 'Thank you for looking after me'. If you offend this type of customer, then you can kiss goodbye to future referrals.

Salespeople who have natural or developed sensory acuity skills will know when to offer financial incentives and when not to. Much safer is the personal gift, but it's got to be something special. For less than fifty pounds today, you can buy a magnum of champagne. Put yourself in the shoes of a customer who has recently given a successful referral to a salesperson that you did business with. One evening, there is a knock at the door and it's your salesperson friend. Clutched in his hand is a magnum of champagne. He greets you and says with a smile: *"Thank you for your referral to Mr Hargreaves, Mr Jones. He took delivery of his vehicle yesterday and this is a personal thank you from me to you for recommending me."*

Now the chances of you being offended by this are fairly slim. As you turn to your wife, it's most unlikely you would say: *"Get a couple of pint pots, Elsie, we've got a magnum to get through."* What you, as a customer, would probably do is put it away and save it for that special occasion. So later, after that family christening or before that meal with friends, out will come that magnum and your best glasses; guess what you will be talking about when you drink that champagne?

It does pay to think about what to give before you give it. The best way to do this is to imagine that you are the customer, and if you were, how would you react. It is amazing how many people would just prefer a 'thank you' and a smile. They are the best customers of all.

The main points again

1 Most customers would be pleased to hear from the person who sold them their vehicle after the sale, although most customers never do.

2 The reason why salespeople should follow up customers is that they will sell more vehicles.

3 The fact that most salespeople don't follow up customers is a very good reason why we should.

4 Salespeople should work as hard to keep customers as they did to get them in the first place.

5 Following up is the best way to nip problems in the bud before they bloom into something totally out of proportion.

6 Salespeople who make negative statements like 'I don't like pestering customers' have got to change or face the consequence of losing customers.

7 Follow-up systems do not work, you have to work them.

8 Computer systems have to be carefully controlled to avoid salespeople becoming frustrated paper shufflers.

9 All sales department staff, including management, should sit down and sensibly work out what is a reasonable level of follow-up. Work out the plan and then work the plan.

10 Having delivered a vehicle to a customer, the very first thing a salesperson should do is to write and thank that customer for taking delivery.

11 Whenever possible and practical, salespeople should make a habit of visiting each new owner personally within a month of delivery.

12 If the customer is satisfied, then this is the best time to ask for referrals.

13 Salespeople should then keep in touch using a combination of telephone, face-to-face and written contacts.

14 Salespeople should always let customers know the outcome of any contact with a referral, whether successful or not.

15 Not all customers want or would appreciate money in exchange for referrals. With some customers a personal gift would be much more acceptable.

16 Many people just prefer a 'thank you' and a smile. They are the best customers of all.

CHAPTER 22
From Acceptable to Extraordinary Service

"If you want more than your share,

give your customers more than theirs"

A friend of a friend owns and runs a fairly large franchised garage on the outskirts of a fairly large town. His business does well. It's well established in an easily accessible location. In addition to this, my friend's friend has built up the most incredible reputation for looking after his customers really well. This has been accomplished by his championing of the customer care cause.

A few years ago, just before Christmas, my friend's friend purchased a china ornament from a large shop that specialised in that type of goods. It was for his wife as an extra Christmas present. He was pleased to see that the ornament came complete with its own, purpose-made protective box. It was gift wrapped and put away safely for Christmas Day.

On Christmas morning, when the present was opened, the china ornament fell into two halves as it was removed from its protective box. Shortly after Christmas, my friend's friend went back to the shop to see if anything could be done about it. He explained to the manager: "*I can't really understand it. I never took the china ornament from its box. Could it have been broken before I bought it?*"

The manager expressed doubt, as each item was inspected upon arrival, prior to storage or display but, nevertheless, the manager offered to talk to the owner of the store to see if anything could be done. My friend's friend said thank you and added that if it could be replaced with a new, unbroken one he would be grateful. If, however, this was not possible, he would be prepared to pay 'cost price' for a replacement, as the broken one was no use to him or his wife. A few days later, he received the following letter from the store owner.

> Dear Mr
>
> The manager of my shop has returned to me a broken china ornament *which you claim was sold to you in that condition.* By making such an allegation, you insult my company and my staff, but above all, you do yourself no credit. Having examined the breakage, it is clear it has been dropped when *outside the protective box.*
>
> Please advise if you require the broken item within fourteen days; otherwise it will be disposed of.
>
> Yours sincerely

My friend's friend immediately sent the following reply:

> Dear Mr
>
> I note from your letter that you are the managing director of your company.
>
> I do not have to insult your company - your letter does this sufficiently. From your letter it appears that your manager did not give you all the facts; perhaps you are not interested or perhaps you cannot afford to put resources into customer care.
>
> I must have an apology for your letter. I have spent over £500 in your shop over the last three years. The product has always been satisfactory in the past.
>
> The only excuse that could be given for such a rude letter is that you have a communication problem with your manager.
>
> Yours sincerely

The next day my friend's friend got another letter:

Dear Mr

I have received your letter of 15 January and I notice you are a director of a motor company. I fully sympathise with you in the present climate and can only think that it is because of this that you have had cause to lower your sights with regard to the subject in hand. If I were to buy a car from your company, drive around the corner, crash the vehicle and then bring it back, albeit two weeks later, and say that it was sold in that condition, I feel I would be making an absolute fool of myself. I rest my case.

I have spoken with my very capable manager. I gather that had you not been so verbosely self-opinionated and allowed her more time to explain, you would not be wasting my time and your own and directing your energies towards selling cars, which I am sure would be more beneficial.

I have no intention of wasting my time further on this subject and further letters will be filed appropriately without reply.

Yours sincerely

So my friend's friend sent a final reply, to be filed appropriately without reply:

> Dear Mr
>
> When I left your shop, your manager and I were polite to one another and she stated that she would 'see what she could do'. Since that day nobody from your company has asked about the facts of the case or even spoken to me, especially yourself.
>
> The product, as you state, had obviously been damaged outside the protective box. I never took it from this box and yet when opened on Christmas Day, it was broken. I did offer to pay the cost of replacement.
>
> I find your tirade of abuse damning to you and your company.
>
> Please return the box and the broken item. I will no longer correspond with you.
>
> Yours sincerely

Let us Consider Good Service

Good service is nothing to do with being servile: it is everything to do with helping customers enjoy the buying experience before, during and after the sale. For the sake of simplicity, let us stick to four levels:

Unacceptable service
Acceptable service
Exceptional service
Extraordinary service

Examples of Levels

Unacceptable service is when you take your vehicle in for service and the vehicle is not ready on time and there is more to pay than you had been told you would have to.

Acceptable service is when the vehicle is ready on time and the bill is what you thought it would be.

Exceptional service is when you are contacted by the service department to inform you that one of your rear tyres is getting close to illegal and asked if you would like them to replace it at a reasonable cost. The vehicle is ready on time and the bill is what you expected. Exceptional service is becoming more normal in today's world of customer care awareness.

Extraordinary service is exactly the same as exceptional service, plus the vehicle has been washed and hoovered out and you cannot see any charge for the clean-up on the bill. There are no stains or finger marks. Everything has been done right first time with parts from stock.

Now it gets Complicated

Unacceptable service can be made **acceptable**, **exceptional** or even **extraordinary**.

Extraordinary or **exceptional services** can be made **acceptable** or even **unacceptable**.

This is going to be easier to see with a few real life examples.

From Unacceptable to Acceptable

There is a five star hotel in a central position that I had heard much about. "*The service is impeccable,*" I was told by more than one person. You can imagine my delight when I was invited to help run a week-long Dealer Principal workshop at the hotel for a leading European manufacturer. Driving up the long drive, I approached a magnificent mansion that had been renovated to the highest standard. I parked my car and registered by filling in a fairly lengthy form. After I had settled in, I went to the bar area to meet my fellow workshop leader and the Dealer Principal delegates.

Being the first to arrive, I sat in the magnificent surroundings, enjoyed a cold drink and perused the set menu for tonight's private dinner that had been pre-booked by the manufacturer for the 12 people attending. There was a problem. The main course was medallions of beef in Madeira sauce, and I did not want to eat beef. I called the person back who had given me the menu when he had taken my drink order and established which party I was with. I explained that I did not want to eat beef and what were the alternatives? The person explained that there were no alternatives since the menu had been confirmed two weeks previously between the hotel and the manufacturer.

I explained carefully that I had no intention of eating beef, and suggested that there must surely be an alternative in a hotel of this size and quality. The person reconfirmed, with the utmost politeness and finesse, that there were no alternatives. I asked the person if he could recommend a good local restaurant as I proposed to eat out that night. The person started to show a little more interest and offered to go and have a word with the chef. He soon returned and stated that I could have some fish. I expressed my gratitude and confirmed that I would eat with the rest of the group. By this time the group had started to assemble and, luckily, all the others were happy with the beef.

We were getting to know one another when a receptionist discreetly approached one of our party and asked him to confirm his vehicle registration number. When he did so he was asked to return to the reception area. He appeared 15 minutes later to explain that the general manager had taken exception to him parking a van in the car park and wanted it removed to the rear of the building, out of sight. We were having a laugh about this when a waiter came to take us to our private dining room which was just off the main restaurant. *"I will have to take you round to your room outside,"* he told us. *"As several members of your party are casually dressed, they will not be able to walk through the restaurant."* He then added: *"Still, it's not raining very hard."*

It was at this point I decided that I was not going to enjoy this hotel.

...And I didn't.

There is another five star hotel that I had heard much about, that was Gleneagles in Scotland. Having recently been the victim of five-star misservice, I approached the hotel with more than a little caution. I pulled up to the main door to ask were I should park, and was approached by this bewhiskered bloke in a skirt. *"Would you be staying with us?"* he asked. When I confirmed that this was the case, he asked me for my name and requested that I open the boot and identify what luggage I would like taken to my room. This I readily did, and once off-loaded followed his directions to park the car. I went up to the reception desk and gave my name. The girl handed me a card that was already completed with all my details and asked me to sign it. I enquired what had happened to my luggage. *"Oh that will be in your room,"* the receptionist told me with a cheerful smile.

It was at this point I decided that I was going to enjoy staying at this hotel.

...And I did.

Unacceptable to Exceptional

A few years ago, I too had cause to write to the managing director, not of a shop but of a very large chain of off-licences. The correspondence is self explanatory, but for people who like to 'chunk down', *See Jiu NgauYuk* is simply quick-fried sliced beef in chilli and black bean sauce.

Dear

I cannot believe the treatment I received in your off-licence on Saturday night in Bath (copy of Access receipt enclosed for your reference).

Both the image that your shop presents and the range of products were absolutely first class. As it was my first visit, I took my time to look around. My main concern was to procure a bottle of decent Chianti to go with a Chinese take-away; you can imagine my delight when I spotted a bottle by Antinori, the perfect wine to complement *See jiu ngau yuk*. As the price was reasonable, £5.79, I went to purchase a bottle. Then I spotted a bottle of Harvey's light sherry, a particular favourite of my wife, so I picked that up as well and put both bottles in front of the lady assistant and proffered my Access card for payment.

As I perused the point of sale material regarding private and company account facilities and pondered over the possibility of opening a company account, which we do not currently have, my eye caught a display of Diamond White cider, and I added four bottles to the growing pile. As an afterthought, a packet of plain crisps and one of nuts rounded off my purchases.

The amount was added up and the bill made out for me to sign, which I did. The assistant handed me my receipt and turned away. I called her back and asked if she could provide me with a bag or something to put my purchases in.

"Bags are 5p," she said and stood there looking bored but expectant.

"I have no change on me at all," I said, "that's why I paid by Access card." On hearing this she shrugged her shoulders and walked back to the man sitting in the rear office.

I did manage to pick up the six bottles and two packets. I even managed to open the door of the shop. It was only when I tried to unlock the boot of the car that I dropped the sherry. I unlocked the boot, put the remaining five bottles and two packets in with the Chinese, cleared up the broken glass and drove away.

I am sure that the Antinori really was superb, I am also sure that the *See jiu ngau yuk* was wonderful, but not for me - not on Saturday. I had somehow gone off eating; in fact I seemed to have quite a nasty taste in my mouth.

Yours sincerely

David Upsher

A few days later I received the following reply:

Mr D Upsher
Director
Mitac Ltd
Station House
Old Station Yard
Bath Road
Box
Wiltshire
SN13 8AE

Dear Mr Upsher

Many thanks for taking the trouble to write to us concerning your recent experience in our Bath branch.

I can only apologise for this experience and state that it is clearly not the standard of customer care we would wish to offer. You can be assured that the incident will be thoroughly investigated at branch level and standards improved rapidly.

However, in the meantime, as some recompense for your loss, I attach a Reserve voucher which is redeemable in any of our branches.

Yours sincerely

Managing Director

Enc £10 Reserve Voucher

From Acceptable to Extraordinary

Nicki Bajel was in the oil brokerage business. His job took him to New York to work most of the time. On a rare visit to England, Nicki offered to take myself and Steven (the estate agent) to dinner one evening. This was an offer you couldn't, and wouldn't want to, refuse. Dinner with Bajel would be an unforgettable experience.

When he had first gone to New York, Nicki had mapped out for me his average working day: he got to his office at 4am, worked through to 9pm, then most nights entertained before going to bed.

"*How long can you keep up such a punishing schedule?*" I asked him.

"*Oh, about three years,*" said Nicki.

"*What will you do then?*" I asked him.

"*Do?*" he said incredulously. "*Do?*" he repeated. "*Why,*" he went on, "*I will retire, of course.*"

So half way through his retirement programme Nicki, Steven and I found ourselves in Wheelers Mayfair Fish Restaurant behind the Park Lane Hilton. Large menus were brought for our perusal and we settled down in the bar area to select our fancy . Nicki looked perturbed and called the head waiter over. "*Is there something I can do for you, sir*" he asked anxiously.

"*Do you have any caviar?*" Nicki asked politely.

"*No sir, I am afraid we don't this evening,*" said the head waiter most apologetically. Nicki looked up. "*Scots in Mount Street have, so why not you?*" he said calmly. The head waiter looked crestfallen for all of three seconds. The lights in his eyes came on again and he positively beamed. "*Oh thank you, sir, for telling me, I will send a runner for some immediately.*"

...And he did!

◆ ◆ ◆

It has often been said (entirely inappropriately!) that a salesperson is only as good as their last deal. The truth is, and always will be, that salespeople are as good as the level of service they give.

Unacceptable salespeople give unacceptable service
Acceptable salespeople give acceptable service
Exceptional salespeople give exceptional service
Extraordinary salespeople give extraordinary service

The level of service that you give is largely a result of your attitude – to your job, your customers, the people you work with and yourself.

Customer Expectations Regarding Service

- Who thinks the builder will finish the entire job early?
- Who thinks the painter and decorator will charge less than his estimate?
- Who jumps up and down with joy the day their vehicle is going in for a full service?
- Who imagines they'll get a cheap drink at the bar in a hotel?
- Who expects to get instant service at the post office counter?
- Who thinks they'll be able to park outside the bank at lunchtime?
- Who expects to find an expert in a high street electrical store?
- Who imagines there will be no queue at the supermarket check-out by the time they get there?

These are all examples of inadequate or indifferent service to which we have become accustomed. They are also the barriers which, once removed, overcome all manner of cost objections and have people buying in large numbers.

- The builder who does a good job AND finishes the job early
- The painter and decorator who does a good job AND keeps to his estimate
- The vehicle garage that does a good job AND makes it a pleasurable experience

...And so on.

All get more than their fair share of business, more than their fair share of recommendations, more than their fair share of repeat business, of profit, of security, of opportunity, of fringe benefits and of loyal staff. Caring for your customers presupposes a purpose for doing so; some reason to behave in a particular way which differs from the norm and it **does** differ from the norm.

Incidents of mediocre or indifferent service are far more commonplace than those of particularly good service. Because of this, customers tend to become indifferent to service givers, expecting average-to-poor service, being made to wait, being let down, promises not kept, jobs not finished on time, the finished job being costlier than the estimate, delivery men and service engineers turning up late for appointments and the vehicle to have more faults **after** the full service than before. Despite these low expectations, people are still disappointed.

From the plethora of customer research available, it becomes very obvious that, given a choice, people will avoid indifferent service and buy from places where they are dealt with:

- Promptly, politely and efficiently
- By human beings to whom they can relate
- With a smile and a 'How do you do?'
- By someone who knows their job
- Who is willing to spend the time to help advise
- By someone who does not pressurise

... and they will pay more for the privilege.

Complaints Can be Good for Business

In a strange way, complaints are good for business.

Consider these facts:

Acceptable Service – No Complaints Scenario

- The customer is satisfied
- He continues to use you unless he is offered what appears to be:
  Better service
  A lower price
  Some other incentive
- He occasionally mentions to his acquaintances that you are good to do business with

This is the kind of business most companies spend their effort trying to achieve and maintain.

Unacceptable Service – No Complaints Scenario

- The customer is dissatisfied
- He decides not to complain
- He takes his business elsewhere
- He tells up to 13 people how bad you are
- End of the line for you

This is obviously bad news – you have lost a customer.

Unacceptable Service – Badly Handled Complaint Scenario

- The customer is dissatisfied
- He decides to complain
- He is treated badly
- He is even more dissatisfied
- He takes his business elsewhere
- He tells at least 13 other people how bad you are
- End of the line for you, but at least you know where you went wrong

Not good news, but better than when he didn't complain, because now you can try to prevent it recurring.

Properly Handled Complaint Scenario

- The customer is dissatisfied
- He decides to complain
- The problem is rectified properly
- The customer is now satisfied
- An additional bond of trust is formed, whereby the customer knows that you are prepared to 'help' as well as 'sell'
- Repeat business occurs until you do something wrong
- It can be proved that he will frequently recommend you to other people.

It's a shame the customer needed to complain in the first place, but, strangely, this customer has proved to be more loyal than the one who never had to complain and have a problem solved. So while you want to avoid problems, more importantly, you need to strive to solve problems promptly, professionally and to the total satisfaction of the customer.

Here is a breakdown of the relevant selling steps giving standards of services for each level.

Customer Expectations	
Unacceptable	Customer expectations not met in any way
Acceptable	Customer expectations met in most ways
Exceptional	Customer expectations met in every way
Extraordinary	Customer expectations met in every way and exceeded

Telephone Enquiries	
Unacceptable	Nobody available to take customer's enquiry
Acceptable	Nobody available but name and telephone number taken and call-back promised shortly
Exceptional	The enquiry is dealt with by competent person and the customer is invited to call in to have a demonstration and for the part-exchange to be priced
Extraordinary	The enquiry is dealt with by a competent person who offers to call to the customer's home to demonstrate the vehicle and appraise the part-exchange

Face-To-Face Enquiries	
Unacceptable	Nobody approaches the customer
Acceptable	The customer is allowed to browse and is approached within three minutes by a salesperson who greets the customer with *'Can I help you?'* or *'How can I help you?'*
Exceptional	The customer is allowed to browse and is approached within three minutes by a salesperson who smiles and says: *'Thank you for calling. How can I help you buy a vehicle today?'*
Extraordinary	The customer is allowed to browse and is approached within three minutes by a salesperson who matches the customer's pace and mood exactly and says the exact right words to make the customer feel safe and comfortable in a strange environment

Qualification	
Unacceptable	The customer is not qualified
Acceptable	The salesperson has a conversation with the customer standing up in the showroom or outside on the used vehicle area
Exceptional	The salesperson invites the customer to sit down away from the product, then proceeds to ask qualifying questions – open-ended questions to gather information; closed-ended questions to clarify understanding
Extraordinary	The salesperson invites the customer to sit down away from the product, then proceeds to ask qualifying questions – open-ended questions to gather information, closed-ended questions to clarify understanding. The salesperson is in rapport with the customer and uses the same 'filters' to process information as the customer

Presentation	
Unacceptable	The customer does not receive a presentation or is pointed in the direction of the vehicle of interest
Acceptable	The customer is shown the vehicle, possibly through the use of a six-step walk-around and/or the salesperson being available to answer questions
Exceptional	The customer is shown the vehicle in a personalised way and the features and benefits that are of particular interest to the customer are emphasised
Extraordinary	The customer is shown the vehicle in a personalised way, the features and benefits that are of particular interest to the customer are emphasised in the same language that the customer uses to process information – visual, auditory or kinesthetic

Demonstration	
Unacceptable	The customer is not offered a chance to try the vehicle in action
Acceptable	The customer is offered a demonstration 'there and then' on a standard route, or very soon, if a suitable vehicle is not available
Exceptional	The customer is given a demonstration in a suitable vehicle on a tailor-made route or is given a 'quality of the product demonstration' plus the opportunity to try the right vehicle in the near future
Extraordinary	The customer is given a demonstration in the right vehicle there and then on a tailor-made route by a salesperson who uses words that the customer easily understands because the words used match the customer's thought processing patterns

The Part-Exchange Appraisal	
Unacceptable	At some point the salesperson leaves the customer to go and look at the part-exchange. The vehicle is seldom driven and an appraisal form is not completed
Acceptable	After presenting and demonstrating the vehicle that the customer is interested in, the salesperson leaves the customer in the showroom and appraises the part-exchange, including driving the vehicle and completing an appraisal form
Exceptional	After qualification, the part-exchange is appraised in the customer's presence, the vehicle is driven and an appraisal form fully completed
Extraordinary	Directly after qualification, the salesperson takes the customer with him; the vehicle is driven by the salesperson, who continues to qualify the customer even more fully, to get to know the customer and to build rapport. The appraisal form is completed fully and handed on to a third party who will value the vehicle

The Part-Exchange Valuation And Negotiation	
Unacceptable	The salesperson asks the customer how much he expects to get for the part-exchange. The salesperson then looks up the value in a trade guide and gives the customer a price based on book value plus any over-allowance available from the new vehicle profit margin.
Acceptable	The salesperson does not ask the customer how much he expects to get for the part-exchange. The salesperson may or may not use a third party to establish what the vehicle is worth ('true value'). A part-exchange price is then given – often as a cost to change or as a monthly payment.
Exceptional	The salesperson does not ask how much is expected for the part-exchange and always uses a third party to take responsibility for the valuation. The customer is told the 'true value' and asked how much more than that figure he would be prepared to do business at.
Extraordinary	The salesperson does not ask how much is expected for the part-exchange and a third party is always used. The customer is told the 'true value' while sitting down with the salesperson over a cup of coffee. If the customer says: *'I want more than that'*, the salesperson: A) Negotiates – if there is room to do so B) Justifies the value by re-establishing all the other reasons for buying this vehicle from this company and from this salesperson. At all times the extraordinary salesperson uses rapport and sensory acuity to talk the customer's language in a way that the customer feels comfortable with.

Objection Handling And Prevention

Unacceptable	The salesperson does not handle objections that are raised by the customer: he ignores them. If, however, the customer does not have any objections, the salesperson always helps out by raising a few of his own: *"These are very hard to get hold of."* *"We could take your part-exchange as long as you are not expecting to get too much for it."*
Acceptable	The salesperson answers the customer's objections as they come up and makes it easy for the customer to buy by not putting obstacles in the customer's way
Exceptional	The salesperson has learnt the ability to turn objections into questions and then answer the question and not the objection.
Extraordinary	The salesperson has identified the common objections and prevents them coming up at all by presenting them as benefits during the presentation and demonstration steps of the sale; uncommon objections are turned into questions and then the questions are answered

Securing The Business

Unacceptable	The salesperson closes early and often, and will sometimes sulk or express his feelings about the customer not buying in some other visual or verbal way. Another unacceptable way to secure the business is to leave it totally to the customer to ask if he can have one. Yet another alternative is to 'hound' the customer 'till he buys or dies', both during and after the showroom visit
Acceptable	Having completed all the selling steps, the salesperson will ask the customer for the order, if they think the customer will say 'yes'
Exceptional	The salesperson will expect the customer to buy and carry out all the selling steps with this in mind; at the 'would you like it?' stage, the salesperson expects the customer to say 'yes'
Extraordinary	The salesperson will do everything the exceptional salesperson does; however, the extraordinary salesperson will have a profound knowledge of what the customer wants and how those wants can be satisfied fully; the salesperson will then help the customer get what he wants with total interest, empathy and rapport

Enhancing The Profit	
Unacceptable	The salesperson will be very good at giving away his company's money. If this type of salesperson was as good at selling profitable deals to customers as he was at selling unprofitable deals to his manager, he would do very well indeed
Acceptable	The salesperson is aware that it is important to sell at a reasonable profit margin and will not give anything away without it being necessary or acceptable to his company
Exceptional	The salesperson will strive to keep the deal profitable by not giving anything away and by offering other items and services to enhance the profitability of the deal
Extraordinary	The extraordinary salesperson will, from the very start, set out their stall to show all their company's goods; they have the ability to raise desire to buy to such a degree that the customer will not only be prepared to pay the price but will also want to purchase other products and services to go with the vehicle

Yes, You've Guessed It

The big difference that makes the big difference to giving good services is 'RAPPORT'.

The main points again

1 Good service is everything to do with helping customers enjoy the buying experience before, during and after the sale.

2 Four levels of service are identified:

- Unacceptable
- Acceptable
- Exceptional
- Extraordinary

3 Levels of service can be changed from:

- Unacceptable to Acceptable
- Unacceptable to Exceptional
- Acceptable to Extraordinary

Or any other combination.

4 A salesperson is as good as the level of service they give.

5 The big difference that makes the big difference to giving good service is RAPPORT.

SECTION NINE

Walking Beyond Your Limits

"Always look and act with confidence"

CHAPTER 23
Introduction

"Who you are used to being

is not necessarily who you are"

My brother Keith is the sailor in the family. He used to crew on an ocean racer called *Whirlwind.* That was limit-stretching in itself, particularly when you are on deck in a force eight in the Fastnet. At calmer times, like all true sailors, the crew swapped stories.

One of Keith's regular colleagues was a naval officer who was based on a carrier. One balmy evening he told me the tale of an aircraft maintenance engineer who was carrying out safety checks inside the cockpit of a jet stored in the below-decks hanger.

He suddenly realised that he had triggered the explosive charge that caused the ejector seat to eject. His problem was that he was sitting on it! He realised that he had probably less than a few seconds to save his life, so he got off the seat fast and crouched in the nose-cone of the cockpit.

The seat went off and up, crashing itself into several pieces on the hanger roof above. The engineer was basically okay – a little deaf for a while, and more than a little burnt down one side of his body and the arm that he had used to protect his face from the blast. When he got out of hospital and returned to duty, he was a little mystified to find a substantial amount of money, in an envelope, in the middle of the mess table with his name on it.

At first he thought that his fellow workmates had had a 'whip round' to treat him to a little rest and recuperation, but he was wrong. The deal, as they explained, was that if he could get back into the nose cone of the aeroplane as he did before, then they would give him the money. They had all tried and found that it just wasn't possible to do what the engineer had managed to do when the seat was about to make a rapid exit.

The engineer said: *"The money is mine! Come on, I will show you how I did it."*

...But he couldn't.

During the mid 1980s, a warm sunny summer day found me driving from the West Country to the Lake District to lead a sales conference. The radio was on, but more as background noise, as my mind was on the conference content. I had just two days to put the 'How to Sell' message across to the delegates. Everything from finding to keeping customers.

After six years involvement in developing and leading such programmes, I had come to a startling, if not frightening, conclusion: a two-day isolated sales training course does not work. This was startling because so much time, energy and money has been put into training courses. This was frightening because I was one of the people responsible for making such programmes work, and also, I made my living from doing so.

I knew that this kind of sales training did not work because it was fairly easy to check for changes in sales effectiveness – by measuring individual volume and profit levels. It is also comparatively simple to check for changes in sales effort by individuals through 'test shopping' activities as well as direct observation. Sure, training did work some of the time with some of the trainees. But most of the time, for most participants, it was very hard to spot the pre-course and post-course difference after about 90 days. I decided to find out why this was so.

There appeared to be three things that stopped this kind of training being as effective as it should have been:

- Time
- Other People
- Intentions

- **Time**
  Salespeople can leave a sales training course with all the best intentions in the world. Then they get back to the reality of the world they earn their living in. Time changes intentions as it erodes good ideas, so that the old less-effective ways of doing things can creep back in again.

- **Other People**
  There are salespeople about who do not believe in training. New sales recruits can get bombarded with 'I tried that once and it does not work' or 'This is the way we do it round here'. It's hard to stay positive when you are constantly hit with negatives.

- **Intentions**

  If people really believe they can't do something, they're going to find an unconscious way to make sure that their belief is true. What this means is that you can have all the best intentions in the world to benefit from training by completing an action plan and then putting your plan into action. Somebody can then stop you, and that somebody can be you.

I had those three pieces, but there seemed to be a bit missing and I could not put my finger on it. Time, other people and intentions, plus what? While I was mentally searching for the answer, I started consciously listening to the radio. It was an interview. The interviewer was talking to a person that I had never heard of. A man by the name of Franz Klammer. I didn't know who he was, but I soon got the gist of it and as it sounded quite an interesting conversation, I started to give it my full attention. Franz Klammer, apparently, was an incredibly fast downhill skier. The interviewer was trying to find out what his secret was. "*After all,*" she said, "*you are a very untidy skier and some of your techniques are rather unorthodox.*" Franz Klammer did not appear to be offended by these remarks. If anything, he was agreeing with them, but he went on to say something rather profound. He told the interviewer: "*The reason why I can win is very simple: I like to walk beyond my limits.*"

I was no more familiar with this phrase than I was with Franz Klammer. But I instinctively knew exactly what he meant. More important than this understanding was the realisation that Franz Klammer had just given me the missing piece of the 'Why sales training does not work' puzzle. So now I had four pieces:

- Time erosion
- Other people's negativity
- Unconsciously scuppering your own intentions
- Inability to 'walk beyond your limits'

Limits Identified

Rather than me write about what these limits are and you just sit there and read about them, let's do something different:

- Let's identify what your own limits are
- Take a look at each limit identified to see how they can effect sales and personal performance

- Discover how you can change you own 'limits' to raise your own level of effort and effectiveness
- At the same time identify how to eliminate time erosion, other people's negativity and the unconscious scuppering of your own intentions to boot

Identification of Your Own Limits

The following quiz will do this for you. There are no right or wrong answers, but it is important that you should answer every question according to the instructions.

Do not be concerned if you find some of the questions a little 'odd': just try to identify with the person in each question and answer as though you are that person.

Quiz – Walking Beyond Your Limits

Identification of Your Own Limits

Please answer the following 30 questions as honestly as you can by allocating a total of five points for each, using any of the following combinations:

Score

A	B	
5	0	If A is completely characteristic of what you would do and B is completely uncharacteristic.
4	1	If A is almost completely characteristic, but you might on occasion favour B.
3	2	If A is only slightly more characteristic than B.
2	3	If B is only slightly more characteristic than A.
1	4	If B is almost completely characteristic, but you might on occasion favour A.
0	5	If B is completely characteristic of what you would do and A is completely uncharacteristic.

Walking Beyond Your Limits

1 You don't have to go to work today and you are still in bed as it is still early. You open one eye and note that it is raining.

Would you:

A Immediately cancel from your mind the outdoor activity that you had decided on before you went to bed and go back to sleep?

B Leap out of bed with the determined thought that you will think of something else to do instead?

A	B

2 You see a little old lady sitting on a wall and she looks as though she's crying. She doesn't look hurt or ill in any way, just distressed for some unknown reason.

Would you:

A Not interfere as it is no business of yours.

B Approach the old lady directly and ask her what the problem is and if you can be of assistance to her.

A	B

3 You go to the fridge at a fat friend's house to get some food, and notice that inside the fridge door there is a picture of a very slim lady. Your friend explains that it is her way of trying to eat less.

Would you:

A Tell your friend that looking at pictures will not help as it is a matter of positive willpower if she really wants to slim.

B Admire your friend's novel approach to slimming and wish her every success.

A	B

4 You have set out to accomplish a task in a particular way. Having half completed what you have set out to do, you realise that you are going the wrong way about it. You still have some time to switch to a different method.

Would you:

A Stick to the original plan and complete the task that you have set yourself.

B Immediately change what you are doing to the way that you now think is best.

A	B

5 You have a violent disagreement with a colleague at work over a matter that could affect your working relationship.

Would you:

A Stick to your own point of view and continue to try to get your colleague to see your way?

B Pretend that you have changed your mind, even though you know that you are right?

A	B

6 You have gone to a good friend's wedding. Unfortunately, the best man is taken ill before the reception and your friend asks you to read out the telegrams and make a short speech.

Would you:

A Turn down your friend as you are totally unprepared and you would not like to make a fool of yourself?

B Tell your friend that of course you will do what he asks to the best of your ability?

A	B

7 You and your partner are driving to have lunch with some friends who live 60 miles away. You have driven six miles when your partner informs you that there is a strong possibility that the gas was left on and there is no-one else there to turn it off.

Would you:

A Do everything possible to reassure your partner that there is nothing to worry about and keep driving?

B Turn around and go back and check in spite of being fairly short of time?

A	B

◆ ◆ ◆

8 You go to buy a newspaper from a street vendor who tells you off in no uncertain terms for not having the right change.

Would you:

A Tell him that he should be grateful to you for your custom and make a point of checking to see if he has given you the right change before leaving?

B Apologise and promise to try and bring the right amount of money with you in future?

A	B

9 You are a small, green, ugly but happy, caterpillar and you do not know that you are destined to become a beautiful butterfly. One day you rescue a fairy from a spider's web. She grants you one free wish.

Would you:

A Tell the fairy that she has got it all wrong: as in all best stories, you should be offered at least three wishes?

B Ask her to grant you the wish that you could stay as you are forever?

A	B

10 A good friend approaches you for advice. He has a difficult choice to make and does not know what to do.

Would you:

A Tell him that the most important thing to do is to make a choice, even if it is the wrong one?

B Tell him that if he cannot decide what to do, he should do nothing until he does decide?

A	B

11 You live four miles from the office and it is a nice evening, so you decide to walk home for a change. Half way home there is a steep hill and you are half way up that hill when your next door neighbour stops and offers you a lift home.

Would you:

A Accept the offer of the lift gratefully, particularly as you are feeling a little out of breath?

B Thank him kindly, but decline the offer, telling him that you must stick to your original decision to walk home, in spite of feeling a little bit puffed on the hill?

A	B

12 You are a salesperson who identifies a local company who could be a very good customer for the goods that you sell. You find out the name of the person who is responsible for purchasing and write a short introductory letter, stating that you propose to telephone the following week to make an appointment to call. When you make the telephone call, the person tells you that you are wasting your time by calling.

Would you:

A Thank the person for thinking of you and explain that you are more than willing to invest 20 minutes of your time if the customer would be prepared to do the same?

B Apologise for the intrusion, thank the customer for being straight with you, get off the telephone and find someone more interested in talking to you?

A	B

13 It is Sunday afternoon and it is raining. You have just decided to read the Sunday papers when your five-year-old daughter comes up and asks you to take her to the local swimming baths so she can practise her swimming in the shallow pool.

Would you:

A Smile at her as you fold up the Sunday newspaper, say yes, and start to get ready to go?

B Tell her of your decision and promise to take her the following week?

A	B

14 Someone you know lets you down badly. They know this and so do you. Shortly afterwards you see the person walking down the road towards you but they have not seen you.

Would you:

A Cross to the other side of the road in an effort to avoid acknowledging or talking to that person?

B Stay on the same side of the road prepared to acknowledge the other person's presence and take it as it comes from there?

A	B

15 You are a salesman and your company gives you an annual profit target to reach to enable you to earn yourself a bonus. This target represents an increase of 10% over the previous year.

Would you:

A Think to yourself there is no point in hitting annual sales targets if as a direct result of this the target will yet again be moved upwards, which makes it very difficult to earn your target bonus?

B Think to yourself that as you 'just' manage to achieve your target every year, perhaps you should set yourself a target of an increase of 20% as opposed to 10%?

A	B

16 You are offered the opportunity to go on a flight to the moon that has a 50% chance of success.

Would you:

A Take this opportunity to be one of the first non-astronauts to land on the moon?

B Turn down the offer because of the lack of 100% guarantee of returning safely?

A	B

17 You receive a surprise invitation from the Queen to a garden party at Buckingham Palace. This unfortunately coincides with your parents' fortieth wedding anniversary, which you have just helped to arrange.

Would you:

A Write to Buckingham Palace apologising for not being able to make it and explaining why?

B Tell your parents of your predicament and ask them how they would feel about you missing this particular family occasion?

A	B

18 You have just gone deep sea fishing on a sunny day with a group of friends and note from the fishing line that you are using that the water underneath the boat must be at least 100 feet deep. Two of your companions decide to go for a swim and invite you to join them.

Would you:

A Say "*Great!*" and be the first to dive in, as the sea is calm, without a current, and you are not in shark waters?

B Stay aboard the boat, prepared to be a little hot rather than swim in such deep water?

A	B

19 You have a message to telephone someone you don't like as soon as you get in.

Would you:

A Pick up the telephone and call immediately?

B Don't return the call straight away, preferring to get yourself in the right frame of mind first?

A	B

20 You are the supervisor of an airline check-in desk and unfortunately you have the job of telling a very famous film actress that you have just let her first class reservations go because she has arrived 12 minutes past the final check-in time. She is far from pleased and has expressed her displeasure by using some very explicit language directed at you personally.

Would you:

A Tell her that you were within your rights and walk away, saying that you are not prepared to take that language from anybody?

B Take the abuse 'on the chin' and wait for the VIP to pause for breath so you can apologise again for the inconvenience that you have caused her?

A	B

21 You wake up one morning after some time off work with your working week ahead of you.

Would you:

A Look forward to the week ahead of you?

B Look forward to your next time off?

A	B

22 You are a Buddhist monk who is forbidden to have physical contact with the opposite sex. One day you approach a fast and isolated flowing river that you will be able to cross without difficulty yourself, but there is a young girl waiting to cross who would be in danger of being swept away.

Would you:

A Agree to her request to carry her across the river safely on your shoulders?

B Turn down her request on the grounds of your religion?

A	B

23 You decide to try out an idea that you have read about because it claimed that you will be better at your job by doing it that particular way and you believe this to be true.

Would you:

A Keep trying out the idea until you prove it works?

B Try out the idea once to see if it works and if it doesn't, forget it!

A	B

24 You are a vehicle sales specialist and have just completed a demonstration. You are now sitting having afternoon tea with your potential customers at their lovely home. Their pet budgerigar is flying around the room. Unfortunately, it flies past your chair just as you cross your legs and you accidentally kick it into the open log fire, where it bursts into flames. As they have not noticed,

Would you:

A Leap up from your chair immediately, and poke the poor bird well in and out of sight, remarking that it is surprisingly cold for the time of year?

B Explain what has happened and that it was a total and tragic accident, confident that after the initial shock and sadness, all will be forgiven?

A	B

25 Your partner wakes up in the middle of the night and claims to have heard a burglar downstairs and asks you to investigate.

Would you:

A Explain that you have not heard anything and there is not much worth pinching downstairs anyway?

B Go down and investigate, even though you do not believe there is any cause for concern, but knowing it will put your partner's mind as rest?

A	B

26 You are driving along a busy road minding your own business when you accidentally cut up another driver, who signifies his annoyance by facial expressions, horn sounding and hand signals that you do not recognise as being part of the highway code.

Would you:

A Resent the totally unnecessary display of bad manners and return the gesture, plus a few more of your own for good measure?

B Do nothing, or possibly just raise your hand in a non-threatening way to acknowledge your mistake?

A	B

27 You want to achieve a particular goal in life and you find that you are spending some of your free time every day imagining that you have actually achieved your goal.

Would you:

A Encourage the thoughts of success and enjoy them?

B Try to stop the daydreams happening as there is not much sense in just dreaming about success?

A	B

28 You are a wise old man sitting by a well outside your village. You are approached by a young man who comes down the road and tells you, to your surprise, that the people in the village he has just come from were very unfriendly towards him. He asks what the people are like in your village.

Would you:

A Suggest to the young man that he should continue to go down the road as he is bound to find the same people in your village as he found before?

B Suggest to the young man that he should come into your village as you are sure that he will be treated with kindness?

A	B

29 You have decided to do something – it doesn't really matter what – but even before you start to do it, you work out a full plan of operation, including contingency plans in case things go wrong.

Would you:

A Expect what you have decided to do to be harder to accomplish than you first thought?

B Expect that what you have decided to do to be easier to accomplish than you first thought?

A	B

30 You are travelling in the Far East, when you come across a group of people who are walking down a shallow pit covered in glowing coals. They appear to be doing this without injury. They then ask you to join them by taking part in the experience.

Would you:

A Take off your shoes and do it, believing that you can, since they have told you that no harm will come to you?

B Not even consider doing any such thing at all. There has to be a trick to it and you think that the group are either drugged or hypnotised in some way?

A	B

Walking Beyond Your Limits

	L		I		M		I		T		S
1B		2B		3B		4B		5A		6B	
7B		8B		9A		10B		11B		12A	
13A		14B		15B		16B		17A		18A	
19A		20B		21A		22A		23A		24B	
25B		26B		27A		28A		29A		30A	
Total											

Record the A or B answer ONLY to each of the 30 questions, as indicated above, then total each one of the vertical columns. Having done this, mark off your total score for each column on the LIMITS illustration on the next page on each 'ladder' above each category, then shade in each ladder from each score line downwards.

L Level of Energy
I Interpersonal Skills
M Motivation
I Informed Decisions
T Tenacity
S Self Confidence

◆ ◆ ◆

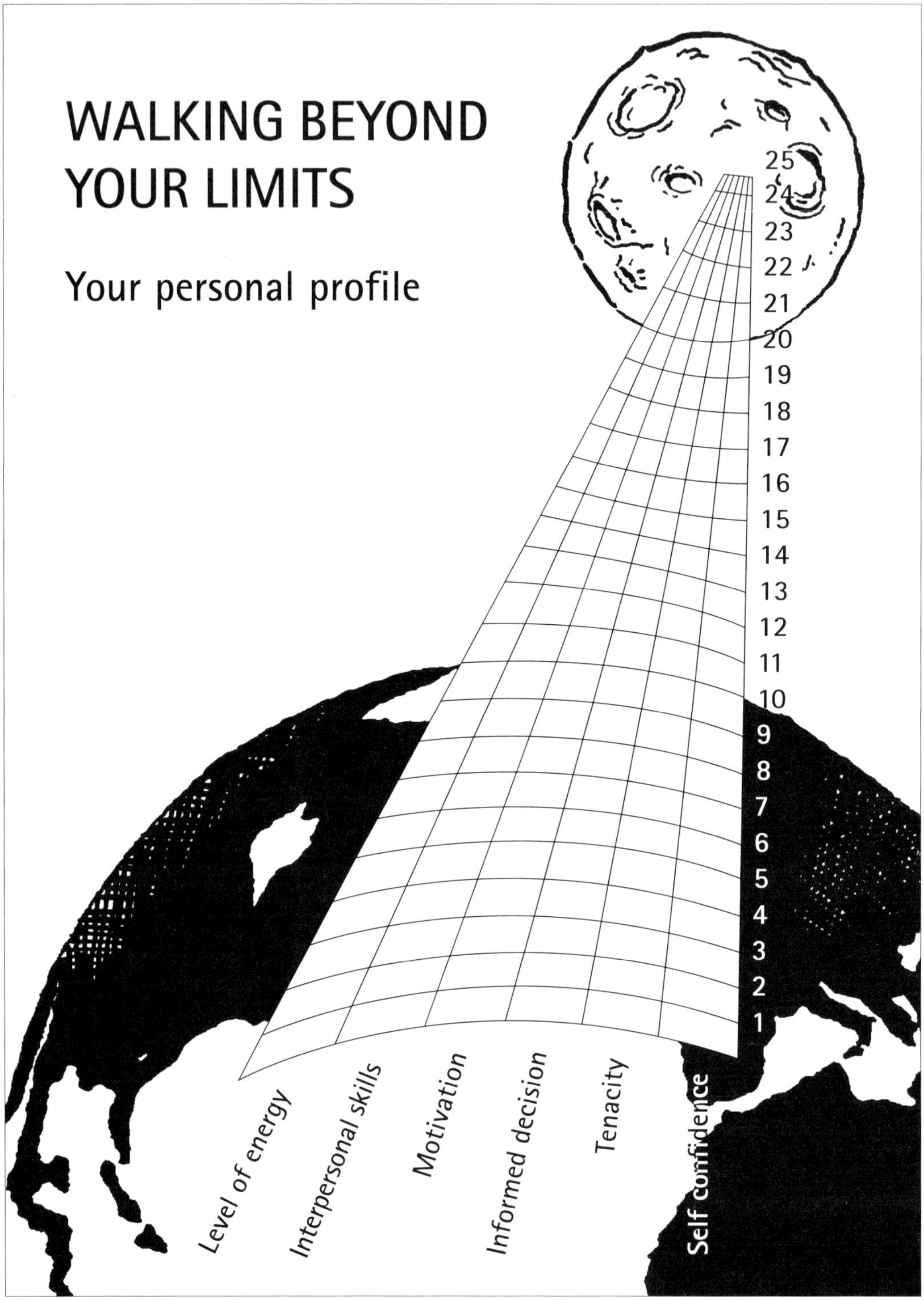
WALKING BEYOND YOUR LIMITS
Your personal profile
25
24
23
22
21
20
19
18
17
16
15
14
13
12
11
10
9
8
7
6
5
4
3
2
1
Level of energy
Interpersonal skills
Motivation
Informed decision
Tenacity
Self confidence

Your Limits

So now you know what your 'limits' are. But what does it all mean?

If you look at your 'personal profile' diagram on page 354, you will notice that there are three parts to the illustration.

- At the bottom you find the main planet
- Then there is a grid (rising to a)
- Satellite or moon.

Your 'limits' scores that finish on the main planet, between one and nine, are the limits that are preventing you from being the sales success that you want to be. Limits scores that finish in double figures between the main planet and the satellite, from ten to 19 represent the norm for most people, and can still be improved. Limits scores that finish on the satellite, between 20 and 25, indicate that you do not have a problem in that area. In fact, you have a positive sales advantage. The good news is that whatever you scored, you can change the limits if you want to.

Six Limits Identified

The six separate contributory limiting factors that have been clearly identified as having a direct influence on sales success are as follows:

- Level of Energy
- Interpersonal Skills
- Motivation
- Informed Decisions
- Tenacity
- Self Confidence

By becoming conscious of your current self-imposed 'limits', you can start to make the changes that will in turn help you achieve the future successes that you want. This can be done because the key factor is that your 'limits' really are self-imposed. You have set your own in the past. Now you can set yourself some new 'limits' for the future. Let us look at them one at a time so you can see how to make the changes if you need to and you want to.

Sales Training Changes

Needless to say, *Limits* has been used to make the changes to sales training courses to give them a better chance of doing some good. These changes include methods of delivery and moving away from teacher based training (chalk and talk) to learner based training (hands on and interactive). Linked training programmes, including distance learning, are now the norm, following a modular format, and can finish with an NVQ qualification. Sales training now works much better than it used to.

The main points again

1 Isolated two-day sales training courses are not the most effective way of training people.

2 Even if the training works, it is hard to spot the effect after 90 days.

3 There are four areas that stop this type of training being effective:

- Time erosion of good intentions by old habits
- Other people's negativity
- Unconsciously scuppering your own intentions
- Inability to 'walk beyond your limits'

4 The limits beyond which you need to walk are:

- Level of Energy
- Interpersonal Skills
- Motivation
- Informed Decisions
- Tenacity
- Self-Confidence

5 'Limits' can be changed because they are self imposed.

6 'Limits' have been changed to make today's sales training much more effective than yesterday's.

CHAPTER 24
Level of Energy

"Don't have nice days, have great days"

At the Park Lane showroom, there was a car lift so that we could store vehicles in the basement. This was controlled by something called a 'tram handle', a horizontal handle situated in the showroom, which you moved left to make the lift go down, right to make it go up and to the centre to stop it – simple enough.

One Saturday I was feeling full of low energy and I got it all wrong. There was a car on the lift at ground level that had just been delivered, to go into the showroom. As well as going down, the lift would also go up three feet, which was the difference in height between the pavement outside and our showroom floor level inside. I moved the tram handle to the right to raise the lift and the car. As I did this, I could not help noticing a most attractive girl walking gazelle-like past the open showroom doors. Her long chestnut hair cascaded down over her shoulders and moved gracefully, like long sea grass being washed by a gentle current over a coral reef on a faraway South Sea island shore.

Now, we have already talked about the brain's capacity to delete, distort and generalise. As far as that girl was concerned, my brain was deleting nothing, but what had been deleted was the fact that the folding showroom doors were open. Now you can't bring a car up above ground level with the doors open because they would get in the way of the lift.

The bang was almighty, and visions of cascading chestnut hair were replaced with the reality of cascading broken glass hitting the ground like pieces of a frozen waterfall. The devastation was total. The four folding doors and the panes of glass they framed ceased to exist. In what must have been an instant but seemed to take forever, the emergency service arrived. They secured the showroom with temporary wooden panels, and we all went home.

On Monday morning the Sales Manager asked me to be on hand as the regional director was coming to see me. I did not have to wonder what that was going to be about, and he did not keep me waiting very long. *"Now, Upsher, I understand that you are solely responsible for destroying the showroom doors on Saturday. Please explain to me exactly how you managed to do this."* So I told him: *"Sheer, utter carelessness, sir."* His jaw dropped. He had obviously been expecting a long and detailed account of what had happened, probably with some justification or mitigating circumstances. So he gave me a verbal and let me go. There was not a lot more he could do.

It could have been worse, I thought, as I walked back to my desk. Like the time a new chauffeur decided to use the lift at the Rolls Royce showroom where I worked to take a Phantom Five down to the basement. He thought it would fit.

...And it didn't.

The Causes of a Low Level of Energy

There are many reasons why some people have more energy than others. Apart from health problems such as blood pressure and vitamin deficiencies, you can choose to have as much energy as you want to.

The Lethargy Top Ten

If you want to have lethargy instead of energy then here is how to get really fatigued.

Make sure that you:

1. Are overweight
2. Eat unhealthy food at irregular intervals
3. Never take exercise
4. Worry about everything
5. Find life and people boring
6. Wake up late to a loud alarm clock
7. Skip breakfast
8. Rush to work and are still late
9. Never take holidays
10. Keep away from fresh air and natural daylight

Salespeople who stick to the lethargy top ten list have interesting days!

Of all the identifiable limiting factors, lethargy has to be the real sales killer. Lethargic people will use self-excuses to hide their lethargy from themselves and from others.

A 'Working' Day in the Life of a Chronic Lethargic:

Typical lethargic self-excuses	What you really mean
I've got nothing to do so I'll stay in bed.	*If I get up I will find something to do.*
I think I've got a bad cold coming.	*I wonder if I can get away with a few days off work.*
I'll just have toast for breakfast.	*I can't be bothered to make myself anything else.*
I'm late for work because I got held up in traffic.	*I'm late because I did not allow enough time to get to work.*
Now I'm here there is no use trying to plan what to do because of the interruptions.	*I'm just too lazy to plan my day.*
It would be better if I left that until tomorrow.	*I don't want to do that now or ever.*
I bet the boss will be late back from lunch today.	*If I get back late the boss won't notice.*
What can I do to fill up my afternoon?	*What will fill up the afternoon without me having to work too much?*
Good Lord, it is only that time?	*The lazier you get the slower time passes.*
I must go early, I have remembered something that I must do at home.	*I would prefer to be at home doing nothing to being at work doing nothing.*
I won't go out tonight if there is something good on telly.	*I won't go out tonight.*
Well, that was the end of another boring day.	*Well, that was the end of another day when I have bored myself silly through personal lethargy.*

The Ten Causes of Boundless Energy

Surprise, surprise, the causes of boundless energy are the opposite of the causes of low energy or lethargy.

Make sure that you:

1 Try and keep to a sensible weight for your height and build
2 Eat healthy food at regular intervals
3 Take some exercise
4 Worry less, be happy more and laugh every day
5 Find life and people enjoyable and interesting
6 Wake up early and, if possible, naturally
7 Never skip breakfast
8 Leave home early and get to work early
9 Always take your holidays and days off
10 Get some fresh air and natural daylight every day

When you ask the question 'How many days do you have on this planet from birth to death?' a surprising number of people just don't know. Others will often say: *'Oh, millions I suppose.'*

The truth is that you have around 30,000 days here – the same as most other people. Doesn't it seem a shame to waste even one of them?

Increasing Your Level of Energy

If you want to raise your own energy level, then the following formula will help you obtain all the energy you want.

1 Change Your Current Behaviour

- To match that of the ten causes of boundless energy.
  That means you will:

2 Change Your Personal Habits

- After around 21 days, you will be in the habit of being brighter and bouncier.
  That means you will:

3 Change the Person You Are

- You will become a different person with different characteristics than you were before.
  That means you will:

4 Change Your Destiny

- You will get a totally different and successful experience from life. Just remember that if you don't make any changes, you will end up exactly where you are headed!

The main points again

1 Things go wrong much more often when your energy is at a low ebb.

2 A lack of energy could be due to a health problem.

3 Apart from that, you can have as much energy as you want.

4 Lethargic people will use self-excuses to hide their lethargy from themselves and others.

5 The causes of boundless energy are exactly opposite the causes of low energy.

6 We have around 30,000 days on this planet, the same as most other people.

7 If you don't make any changes, you will end up exactly where you are headed.

CHAPTER 25
Interpersonal Skills

"You can make more friends in two months
by becoming interested in other people,
than you can in two years by trying to get
other people interested in you"

As soon as she walked through the door, I recognised her. She was there in my living room every time I switched on the television, singing her latest song, her face a picture of sweetness, her voice warm and rich. Today she looked different. Her face resembled the mental picture of a bulldog sucking a wasp. Something appeared to be wrong. Today her voice was different. The sweetness had been replaced with a sound similar to a lorry-load of chickens colliding with a truckload of empty milk bottles. Boy, was she angry, and all of her anger was directed at me, personally, and my parenthood!

Apparently, the radio in the car that she had recently bought from my colleague was not meeting the standards she expected. As my colleague was out, it was me that had to face the tidalwave of her emotions that threatened to swamp me and send me crashing back against the showroom wall.

Our service department had checked the radio and had had the audacity to report 'No fault found'. She blasted at me: "*What kind of twits do you employ in aftersales? Stone deaf monkeys?*" Every time I tried to say something or ask a question, I was shouted down as she continued to direct her venomous flow of abuse at me. She cared not for what I thought, or wanted to say; her only desire was to continue her hysterical outburst at me – who was, at that moment, the sole occupant of the showroom where she had purchased her car.

I gave up and decided to say nothing and just listen. That really made her mad, and she accused me of not being interested or concerned about her problem. I decided to speak and was rebuked for not letting her finish. So I just stood there trying to look concerned and interested in an effort to ride out the storm. It was a long storm! As abruptly as the storm had started, it abated. She tossed her head and stormed out of the showroom. *"That lady has a problem,"* I thought, *"and it's not her radio."*

When the salesman who had sold the lady the car returned, I explained what had happened. He talked to the electrician who had checked and tested the equipment, who reconfirmed that everything was working perfectly. My colleague then wrote a very nice letter apologising for all the trouble and inconvenience we had caused her and offered to replace the radio for a model of her choice.

Two weeks after all this happened, I was sitting with a group of friends in a popular Chinese restaurant in Soho. As soon as she walked through the door, I recognised her and she recognised me! I said: *"Hi, it's good to see you again."* as I stood up. She knew that she knew me but could not remember who I was. Her face was a picture of sweetness, her voice warm and rich as she returned my greeting and a light kiss that brushed her cheek with a generous and slightly shy smile before she and her partner were swept away by a highly excited waiter.

"Do you know her?" one of my friends asked incredulously. *"Just a passing acquaintance,"* I said nonchalantly, *"just a passing acquaintance."*

I still see her occasionally on television today. Her face is older and more sickly than sweet; her voice more gaudy than rich. *"If I press that little button,"* I think, *"she will disappear."*

...And she does!!

◆ ◆ ◆

Interpersonal Skills

Interpersonal skills are all about RAPPORT. You already have a chapter devoted to this, and much more information besides. Rapport really is one of the greatest and most useful of all the selling skills.

...So, how well do you know how it works and how to use rapport?

Let's Find Out

Here are 25 questions on the subject of rapport; all the answers are in this book. When you can answer all the questions correctly, then you will know something about rapport. When you know something about rapport, you will have all the tools you need to polish up your interpersonal skills and make them really shine out there in the selling world, like a beacon on a dark night.

Interpersonal Skills and Rapport

Please indicate your answer to the following multi-choice questions by placing A, B or C in the box provided. If you seriously want to improve your interpersonal skills, then please feel free to try and find the answers in the book.

1 Rapport is:
- **A** Pretending that you like someone when you don't?
- **B** Liking someone and pretending that you don't?
- **C** The naturally occurring 'dance' that happens when two people meet? ☐

2 Without exception, every great salesperson has the ability to:
- **A** Create a high level of sales without rapport?
- **B** Create a high level of rapport with customers?
- **C** Create a low level of complaints? ☐

3 Rapport is when you feel that you are in harmony:
- **A** In some way with someone else?
- **B** In some way with yourself?
- **C** In some other way? ☐

4 When you are in harmony with someone, you will create:

A A sense of acknowledgement and mutual respect?

B A sense of achievement and demand respect?

C A sense of humour and sometimes sadness? ☐

5 The reasons why there is rapport between people:

A Are always conscious and easy to see?

B Are sometimes conspicuous and difficult to fake?

C Are normally outside conscious awareness? ☐

6 If you get good at creating rapport with customers:

A You might be able to give up selling?

B You might get better at selling?

C You might be easier to sell to?

7 People do quite naturally often adopt the body posture:

A Of their favourite film star?

B Of the person they are talking to?

C Of someone they once knew? ☐

8 If you match someone else's body posture, they will:

A Adopt yours in turn?

B Know what you are doing?

C Not be aware of what you are doing? ☐

9 If you are matching arm movements and the person you are talking to uses their right hand, then you:

A Should use the right hand too?

B Should always use the wrong hand?

C Should use your left hand? ☐

10 If a person uses exaggerated movements, then:

A You should use exaggerated movements too?

B You should use a gentle reflection?

C You should do nothing at all? ☐

11 Start to match customer's energy levels if you want to:

A Maximise and harmonise your rapport skills?

B Minimise and synchronise sales success?

C Or don't if you don't want to? ☐

12 If you are with a customer who is a bit down in the dumps:

A Crack a joke and try and cheer him up a little?

B The first thing you should do is to break rapport before his mood affects you?

C The last thing that person wants is to have a conversation with a fireball? ☐

13 If your customer is very enthusiastic and full of the joys of spring:

A You are not going to hit it off if you had a very heavy, late night last night?

B You should be very wary: there might be something wrong with his part-exchange and you have failed to notice it?

C It is important to calm the customer down before trying to sell him anything? ☐

14 If you start matching a customer's energy level:

A Then there will come a point when you can start leading the customer?

B They will think that you are a little odd?

C You will always find that you both move and talk faster? ☐

15 If a customer says something that a salesperson does not like, then:

A It is more than likely that the customer will unconsciously know from the expression on the salesperson's face?

B It is easy for the salesperson to hide the fact from the customer through controlling facial expressions?

C It is important to break rapport and put the customer straight? ☐

16 There is not one but three different English languages in everyday use. These are:

A Southern, Northern and Western?

B Scottish, Welsh and English?

C Visual, Auditory and Kinesthetic? ☐

17 These three main ways of talking are influenced:

A By the area people live in?

B By the way people think?

C By the way people have been brought up? ☐

18 Visual preferers will say:

A I see what you mean?

B I hear these are economical?

C I feel that would be okay? ☐

19 Auditory preferers will say:

A Can I just grab a brochure?

B Give me a call on Friday?

C Let's look at it this way? ☐

20 Kinesthetic preferers will say:

A I will get in touch with you?

B That sounds like a good idea?

C What a nice bright colour? ☐

21 If you really want to see 'eye to eye' with your customers, try using more words:

A That will make them jump?

B That will match their own processing preference?

C That they don't understand in order to make them think? ☐

22 Matching a customer's volume and speed of delivery works very well:

A All the time, but particularly during presentation and demonstration?

B Unless it sounds like you are trying to mimic someone?

C Particularly if you try and mimic someone? ☐

23 One of the least known and most powerful methods of creating rapport is to:

A Keep very silent after you have asked for the order?

B Ask them how much they want for their part-exchange as they are turning right in heavy traffic?

C Match the breathing of the person you are talking to? ☐

24 When you first meet a customer who is breathing fast through 'fear of the unknown':
A Match their breathing for a while and then start to slow down?
B Breathe slower than they are to show them that you are confident?
C Breathe faster than they are to make them feel more relaxed? ☐

25 Another good time to 'breathe in harmony' is when:
A The customer is trying to make the decision whether to go ahead or not?
B The customer calls back in and tries to cancel the order?
C When another salesperson tells you that the order you got is his? ☐

(Answers on page 370)

Six Steps to Improving Interpersonal Skills

People who have poor interpersonal skills don't really want to communicate with others. This could be due to shyness, but it could also mean that they are unaware or apathetic regarding other people's feelings. Not knowing or caring for other people is a tremendous limiting factor in life, particularly if you are in any face-to-face type of career.

Apart from rapport, there are six excellent ways to avoid falling into the lonely trap of a low level of interpersonal skill. Use it like a formula to make the most out of all your relationships with all the people you know and would like to know. Not just your customers.

The Six Steps are:

1 Smile easily and often at other people you meet

2 Communicate with everyone you meet

3 Ask open and closed questions

4 Remember to listen to the answers

5 Show respect for other people's opinions

6 Always take advantage of any opportunity to give someone praise and recognition

Let's flesh these out a little, to help you understand both the simplicity and the importance of these six steps.

1 Smile easily and often at other people you meet

This is not to say you must walk around with a permanent grin on your face. It is amazing, though, when you do smile at people, you will virtually always get a smile back. And that's from people you don't and won't know. With people you do or will know, you should always greet them with a smile – every time you meet them.

2 Communicate with everyone you meet

With people you don't and won't know, this is usually a nod of the head or a '*Goodnight*' or a '*Good morning*'.

Living in a country village has made this very easy for me to do. If you didn't, then other people would think that you were most peculiar. The funny thing is, I forget and do the same thing no matter what part of the country I happen to be in. The truth is that virtually all people in all areas and all places are happy to communicate with you at the slightest sign that you are willing to do so.

3 Ask open-ended and closed-ended questions

One of the first questions you should ask is the name of the person you are talking to – and not just in showrooms. If you want to find out the power of finding out someone's name, try it in restaurants. Chinese and Indian restaurants are as good a place as any. As the waiter takes your order, ask him for his name. Notice the look of puzzlement mist across his expression as he looks for the reason for such a strange question. Then he will give you his name. Then you can say, with a smile. Thank you, Sam or Khan, and the magic is done. You will get fabulous service and a better meal. It's guaranteed. And all you did was to ask the question 'What is your name?'

4 Remember to listen to the answers

We have already discussed the importance of listening to people when they talk to you. Not just listening, but *hearing* what the person is saying and understanding the meaning of the words. If you do not understand, then you must ask for additional information or clarification. It may take a little longer, but it will always save time in the end for both the giver and the receiver of the message.

5 Show respect for other people's opinions

As stated elsewhere in this book, great salespeople don't have opinions. You will, however, meet many people who have many opinions. Some of those opinions will be very odd indeed to you. Everybody thinks differently. Show respect for that difference. Listen to people's opinions and ask them questions without criticising them. You do not have to agree, only to listen and show respect.

6 Always take advantage of any opportunity to give someone praise and recognition

When was the last time you said 'thank you' to your boss? If the answer is 'I can't remember', then think of a reason for saying thank you to him – and go and do it. *"Thank you, George, for getting me that book. It has been really useful and I am truly grateful."* Or *"Thank you for sending me on that course last week. I learned a few things and we will both make some money out of my attendance."*

As you walk away from your boss, he will look at you with new eyes, and he will probably say gently to himself: *"What's that snivelling little rat been up to now?"* The problem is that your boss has not experienced praise and recognition from you for some time – if ever!

All people, not just bosses, love receiving praise and recognition. Give it out generously when it is deserved. The receiver will be pleased to know you and will give you some praise and recognition back.

The Answers to the Rapport Quiz

The more you consciously practise rapport, the quicker and better you will be able to use it.

1 = C	6 = B	11 = A	16 = C	21 = B
2 = B	7 = B	12 = C	17 = B	22 = B
3 = A	8 = C	13 = A	18 = A	23 = C
4 = A	9 = C	14 = A	19 = B	24 = A
5 = C	10 = B	15 = A	20 = A	25 = A

If you scored 20+, you've got it! 15 to 20, you're getting it! Less than 15, you need it!

The main points again

1 Interpersonal skills are all about rapport.

2 When you know something about rapport, you will have all the tools you need to polish up your interpersonal skills.

3 People who have poor interpersonal skills don't really want to communicate with others.

4 Not knowing or caring for other people is a tremendous limiting factor in life.

5 There are six ways to avoid falling into the lonely trap of ignorance:

- Smile easily and often at other people you meet
- Communicate with everyone you meet
- Ask open-ended and closed-ended questions
- Remember to listen to the answers
- Show respect for other people's opinions
- Always take advantage of any opportunity to give someone praise and recognition

CHAPTER 26
Motivation

"Things look better

now I have given up hope"

Personalised number plates do not motivate everyone, but in the last flush of youth I did get smitten when I fell in love with MAD 2. I was determined to make that number plate mine, but it was not going to be easy!

Both MAD 1 and MAD 2 lived on Rolls Royces at that time. The two cars were owned by two brothers who worked and lived in London. The MAD 2 brother must have become disenchanted with his number plate, so when he part-exchanged his old Rolls Royce for a brand new one, he did not transfer the number plate to the new car.

So there sat MAD 2, surrounded by the opulence of its temporary home in a West End showroom. I could not help but notice it, for I was the most recent addition to the selling team. My desk was not more than ten feet away from the front of the MAD 2-bearing Silver Shadow. I had just bought a blue Mini for my wife and I to use. *"How grand,"* I thought, *"MAD 2 would look on our new little car."* So I approached Mr Gold, our Financial Director (a very daunting thing to do without good reason!) in suitably respectful fashion.

"Mr Gold," I began, in what I hoped was a conversational tone.

"Yes, dear boy," he replied, without looking up from his ledger – he always called me 'dear boy', although I knew for certain that he knew my real name.

"That number plate on the previously owned Silver Shadow," (we did not sell used Rolls Royces, we sold 'previously owned') *"in the centre of the showroom..."*

"What about it, dear boy? Is it crooked, cracked or even half-cocked, or something?" he asked, beginning to take notice.

"No, it's nothing like that," I continued. *"It was just that I was just wondering how we can expect to sell a nice car like that with such a silly number plate."*

I had his attention. *"What do you mean, 'silly'? Please justify your opinion at once, dear boy."*

"*Well, Mr Gold,*" I said, "*the person who buys that car will be telling everybody he meets that he is mad too... get it?*"

He eyed me curiously, and I pressed my advantage. "*We can't possibly sell that car with that number plate. It's too downmarket; it could even cost us money.*"

That was it: he was suddenly very interested. I had mentioned the magic word – money. He looked at me with totally wide-awake eyes, rather like a mongoose closing on a cobra. "*Cost us money, dear boy? Do you really think so?*"

"*Yes, I really do.*"

"*What then, dear boy, do you suggest we do? You have a suggestion – don't you? Otherwise we would not even be discussing the matter – would we?*"

"*Yes, I do happen to have a solution, Mr Gold. Why don't I get the number plate transferred to my car – then the licensing people will give the Rolls a nice new number plate with a more dignified set of digits?*"

He must have been totally satisfied with what he heard. "*All right, dear boy,*" he agreed. "*Will you arrange for that to happen straight away?*" then added: "*You will of course be paying the five pounds transfer fee, and for a new set of number plates for the Shadow, won't you?*"

...And I did.

So What Motivates You?

There are ten motivational areas or factors which are, by common consent, those which have the greatest impact on the motivation of individuals in a working environment:

1 Good working conditions
2 Security in the job and for your old age
3 Opportunity for advancement
4 Status as a person
5 Satisfying work
6 Recognition by superiors
7 Income level
8 Responsibility and authority
9 Competent management and supervision
10 Impact of your work on your personal life.

Salespeople on sales courses are often asked to rank these 'Motivators' in order of importance to them personally. The current top three motivators are:

9 Competent management and supervision
6 Recognition by superiors
7 Income level

Competent Management and Supervision

Salespeople do look to management for motivation. There are times when they want to be told what they have to do; they sometimes need to be sold ideas. There are occasions when they need to be coached by their manager through participation. There are also times when salespeople need to be allowed the freedom to get on with the job with minimum interference.

If your manager knows when to: tell, sell, coach and delegate... all at the right time and to the right degree, then you will be a highly motivated salesperson.

If you are a manager, then you now know one of the secrets of leading a highly motivated team.

Recognition by Superiors

A managing director once asked me: "*Why should I thank people for doing what I pay them to do?*" He missed the point there really. People, and that includes salespeople, absolutely adore praise and recognition, when deserved. It is truly amazing how the odd "*Hey, thank you*" or "*Thanks, I appreciate that*" helps to brighten dull days.

Income Level

Income is always high on the list, but seldom first. Most salespeople still work on commission and basic salary. So, to a degree, how much they earn is in their own hands; money is only considered a problem when there is too much 'month' left at the end of it. Then you have a problem. That could indicate the need for an 'outcome'.

'Problems' vs 'Outcomes'

In general, people and businesses today are more aligned towards problem solving. There is a bias towards looking for what *isn't* working, for problems to solve and people to blame. Such institutions and individuals are less likely to model excellence. The price they pay is that they do not notice what is working. Some of our larger companies, for instance, have whole departments staffed by many people, whose sole reason to exist revolves around handling customer complaints. How many companies do you know that have customer compliment departments?

- What do you pay attention to?

Your problems and failures OR The things you do that work

Start to notice the success and excellence that you already have and the resources that you already have, and build on those. If you do this, some 'problems' will become less of a problem. Others will simply fade away.

'Problem Frames' vs 'Outcome Frames'

Einstein, who was a bit good at solving problems, once wrote: "*You can't solve a problem with the same thinking that is creating the problem.*" The best way to solve a problem is to use 'an outcome frame'.

Take the example of too much month left at the end of the money. Let's run it though both frames in order for you to notice the difference:

Problem Frame	
1 What is your problem?	*"I often find that I do not have enough money to do what I want to do."*
2 How long have you had it?	*"As long as I have been involved in selling."*
3 Whose fault is it?	*"My company's for the silly payment structure they use. Do you know, I can wait for up to two months to get paid the commission for a vehicle that I have delivered."*
4 Who is to blame?	*"Well, apart from my company, the manufacturer is also to blame – sometimes I can't even get the vehicles to deliver."*
5 Why haven't you solved it yet?	*"Who me? What can I do about it, I'm just a salesperson."*

Now notice the difference when you take the same problem through an outcome frame.

Outcome Frame	
1 What do you want?	*"I want enough money to do what I want when I want to do it."*
2 How will you know when you have got it?	*"That's simple – I will not get those letters from the bank manager any more. And I won't have to worry about money, and that would be truly wonderful."*
3 What resources do you already have which can help you achieve this outcome?	*"It would be less of a problem if I sold from stock. If that's not possible, then I could sell the idea of waiting for delivery. It can take some time to get paid, so it would pay me to plan ahead and work out what I will need to take home in three months' time instead of thinking of this month all the time."*
4 What is something similar which you succeed in doing?	*"Oh, I get it. I needed money for that trip. I planned that ahead and didn't have a money problem when I went. What a great time that was, and no money worries."*
5 What is the next step?	*"Repeat what I did successfully in the past. Plan to have no money worries in three months' time through sales ability and a little bit more care on what I spend my money on today."*

Following are two blank frames for you to work out your own problems and outcomes.

Problem Frame
1 What is your problem?
2 How long have you had it?
3 Whose fault is it?
4 Who is to blame?
5 Why haven't you solved it yet?

Outcome Frame
1 What do you want?
2 How will you know when you have got it?
3 What resources do you already have which can help you achieve this outcome?
4 What is something similar which you succeed in doing?
5 What is the next step?

The Change Process

Just the fact that you have completed the outcome frame will be enough to start a change process. If you concentrate on what you want, your unconscious mind will endeavour to organise your behaviour to achieve the outcome that you have set for yourself.

Present State (Not enough money)

+

Resource (Planning ahead and managing better today)

=

Desired State (More money left at the end of the month)

Both Frames Have Their Uses

When you start to use these frames, you will notice that the problem frame also has its uses and is sometimes more appropriate to use when solving problems. This particularly applies when it is 'your fault' and 'you are to blame'!

Outcome frames are normally the more motivational, particularly when used in conjunction with a 'motivation formula'. Here is a simple to use, easy to follow example for you:

Motivation Formula

1 Be conscious of the need for personal targets

2 Set yourself realistic targets

3 Write down your targets and read them every day

4 Take the time to imagine yourself achieving your targets

5 Set yourself time limits to achieve your goals

6 Replace achieved targets with something new to aim for

...And that's it.

Let's examine each step with you one by one. Then you will be able to fully see, understand or feel the ladder of success, rung by rung, before you.

1 Be conscious of the need for personal targets

Life without goals is a trip without a destination. Everybody needs some form of motivation, something to live for, to work for, to enjoy, to achieve and to fulfil.

2 Set yourself realistic targets

There is little point in setting yourself impossible goals that you will never achieve. The best way to avoid this sale-destroying situation is to set yourself achievable 'outcomes'.

The best way to set yourself an outcome is to complete an outcome frame as discussed which leads us to part 3 of our formula.

3 Write down your outcome and read it every day

Apart from completing an outcome frame, many salespeople have benefited by placing a one sentence statement of their outcome on a small card, something like an A5 size. This card would simply re-state what they wrote in the 'What do you want?' section of their outcome frame. The statement would be positive and in the present tense:

- I have enough money to do what I want when I want to do it
- I am the owner of a Nickleson 31
- I own a large house with four bedrooms, a study and a large garage
- I weigh twelve stone

This has far more positive results than using the future tense – 'I want enough... ', 'I will be the owner... ', 'I will own... ', 'I will weigh... ' and so on.

The trick is now to stick this card up where you can see it every day. Somewhere like the inside of an opening door of a wardrobe. Or perhaps as a page marker in your day-to-day diary.

You will start to read it consciously and after a while, when you think that you do not notice it, your unconscious will take over and read it for you. That will reinforce your unconscious mind's natural ability to organise your behaviour to achieve your outcome. That's why the statement has to be positive and in the present tense.

4 Take the time to imagine yourself achieving your targets

See, hear and feel yourself achieving your outcomes. If your target is to buy a boat, then go and look at boats. If it is to own a larger house, then go and look at larger houses. If your target is to be slimmer, then by all means stick pictures of slimmer people in your fridge for you to see and as a reminder to you.

The human mind has difficulty in recognising the difference between role-play and reality. This is why seeing, hearing and feeling your success 'inside' has such a positive effect on what happens 'outside'.

5 Set yourself time limits to achieve your goal

Some goals are ongoing; others need a time limit, otherwise they can drag on for ever. Even though statements can be made positive and in the present tense, somewhere in your mind you should be aware of a time limit to achieve your outcome if appropriate.

6 Replace achieved targets with something new

When you have the money, you will no longer be motivated by it or worried about it. When you have the boat, it will be very nice but it will not motivate you in the same way as it did when you were trying to get it. When you live in that house, you will be very pleased and will feel a great sense of achievement, but you will want something else to aim for. When you weigh twelve stone, you could think 'Great' and, like most people, put it all back on again because you have achieved what you want.

Can you see the danger? Human beings need motivation. Personal motivation comes from striving to achieve outcomes that you have set for yourself but have yet to achieve.

The main points again

1 The top three 'motivators' of salespeople are:

- Competent management and supervision
- Recognition by superiors
- Income

2 Income is always high on the list but seldom first.

3 There is far more emphasis today on noticing what is not working – the problems.

4 Start to notice the success, the excellence and the resources that you already have, and problems become less of a problem.

5 The best way to solve a problem is to use an 'outcome frame'.

6 If you concentrate on what you want, your unconscious mind will endeavour to organise your behaviour to achieve the outcome that you have set for yourself.

7 Outcome frames are more motivational when used in conjunction with a motivation formula:

- Be conscious of the need for personal targets
- Set yourself realistic targets
- Write down your targets and read them every day
- Take the time to imagine yourself achieving your targets
- Set yourself time limits to achieve your goals
- Replace achieved targets with something new to aim for

◆ ◆ ◆

CHAPTER 27
Informed Decisions

"Give me the courage to change the things I can,
the grace to accept the things I can't
and the wisdom to know the difference"

There was nothing indecisive about Mr Gold the day I told him that I was going to Bologna in Italy to pick up Lucki Takis' new Lamborghini. It was an emphatic and instant *"Not on your life, dear boy"*.

It had all started around two weeks before, when Lucki called in at the showroom. *"This Rolls Royce you sold me last week, she is great to drive and also very big as well I think."* My face fell. If Lucki was thinking of asking me to buy back the Rolls Royce, then I hoped for his sake that he was as well funded as he appeared to be. Apart from that, I hadn't even been paid the commission for selling it yet.

"What do you want me to do, Lucki?" I asked cautiously.

"I want you to get me something more sporty, a Lamborghini or something. I want a car that is fun to drive."

"What about the Rolls Royce?" I asked, endeavouring to work out mentally a part-exchange price on a car I had delivered a week ago against another car on which I didn't know our profit margin. I needn't have bothered.

"Oh, the Rolls Royce, I keep her. I think I will have the Lamborghini as well."

I breathed a force eight sigh of relief as Lucki went on: *"Can you arrange for me to see and try the car first?"*

I agreed to this and, after Lucki had left, got on with the task.

I telephoned the Lamborghini concessionaires and explained who I was, who I worked for and what I wanted. *"Sure,"* said the cool, educated voice, *"a demonstration from your showrooms next Wednesday will not be a problem."*

"What about our commission?" I enquired, *"I mean, if our customer decides to go ahead."*

"Yes, well we would pay you a ten per cent commission on the basic price of the car," said the cool, educated voice flatly.

"That would be acceptable," I replied, trying to sound cool, educated and unexcited. 10% of the basic price of a Lamborghini then was around £8,000 in today's money, and £800 of that was going to be mine. Not bad wages for making a phone call, I thought.

Wednesday came around and so did the Lamborghini. It was an Espada in metallic flecked white paint. It was brash, but it was also beautiful. The cool, educated voice did not look as I had expected. More like an Italian heavyweight boxer who wasn't very good at guarding his face in contests. He was immaculately dressed and adorned with fruit salad (the then motor trade term for gold jewellery), a heavy gold Rolex on one wrist and heavy gold chains on the other, balanced by two gold rings on the smaller two fingers of each hand.

"Hi," he said, *"are you the chappy with the punter for the Lambo?"*

Having exchanged greetings, we both waited for Lucki to show, which he did, shortly after eleven.

"Sorry I'm late," he said, *"I had trouble buying a ship I wanted. Let's get on with it, I haven't got long."*

We got on with it. Lucki looked the car over and looked pleased. Then he opened the door. Suddenly he looked a little less than pleased. *"What's wrong?"* I asked him, thoughts of a massive commission fading rapidly like a Lamborghini on full chat heading for the middle distance. *"It's a long way down to get into it,"* he said, *"and when you do, there is not much space to get in."*

"But you've still got a Rolls Royce as well," I blurted out in desperation (thinking which is better, to think you have made eight hundred and then not make it or never to think you have made it in the first place?). *"You're right, I'll have it,"* said Lucki.

Cool educated drove the Espada away, and Lucki and I sat down to sort out the details. There was an Espada being built at that moment, and it would be ready at the factory in Bologna in three weeks' time. *"You collect it for me,"* said Lucki, *"I don't want someone I don't know to drive it. I will pay all your expenses, of course."* This I readily agreed to do, as Lucki wrote out a deposit cheque that was equivalent to our commission on the deal. I took the signed order and cheque up to Mr Gold's office for him to approve.

"*What's this, dear boy?*" he said as he looked at the order in a puzzled kind of way.

"*It's an order form for a new Lamborghini Espada,*" I told him.

"*What is a what did you call it?*" he said, looking up.

"*It's a kind of sports car. It's a Lamborghini,*" I reconfirmed.

"*We don't sell Lamborghinis,*" he told me. "*Why don't you sell him a Rolls Royce?*"

"*I did – last week,*" I told him. "*Now he wants a Lamborghini.*"

"*Well tell him to go to the Lamborghini people then, dear boy,*" said Mr Gold, with a hint of agitation in his voice. "*Give me one good reason why we should get involved with the transaction,*" he added, as he held out the order and deposit cheque for me to take back.

"*You're holding it, Mr Gold,*" I said calmly.

"*Holding what, dear boy? Please talk sense if you will.*"

"*That cheque you are holding is our commission from the Lamborghini people for selling the car.*"

Mr Gold looked at the cheque for the very first time and he actually blinked. I saw it. It was not something he was ever supposed to do. He sat back in his chair and held his chin, as though he was trying not to let his jaw crash into his rib cage. "*Well, I suppose we could make the odd exception, dear boy.*"

...And we did.

What is an Informed Decision?

An informed decision is an outcome that you have thought through fully and written out in full. It is an outcome that you can 'see', 'hear' and 'feel'. There is something magical about writing down what you want to achieve.

When you just think something through, or just talk about it, it just doesn't happen in the same way. Once you write down your objectives, you are far more likely to achieve what you want.

There is the classic and well documented case of the graduate who as long ago as 1953 wrote a masters thesis on goal-setting. The graduate found that only 3% of the students had written down their lifetime goals. Twenty years later, someone checked with 'the class of '53' and found that the 3% of students with written goals had made more income than all the rest of the class put together.

Anybody can make a decision – it's easy. You simply say 'Yeah, I'll do that', then nothing happens. After all is said and done, a lot more is always said than done. This is the reason why you should decide to carry out more demonstrations from potential purchasers' homes or business premises. If you leave it to the customer to come to you, then you too can become the victim of 'the brain that makes appointments the body never keeps' syndrome.

The problem is that we are faced with decisions to make every day. These can range from small to life threatening. Hardly anybody is really taught to make a decision: it is often left to each individual to work it out for themselves.

The solution is to use an 'outcome frame' to help you establish the best way to decide what to do and to get what you want for small and short term decisions. This is illustrated and explained in the previous chapter, *Motivation* (see pages 375-380).

If, however, you are faced with establishing long term goals or have to make decisions that are crucial to your future, then it is rather like surfing the North Shore in Oahu on a big wave day. You are going to need a 'Big Gun'. In decision-making circles, that big gun is known as a 'well informed outcome frame'. This frame is illustrated here, and gives you the opportunity to gather all the facts and information that you will need to help you make an 'informed decision' – one that has every chance of being put into motion and achieving a satisfactory outcome.

Well Informed Outcome Frame	
1 Stated in the positive	"What do I want?"
	"Why do I want it?"
	"What will that do for me?"
2 Sensory specific	"How will I know when I've got it?"
	"What will I see?"
	"What will I hear?"
	"What will I feel?"
3 Started and maintained by me	"What will I be doing to achieve my target?"
	"How do I start and maintain the process?"
	"What do I need?"
	"What stops me from having it right now?"
	"What's my first step?"
4 What must I keep?	"What do I get out of my present behaviour, that I would wish to preserve?"
5 What context?	"When, where and with whom do I want it?"
	"When, where and with whom do I not want it?"
	"How long do I want it for?"
6 The safety checks	"If I could have it, would I take it?"
	"What will I gain?"
	"What will I lose?"
	"Is it worth the cost to me?"
	"Is it worth the time it's going to take?"
	"Is this outcome in keeping with how I see myself?"

The Six Steps to Well Informed Outcomes

1 Stated in the positive

Always state any outcome in the positive. If you consciously focus on what you don't want, your unconscious mind will give you that. If you focus on what you do want, you are likely to get that instead.

"Whatever you do, don't imagine a green mushroom with large red spots, and don't even think of putting a little yellow frog on it with big black eyes."

This sentence is an example of focusing on what you don't want. Your brain is organised in such a way that you can't think about what you don't want without imagining it. How was your frog for you?

2 Sensory specific

The question 'How will I know when I've got it?' will start the process of imagining what it will be like to achieve your outcome. An outcome is a goal or target that you can 'see', 'hear' and 'feel'. It has been said that you can imagine anything and master it. Take the time to imagine that you can 'see' the results of your achieved outcome. That you can 'hear' and can 'feel' your future success. This behaviour alone will be a tremendous help for you to achieve your outcome.

3 Started and maintained by me

Continue to use your imagination to see, hear and feel. Decide exactly what you will be doing to achieve your target. Think over the best ways to get started and continue the process and start to rank choices and options.

Work out what you will need to be successful in achieving what you want, what resources, what help, what knowledge and what methods of working. Ask yourself the question 'What stops me from having it right now?' Work out what you need to do first to put the whole process into operation.

4 What must I keep?

It is very important to establish what you wish to preserve relating to your current circumstances. What are the positive things that you would wish to keep? Things like free time, sports, hobbies, time with friends and family spring to mind. Anything that is important for you to keep or continue to enjoy should be clearly established at this point.

5 What context?

The next thing to establish is with who else you want to achieve your outcome. There could be no-one. It might be a solo performance, or it might be important to include others. The time and place to achieve your outcome will have to be established. It is vital to decide if there are others that you would not want to include and if there are times and places that you would wish to exclude. You also need to establish for how long you would wish to do all this. Some outcomes could be permanent changes, as in *"I am a healthy, socially acceptable non-smoker."* Other outcomes could be terminal, as in *"This year I am going to sell 'X' number of cars."* Or better still, *"This year I have sold 'X' number of cars."*

6 The safety checks

Don't forget to complete the safety checks, for they will confirm to you that you really do want to achieve the outcome that you have set for yourself. Ask yourself the question: *"If I could have it, would I take it?"* Work out what you will gain and lose. Consider what it will cost you in time and money to achieve what you want.

Once, while working with a highly successful heavy truck sales specialist, he decided that the only thing that he had left to achieve was a break of 147 at snooker. So he started to fill in his well informed outcome frame. Everything was going well and smoothly until he got to the second-to-last safety check question: *"Is it worth the time it's going to take?"* His pen faltered in mid air and a horrified look came over his face. He put the pen down and said *"In order to achieve my outcome of a break of 147 at snooker, I would have to practice for six hours every day. Stuff it! It's just not worth it."*

The very last question is *"Is this target in keeping with how I see myself?"* We all have this sense of ourselves. Any changes that we make to our behaviour will change this self image. The point is, will you still be happy with the person you will become if you achieve your outcome?

Completed Example

On this page you will find a completed example of a well informed outcome frame. This relates to a vehicle sales specialist who would like to raise the number of vehicles sold over a one-year period.

'(X)' is used in this illustration. If you decide to work on a similar outcome, then you will need to establish the number of units or the volume of profit to aim for.

Although the outcome is for the year ahead, the vehicle sales specialist in this example has stated the target as if it were already achieved.

"I have sold (X) vehicles this year."

This is a statement of intent and will carry more weight with your internal state than *"I want to"* or even *"I will"*.

Well Informed Outcome Frame	
1 Stated in the positive	
"What do I want?"	*"I have sold (X) vehicles this year."*
"Why do I want it?"	*"I'm fed up with being 'average' – the best of the worst, the worst of the best."*
"What will achieving this outcome do for me?"	*"I will earn more money and obtain job security."*
2 Sensory specific	
"How will I know when I have achieved it?"	*"The vehicles will be sold, the money will be earned, my job will be secure."*
"What will I see, hear and feel?"	*"I will see my sales target achieved."* *"I will hear the praise and recognition."* *"I will feel financial and job security."*

Well Informed Outcome Frame	
3 Started and maintained by me	
"What will I be doing to achieve my target?"	*"Taking advantage of every sales opportunity and making full use of the time available."*
"How do I start and maintain the process?"	*"Find out how many prospects and enquiries I need to see, break it down as a daily target, and make sure that I do see that number of people."*
"What do I need?"	*"I need more selling opportunities. I need to become better at selling."*
"What stops me from having it right now?"	*"Lack of personal motivation and commitment."*
"What is my first step?"	*"To take full advantage of all the now identified personal, company and manufacturer resources."* *"Learn and remember all the selling skills and product knowledge that will be essential to achieving my target."*
4 What must I keep?	
"What do I get out of my present behaviour that I would wish to preserve?"	*"I want to preserve my free time as much as possible – for both my family and my relaxation."* *"I want to continue to enjoy coming to work."* *"I want to stay healthy and enjoy life."*

Well Informed Outcome Frame	
5 What context?	
"When, where and with whom do I want it?"	*"From now, with my existing company, working with the people I know and the customers that I will get to know."*
"When, where and with whom do I not want it?"	*"I want to stay in the same job; I don't want to start again somewhere else to achieve my target."*
"How long do I want it for?"	*"The target is set for one year. I will achieve it. Then I will decide what I want to do next."*
6 The safety checks	
"If I could have it, would I take it?"	*"Like a shot."*
"What will I gain?"	*"A great deal of job and personal satisfaction, plus the money and job security."*
"What will I lose?"	*"Just a little time, that's all."*
"Is it worth the cost to me?"	*"It's about time I put my skates on. I have a reasonably pleasant life at the moment, but I'm not going anywhere. Yes, it is worth the cost to me because I want to succeed."*
"Is it worth the time it is going to take?"	*"Yes, because I can gain much time from just using the hours in the day better."*
"Is this outcome in keeping with how I see myself?"	*"Oh yes! I want to be successful. It's about time I started."*

This is your Opportunity to Get What You Want

On the following pages you will find a blank 'well informed outcome frame'. If you really do want to make some changes in what you do and how you do it, then here is your chance. It is recommended that you photocopy the well informed outcome frame and enlarge it onto A4 paper (110%) for your own use.

But be warned: If you do take the trouble to think through fully and complete a well informed outcome frame, there is a very grave danger that you will get what you want.

Well Informed Outcome Frame	
1 Stated in the positive	
"What do I want?" "Why do I want it?" "What will achieving this outcome do for me?"	
2 Sensory specific	
"How will I know when I have achieved it?" "What will I see, hear and feel?"	

Well Informed Outcome Frame	
3 Started and maintained by me	
"What will I be doing to achieve my target?"	
"How do I start and maintain the process?"	
"What do I need?"	
"What stops me from having it right now?"	
"What is my first step?"	

Well Informed Outcome Frame	
4 What must I keep?	
"What do I get out of my present behaviour that I would wish to preserve?"	
5 What context?	
"When, where and with whom do I want it?" "When, where and with whom do I not want it?" "How long do I want it for?"	

Well Informed Outcome Frame	
6 The safety checks	
"If I could have it, would I take it?"	
"What will I gain?"	
"What will I lose?"	
"Is it worth the cost to me?"	
"Is it worth the time it is going to take?"	
"Is this outcome in keeping with how I see myself?"	

The main points again

1 The discipline of writing something down is the first step of making it happen.

2 People who write down their goals have far more chance of achieving them.

3 Hardly anybody is really taught to make a decision.

4 Using an 'outcome frame' will help you to establish what to do and to get what you want.

5 Bigger ambitions need a bigger frame, known as a 'well informed outcome frame':

- Stated in the positive
- Sensory specific
- Started and maintained by me
- What must I keep?
- What context?
- The safety checks

6 Using this frame will help you to gather all the facts and information to help you make an 'informed decision'.

7 If you do take the trouble to think through and complete fully a well informed outcome frame, there is a very grave danger that you will get what you want.

CHAPTER 28
Tenacity

"When the going gets tough,
the tough get going, but only
when the going gets tough.
When things are easy,
the tough are a total mess"

Mr Selby telephoned for the first time on a Monday morning. You know the type of call: *"Have you got?"* and *"How much off?"*.

Mr Selby's quest was for a white 320 with a blue cloth interior and some extras.

"If there is one in the country I will find it for you," I told him.

"You haven't got one there then?" Mr Selby sounded surprised.

"No, I'm afraid not, they are a bit short at the moment." Then I added: *"Look, Mr Selby, give me your order and I will find the car for you. It shouldn't take too long."*

"What do you want my order for?" he said suspiciously, *"you haven't got one, you don't know if you can get one and you haven't told me what discount you are going to give me yet."*

"I need your order," I said patiently, *"so that I can justify the time that it will take to track one down. I think I can get one for you – I will certainly try very hard to do so."*

"And how much off?" he said. Vehicle salespeople need to have the patience of a saint, I have been told, and boy was I patient.

"Mr Selby," I replied, *"we can certainly discuss the price of the car. The best time and place would be face-to-face, preferably when you have your cheque book in one hand and your pen in the other."*

This was all said in a most pleasant manner and did not sound at all aggressive or disagreeable. Mr Selby did not see it that way. He positively exploded: *"Look here,"* he said, *"you don't have the car I want and you won't give me the discount that I want, I just know it. You are wasting my time."*

"Mr Selby... " I began again, careful to keep my voice calm and reasonable, but he wasn't interested in hearing what I had to say.

"Look here," he said, *"there is more than one BMW dealer in London. I can do my own phoning around. Give me some names and numbers."*

Now what would you do? Think about it while I tell you what I did.

"Well, the three local to here would be Cheyney Motors at Putney, First-Front at Vauxhall or, going the other way, Hexagon at Highgate." I also gave him the telephone numbers as requested. I already had his name, business address and office telephone number, so I was not bothered when he terminated the call with a gruff 'thank you' and put the phone down on me.

I kept the phone in my hand and telephoned the new car allocations department.

"Morning Anne," I said, *"how are you today?"*

"Very well, thank you, what do you want?"

Anne was a very busy person so I didn't waste her time. *"Who has an unsold 320 manual, white, blue cloth trim with tint and a sunroof?"*

"There is only one," she said, *"Agnews in Belfast"*. *"Ta, Anne,"* I told her, *"I will give them a bell."* And I did.

"Morning Reggie, how are you today?"

"Couldn't be better, it's good golfing weather," came the happy smiling reply.

"You have, or did have, an unsold 320 in white. Do you still have the car?" I asked.

"Ah yes," he said, *"did you want it?"*

"Yes, I think so," I replied. *"Would you take a maroon or blue to the same spec?"*

"Sure," he said, *"Put me down for the blue one. When will you know?"*

"Give me twenty-four hours to sell it. I will confirm this time tomorrow, okay?"

It was, so I had a car if I wanted it. The next step was to get back to Mr Selby, and that wasn't easy. His phone was constantly engaged. He appeared to be telephoning every BMW dealer in the country. His phone bill alone will be more than the discount he might get, I thought. Eventually I got through to him. *"Hello there, Mr Selby,"* I said, *"I have found the car that you are looking for. Do you want it?"*

"You've got one?" he exclaimed. *"What, with the sunroof?"*

"Yes, Mr Selby, this car is exactly what you are looking for. Do you want it?"

"When will it be there?" he asked.

"I can get it before the end of the week," I told him. *"In fact, give me your order today, and you can have it on Friday. Do you want it?"*

"I've been offered seven and a half per cent discount, you know," he said with satisfaction.

"That's wonderful," I replied. *"That's a very good offer. Have they got the car you want?"*

"*No,*" he said, *"they haven't."*

"*Well, Mr Selby,*" I said *"If I hadn't got the car, then I would offer you seven and a half per cent discount too."*

"*What do you mean?*" he asked, puzzled.

"I mean that anyone can offer as much discount as they like on stock they haven't got because they are not in a position to do business. I am, and do you want the car?"

"*Yes I do,*" he said at last, responding to the fourth 'do you want', *"but I always get a discount when I buy my cars."*

"*What is more important to you, Mr Selby, getting the car or getting the discount?*"

"*Well both,*" he replied.

"Then I can't help you," I told him.

"You really won't give me anything off?" he asked in a tired sort of way.

"To discount the car would be to demean the BMW, you see," I explained. *"Today's discount is tomorrow's depreciation. If you discount today, then the discounted car will be worth that much less when you come to sell it."* Mr Selby said nothing. I knew he was there because I could hear him breathing. I let him take his time.

"*Okay,*" he said at last, *"can you pop around to my office and we will sort out the details."* His office wasn't far and as I went I wondered if he would have his cheque book in his hand.

...And he did.

So What Exactly is Tenacity?

If you look up the word in the dictionary, you will discover that it means 'the ability to hold fast, to be retentive, to see it through, to stick to it' and yes, even 'to be stubborn'. Salespeople can be nice as they like, but there comes a time when all of us need a little tenacity.

- Not all customers throw their hands up in the air and say 'I'll take it'. Many need a little push. That's tenacity.
- If the last three people you saw in the showroom were a man to read the electric meter, a lady that wanted brochures for her grandson's school project and a test shopper sent by your manufacturer, then you will need a little tenacity for the next enquiry.
- When you telephone someone to make an appointment to call and see them and they tell you that you would be wasting your time, you say: *"Thank you for thinking of me, Mr Aston, I am more than happy to give twenty minutes of my time if you are."* That's tenacity.
- When you knock on a prospect's door and they tell you to 'push off', and you say with a smile: *"Is that push off for good or push off now and come back later?"*, you have tenacity.

There comes a time in many selling situations when a firm but friendly approach is required. If you've got it, then you will be more successful than other salespeople that don't have it. If you haven't got it and would like it, here is how to get it.

The Tenacity Formula

1 Always make sure that what you are about to do has the maximum chance of success.

2 Believe that you can do what you have decided to do and then do it to the best of your ability.

3 Expect what you are doing to be more difficult than you thought it would be.

4 Make sure that you allocate enough time to complete the task that you have set for yourself.

5 Whenever possible, have some way to measure your performance or results.

That's the formula: let's take a closer look at it one step at a time.

1 Always make sure that what you are about to do has the maximum chance of success

This is a question of planning things out:

Proper Planning Prevents Poor Performance

You already have the answer to planning things out properly in the preceding chapter, *Informed Decisions*.

2 Believe that you can do what you have decided to do and then do it to the best of your ability.

In order to achieve the results that you want to achieve, you will need four things. You need:

- To want to achieve it
- To believe that you can achieve it
- To know how to achieve it
- To give yourself the chance to achieve it

Once you have got those four needs firmly in mind, then you have every chance of success.

3 Expect what you are doing to be more difficult to do than you thought it would be

It very well might not be more difficult, but expecting some difficulties will help you retain the tenacity to carry things through to a successful conclusion. The following diagram will illustrate what often happens when you change your behaviour.

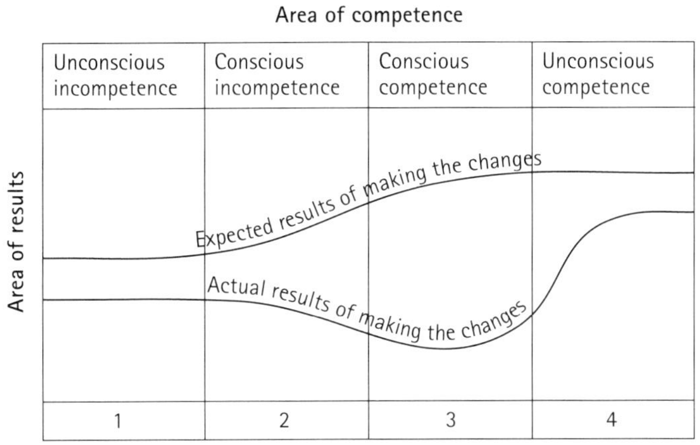

There are four levels of awareness in selling:

Unconscious Incompetence	This is where a salesperson does not know that he is not good at doing something.
Conscious Incompetence	This is where a salesperson becomes aware of the fact that he is not good at doing something and starts to make changes, in an effort to achieve better results.
Conscious Competence	By now the salesperson is conscious of what he needs to do and puts that plan into operation.
Unconscious Competence	The new behaviour has become a habit and is done automatically, outside conscious awareness.

The Unconsciously Incompetent salesperson is not aware of his incompetence and therefore is not in a position to do much about it.

The Consciously Incompetent salesperson has become aware of his incompetence and starts to make changes. The results of this can often be a fall in sales performance. The reason for this is that selling consciously takes more time and effort since new behaviour takes time to master.

The Consciously Competent salesperson still finds it harder to sell consciously, as progress is often two steps forward and one step back. This is where many people give up new behaviour and go back to old, more familiar and ineffective ways. This is a great pity because if they had just stuck it out a little longer, they would have reaped the rewards of success. Salespeople who do keep going at this point will find that the results of their efforts start to show in the results of their sales performance.

The Unconsciously Competent salesperson, who does see the plan through to the end, will continue to improve performance as new methods become more natural behaviour. There will then come a point where performance will level out. Sometimes a salesperson can slip back to Unconscious Incompetence all over again. For this reason, it really does pay salespeople to revert back to Consciously Competent from time to time and check themselves out.

4 Make sure that you allocate enough time to complete the task that you have set for yourself.

Time is one of the most valuable resources we have. As stated earlier in this guide: 'Nobody has enough time and yet we all have all the time there is'. If you waste a minute, an hour or a day, then it's gone for ever and you can never get it back. Use your time wisely and use it to help you get what you want. The time will come when you won't regret it.

5 Whenever possible, have some way to measure your performance or results

A visual method is best. Something that you can look at that will instantly identify how you are doing in relation to the target that you have set yourself.

Do you know these 'church roof fund' target boards that you see around from time to time? This type of thing would make a grand visual results chart as you can see from the following diagram.

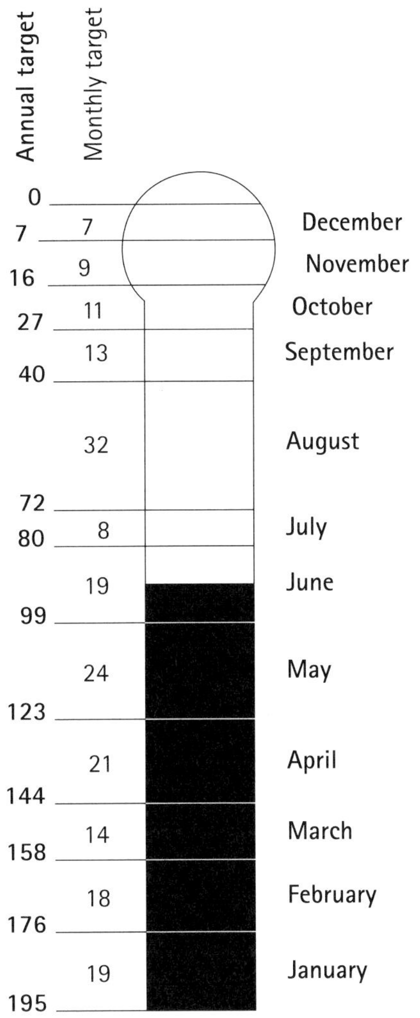

Explanation and How it Works

On the left-hand side of the diagram you will see a total figure of targeted sales for the year. This salesperson has a target of 195 units, which is not a norm or a recommendation. It is up to you to work out what your target would be. This target has been broken down into months, in volumes that follow the traditional monthly flow of a company's sales.

The full annual target is at the bottom, and the salesperson 'aims for zero' by the year end. This is because the closer you get to hitting your target, the bigger the impact each sale will make on the reducing balance. To make it work, the salesperson simply shades in the column to represent sales made towards achieving his target. It does not have to be units: it could be retained gross profit or even personal earnings. It is entirely up to you to decide what you want to measure. Being able to measure your present results will always help you to improve your future results.

Where to Put your Results Chart

It could be on a wall. It could be on a page at the back of an A4-size diary. As long as it is somewhere that you can see it, use it and benefit from it.

The main points again

1 A frightening frame of mind for anyone to get into is the 'I tried that once and it did not work' routine.

2 Tenacity means the ability to hold fast, to be retentive, to see it through, to stick with it and even to be stubborn.

3 There comes a time in many selling situations when a firm but friendly approach is required.

4 The Tenacity Formula:

- Always make sure that what you are about to do has the maximum chance of success
- Believe that you can do what you have decided to do and then do it to the best of your ability
- Expect what you are doing to be more difficult than you thought it would be
- Make sure that you allocate enough time to complete the task that you have set for yourself
- Whenever possible, have some way to measure your performance or results

CHAPTER 29
Self Confidence

"It is such a delight to deal with confident people who offer solutions to problems and have the initiative to complete tasks successfully. Those who are forever whining about their difficulties are rather depressing – they do not make my day."

"Now listen, you boys," said Steve, *"this is very important. Next April, the first ever British National Karate championships will be taking place at Crystal Palace and we are going to be there."* Steve had our total attention. Everybody had taken in the challenge in his statement. We were a fairly new club and none of our members had had more than a year's experience of Karate; a few had come from other martial arts – mostly Judo or Aikido – but it wasn't going to be easy.

"It's not going to be easy," Steve, as usual, showed his absolute ability to read our thoughts. *"But it is going to be, and this is how we shall do it."* Steve explained his plan. He talked about training harder and longer, circuit training to firm us up, *Kata* (formal exercises), to speed us up and improve our techniques, plus plenty of *Jiyu-Kumite* (free fighting) under contest conditions, to get us used to the experience.

We were keen and we went for it. In addition to the usual weekday evening training sessions, we would go away at weekends, sleep in barns by night and train by day. It was quite an experience to run through the dawn down a country lane as part of a white-suited, barefoot squad. Steve and Bob would get up the chant *"Hezo"*.

"He" on the left foot, *"Zo"* on the right.

"Hizo," we would reply.

"Hi" on the left and *"Zo"* on the right.

Then we would shower using the farmyard hosepipe and have a hearty farmhouse breakfast followed by a little free time before the real work of the day began. We would work the farm most mornings to pay for our barn floor and food, chopping trees, shifting wood, clearing stones from fields and digging ditches – anything that was manual and heavy. In the afternoons we 'free fought' in fields, river beds and on river banks. Boy, did we get fit fast!

When the day of the championship arrived, we were all ready and raring to go. Who could have known then that among our number was a future world champion and another who was destined to become an eighth dan?

In my first bout I was up against a tall, gangly youth with long legs and arms. There was not much to him compared to my own 12st 12lbs. *"Watch his legs,"* said Steve, *"he looks very fluid on the hips."*

"Don't worry," I replied with confidence and conviction, *"he won't be a problem!"*

I had every right to be confident, I thought, I was at my best fighting weight – at least a stone of usable muscle power over my undernourished-looking opponent. I had trained as hard as anyone. I had a developed my speed and techniques beyond anything that I could have imagined eight months ago. On top of all that, my chief instructor and mentor was the highest ranking non-Japanese black belt in the world.

"Still watch his legs," said Steve, thoughtfully.

He led with his right foot and right hand forward. I mirror-matched his stance with my left foot and left hand. The contest would only last for two minutes, not a long time in terms of time, but a long time not to blink. I refocused my eyes to allow my peripheral vision to take in the whole of his long, lanky frame. I could see all of his body well enough to detect the physical signal that would precede any attack. We had also been taught that all physical movement was preceded by eye movement, that's why it was wise not to blink, as you might just miss something!

And there it was, almost imperceptible, a very rapid flick of his eyes to my right. Not once, but twice, in very quick succession. The first flick gave me the direction, the second the target area he was aiming for – the exposed right side of my head. His stance and my cover gave him two choices: *Shuto*, an open hand chop to my right temple, or *Mawashi Geri*, a round house kick to just under my right ear.

My eye caught the next movement as his left knee had started to rise. It looked like the *Mawashi Geri*. His left knee had started to move outwards, and his ankle upwards, leaving his toes still planted to the floor. It was going to be the *Mawashi Geri* for sure.

Instinctively, in a time that it takes far less to think, my right elbow started to rise in harmony with his foot. My right hand stayed down to block any sudden change to a frontal attack.

At the same time, my body started to swivel to my left and my left hand started to draw back and would continue to move until the little finger of my upward clenched fist would brush my left nipple. I had instinctively started to get my body set up to deliver *Chudan Tsuki*, a straight punch that would revolve towards his solar plexus and score a full point to win the contest.

His foot was still coming outwards and upwards, following the momentum of his knee that preceded it and disclosed its path. There was suddenly a slight change of angle – it was not going to be the side of the head after all, he was going to try to come under my guard and score his point by connecting with the side of my rib cage, under my arm. Cunning, I thought, as I rapidly changed the direction of my elbow to downwards to prepare...

Then the impossible happened. It was like watching a flat pebble skip on a perfectly calm sea. His foot 'bounced' on nothing but thin air and, with gathering momentum, smashed against the side of my head, knocking me down and out of the contest! My neck was sore and my ego bruised, but as a team we did well!

By the next day I was in trouble with my neck and ended up in hospital. An X-ray showed that I had chipped a bone in my neck, which ended up in a protective collar for a long time. When the collar was removed, I went back to the *Dojo* to resume training, but something had changed. I just could not fight the same way. In spite of all my efforts, and those of Steve, I was far too protective of my neck and spent far too much of my time on the defence rather than the attack. I had lost my edge and my confidence with it, and I drifted away. I bought a surfboard, swapped *Dojo* floors and opponents' feet for soft waves to fall into, and fell in love with the sea. I did still miss Steve and the gang, but felt that there was no way that I could settle for being just another 'also ran' in karate circles.

The whole point of this story is that if I had been aware then of the knowledge and techniques that are contained in these pages relating to *Walking Beyond Your Limits*, then I would have been able to go back fully to competitive karate.

...But I didn't.

When Katherine was five years of age and her brother James was two, we got into the habit of having boiled eggs and soldiers for breakfast on Sundays. To make the eggs more interesting, I started to draw pictures on the eggs with a set of indelible felt tipped pens.

One Sunday morning, as I was preparing the breakfast eggs, Katherine turned up asking if she could draw her own picture. I readily agreed and handed her a felt tipped pen and an egg. "*I'm going to draw a flower,*" she told me as she started to draw on the egg that was resting on the kitchen worktop. The worktop was high, and Katherine was not very tall. The egg slipped from her fingers and rolled off the worktop to splat on the floor. Katherine burst into tears: "*I've broken my egg and now you will be cross with me,*" she sobbed. Well, even if I was, I couldn't be cross now, I thought, as I dried her tears and handed her another egg. Katherine was delighted and successfully drew her flower, mostly on her egg, without further mishap.

Raggs, a large black cat that we had at the time, was also delighted and cleaned up the contents of the broken egg. We all had a pleasant breakfast that morning, with Katherine proudly showing the results of her handiwork to James. As this was all happening, a sudden thought crossed my mind: in similar circumstances, in other houses around the world, what would have happened to all the other Katherines who dropped their eggs that day?

I know the answer: "*That's it – you've dropped your egg, now you can't have one. You will have to have just soldiers for breakfast while you watch James eat his egg.*" Just how important do you think Katherine would have felt that morning if the same had happened to her. Just a little less important than an egg?

By the age of seven, most children have developed some kind of doubts about their own importance. This results in anything from a lack of confidence to a downright inferiority complex. Parents, teachers and, later in life, friends, workmates and bosses can destroy or reduce your level of self confidence without meaning to or even realising it. What a pity that many of us are taught from an early age that we are not that clever. Kids will grow up to be exactly what you tell them they are.

James came in not that long ago and gushed out: "*I'm sorry, Daddy, I have scratched your new car.*" I rushed out with him to survey the damage, a nasty jagged scratch down the front wing. I just looked at in horror (the car was three days old). James saw my face and started to explain how it had happened. "*It was Scot's fault,*" he told me, "*he left his bike on the pavement and I had to swerve around it to stop hitting it and that's when I hit your car.*" Then he quickly added: "*But I'm more important than a car, aren't I Daddy!*"

"*Only just,*" I told him, but I knew he was right.

Unless you do something to restore or increase your own level of self confidence, you could spend the rest of your 30,000 days suffering from a lack of confidence. Here is a formula that will help you find or regain all the confidence you need – and then some.

The Self Confidence Formula

1 Tell yourself that you are great – every day.

2 Always look and act with confidence.

3 Get rid of the baggage of your own negative thought viruses.

4 If you want to fly with the eagles, don't mix with turkeys.

5 Remember that nobody can make you feel inferior without your permission.

6 Do not try – do!

7 Always believe that you are more important than an egg.

Let's take it one step at a time:

1 Tell yourself that you are great – every day

If you are not getting your share of praise and recognition from others, it is about time that you started to praise and recognise yourself. Go on – pat yourself on the back as often as you can and as often as you deserve it. It will do wonders for the way you feel about who you are and what you do. If you can start to feel good about yourself, then it is far more likely that others will feel good about you too.

2 Always look and act with confidence

The secret of being successful is to look successful, and the same rule can be applied to confidence. If you would like to be more confident, then just imagine that you are.

The following words are based on the thoughts of Milton H Erikson. They are very powerful, and an excellent way to help you gain more confidence. Read them as often as you feel you need to.

> *"You don't consider yourself a confident salesperson who always achieves sales excellence, do you? Well let's pretend that you are an excellent salesperson who is very good at your job. One of the best, in fact, if not the best salesperson who ever sold.*
>
> *The most important thing... when you are pretending this... is to understand... that you are REALLY not... you are just pretending... and if you pretend really well, the people you are selling to will start to pretend to be buyers. And then they will forget that they are pretending... and become your customers.*
>
> *But don't be fooled by all this."*

3 Get rid of the baggage of your own negative thought viruses

We don't have to be prisoners of our own negative emotions.

People weigh themselves down with bag after bag of negative beliefs about themselves. No wonder they never get anywhere fast.

Negative beliefs like:

- *"I'm not much, but I'm all I've got"*
- *"Nobody loves me"*
- *"I'm not very important"*
- *"I can never get anything right"*
- *"I'll never make anything of myself"*

Your unconscious mind has difficulty in distinguishing between what you imagine and what is really true. So when you hit it with a thought virus, it says to itself: "*Message received and understood. I'll make sure:*"

- *"That you're not much"*
- *"That nobody will love you"*
- *"That you are not very important"*
- *"That you will never get things right"*
- *"That you will never make anything of yourself"*

Your head, just like a computer, can be programmed. Kick out the negatives and replace them with positives. It does not matter a bit if you think the positive statements are not true, the end result will always be the same:

- *You will be much more than you thought*
- *People will love you*
- *You will be important*
- *You will get things right*
- *You will make something of yourself*

Your unconscious will take care of that for you: *"Positive message received and understood."*

4 If you want to fly with the eagles, don't mix with turkeys

There is always somebody about that wants to put you down, isn't there? Stop listening to those people. Leave them to get on with their own negative thoughts and behaviours. Think of the people that you like and enjoy spending time with. Ask yourself the question why this is so. The answer is always the same. The people you like to be with are the ones that make you feel important to them personally. Spend more time with these people. It will do you and your self confidence the power of good.

5 Remember that nobody can make you feel inferior without your permission

A pal of mine in the industry got into a terrible state a few years back. He worked for a boss who was always putting him down. As time passed, my poor pal went from bad to worse to feelings of total inferiority. It got to the stage where one night, as he was driving home, he started to work out the various ways of killing his boss, and then he realised that he wasn't kidding. That's when he left and started his own business; he regained his confidence and is now doing very well indeed.

Hopefully you will not find yourself in this situation. If you do start feeling that someone else is making you feel insecure, inferior or uncomfortable, then please remember that this cannot be done without your consent.

They have the problem, not you. So

- Stay feeling confident
- Stay feeling as good as anybody
- Stay feeling comfortable

6 Do not try – do!

This is based on the thoughts of Yoda, that famous 20th century American philosopher who once told Luke Skywalker:

"Try not: Do or do not – there is no 'try'."

Just try a little experiment to prove this to yourself right now. Put this book down and try, really try, to pick it up again. Do you get the point of Yoda's message? Either you do it or you don't, either you have self confidence or you don't. Don't even think of trying to be self confident.

"I will try to be more self confident" will not work for you. *"I am self confident"* will.

7 Always believe that you are more important than an egg

A Fabergé egg, a racehorse or a Rolls Royce, because like Katherine, you are, you know.

Have you ever stopped to think what an incredible person you are? You have a brain that is far superior to any computer that has ever been built. You have a body that lives and breathes totally automatically. You are a very special person; you are unique. There is nobody else in the world just like you... you are one of a kind.

The main points again

1 By the age of seven, most children have developed some kind of doubts about their own importance.

2 You could spend your life suffering from a lack of confidence unless you do something about it.

3 The self confidence formula:

- Tell yourself that you are great – every day
- Always look and act with confidence
- Get rid of the baggage of your own negative thought viruses
- If you want to fly with the eagles, don't mix with turkeys
- Remember that nobody can make you feel inferior without your permission
- Do not try – do!
- Always believe that you are more important than an egg

4 There is nobody else in the world just like you... you are one of a kind

SECTION TEN

Out into the Unknown

"We chatted away like two old friends, the MP and I."

CHAPTER 30
Non-Showroom Traffic

"The more you expose yourself
to the risk of selling something,
the more you will succeed"

Reading the evening paper the other decade, I happened on an article about the new chairman of the House of Commons Motor Club. Now I didn't even know that the House of Commons had its own Motor Club, but I did recognise the name of its new chairman. The name was Sir Gerald Nabarro. Sir Gerald was a larger-than-life character who loved motor cars. He had at least three with the consecutive number plates; NAB1, NAB2 and NAB3. When he wasn't messing about with motors, he spent the rest of his time being a Conservative MP.

As I read the article, I was struck with quite a forceful thought: *"What would it be like if I cornered the House of Commons Motor Club? You know, become the recognised supplier of cars to its members?"* It all seemed quite reasonable to me, so I decided to write to Sir Gerald to set up a meeting to discuss the possibility.

> Dear Sir Gerald
> Many congratulations on your recent appointment as chairman of the House of Commons Motor Club.
> I would be most grateful if you could spare a few minutes of your time to discuss the possibility of supplying cars to your members.
> Please do let me know when and where we could have our meeting.
> Yours sincerely

My Sales Manager gave me his 'Gosh, you're weird' look when I showed him the letter, but agreed to let me send it off, shaking his head sadly, but not unkindly. Much to my Sales Manager's surprise, but not to mine, a reply on House of Commons notepaper duly arrived.

4th January, 1968

Dear Mr. Upsher,

HOUSE OF COMMONS MOTOR CLUB

Many thanks for your letter on 27th December, 1967, and perhaps you would telephone my Parliamentary Private Secretary, Miss Margaret House, at 222 7643 to make an appointment for us to meet at the House of Commons, for a chat for ten minutes on a mutually convenient date, following reassembly of Parliament on 17th January, 1968.

With warmest regards and very best wishes for the New Year,

Yours sincerely

Gerald Nabarro

David Upsher, Esq.

That can't be bad, I thought, it's not every car salesman who has important MPs who they don't know sending them warmest regards and best wishes. "*Only the weird ones,*" said my Sales Manager. So I rang Miss Margaret House and fixed up an appointment to call and meet Sir Gerald.

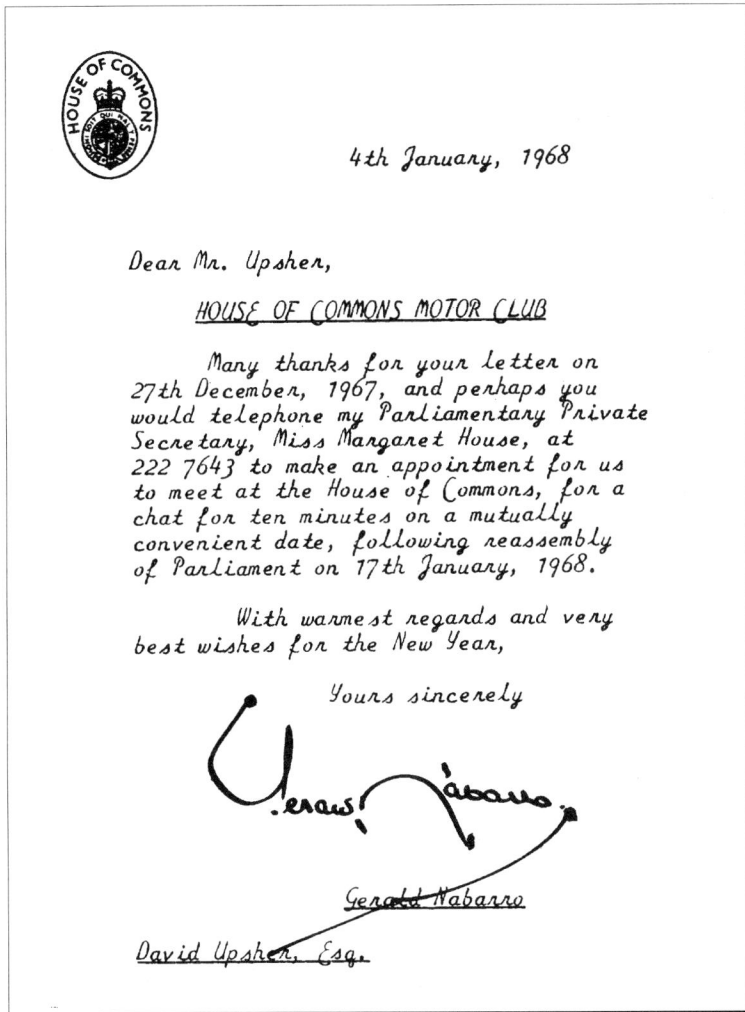

The day of the appointment arrived and it felt special. It was going to be an enlightening and exciting day. I had never met an MP before, let alone visited the House of Commons. I told the policeman on the gate who I was and who I had come to see, and I was directed to a long room with tables and chairs and many people milling about.

A man dressed like a cross between a penguin and a hotel porter went off to tell Sir Gerald that his guest had arrived. In next to no time at all I was shaking the hand of Sir Gerald himself. He invited me to sit down and tell him more about my idea. *"It's simple,"* I explained, *"MPs need cars but don't have much spare time. My company has plenty of cars, we're just down the road and I have the time to arrange demonstrations, take orders and deliver cars. I would be happy to help with the House of Commons Motor Club members' motoring needs. Particularly as they are often a long way from home and might appreciate having a local person to look after them."*

"It is a good idea and I commend you for it," said Sir Gerald stroking his abundant moustache thoughtfully. *"But,"* he added with a sigh, *"there is a problem. MPs, as you say, are often a long way from home and their constituencies. Now, if you were an MP for Preston and you bought your car in Putney, how do you feel the population of Preston would feel?"* He went on to answer his own question: *"They would feel let down, that's how they would feel."*

Well, I hadn't thought of that one, and I could see the sense in Sir Gerald's words. He could obviously see the disappointment in my face. *"Now you're here,"* he said in a large and interested voice, *"tell me all about yourself and what you think of the motor industry."* My sadness diminishing, we chatted away like two old friends, the MP and I. I did tell him about myself and we talked about the motor industry. We both marvelled at the fact that the sale of vehicles in this country that had not been built in Great Britain had just gone into double figures for the first time, ten per cent would you believe it. Where would it all end? We parted company with firm handshakes and soft smiles. Sir Gerald returned to helping run the country; I returned to a scornful Sales Manager.

It was three weeks later that the showroom door was opened by a well suited distinguished looking man: *"I'm looking for David Upsher,"* he said.

"That's me," I replied.

"Ah, just the person. I was asking my friend Sir Gerald Nabarro where would be a good place to buy a car and he mentioned your name. I want to buy a new Rover..."

And he did.

And he wasn't the only one from that source either.

David Heslop, Managing Director of Mazda Cars UK Limited, often asks Dealer Principals and sales staff: *"How's business?"* If the reply is anything to do with a shortage of showroom traffic, David will then ask: *"How's your non-showroom traffic?"* A salesperson's job is all about finding a customer, helping that customer buy a vehicle and then keeping that customer. If not enough customers are coming to you, then you will have to go to them.

A few salespeople can live off showroom traffic. It depends on the franchise, the dealership and the methods of marketing employed. The rest of us should adopt the mentality of the vulture who was sitting in a tree and who turned to his mate and said: *"Stuff all this hanging about, I think I'll go and kill something."* You don't have to live off showroom traffic alone. You can control your own volume and profit opportunities.

The Vital Need to Find Customers

The deals that you do not do are never really 'lost deals'. They usually end up safe in the hands of your competition. That's business, and should be both acceptable and expected. You can never *'win them all'*. Whatever you do and however you try, a proportion of customers will buy elsewhere. That's not always your fault. It could be that you don't have the right vehicles for the right people. But what about the customers who never think of coming to you in the first place?

A pal of mine worked for a Vauxhall dealer in a fairly large town. One day a man came in and said that he wanted to look at a particular vehicle in the showroom. He explained to my friend that he had been into the other Vauxhall dealer on the other side of town, but they could not show him what he wanted to see. In fact, it was the salesperson there that had told him to call in at my friend's showroom to see the vehicle that he was interested in. The suggestion was that the man should go back to the other showroom and order the vehicle from there.

As my pal was showing the customer the vehicle, the man appeared fascinated that there were two Vauxhall dealers in town. He had had no idea that they were there, in spite of the fact that he had lived on the other side of town for 14 years. My pal explained that they too had been in business for about the same amount of time and was fascinated that anybody did not know that his company existed.

The whole point of all this is:

"How many deals do you lose because the customers never even think of coming to you in the first place?"

There is a secondary learning point to this particular story. And that is, not to do what the other salesperson did. By the time my pal had finished, the customer never made it back to the other showroom to order his new vehicle.

Every salesperson who seeks to become very successful and truly professional is best advised to master the art of creating 'non-showroom traffic'. You will never be the success that you really could be by waiting for all the business to come to you.

The problem is that most salespeople in the motor industry are not all that keen on prospecting. That probably includes you, and it would be well worth your time to ask yourself why this is so. In order to help you identify why, here is a 'Top Ten Reasons Not to Prospect' checklist to help you. Tick as many reasons as you like.

I am not all that keen on prospecting because:

- ☐ *"My boss expects me to do it"*
- ☐ *"If I go out, I might miss something"*
- ☐ *"It's a total waste of time"*
- ☐ *"Customers don't like being pestered"*
- ☐ *"I haven't got the time to prospect"*
- ☐ *"My company should find the customers for me"*
- ☐ *"I just get paid for closing deals"*
- ☐ *"If I do find some customers, they could be 'nicked' by other salespeople I work with"*
- ☐ *"I just don't like doing it"*
- ☐ *"You don't get good enough results to justify the effort"*

That's a pretty powerful list, isn't it? Most salespeople could tick most of those boxes. So that's it then, prospecting is out for you. Let's skip this chapter and move on to something more useful... Unless:

- Living up to my boss's expectations could be no bad thing
- If I go out, I might find more business than I miss
- Done properly it could be my time well spent
- Customers respond positively if I approach them properly

- I could find the time to find customers
- For every customer the company finds me, I should find one for my company
- I could close even more deals if I could find more deals to close
- I could make sure that customers I find want to do business with me personally
- I could find ways of prospecting that were enjoyable
- I could get good enough results to justify the effort

Perhaps we had better read this chapter after all.

The Real Reason Not to Prospect

The real reason why most motor industry salespeople don't like prospecting is that very few know how to do it properly. Also, most salespeople think prospecting is something to do with selling. This chapter is all about how to prospect properly, which has got very little to do with selling.

Prospecting is all about finding people to sell to. It's the 'opening a relationship' stage of the sale. It's getting in contact with people you don't know, so when they do want to buy a vehicle, they think of coming to you.

If you **can** get face-to-face with more potential customers before they even consider finding somewhere to buy a vehicle, then you will have a very good chance of helping that customer buy from you and not your competition.

Picking the Right Targets to Aim At

There are Customers Who Seek You Out

- Incoming telephone enquiries
- Showroom enquiries
- Enquiries forwarded by manufacturers
- People you know
- Referrals

These are the easy ones, but let us explore each opportunity. You don't have to do them all. It would be far better if you concentrated initially on a few methods that appeal to you personally.

- **Incoming telephone enquiries**

Already dealt with under *The Telephone Enquiry* (see page 62). Worth mentioning again as an incoming telephone enquiry is one of the 'hottest' prospects that you will ever get.

- Find out what the customer wants
- Establish how you can help the customer get what he wants
- Get face-to-face
- Help the customer to buy what he wants

Showroom enquiries

- Dealt with under *Meeting and Greeting* (see page 96). The 'very hottest' prospect of all. Always take full advantage of every face-to-face selling opportunity.

Enquiries forwarded by manufacturers

- Real hot chestnuts, these ones. Considered to be a total waste of time by all but a few enlightened salespeople. The true value and how to handle can be found under *Demonstrating your Product* (see page 174). Dealerships and salespeople who take manufacturer generated leads seriously do very well indeed. In the dim and distant past of the Rover SDI, Rover came up with an offer that was very hard to refuse:

"Try one of our vehicles and we will give you a side of smoked salmon"

A brilliant mailshot was sent out to the right potential customers, mostly local professional people, including doctors, dentists, vets and so on as well as business people. The response was enormous – a side of smoked salmon for nothing was an offer few could refuse. There were the dealers who took the campaign seriously and insisted that in order to get your salmon, you had to have your demonstration. There were other dealers who simply signed the salmon order forms without the need for a demonstration.

Many vehicles were sold as a result of this campaign. When it came to signing vehicle order forms, which of the dealers do you think got the business? Those who gave the demonstrations or those who didn't?

- **People you know**

  These could include:
  - Business connections
  - Current customers
  - Current prospects
  - Family connections
  - Former business contacts
  - Friends
  - Neighbours
  - Organisation/club contacts
  - Personal contacts
  - Church contacts
  - School/college connections
  - Social contacts
  - Sport/hobby contacts
  - Tradespeople
  - Everybody and anybody

It is not suggested that you should ram it down everybody's throat what you do for a living. That would be a great way to end up very lonely. Nevertheless, people you know should know what you do for a living and that you would be prepared to help them in relation to a vehicle purchase. A soft approach is normally called for, and if you know people really well, leave it for them to come to you, when and if they want to.

The best way to remind people you know what you do for a living is to tell the odd story about your working experiences. If you haven't got any to tell, then borrow someone else's. There should be enough in this book to keep you going for more than a while.

- **Referrals**

Well covered under *From Delivery to Repeat Business* (see page 314). All referrals should be taken very seriously. Always make sure that the person that gave you the referral knows the outcome.

If you have got what the referred person wants to buy, then you have a very good chance of helping them buy it. Apart from having the need for a vehicle, they will have a desire or need to please the person that recommended you – by taking their advice.

There are customers you go to

Not all customers will come to you, so you have to find ways of going to them. Approaches that will be acceptable to the potential customer – in order to give them the inclination to allow you to open a relationship – and to you the salesperson – in order to give you the inclination to make the effort to open relationships with people that you have to get to know.

There are acceptable approaches that satisfy both customers' inclinations and your own. Not all the methods will work for everybody all the time. The recommendation is that you select just two or three ways of finding customers that appeal to you personally. This will give you some variety, plus the opportunity to measure the results of each selected way. Listed here are your options to select from. After the options list, you will find details of the recommended method of approach for each source.

Non-Showroom Traffic Sources

Sources from your dealership

- Owners
- Lapsed owners
- Previous salespeople's owners
- Service and parts department
- Existing long term prospects
- Bodyshop
- Forecourt
- Company staff
- Companies you buy from
- Providers of professional services

Sources outside your dealership

- Publications
- Local shops
- Local householders
- Local temporary displays
- Professional people and partnerships
- Societies, associations, groups and amenities

- Sports clubs, social clubs and other meeting places
- Prospect locators
- People you buy from
- Cold spearing

The choice is yours

As you can see, there are plenty of ways to choose from. So you can see even more clearly, let's flesh out each non-showroom traffic source for you.

Sources from your own dealership

Owners

Your best potential customers are your own customers. That's why it is so important to keep in touch with them. The methods of doing this are amply covered in *From Delivery to Repeat Business*. This is one of the easiest ways of increasing non-showroom traffic.

Lapsed owners

These are the people who used to buy from you or your company and who no longer do so for some reason. Find out the reason by direct contact, unless you already know it. The reason could range from dissatisfaction with past buying or aftersales experience to the fact that their motoring needs have changed to fall outside your product range.

Once you know the reason, you will have the opportunity to do something about it.

- Time can erode dissatisfaction with past experiences
- Product ranges change just as customers' motoring needs change. The two could be in harmony again.

Telephone lapsed owners and find out why they are lapsed owners. Then you will have the opportunity to win them back. Quite often, the fact that you have taken the trouble to get back in touch will be the difference that makes the difference.

Previous salespeople's owners

Often referred to as 'orphaned owners' – with good reason. The person you replaced left your company and you get his old customers to follow up. You did not create them, you do not know them. Let's face it, you don't have that much inclination to get in touch. On joining one company, I was given a whole box of orange, eight by five owner/prospect cards that had been 'owned' by the salesperson that I had just replaced.

I was instructed by my new Sales Manager to make contact with all of them and tell them that I was now the person who would be responsible for looking after them. This did not strike me as being an exciting or interesting task, and came well down my list of priorities. When my Sales Manager started to ask what I was doing about the cards, I decided to go in for some 'creative follow-up'. How that works is you sit there, select about eight of these cards and 'imagine' getting in touch with these people. Then you write the 'weather report'.

"Happy with car"
"Not changing at the moment"
"Will call me when interested"
"Not in the market at the moment"
"She said he was out and will let him know I called"
"He said she was out"
... and so on and so on.

After a couple of weeks, I had made quite a big dent in the box of prospect cards. It was then that the Sales Manager called me into his office. He gave me a right going over and in no uncertain terms told me what he thought of me and how disappointed he was that I was not doing what he had asked me to do. He asked me why I had been writing false information on the cards and I told him rather sheepishly that I thought the cards were a bit of a waste of time. He took a handful of the cards and went through them with me.

He knew most of the people, and told me all about them. They sounded quite interesting and well worth talking to. I grasped at the second chance I was given and started to make contact for real. Without exception, the people that I contacted were delighted that I had got in touch. Promises of future business were made and enough of these promises were kept to make the effort well worthwhile.

Service and parts department

Many customers use your aftersales facilities but do not buy from your sales department. There could be some good reasons for this, but not always. I had my cars serviced by one company for six years. The service was brilliant, but never once in that six year period did anybody from sales get in touch and offer to supply my next car. Find out who uses your aftersales facilities, including your bodyshop if you have one. If you did not supply the car, then make direct contact by telephone (or face-to-face when they call to collect) and offer to help them the next time they are in the market for a new or used car.

Existing long term prospects

These are the people with whom you have had some contact at some time, and they have yet to buy. It is important to establish exactly what your chances are of doing some business at some time in the future. If there is little or no hope of converting a long term prospect into a customer, then you should seek management permission to terminate the prospect. Those who look like they might buy should be followed up with as much care as those customers who have already bought.

Bodyshop

It is truly amazing that some customers go off a vehicle completely if it has been in even the slightest accident. If you do have a bodyshop, it would certainly pay you to find out who has had, or is about to have, an estimate for bodywork. Then, before the repair is even carried out, get in touch with the owner and ask if they would like to part-exchange their damaged vehicle for a nice new or nearly new shiny one. Everybody wins this way:

The customer:

- They get an undamaged vehicle and no hassle

You, the salesperson:

- You make a sale and a satisfied customer

Your company:

- They get a part-exchange for the right price and the insurance company pays for the repair

Forecourt

If you have a forecourt, it can be an excellent source of non-showroom traffic – fuel account customers who do not buy from you, for instance. Telephone and find out the reason why they do not buy their vehicles from your company. If you are close to the forecourt and see an interesting potential part-exchange pull in, go and introduce yourself to the driver. Tell him who you are, give him your business card and offer your help the next time he is in the market for a vehicle. Most people have no objection to this kind of approach if it is friendly and sincerely meant.

Company staff

Some companies have staff introduction schemes: 'If you bring us a customer, we will pay you a reward'. Irrespective of whether your company has such a scheme or not, it will pay you well to take the trouble to get to know the people you work with. Let them know that you would be pleased to help anybody they know in relation to a new or used vehicle sale. Live up to the promise of good service by looking after the customers that you already deal with. The people you work with will notice, and you will get in-house referrals.

Companies you buy from

Your company does business with many other companies. How about generating a little reciprocal business? One slightly unusual way of doing this could be classed as being a little cheeky. If you have got the cheek, try this idea out. Find out when and where your company pays for the goods and services that you purchase. If it is a local business, take the payment cheque around by hand. Ask to see somebody important. (The owner in a small business, a departmental manager in a company a little larger.) Explain that you have called to give them some money.

They will see you all right, and then you have the opportunity to say something like:

"My Managing Director has asked me to bring this to you personally and to thank you for the way that you have looked after us. The opportunity to help you in return and perhaps your company would be very much appreciated. May I ask what vehicle do you run?"

Take it from there. If the person you are talking to is not in the market, then perhaps someone else in the company might be. Perhaps the company itself might be in the market. If you don't ask, you will never know and if you don't know, you will never get.

Providers of professional services

This would include auditors, accountants, solicitors, consultants and bankers. All of these services involve potential purchasers, people who have good reason to buy from your company if at all possible. Write a letter offering to help the next time they are in the market to buy. Follow that letter up by telephone to confirm your interest and to gauge the chance of doing some business at some time in the future. Then keep in touch according to the chances of doing some business.

Sources outside your own dealership

Some salespeople appear to be chained to the showroom, terrified of going out in case they might miss something. Outside the showroom is a big wide world full of potential customers. So who in your area should you be talking to? How do you find them? And how do you convert them from people you don't know into warm friendly prospects?

Publications

One very useful publication is your local newspaper. People sell vehicles privately by advertising them. There is nothing to stop you telephoning those people and asking why they want to sell the vehicle. If it is anything to do with purchasing another one, then offer your services. Some salespeople who use this method prefer to use last week's paper. Then they are talking to people who are more than keen to move on a vehicle that they still have.

If a local company is advertising for staff and is offering a company vehicle as part of the package, there is no reason why you can't telephone and explain that you don't want the job but you could provide the vehicle.

If somebody is in the news for a positive reason, such as promotion, winning an award or a lottery prize, business expansion or any form of praise or recognition, write and congratulate them. Ask them if they would like to buy a new vehicle to celebrate their success. The bigger they are, the bigger they fall for this one. So make sure they fall in your direction.

Local shops

This is the 'BBC' of prospecting. The butcher, the baker, the candlestick maker. Bigger companies are dealt with under *Finding Your Own Business* (see page 462). This is the very best way for salespeople who are new to selling vehicles to get their 'feet wet' and gain confidence in the art of creating non-showroom traffic.

Here is the plan:

- Call into the local shops and small businesses in your area
- Make contact with the first person you meet
- Ask: *"Are you the guv'nor?"* (The reason for this is *'bitter personal experience!'* If you ask the man in the white coat who is sweeping the floor *"Is the guv'nor in?"* and he says *"I am the guv'nor"*, you have just lost all your brownie points.)

- If the person you are talking to is not the guv'nor, find out who is. Get the name and get face-to-face
- Hand over your business card, company information, catalogues, used car stock list and so on
- Thank the guv'nor for seeing you and offer your help the next time a change of vehicle is being considered
- Offer this in a very friendly way, and keep the conversation short and to the point
- Then keep in touch with all the warm prospects, in an effort to kindle them into happy customers

Local householders

This is the most successful way ever invented to increase your non-showroom traffic. Yet so few salespeople use it. It's a good job they don't, because if they did, then it would no longer be worth doing.

If you are one of those very rare people who is prepared to make this part of your daily sales activities, then you too will increase you sales by an extra vehicle a week, every week, which is the norm for all but the most specialised franchises.

This is how you work it:

Phase One – Planning

- Drive out into the area that surrounds your business and select an area where the kind of people who like to buy what you sell live.
- Park your vehicle and start to walk the area on foot.
- Start to 'pick off' potential purchasers on a residential basis. In other words, match your product to the types of houses that you see, plus what's parked outside or on the drive.
- Take your list of selected residences to your local library and ask to see the electoral roll for that area.
- Note down the names to go with the houses.
- Use the telephone directory to find the numbers to go with the names.

Phase Two – Implementing Your Plan

◆ Sit down in a quiet office and telephone five people from your list every weekday.

◆ Get through to the person you wish to speak to and use a script similar to the one produced here.

◆ Remember that you are not trying to sell. The whole purpose of this exercise is to identify the prime people to open a relationship with.

◆ Telephone at the best time, which can vary from area to area – in most areas between ten and twelve in the morning would appear to be best. You will speak to the lady of the house, who will give you the information you want 95% of the time.

◆ Say: *"Good morning, Mrs Hawk,"* as opposed to *"Is Mrs Hawk there?"* If it is not Mrs Hawk, then the 'lady what does' will tell you and get Mrs Hawk. If it is Mrs Hawk, she will unconsciously feel that she knows you and start the conversation more readily.

◆ Make your opening statement with style and confidence, making sure that you get both make and model of the vehicle.

◆ Then ask the other questions, none of which can be classed as 'selling'. At this stage, all we are getting is information.

◆ If you are challenged (which is very rare) as in *"What's this all about?"*, explain: *"Well, Mrs Hawk, what my company is trying to do is to find our future customers but without being too pushy about it... and did you have the vehicle you drive from new?"* That's right! Straight on with the questions... with confidence.

◆ That 'one last question' is optional, but could be of great use to companies who are keen to develop their businesses to cover all the services that local people would like to be provided and be prepared to pay for.

◆ ◆ ◆

Local Householder's Contact Report

Date of Call ______________________ Customer's Name ______________________

Time ______________________ Telephone Number ______________________

Address ______________________

____

____

Important:

You are not trying to sell – but do not miss an opportunity!

Good morning, Mr/Mrs ______________________

My name is ______________ of ______________, your local dealership.

I would be grateful if you would help me. My company is trying to obtain some idea of the makes of vehicle that both you and the other people are driving in the ______________ area, so could you spare me a minute and tell me what vehicle you drive?

---

1 Make and model of vehicle? ______________________

2 How long have you had it? ______________________

3 What other vehicles are there in the family? ______________________

4 Did you have the vehicle you drive from new? ______________________

5 Do you buy locally? ______________________

One last question: are there any services that you think should be available to local motorists but are not currently on offer? ______________________

Other remarks

____

____

____

Action to be taken

____

____

____

◆ Space on our example form is provided to make other notes and decide what to do with each new contact.

◆ 'Hot prospects' will be followed up fast. It really does happen. It is a mathematical certainty that someone will say to you: *"It's a funny thing that you should ring, but..."*

◆ Totally cold (*"We haven't got a vehicle and have no intention of getting one"*) should get a polite 'Thank you for your help' letter. You've got nothing to lose by giving local people that kind of courtesy. Even if they don't drive, they will know people who do.

◆ With other people, you will have to decide what to do as you make contact. It could be a case of taking round catalogues. You might decide to offer a demonstration. You might desperately want the vehicle that they currently drive and get back in touch and offer a good deal. You might even decide to knock on the door so that the more interesting sounding people will have your face to go with your name.

◆ Everybody, unless they come in the 'hot' or 'totally cold' examples discussed above, should get a letter similar to the example shown here.

> Dear Mrs Hawk
> Thank you so much for your help when we telephoned today to enquire about the makes of vehicles that you and other people are driving in our area.
> As you may know, apart from being the official dealer for this area, we do specialise in used vehicles of all types, and offer a comprehensive range of parts and service facilities.
> We will be inviting you to come and meet us in the very near future, on the occasion of our next showroom promotion, but if in the meantime we can help you, then please contact us.
> Looking forward to having you as a customer.
> Yours sincerely

That's right, you invite the *'right'* people to your showroom and other promotional events. There is always the need to find good potential prospects to invite. This method will certainly identify these people for you. Mix them in with your existing customers and let the people who you have already sold to do some of the future selling for you.

What's in it for you?

You can most likely recall the opening statement on this section about local householders: *The most successful way to increase your non-showroom traffic…* . Prospecting, just like selling, is a mathematical certainty.

If you spend half an hour a day doing five calls, as described, you will be making 25 calls a week, or 1,200 calls per year. Some of these calls will be a waste of time, but from the total of 1,200 calls, you should be able to achieve a 4% success level, based on our experience. It doesn't sound like a lot, but in actual fact, it is a vehicle a week. It also means that if you get £50 for selling a vehicle, every time you pick up the phone you earn another £2.

You will also end up, at the end of a year, with a list of what 1,200 local people currently drive, quite useful marketing information for your company. Also, you could consider that useful information when looking for a particular used vehicle for a customer. You could even end up doing two deals. A new vehicle to a new customer, their part-exchange to the used vehicle enquiry.

Local temporary displays

What a great way of creating non-showroom traffic. There are all sorts of places that this can be done – railway stations, shopping malls, large food supermarkets and DIY stores – and all sorts of ways of doing it.

The simplest was the Ford salesman at our village fete a few years ago. It was a 'Guess how many balloons are in this vehicle' competition. I paid my money and had a go. The Ford man asked me for my name, address and telephone number. I asked him why he wanted my number. He told me that if I won, he would ring and let me know. I didn't win, but the Ford salesman did. He must have collected, at the very least, one hundred names, addresses and phone numbers of potential future customers.

Shortly afterwards, I received a lovely letter and an information pack on the Ford range, plus the invitation to come on down. I followed the Ford man up six weeks later out of curiosity. He told me that he could trace two sales back to our village fete, but would expect to do at least one more shortly.

Slightly more formal was the beautiful Honda display of three highly polished red cars at our local garden centre. In the middle of the triangle they formed was a high quality patio set complete with shade and cushions for the chairs. All you had to do to have a chance to win the patio set was to leave your name and address. This would be entered into a draw. I got a letter to tell me that I hadn't won the patio set but was welcome to have a complimentary test drive without obligation in the Honda of my choice.

This type of activity always generates non-showroom traffic. The kind of non-showroom traffic that always generates sales.

Professional people and partnerships

There are many of these, for example:

- Accountants
- Acupuncturists
- Auctioneers and valuers
- Auditors
- Business consultants
- Chiropodists
- Chiropractors
- Dental surgeons
- Estate agents
- Insurance brokers
- Investment consultants
- Life Assurance brokers
- Management consultants
- Mortgage brokers
- Motor insurance brokers
- Osteopaths
- Physicians and surgeons
- Physiotherapists
- Psychologists
- Psychotherapists
- Publicity agents
- Quantity surveyors
- Solicitors
- Surveyors and valuers
- Training centres
- Transport consultants
- Veterinary surgeons

Everybody wants these people as customers. They get bombarded with 'junk mail' and 'selling' telephone calls. A very specialised showroom promotion could work where you just invite this type of customer. The most successful way to get some business out of this section is through existing customers, referral business and the 'local householder' method of contact. Simply pick the kind of area where the local professional people live, and go there.

Societies, associations, groups and amenities

Another area to find non-showroom traffic, for instance:

- Citizens' advice bureaux
- Community centres
- Community councils
- County councils
- District councils
- Government departments
- Hospitals
- National societies (branch offices)
- Nursing and old people's homes
- Old peoples' welfare
- Probation and aftercare
- Samaritans
- Schools, colleges and universities
- Tenants' associations
- Voluntary services

Many of these organisations purchase vehicles, ranging from the district nurse car to the school bus. They are usually much easier to approach than the professional group. If you want to work in this area, then try to find out the name of the person responsible for vehicle purchases and use a similar approach to the 'local householders' method. If it's a fairly substantial organisation involving multiple sales, then use the techniques to be found in the chapter *Finding Your Own Business*.

Sports clubs, social clubs and other meeting places

Every salesperson should belong to at least one local sports or social club; the small cost can be greatly outweighed by the profits that come from meeting and mixing with groups of local people. Some places, like pubs, are even free to go into. Make sure that you become a remembered person for all the right reasons. You work during the day, but you are always a 'goodwill ambassador' for your company and yourself wherever you are and whatever you are doing.

Dave had a good idea. He put a sign up in his local pub which read

```
    Dave does not sell cars
      after eight o'clock
```

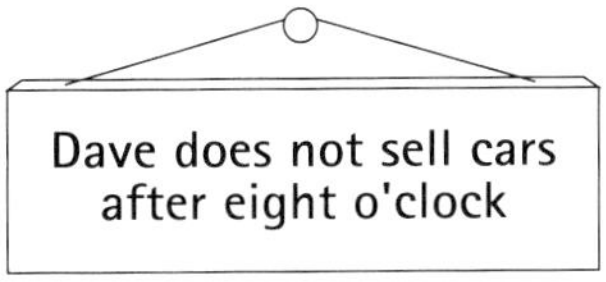

When people who knew Dave saw the sign, they remembered what he did for a living; people who did not know Dave would often ask what the sign meant. The result was that Dave did a lot of business after eight o'clock.

Try to get your company to invest in a small and inexpensive trophy or shield for a club competition. This is a great way of subtly keeping your company's name known. There was one company who had their name printed on dart boards and then distributed them free to all the local places that used or would use them for the same reason.

When talking to club members, you would be best advised not to keep touting for business, because your fellow club members will go off you. Squash played by yourself is such a solitary game! Remind people what you do for a living by telling the odd story about your work, as already suggested in this chapter. Then leave it to them to come to you.

◆ ◆ ◆

Prospect locators

Sometimes called 'bird dogs'. Salespeople have been known to say: *"I don't know anybody suitable"*. Here are just a few of the many people who can make brilliant bird dogs:

- Accountants
- Barbers and beauty shops
- Bartenders
- Body shops
- Car park attendants
- Car wash attendants
- Church connections
- Driving school instructors
- Estate agents
- Fellow club members
- Former business associates
- Friends
- Golf professionals
- Independent garages
- Milkmen
- Neighbours
- Newsagents
- Other salesmen
- Owners
- Part time workers
- People with whom you do business
- Policemen
- Pools collectors
- Postmen
- Service station attendants
- University students
- Waitresses and cafe owners

All these people know other people. Ask these kind of people, if you do know them, to let you know if they hear of anybody who is in the market to buy a vehicle. If your company has an introductory scheme, then you can offer a reward for successful introductions. The best bird dogs of all will do it for free because they like you and want to help.

People you buy from

What do you buy? All sorts of things from all sorts of people. Most of these people have vehicles. The person who cuts your hair certainly does, so does the man who runs the corner shop. Whatever happens, make sure that all the people you buy from know what you do for a living. Find out what they currently drive, what they think they will buy next and when. Simply offer your help and keep in touch.

Your doctor, dentist, hairdresser and so on should all have your brochures. People who have to wait to be seen will read those brochures as a change from a three-year-old edition of *Country Life*. Pin four or five of your business cards inside the front cover. They might not take the literature, but they will take a card if they want to talk to you.

Cold spearing

Gone out of fashion? Perhaps it's time to give 'cold spearing' another go. It's a funny technique, but one that can work well when done properly. All you do is find a vehicle that you would like to have as a part-exchange and leave a message on it. The back of your business card will do fine. The message is as varied as you are creative. It could be formal:

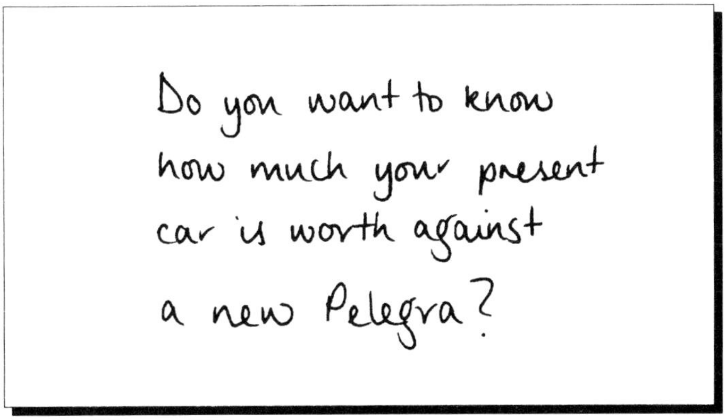
Do you want to know
how much your present
car is worth against
a new Pelegra?

It could be dramatic:

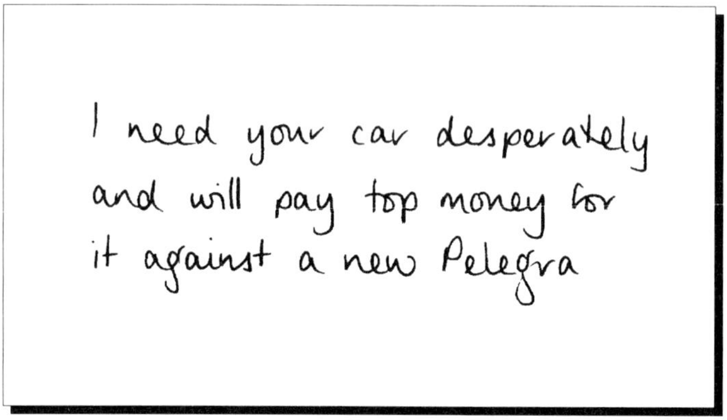
I need your car desperately
and will pay top money for
it against a new Pelegra

It could be frantic:

I HAVE SOLD YOUR CAR!!!
Please contact me
urgently

Write out your chosen message by hand and place it hand-written side out in the rubber of the driver's window near the door lock. This is a far better place than leaving it under the windscreen wiper.

Take your pick

So now you have plenty of choices. Remember, start with not more than three and see how you get on. There is one thing you will soon discover for sure: creating non-showroom traffic is much more interesting and rewarding than waiting for business to come to you. It's more profitable too.

The main points again

1 Ask yourself the David Heslop question: *"How's my non-showroom traffic?"*

2 You don't have to live off showroom traffic alone. You can control your own volume and profit opportunities.

3 You can't win all the business, but what about the customers who never think of coming to you in the first place.

4 Most salespeople in the motor industry are not all that keen on prospecting. The reason is that very few know how to do it properly.

5 Prospecting is nothing to do with selling. It's all about finding people to sell to.

6 There are customers who seek you out.

- Incoming telephone enquiries
- Showroom enquiries
- Enquiries forwarded by manufacturers
- People you know
- Referrals

7 Not all customers will come to you, so you have to find ways of going to them.

8 Not all methods work for everybody. Select two or three ways that appeal to you.

9 Non-showroom traffic sources, dealership:

- Owners
- Lapsed owners
- Previous salespeople's owners
- Existing long term prospects
- Bodyshop
- Forecourt
- Company staff
- Companies you buy from
- Providers of professional services

10 Sources outside your own dealership:

- Publications
- Local shops
- Local householders
- Local temporary displays
- Professional people and partnerships
- Societies, associations, groups and amenities
- Sports clubs, social clubs and other meeting places
- Prospect locations
- People you buy from
- Cold spearing

11 There are plenty of choices to pick from.

12 Creating non-showroom traffic is much more interesting and rewarding than waiting for business to come to you.

CHAPTER 31
Finding Your Own Business

"A foot in a customer's door

is worth two on your desk"

Business was a little slow; in fact, business had almost stopped. It was time to do something instead of waiting for something to do. But what to do? Then I remembered that I had recently read an article about a very large group of companies that had seven thousand company vehicles. Can you imagine it? Seven thousand company vehicles. To park one vehicle, you need 200 square feet. To park seven thousand you would need fourteen hundred thousand feet. That is twenty eight football pitches worth of parking space. What on earth would happen if everybody who had a company vehicle wanted to go to head office on the same day at the same time? The queue for the car park would be around twenty seven miles long. Some fleet, I thought. Some business opportunity. Think big, I reminded myself as I reached for the telephone.

Directory Enquiries had their head office number, and their head office number had the name of their head transport buyer, a Mr Savage. So far, so good. "*Where do I find Mr Savage?*" I asked the bored, busy, tight voice that represented their head office. "*Well here, of course, do you want me to put you through?*" she said fast and thin.

"*How kind,*" I said. "*Yes, please.*" And she did, as easy as that.

"*Savage,*" said the phone, loud in my ear. I re-tuned my ear to fit the larger volume. "*Mr Savage,*" I replied in BMW best, "*we haven't met yet. My name is David Upsher of BMW Park Lane. I understand that you are responsible for the acquisition of seven thousand company vehicles.*"

"*Well, something like that,*" Mr Savage said, "*but I do have help you know. What do you want anyway?*"

"*Well, like I said, we haven't met yet. If you and your department are responsible for the acquisition of seven thousand company vehicles, and my job is to supply vehicles to companies, then perhaps we should.*" I paused for breath and waited for some feedback. "*BMW you say?*" said Mr Savage.

"That is correct," I replied.

"In that case, we can't really be of help to each other," said Mr Savage, adding not unkindly, *"you are a bit previous, old son, because in the UK we operate a strictly 'Buy British' policy."*

Stuff it, I thought, as pictures of supplying the odd football pitch full of BMWs rapidly faded from the front of my visual mind. *"Do you think that the 'Buy British' policy will ever change?"* I asked, more in sorrow than hope.

"Could do, could do," he said thoughtfully. *"Nothing is forever. It depends on the big daddies."*

"The big daddies?" I repeated, with a puzzled look on my voice.

"Yeah, main board directors to you. It depends on them. They decide what to do. I just do it," he told me matter of factly. *"Mind you, if you want to discuss the possibility of a possible but improbable change of policy, then why don't you call in to the branch office today at any time between twelve and two."*

"Where is the branch office?" I asked uncertainly. He named a pub near his company's head office which was not far from the city of London *"I'm always there between noon and two, Monday to Friday."*

"Sure" I said, nothing to lose, *"I'll pop in and say hello. How will I recognise you?"*

"That's easy," said Mr Savage, *"I'm the little bloke with the pint of Guinness, you will find me right at the end of the bar to the right as you come in."* I told him that I would be there and thanked him for the invitation to come and meet him. *"Where can I park?"* I added as an afterthought.

"You can't. We are a bit short of space and the public car park is full by eight in the morning. Come by tube," he suggested. I wasn't surprised.

I got to the branch office, as Mr Savage had called it, shortly after midday. That was a decision that I would shortly regret. As he said, Mr Savage was easy to find and was instantly friendly as I offered to buy him a second pint. *"You mean a third,"* he said, as he dipped his moustache into the creamy foam that covered the black liquid.

We had a long chat about everything and anything. We took turns to buy rounds. Mr Savage had pints of Guinness, I had halves of light ale. It should have been okay apart from the fact that we had a total of twelve rounds during the time I was there. Nobody forced me to drink. Somehow I had come to the conclusion that Mr Savage would have been upset if I had refused to drink with him. I was probably right.

At 2.00pm we parted company. Mr Savage headed back to his head office and I headed in the direction of BMW Park Lane. I could not do the tube station steps, but as I could get one foot in front of the other I decided that it would be a good idea to walk. I think it took a long time, but I can't really remember. What I could remember was a secondary gut feeling to the beer gut feeling that there was a deal to be done here sooner or later.

I do remember that the next day, when I felt less confused, I wrote to Mr Savage and thanked him for his time, promising to keep in touch. This I did on an 'every so often' footing. Naturally, I did not get there too early. About twenty to two seemed about right. Mr Savage and I got to know each other quite well. He was a fascinating character. I never saw him eat anything. *"What do you eat, Tony?"* I said one day. *"Don't you ever have a proper lunch?"*

"Listen, old son," he said, *"there are a lot of vitamins and minerals in a pint of Guinness."*

I took his point: at an average of 14 pints a day, Mr Savage was getting more than his fair share of whatever vitamins and minerals inhabited his liquid lunch.

It was around 18 months and (for Mr Savage) 5,460 pints of Guinness later that I got my first sniff of the deal that I had always felt was somewhere there to be had. It came in the shape of a telephone call. *"There you are, old son."* I recognised Mr Savage's gravelly voice and salutation. *"One of the big daddies has asked me to arrange a demonstration in a BMW 318 for his daughter. Are you interested?"*

"Of course," I said excitedly, *"just tell me when and where."*

"It's out at Guildford. Next weekend if you can make it," he told me, *"but don't get too excited, it all sounds a bit vague to me."*

We fixed up a time and I took the address and other details. The next Saturday I called on the big daddy and his daughter. *"Are you sure that this is the one you want?"* said the big daddy to his daughter after the demonstration. She was sure and the big daddy signed the order and paid the deposit.

I went back the following weekend and delivered the vehicle and that was the end of that, I thought. That was the second time I made a wrong decision regarding this particular group of companies. Three days after the delivery, Mr Savage came on the telephone again: *"You could be in luck,"* he said, *"The big daddy loves his daughter's car so much that he would like to try a new Seven Series for himself. Can you oblige?"* I could, and I did and the group acquired its first non British vehicle.

The BMW driving big daddy's action set off a chain reaction within the group, and

BMW was added to the approved vehicle list at senior management level. They did not buy a massive amount of BMWs, but they were all supplied by yours truly through Mr Savage's office. The discount agreed was reasonable and the deals were profitable. I had that business for a further 18 months. Then Mr Savage retired. His replacement had his own contacts who were keen to buy the business with ever increasing, forget about competing, discounts.

... And they did.

Let's Start at the Beginning

I was fresh into vehicle sales, selling both cars and light commercial vehicles. When a customer did happen to call in, my older, well established colleague would say: *"It's all right, Dave, I know them."* The result of all this was that three months later, I had accomplished a lot of waiting, but not much action; so I talked to my Sales Manager about it. *"You will have to find your own business, David"* he told me.

"How do I do that?" I asked.

"Well, it's simple," he said, *"you go out and knock on doors."*

"Any particular doors?" I enquired.

"No," he said, *"any door will do, just knock on a door and ask the person who opens it if they would like to buy a car."* This didn't sound too hopeful to me, but it would make a change from sitting around waiting for something to happen.

It seemed logical that the best doors to knock on would be BIG doors. Those people might want more than one car and possibly a van or two as well. The biggest door for miles was a construction company not far from my dealership. So I leaped in my car and shot off to knock on their door.

"Good morning," I said to the cheerful-looking receptionist, *"I want to talk to the person who is responsible for buying your company cars and vans."* She asked me who I was and I told her. She picked up the telephone, spoke briefly and turned her gaze back to me and said: *"Mr Martin, our transport buyer, can spare you ten minutes."*

Mr Martin turned out to be as cheerful as the receptionist. He wanted to know who I was, who my company was, what franchises we had, what discount we offered, plus any other benefits of buying from my company. I could only answer the first three questions, which I did, and then admitted that I did not know about discounts and benefits. I went on to explain that this was the very first business call that I had made, and offered to go and get the information for him. He looked puzzled for a few seconds and them smiled again as he asked me to come back with the information he wanted.

I left and went back to my Sales Manager. "*Given up already?*" he said. I explained where I had been, the outline of the conversation and the information I had been asked to take back to Mr Martin. The Sales Manager and I sat down together to put the information required into writing. "*It saves any misunderstandings,*" he told me.

I took the information back to Mr Martin, who read it through carefully and looked thoughtful. He nodded at me and said: "*This looks okay. I'm not happy with the service I am getting at the moment from one of the companies we do business with. I might give you a try when I need something.*"

Three weeks later Mr Martin telephoned and offered my company the opportunity to supply his company with three new cars. We managed to agree to the discount he expected and the deal was done. The Sales Manager was very pleased with the outcome, but my older well established colleague wasn't. He claimed that he knew Mr Martin but he didn't. So that deal was mine along with many other vehicles sold to that company over the next few years.

People tell me that I was lucky to hit it off on the very first call that I made, and I accept that. Success breeds inclination, and in the ten years that I knocked on doors as a salesperson, many did not open. But the ones that did more than made up for the effort expended, as my 'luck' continued.

All this happened many years ago, and times change. You cannot rely on luck to get you through doors any more. What is needed is a more subtle approach. If you really want to find yourself some company business, then this chapter is for you. What follows is a blended collection of all the best practices of all the best 'company door knockers' I've ever met on my own journey through sales and sales courses. By copying or modelling excellence, you too can become excellent if you want to.

◆ ◆ ◆

The Incoming Business Enquiry

It can and does happen. Business customers will make the first contact. This could be on behalf of a company or it could be an enquiry from an individual whose company is buying them a vehicle. The following two incoming business enquiries are based on real experiences and illustrate the right and wrong way to handle such a call.

Telephone Call 1

All the caller wants is a quotation for a new vehicle, to be used to obtain board approval before an order is placed. The call is made, and the telephone is answered by a receptionist who uses the company name only as she takes the call.

"Oh, good morning. I need to get a quotation for a new car."

"Sales, service or parts?"

"Sales, please."

"Can I ask who's calling?"

"Yes, my name is David Upsher."

"Let me put you through."

(28 seconds later)

"Hello."

"Hello."

"Yes, good morning, it's Mr Upshire?"

"Yes, I wonder if you could help me"

"Yes."

"I need a quotation for a car. Can you help me with some information first? When is the new 2.2 multi valve coming out?"

"Um – as of motor cars built in the month of September."

"September."

"Um – so the first cars are going to be available for customers during October?"

"Right, okay. And the 2.5 will continue, will it?"

"To the best of my knowledge, we've not been told it won't. But I must admit when I think about it, one thinks – well – if the new 2.2 multi-valve is going to put on a lot more power than the current 2.2 – then one wonders, what's happening to the 2.5… "

"Yes."

"But I don't know – I mean I worked with this franchise for donkey's years – Um – and they really don't give out a lot of very specific information."

"Right."

"Until the eleventh hour."

"Right – okay then I can't get a quotation on a 2.2 multi valve because you won't have prices yet?"

"No – I mean I have quoted people on them. I've just quoted them today's prices plus manufacturer's price increase."

"Ah – that would do."

"But it doesn't help anybody."

"No?"

"It doesn't help anybody at all."

"Yes, I really wanted a car for the first of August, or August would be sensible."

"Right, in that case all I can do is talk to you about a regular 2.2 or a 2.5. Um – I tell you what we are really expecting, we are expecting that there is going to be one hell of a difference in price."

"Yes?"

"Between, you know between the current model and the new multi valve model."

"Right, I think what would be sensible to do, as I need a car quickly, is to go for the 2.5. You could get a 2.5? There's a very bright red I noticed."

"Oh right, red."

"What sort of delivery would there be on a … ?"

"Well, if you want a car for the first of August, number one thing is that you are going to have to be incredibly open minded on colour and specification."

"Well, I don't mind what colour it is as long as it's that red."

"Ha ha, right – um – I mean – one wonders – one never knows I mean – all I can do is – ah go into the computer and see what I come out with."

"All right, let's get the car approved by the company first."

"Right, now, Mr Upshire."

"Yes."

"And your first name, Mr Upshire?"

"David."

"David – Hello, I'm Kevin, by the way. Um, who are you with, Mr Upshire? What company?"

"The company is called Mitac."

"M.I.T.A.C." – (spells it out)

"That's right."

"Right, and where is Mitac?"

"Mitac is at Station House."

"Station House."

"Old Station Yard."

"Old – that's Westbury, isn't it? Westbury, Wilts?"

"No, Bath Road."

"Oh, right."

"Box."

"Yup."

"Wiltshire."

"Right."

"Postcode?"

"Please."

"SN13 8AE."

"Right."

"What I need is a quotation – a written quotation."

"Yup."

"We have a fax number, if that helps."

"Yes, please give me your fax number."

"The fax number is 01225 743544."

"And your regular telephone number is, Mr Upshire?"

"It's 01225 743894."

"743894."

"Right, okay."

"Right, first of all, do you want the 2.5 as a manual or as an automatic?"

"Manual."

"Do you want it as a special model, or the reg… "

"Yes."

"Ah, right."

"I know exactly what I want."

"Right, fire away, tell me exactly what you want."

"It's easier if I do that. It's the 2.5, preferably the red, but there could be choice on that."

"Well yes, I mean, I always try and get people what they want, but give me… "

"Red, white or black."

"Right."

"A non-metallic colour, a primary colour."

"Right."

"I want it… "

"As a special model."

"Yes, the difference is, I believe you can have it with the ABS?"

"Yes, but the likelihood of that… em. I mean, one never knows until one tries, but ideally you would like the ABS option?"

"If that's possible."

"Yup, okay."

"Oh, I would prefer it without badges."

"Oh, that's neither here nor there, cos' even if I can't find you a car without badges, we can whip 'em off when they arrive here."

"And to be really awkward, an adjustable lumbar support."

"I think that's incredibly unlikely."

"Right, okay, I'll buy a cushion."

"Ah ha, right. Just bear with me a second, there are so many models."

"It's the quotation I need more than anything, so I can get the price approved from the company. Then I can go from there."

"Well, okay. If I quote you with all the bits and bobs that you've requested – ABS and what was it, lumbar support?"

"That's it."

"Then you know, if I quote on the high side – um – and you can get the approval for that."

"Yes, then we can sort it out from there."

"Right, so in an ideal world, you would like a 2.5 manual, a non-metallic colour, red being first choice, with ABS and the lumbar support."

"You've got it."

"Right, what about a stereo?"

"I usually have one fitted myself actually."

"Do you? Ah – who does that?"

"There's a chap in town. A friend of mine, who does them."

"Not Lows Hi-Fi?"

"Ah no, an independent guy."

"I mean you – I have this to say to you, that you could – possibly run a risk of – ah warranty problems – I mean with the new model, particularly – ah, I mean the electronic wizardry going on behind the scenes is quite unbelievable."

"Right."

"And if somebody who doesn't know what's where."

"If you could leave the radio and stereo off the quotation, I would be grateful."

"Okay, right, and mudflaps, overmats?"

"Mudflaps – no, overmats – yes."

"Remote control alarm?"

"Not bothered, I'm not used to it, I'm not bothered."

"Right, look, I will – ah – I'll talk to you during the course of the day. I mean the very first thing I'll do is just whiz across to the computer and see what it comes up with."

"Sure, but what I must have first is some sort of written quotation."

"Ah, I'll get that faxed through to you today. But let just me see what is about first of all. That's not going to take me very long."

"Yes, but getting approval is more important than seeing what is about."

"Right, well okay, alright, I'll just do the quotation on that car."

"I would be grateful and then we can sort it out from there. If it changes that much, it does not matter. It's company policy to get written quotations."

"Okay right. Now the name of the company. It is Mitac Ltd."

"M.I.T.A.C. Ltd. Yes."

"Right okay, I'll get that done, rapidly."

"Right, thank you."

"Do you want me to phone you and say 'Right, the fax is about to be sent'?"

"No, I'm in all day today."

"Oh right. I mean a lot of people want that to happen in case the wrong person is standing by the fax machine."

"No that's quite all right."

"Okay, I'll get it done, you know, within the hour."

"I would be grateful."

"Okay, thank you for phoning."

"Bye, bye."

"Bye, bye."

END

This example is not the best of calls, and it's certainly not the worst of calls. In less than ten minutes, Kevin managed to raise 15 objections to me buying a car from his company. It's not surprising that the car was sourced from another company.

Telephone Call 2

"Good morning, New Town Motors."

"Oh, good morning. I need a quotation for a new car. Can you put me through to sales please?"

"Certainly, may I ask who is calling?"

"My name is David Upsher."

"Mr Upsher, I will be putting you through to our Mr Sammy Chamberlain."

"Thank you."

(10 second wait)

"Good morning, Mr Upsher, how can I help you?"

"Yes, I need a quotation, so I can get a price approval from my company."

"For what car, Mr Upsher?"

"Well, either a 2.5 or a new multi valve 2.2. But I want a car for August, ideally."

"I see. Well, there are 2.5s available for August, but not a lot of choice. A new 2.2 multi valve could be yours before the end of October. Are you familiar with the current range?"

"Yes, I have a 2.2 at the moment. In fact I have had several Pelegras."

"Oh good, then that makes it much easier to help you get what you want. Can you get to us, or would you prefer me to come to you?"

"What for?"

"Well, to discuss your exact requirements and to look at cars rather than just talk about them."

"Well, my office is quite a long way from New Town. All I need at the moment is a quotation for a car in writing initially. Can you fax me something?"

"How far are you? I mean, where exactly are you based?"

"Box, in Wiltshire, about 25 miles from you."

"That's not far. I would prefer to come and discuss the specifications, delivery and funding options with you, if you don't mind. Then you will also have a face to go with the name. How did you hear of us, by the way?"

"Your company was recommended to me by someone I know who bought a car from your company."

"That's good. Who was that?"

"Jonny Morrison. He bought a 1.8 for his wife from you."

"Mr Morrison, Mr Morrison, not one of mine. Ah, here he is. He bought a car from my predecessor, so I can help you get the car you want. If you are serious about buying a new car, then I can be with you about 4pm, say, today."

"Ah. Look, I am serious, I do want a new car, but I don't want to make you travel 50 unnecessary miles to take an order."

"It would be no trouble. Perhaps I could pop in and thank the Morrisons for their recommendation while I'm there."

"Look, let me have a quotation first, to get price approval from my company. Having done that, I've got to go to New Town next week. I can call in and sort everything out then."

"Well, okay. Do you know what you want?"

"Yes. Specification wise anyway."

"And what's that?"

"A current 2.5 or a new 2.2 multi valve in red, the special model plus ABS, no badges, and a lumbar support."

"Okay Mr Upsher, now you mentioned wanting a car sooner than later."

"That's right."

"You obviously have a reason for this, may I ask what it is?"

"Well, no real reason. The new plate comes out in August, so I wouldn't want it before then. But then again, having decided to get a new car, I would like to get it as soon as possible."

"How long do you keep a car, Mr. Upsher?"

"Normally around three years, but you know how it is when you want something."

"Yes, I see what you mean, I know how you feel. May I ask you a question, that could be important to you?"

"Yes of course."

"What is more important, a car as quickly as possible, or getting the car exactly as you want it? Bearing in mind of course that you are going to have to live with that car for three years."

"Oh, getting the car I want I suppose."

"Fine, let's do it your way. I will provide you with a full proposal for both cars with accurate delivery times to your full specification."

"Thank you."

"Now what will be happening to your present car?"

"Oh, we already have a buyer for that. So don't worry about it."

"Good. Well if that does go wrong, then do let me know, and also how do you propose to acquire your new car? I mean, do you want ownership, or are you thinking of a lease of some sort?"

"We have a finance company that we use. It will be done on a lease."

"Is that with or without maintenance?"

"Without."

"Fine, would you mind if I include details of our own funding options in our proposal? It doesn't commit you, but it will give you some comparisons, in fact you might be pleasantly surprised."

"Yes, include those if you will."

"Fine, so I will call in and see you and talk you through everything at 4pm today then. What's the full address?"

"Call?"

"Yes, call. You did say you are a serious customer, didn't you?"

END

Sammy got the address.

Sammy called at four.

Sammy went away with the order.

◆ ◆ ◆

Dealing with the Incoming Business Enquiry

Recommendations

Very similar to handling the incoming retail enquiry.

- The reason to have a telephone in a sales office is to enable you, the seller, to get face-to-face with the enquirer, the buyer.
- If you have a telephone receptionist, ask to be given the name of the caller before the call is put through. Then you can open by saying: "*Good morning, Mr Upsher, How can I help you?*"
- It is not necessary to give your name at this stage. The customer at this point is far more interested in what he wants rather than who you are.
- Find out what the customer wants. Ask the right questions, listen to the answers and make notes of key points.

Find out:

- Who the customer is
- What the customer wants
- What the customer drives
- What will be happening to the current vehicle

Then find a good reason to get face-to-face, so you can really start to help that customer buy your product, from you and from your company.

Business Users

By definition, a business user is a company or business that uses and provides payment for anything from one vehicle upwards. Sometimes they come to you. Most of the time, though, you will have to go out and find your own business users. Lists of businesses are available; there is a vast variety of publications around to help you identify potential business users. The best list of all is the one that you take the trouble to create for yourself.

Finding Your Own Business Users

Just get round there and knock on the door

Very traditional and it works; it is a numbers game after all. Some salespeople make a good living at it.

Take the double glazing salesman who knocked on Norman Barnard's door. Norman did not need double glazing. He had just sold the house and had double glazing where he was moving to. The salesman said: *"Don't worry, guv, you've just earned me a pound."* Norman asked the salesman to explain what he meant. The salesman said: *"It's simple really. I go out and knock on a hundred and eighty doors. From that I get ten presentations. From that I get three orders. I make an average of sixty pounds for an order. Three times sixty is a hundred and eighty, that means every time I knock on a door I earns a pound. Thanks for the pound, guv."* He walked off down the road whistling a happy tune. Some salespeople find the high level of rejections using this method a little off-putting.

Success rate – Face-to-face with decision makers 12%

Telephone first to make an appointment

Used with great success by insurance salesmen for the past two decades, but not so successful as it used to be because of misuse – and the resulting mistrust.

Take the timeshare lady who telephoned Jules Cardigen-Fitzim-Baddly one evening right in the middle of *Blind Date*. *"Congratulations Mr Baddly, you have just won a brand new Ford Escort. All you have to do to confirm your win is to call to our luxury leisure development at Sellafield to collect your car personally. Bring your wife with you, be prepared to attend a short, two-hour presentation on the benefits of eating fluorescent fish and to make sure that the winning number that I'm about to give you matches the one that relates to the car that you have won."*

Get the picture?

Success rate – Face-to-face with decision makers 19%

Telephone first to get some information then write to suitable potential customers

Can be quite successful: you can certainly pick up plenty of information over the telephone. Or you can use this method to check information that you have already researched. You could use this method to bypass unhelpful receptionists. There are some problems though:

- The information you receive is all verbal
- You can't 'see' the whole picture
- Some people will not talk to you
- Some that do will not tell you much
- You can waste time getting through to and talking to the wrong people
- It is very easy to start selling on the telephone
- If you do get tempted to try and make an appointment there and then and get rejected, you have closed the door on yourself.

Success rate – As long as the telephone call seeking information is followed up by a letter, telling the customer that you will be in touch to make an appointment, then you will achieve a much higher success rate than cold calling or just telephoning.

Note
An example of a telephone contact sheet follows on the next page.

Identification of potential company buyers before face-to-face contact analysis

Contact ____________________ Company Name ____________________
Position ____________________ Telephone ____________________
Address ____

____

"Good morning/afternoon"
"Can you help me?"
"I have been asked to contact the person in your company who is responsible for the disposal and acquisition of the vehicles that you use."

"May I have their name, please?" ____________________

"And what is their position within your company?" ____________________
"Thank you, that is most helpful."
"Is he available at the moment?"
(He is not, or is, but is not available to talk for any reason)
"Don't worry, I will drop him a line, thanks for your help."
(He is)
"Can you put me through, please?"
"Good morning/afternoon Mr/Ms ______________"
"My name is ____________ of ______________, your local distributor."
"My company is trying to find out what makes and types of vehicles that both you and other companies in your area are using. So could you spare me a minute to tell me which makes you are currently running?"

Which makes? ____________________________________
Which models? ____________________________________
How many do you run? ______________________________
How do you use them? ______________________________
How do you usually fund your purchases? ____________________

"Thank you for your help."

Recommendation – only use this sheet if you really can't call in person as described in the next method, which is highly recommended.

Recommended Way to find Business Customers

There are, of course, many different ways of looking for potential customers. You will have your own style and ways of implementing it. Remember that your goal is to find the prospects and retain their ongoing interest before someone else does – or they may go to the competition. If you are not happy with the results of the way you currently look for business, then the following method will be well worth a try.

Leave the sales office

It is not generally possible to do it all from your office. Havimg decided on what you want to do, you need to get out into the marketplace and establish your new areas for development. Only you will know the local area and the territory for which you have the responsibility. There is generally a substantial marketplace to work in with businesses across the whole spectrum of commerce. Choose your territory to have a look at – and then go there.

Park the vehicle

In a populated area, the best way is to walk your target area. Have a notebook or a mobile dictating machine and keep your eyes open. Look for potential prospective customers. It has often been said that salespeople are inclined to walk past far more business than they close. Take care that this does not happen to you. Visit local businesses personally to establish the 'worth' of the business as a potential customer. That can be any business and any size.

Look for clues:

- What's parked up?
- Size of company?
- On-site service workshop?
- Where are they buying from?
- How old are the vehicles?
- General impression of the company?
- What do they do?
- Any special requirements?
- Head office or branch?

Find someone to talk to

- Preferably a receptionist
- Anyone will do to start with

Then

- Say who you are, and give your company's name
- Hand over your business card
- Say that you want to write to the person responsible for buying the vehicles
- If no one person is responsible, then start at the top (the managing director, for instance)
- Get the name and correct spelling and job title
- Seek other useful information
- Find out the name of the person you are talking to
- Thank them for their help
- Leave the premises and find another one
- Repeat the whole exercise

Write the appointment letter

- To say that you will telephone shortly
- To make an appointment

Make the appointment telephone calls

- Between three and five working days later

Success rate – This technique has been used by other motor industry business sales specialists. Normally, the success rate of face-to-face appointments to decision makers contacted is 40% or more... why not you?

The double key that unlocks the 40% success rate

Key 1 – The Quality of the Letter You Write

- Get it wrong and it ends up in the wastepaper basket
- Get it right and it will end up on your prospect's desk

Key 2 – The Clarity of the Telephone Call You Make

- Get it wrong and you will be rejected
- Get it right and you will get face-to-face

So let's look at each of these keys in detail.

Key 1 – The Appointment Letter

Having done my fair share of door knocking, I was aware that too many salespeople were at it. Getting face-to-face was getting harder and harder, particularly as most of the really good business prospects had taken to employing 'dragons' to keep the likes of you and me from bothering their bosses. As luck would have it, I just happened to know one such dragon. In fact I was dating her on a regular basis. So one day I asked the dragon what was the best way to get past her and face-to-face with her boss. This is what she told me:

"My boss will not see anybody without an appointment. I always have to get rid of those people who just call and expect to be seen."

"So how do I get an appointment? Would it be better if I telephoned first?" **I asked.**

"No," she said, *"my job is to get rid of those people too. He will not talk to people on the telephone that he knows nothing about."*

"I get it," I said, ***"so what I should do is to write first to say that I am going to telephone to make an appointment."***

"Well," she said, *"It's also my job to throw that kind of letter in the bin."*

"Oh this is hopeless," I said. ***"Do you mean to tell me that you throw every letter asking for an appointment in your wastepaper basket?"***

"Well not quite all of them," she replied. *"Sometimes I open a letter and I don't know what to do with it, so I put it on my boss's desk for him to decide. There are other occasions when the letter sounds quite interesting, so I let my boss see those too."*

"Ah," I said, ***"so if I was to send your boss an interesting letter that you were not quite sure what to do with, then your boss would see it?"***

"Yes," she told me, *"but it doesn't happen all that often."*

"Would you help me write one of those letters that would get past you?" I asked. And that is precisely what she did – and here it is.

Dear Mr MacKintosh

Choosing the right company car or transport generally can be most difficult in today's ever-changing marketplace. Just keeping up-to-date with your various options can be very time consuming.

In order to assist you, I will contact you by telephone during the next few days to ask for twenty minutes of your time to introduce myself, my company and our range of products and services.

During our meeting, the main objective would be to show you how we have helped other companies, similar to your own, to save both time and money regarding transport costs.

Yours sincerely

David Upsher

P.S. If more urgent help is required, please call me

The Dragon's Rules for Dodging Dragons

Start with 'Dear Mr MacKintosh'

◆ The letter must always be addressed to her boss. 'Dear Sir' or 'For the personal attention of the Managing Director' always were classed as bin letters.

The letter must have an interesting opening

◆ Any letters that started 'I am writing to introduce myself and my company' hit the bin really fast.

The letter must have no enclosures

◆ Anything with catalogues, price lists or other printed information also ended up binwards.

The letter must have plenty of 'you' and 'your' and very few 'we' and 'I'

- 'I' letters sound selfish, even if it is not meant. A letter with lots of 'you' is far more interesting to read, particularly as it will be all about the receiver and not the sender.

The letter must be well laid out, clear, concise and properly typed

- Dragons are usually very good at letter-writing themselves, and will have some respect for the writer of a properly presented letter.

The letter must have some good reasons in it for her boss to see the writer

- In this case 'time and money', two things that most people would love to save.

The letter must be proactive

- It has to point the way ahead; in this case the writer will be contacting the receiver. Letters that expect the receiver to do the contacting seldom reach the appointment stage.

The letter must be written by the same person who will be making the follow-up call

- Anything less than this is too impersonal and will make the caller 'less important' in the eyes of the customer.

The letter could benefit from a 'hand-written' PS

- Because it will draw the reader's eye through the letter and make the letter 'feel' more personal.

The letter must look important

- A white envelope, not a brown one
- A typed address, not a label
- A real first class stamp, not a frank
- Quality paper
- Perfectly written

"So if I do all that," I asked the Dragon, ***"my letter will get past you and end up on your boss's desk?"***

"Oh yes," she said.

"If you are right about this," I told her, ***"I will sell so many cars that one day I will be able to afford to marry you."***

... And she was.

Key 2 – The Appointment Telephone Call

One of the joys of teaching is that you learn so much. For the past ten years, my company has been running 'live' telephone workshops. Delegates come on the courses having written dragon dodging letters, make real calls to real customers and walk away with real appointments, not just a few. Get the letter and the appointment telephone call right, and you can expect more than a 40% success rate.

Some very good ideas on how to get face-to-face with business people you have written to have come out of these workshops – and from other sources. Good ideas never mind who had them, so pick the ideas that appeal to you, practise them, master them and make them your own.

1 Pre-telephone Call Guidelines

Keep the commitment

If you write to a potential customer to say that you are going to telephone, then you must telephone. A far too easy way of destroying your local business opportunities is to get as far as writing letters to potential customers and then not telephoning to make the appointment as promised.

Have a clear objective before telephoning

Before you pick up the telephone, know exactly what the objective of the call is. In this case it will be to make an appointment to introduce your company and its services.

Review what you know about who you are calling

Determine what you know about the prospect and his company before you make the call. Make notes of anything that might be of help to you.

Choose the right time

In an ideal world, you would probably be more successful in making contact with a director of a company at his own premises between 10am and 12 noon or between 4.30 and 5.30pm. For most businesses, Tuesday, Wednesday and Thursday appear to be better days to call than Monday and Friday. Executives can often be approachable outside normal office hours when their dragons are out! – after 5pm, before 9am and at lunchtime.

Pick the right place

Try to make your appointment telephone calls from a quiet office, away from interruptions.

Have everything to hand

The telephone is used to get face-to-face, not for selling purposes, so you need your diary and something to write with. (Two pens may be useful.) But just in case, it would be sensible to have product information and price lists to hand.

Know what you are going to say

Unless you are very experienced in making appointments by telephone, it will be very beneficial to always write down what you propose to say to your potential customer as an opening statement.

Know how much rejection you need

No matter what you do, you will get rejected. If you track your calls and find out how many calls equal an appointment, how many appointments equal a sale, each 'no' will carry less weight.

Break down your calls on a daily basis

Once you find out how many calls you need to make, break it down by calls per day. It's easier to pick up the telephone and start calling every day if you know when you can stop.

When you reach your daily goal – STOP

If you make the amount of calls you set out to make every day, you'll develop a sense of accomplishment and feeling good about your day. This will make you want to come back and do it again tomorrow.

Be consistent

You are very much better off doing a little bit every day than a lot every once in a while. By doing little bits daily, you create a habit and avoid hating what you are doing. You only fail if you give up.

Don't put the telephone down between calls

It gives you too much time to deliberate over the next, wastes time and creates fear and anxiety. Keep the telephone in your hand, disconnect with your finger and go straight on with your next call.

Always let your prospect hang up first

If they hear your phone go dead, it tells them that you're already moving on to something more important.

2 First Contact – The Receptionist

In most cases the first person that you will speak to will be a telephone receptionist. So here are some simple rules to make this part of the call successful.

Use the receptionist's name

If you have carried out direct research on a local company, either face-to-face or by telephone, it is more than likely that you will already have spoken to the receptionist. Try to make it your usual practice to find out the receptionist's name, and then use it as an ice-breaker when you call.

Give your full name and the full name of the person you are calling

Do not ask *"Is John MacKintosh in?"*, or *"May I speak to John MacKintosh?"* Simply say *"Good morning / afternoon, this is David Upsher calling for John MacKintosh."* It is not necessary to use your company's name at this stage, unless it is well known and will be to your advantage. If the receptionist asks for the company name, then give it.

Handling 'What's it about?'

Receptionists will often ask why you want to talk to the person you are calling. They need to tell the prospect something. Simply say that the prospect is expecting your call, which is the truth. You wrote and said that you would be telephoning. As long as you are pleasant, she will probably put you through.

3 Getting Past the Managing Director's Dragon

This can be a minefield for the unwary. Sometimes you will get straight through; other times you will be talking to a person who sometimes thinks their main aim in life is to stop people like you from bothering their boss.

- The receptionist techniques still apply
- Get the secretary's name and use it
- Say *"Good morning, this is David Upsher calling for John MacKintosh."*
- Use *"He is expecting a call from me."*
- Expand if necessary by saying *"I wrote to John MacKintosh to say that I would telephone to discuss the possibility of doing some business together."*

  (Now, who is the customer?)
- Stay pleasant at all costs. In difficult cases you can always try again later

4 Making the Appointment

Normally start with Good morning/afternoon

It gives the prospect time to get situated and ready to talk to you. It is far more professional than just *"Hello"*. If the customer starts with *"Hello"*, then you could certainly use the same word back to help create rapport.

Don't say "You don't know me"

When you begin your conversation with the prospect, say *"We haven't met yet"* instead. It is far more positive.

Don't say "How are you?"

Far too many sales calls start that way, and it's none of your business anyway.

Don't say "Did you get my letter?"

The usual response is *"What letter?"*, and the explanation that you will now have to give will only go against you in most cases.

Do use your written opening statement

For example:

"Mr MacKintosh? Good morning/afternoon. This is David Upsher here of Pelegra Motors. I wrote to you last week to say that I would telephone you to make an appointment to call and see you regarding our range of vehicles and services. When would be a good time for you? This Thursday, perhaps? Or would one day next week suit you better?"

Make the prospect want to see you

- Expect him to see you
- Be friendly and enthusiastic
- Be very polite and courteous
- Sound business-like but not stiff
- Make the prospect feel important

5 Overcoming Appointment Barriers

Many people will still be reluctant to see you. This is perfectly natural, but the more you talk, the more chance you have of opening a relationship.

If the customer uses an excuse to not see you, you have two alternatives:

- You can roll over and die
- You could try to overcome the excuse

The following ideas may just help you:

"I'm not changing my car currently"

"Mr MacKintosh, it would be my lucky day if I telephoned you just as you were thinking of buying. The main purpose of our meeting would be to discuss how we could possibly be of help when you are thinking of changing. A brief meeting at this stage could be most worthwhile for you at some time in the future."

... Ask for the appointment again.

"I'm too busy to see you"

"That is fully understood, Mr MacKintosh. That's why I have telephoned you to make an appointment to call and see you when you are not so busy. We will only need about twenty minutes."

... Ask for the appointment again.

"I always buy from your competitors"

"Some people do, Mr MacKintosh, but then again, there are local companies who have found some good reasons to place their business with my company. I would appreciate a short meeting with you to try to explain what those reasons are."

... Ask for the appointment again.

"We used to buy from you but don't now"

"Thank you for your past support, Mr MacKintosh. We constantly strive to improve both our products and services so that we can offer more benefits to customers, both past and present. I would be grateful for the opportunity to explain what those benefits will mean to you in today's terms."

... Ask for the appointment again.

"Talk to my assistant"

"That's very kind of you, Mr MacKintosh. I would welcome that opportunity if you would like to give me the name of the person I need to speak to. I will make an appointment to call."

... Make the appointment with the assistant.

... Make sure that you get face-to-face with Mr MacKintosh while you are there.

"We can't afford to change anything"

"I know just how you feel, Mr MacKintosh. However, it might just be that my company could save you some money, if not now, then possibly in the long term. It would certainly be worth discussing."

... Ask for the appointment again.

"You would be wasting your time"

"It is kind of you to think of me, Mr MacKintosh. However, I am more than willing to invest twenty minutes of my time if you are."

... Ask for the appointment again.

"I am not interested"

"Thank you for being straight with me, Mr MacKintosh. You obviously have a reason for not being interested. Before I get off the telephone I would be grateful if you would spare a minute of your time to tell me what that reason is?"

- Don't ask for an appointment yet
- Become a good listener
- If it's one of the excuses, use the ideas here to counter it, and ask for the appointment again.
- If it really is a problem, try to overcome it, short term or long term.
- If you really are wasting both your time and your company's, you would be better off looking for other sales opportunities.

6 Confirming the Appointment

Having made an appointment, always write and confirm the date and time. If you don't make an appointment, write and thank the prospect for his time and try again later.

7 Planning and Preparation

The first step in selling should always be planning and preparation. Being well organised and prepared helps you avoid embarrassment, gives you more control, saves time, increases your confidence and increases your sales.

You can't sell to them all, but if you research companies, write introductory letters to named people and then telephone to make the appointment, you can look forward to getting face-to-face with four out of ten prospects. That means that making appointments is a mathematical certainty: each 'No' brings you closer to a 'Yes'.

8 Keeping the Business Appointment

Once you get face-to-face, keeping the business appointment is very similar to dealing with a showroom enquiry. You may know what those similarities are. Just in case ...

Write and confirm the appointment

- Well worth saying twice. It reminds the customer that you will be calling
- It promises professionalism
- It is a courteous thing to do

Arrive early

- Give yourself plenty of time, it will not matter if you are early
- It can matter very much if you are late, because it will knock out that promise of professionalism
- Tell the receptionist who you are and who you have come to see
- If you are early, tell her that you are happy to wait
- Always carry something with you to read or do
- Alternatively, read any company information that is provided in the reception area or review your notes relating to the person you are about to meet

Relax and prepare

- Sit back in your chair, let your body hang loose and take a few deep breaths
- Imagine a picture of yourself looking relaxed and confident. Then make that picture bigger and brighter – and notice the difference
- Hear yourself talking to the person you have come to see. Then make that voice stronger and more confident – and notice the difference
- Feel how confident and relaxed you are. Then make that feeling stronger – and notice the difference
- Those are the differences that will make the difference when face-to-face.

Face-to-face

◆ Meet and greet your customer using his surname

◆ It is normal to shake hands in business circles... unless something tells you not to

◆ Hand over your business card straight away, to save the customer the trouble of remembering your name

◆ Wait to be asked before you sit down

◆ Use 'sensory acuity' to establish what kind of state or mood your customer is in

◆ Use 'rapport' to match your customer

Opening the relationship

◆ Always accept the offer of tea or coffee

◆ Start by reminding the customer why you are there

◆ Focus your attention on the customer

◆ Avoid spending too much time on small talk, unless that is what the customer wants to do

Qualify the customer

◆ Well covered under *Qualification* (pages 118-121); the only difference is that you will need to find out about the company as well as the person

◆ Start by saying something like *"Before I tell you about what we do, do you mind if I find out a little bit more about what your company does?"*

◆ Ask the customer if it's okay to take notes *"just to remind me of the key points to identify how we can help you best"*

◆ Ask your qualification questions. For example:

"What vehicles do you run?"
"How many?"
"How often do you change them?"
"How do you use them?"
"Any current needs?"
"If not now – when?"
"How do you fund your vehicles?"
"Happy with present suppliers?"
"Anything that you are not getting in the way of service that you would like to get?"
"What do you know about our range of vehicles?"

and so on ...

Give the customer a good listening to

- You are asking interesting questions that the customer will want to answer
- Give the customer your full attention
- Don't make notes as the customer is talking. It looks like you are not listening and the customer could get bored looking at the top of your head

Start raising desire

When you have qualified your customer and fully understood what he wants or how you can help, by all means show the customer pictures. The true art of selling to companies is to get the customer to see and try the product in action. This could take more than one visit. Just in case, it would not hurt to take an example of your product range for the customer to see and try there and then, if the opportunity does arise:

"What you have told me, Mr MacKintosh, is very interesting. Do please come with me, I want to show you the car I have brought with me today. It's just downstairs and it won't take long."

Alternatively, offer a demonstration later or the loan of a vehicle for a short period of time.

Sell All Your Services

Before you leave, make sure that the customer is fully aware of all your company's goods and services.

The customer might not be interested in buying vehicles today, but there could very well be some other way to start a business relationship. This could be:

- Fuel account
- Valeting service
- Servicing of vehicles
- Repair and bodyshop work
- Disposal of unwanted vehicles

By taking the trouble to sell all your services, you will come across as a complete company rather than just a sales department. This will enhance the value of what you are offering and will give you the status more of a transport adviser than just another salesperson.

Keep the Door Open

After the customer has had the opportunity to assess the product and has an understanding of what you and your company can offer, ask what the chances are of doing some business

◆ Customers usually say the same thing at this point:
"We are not in the market at the moment."

◆ Your reply should be:
"If you were in the market, do you think you would now consider buying our product, from my company, from me?"

◆ Customers must learn a script from somewhere: 90% will say:
"Yes, of course, it depends on the deal you offer though." And that's what you wanted – to keep the door open

◆ *"That's fine, Mr MacKintosh. In that case, I had better keep in touch – thank you for your time."*

Notes

The deal you offer is covered under *Securing Business Customers* (pages 487-488).

The basic 'presentation' and 'demonstration' rules still apply equally to business and showroom customers.

The only difference is that the sales process takes longer when you are 'finding your own business'. You would be best advised to take the lead from the customer, and let him set the pace initially.

◆ ◆ ◆

The main points again

1 Not all the doors you knock on will open, but the ones that do will more than make up for the effort.

2 By copying or modelling excellence, you too can become excellent.

3 If you are approached by a business customer by telephone, get the information and get face-to-face.

4 Normally, you have to go out and find your own business users.

5 The recommended way to do this is:

- Leave the office
- Drive to the target area
- Park the vehicle and walk your area
- Visit local businesses
- Establish your chances of doing business
- Find out the name of the person you need to talk to

6 When you have found some potential business:

- Write an appointment letter
- Make an appointment telephone call
- Write and confirm the appointment
- Arrive early
- Relax and prepare
- Open the relationship
- Qualify the customer
- Give the customer a good listening to
- Start to raise desire
- Keep the door open
- Keep in touch

CHAPTER 32
Securing Business Customers

"When it comes to asking for the order time,
you should give your customers the absolute freedom
to do exactly what you suggest,
in any way that you want them to"

Securing Business Customers

I'd secured the business all right. It was a large advertising company not far from our showroom. The office manager had telephoned to confirm that one of the partners, who had recently had a demonstration, wanted to place an order immediately and take delivery in the New Year.

So a late and dismal December evening found me on foot on my way to get the signature on the line that is dotted. The shop windows were a delight with their lights, as I fought my way through throngs of late Christmas shoppers and early evening revellers. I did not mind a bit. I had the business and, as usual, I started mentally to spend the commission that I would not see until the end of January. Who cares, I thought, as I turned into the advertising agency's doorway, the money is in the bag anyway.

When the office manager came out to see me, you could see that something had gone wrong. It really was written all over his face. *"Bad news, I'm afraid,"* he told me grimly. *"Mr Monk has changed his mind and doesn't want the car after all."* I was totally stunned by this news. Not ten minutes before, this same man had telephoned and told me to call round and collect the order.

The office manager could see that I had taken the news badly and had started to apologise for the fact that one of the bosses was, as he put it, 'mucking me about'. In a fit of inspiration, or was it desperation, I blurted out: *"Very well then, if Mr Monk is not going to have it, which of the other partners is?"* The office manager was taken aback by this question. He shook his head and said he would go and see what he could do, and took the order for the new car back to the main office, leaving me in the reception area. When he returned, you could see that something had gone right. It really was written all over his face.

"*Good news, I'm pleased to say,*" he told me happily, "*Mr Silver will take the car.*"

...And he did.

Keeping in touch

Having opened a relationship and left the door open, as outlined in *Finding Your Own Business*, it is really a question of keeping in touch. Enough to be remembered, not enough to be avoided.

Try and have a reason to re-contact potential customers:

- New product
- Pending price increase
- Show or event
- Special offers and campaigns
- Free service checks
- Local news that might be of help or interest

If you get the balance of contacts right, and form a good relationship, then the day could very well come when you will get the 'Can you pop in and see me?' call that indicates that the opportunity to do business has moved a little closer.

Become a Good Listener

When the potential customer has a need, give them the opportunity to tell you what they want. In most circumstances it will probably mean a re-qualification, plus a presentation and demonstration, if this has not already been carried out.

It is dangerous to try and cut desire-raising corners in a headlong rush to get down to the nitty gritty of pounds and pence. Give the customer the time and attention he wants. The arrival at the 'So what's it going to cost me?' stage is inevitable. That's the point at which you can really get down to winning the business.

How do you want to fund your purchases?

If you ask a customer how they propose to pay for the vehicle or vehicles, most will have some idea, some will want advice. This is where you can win some credibility and some time. You can do this by completing a 'How to fund your purchase' matrix.

Ask your business customers the questions overleaf. Copy the master score against the most appropriate answer in the customer's score boxes, to the right hand side of the matrix. When you have finished asking all the questions, total the customer's score for each type of finance.

In the example that follows, you can see that the fictitious customer scored:

Cash	Hire Purchase	Lease	Contract Hire
29	38	35	35

The higher the score, the more appropriate the type of finance, but it would be sensible for you to give your customer two methods of funding to chose from.

"From what you have told me, Mr Nash, it looks to me like you have a choice of two options, contract hire or hire purchase. May I propose that I go away and work out some figures for both options for you to choose from?"

Most customers will find this acceptable and professional. This gives you the chance to escape and seek advice from your manager and/or finance house. It also takes care of the 'How much off?' question. You can side-step that for the moment using this method. Get a little breathing space and the chance to put together some figures, along with some very good reasons for doing business with you and your company.

Then...

Write a Proposal, not a Quotation

A quotation gives the cost but a proposal shows the value and gives further reasons why the customer should buy from you.

Also included here is a blank example of the 'How to fund your purchase' matrix for you to photocopy and use, if you feel that it would be of benefit to you and, of course, your customers.

	Master Score				Your Customer's Score			
	Cash	Hire Purch	Lease	Contract Hire	Cash	Hire Purch	Lease	Contract Hire
1 Has the business been established long? *or*	4	3	2	2				
Is it a relatively new company?	1	3	4	4	1	3	4	4
2 Does the business own its premises wholly? *or*	4	3	2	2				
Are they still subject to a mortgage? *or*	2	3	3	3				
Are the premises rented?	1	3	4	4	1	3	4	4
3 Is the business expanding rapidly? *or*	1	2	4	4				
Is the business expanding slowly? *or*	3	4	2	2	3	4	2	2
Is the business not expanding at all?	4	4	2	2				
4 Is the business high turnover, low profit? *or*	3	3	4	4	3	3	4	4
Is the business low turnover, high profit?	3	4	3	3				
5 Has the business bought equipment recently? *or*	2	3	4	4	2	3	4	4
Has it not recently bought significant fixed assets?	3	4	2	2				
6 Is the business mainly a cash sales business? *or*	3	3	3	3				
Is it mainly a credit sales business?	2	4	4	4	2	4	4	4

	Master Score				Your Customer's Score			
	Cash	Hire Purch	Lease	Contract Hire	Cash	Hire Purch	Lease	Contract Hire
7 Are the business suppliers mainly cash suppliers? *or*	1	4	4	4				
Are they mainly credit suppliers?	3	3	3	3	3	3	3	3
8 Has the business had vehicles through HP before? *or*	2	4	3	3	2	4	3	3
Through leasing/rental? *or*	2	3	3	4				
Cash purchase?	4	3	2	2				
9 Is the business able to use capital allowance? *or*	4	4	2	2	4	4	2	2
Is it carrying low taxable profits, or even losses?	2	3	4	4				
10 Is the business paying tax at a low rate? *or*	2	3	3	3				
Is a high tax rate being paid?	4	3	2	2	4	3	2	2
11 Does the business have a high level of borrowings? *or*	2	3	5	5				
Does it have a low level of borrowing?	4	4	3	3	4	4	3	3
Total Score					29	38	35	35
Additional notes								

		Master Score				Your Customer's Score			
		Cash	Hire Purch	Lease	Contract Hire	Cash	Hire Purch	Lease	Contract Hire
1	Has the business been established long? *or*	4	3	2	2				
	Is it a relatively new company?	1	3	4	4				
2	Does the business own its premises wholly? *or*	4	3	2	2				
	Are they still subject to a mortgage? *or*	2	3	3	3				
	Are the premises rented?	1	3	4	4				
3	Is the business expanding rapidly? *or*	1	2	4	4				
	Is the business expanding slowly? *or*	3	4	2	2				
	Is the business not expanding at all?	4	4	2	2				
4	Is the business high turnover, low profit? *or*	3	3	4	4				
	Is the business low turnover, high profit?	3	4	3	3				
5	Has the business bought equipment recently? *or*	2	3	4	4				
	Has it not recently bought significant fixed assets?	3	4	2	2				
6	Is the business mainly a cash sales business? *or*	3	3	3	3				
	Is it mainly a credit sales business?	2	4	4	4				

Master Score					Your Customer's Score			
	Cash	Hire Purch	Lease	Contract Hire	Cash	Hire Purch	Lease	Contract Hire
7 Are the business suppliers mainly cash suppliers? *or*	1	4	4	4				
Are they mainly credit suppliers?	3	3	3	3				
8 Has the business had vehicles through HP before? *or*	2	4	3	3				
Through leasing/rental? *or*	2	3	3	4				
Is it run on a cash basis?	4	3	2	2				
9 Is the business able to use capital allowance? *or*	4	4	2	2				
Is it carrying low taxable profits, or even losses?	2	3	4	4				
10 Is the business paying tax at a low rate? *or*	2	3	3	3				
Is a high tax rate being paid?	4	3	2	2				
11 Does the business have a high level of borrowings? *or*	2	3	5	5				
Does it have a low level of borrowing?	4	4	3	3				
Total Score								
Additional notes								

A Quotation

Mr David Upsher
Mitac Ltd
Bath Road, Box
Corsham
Wiltshire SN13 8AE
Our Ref:

Dear Mr Upsher

With reference to our telephone conversation today, herewith are quotations for your perusal.
To supply one new vehicle as specified below:

Make & Model:	Pelegra 2.2 Multi Valve	
	Cash Price	£17,500.00
	Advance Deposit	£1,750.00
	PAYMENT SCHEDULE:	
	Maintenance Excluded	23 Monthly Payments of: £498.20.00
	Guaranteed Buyback	£7,690.00
	Administration Fee (payable with first payment)	£25.00

Based on 15,000 miles per annum, total mileage 30,000 miles.

This quotation is valid for 14 days. All credit subject to status.

Please do not hesitate to contact me if we can be of further assistance to you.

Yours sincerely

Vick Brit

The Proposal Alternative

(Example figures only - not accurate)

Vehicle Proposal

Proposed Vehicle

Pelegra 2.2 Multi Valve 'Special Model' finished in 'Bright Red', fitted with ABS, Driver's Lumbar Support and De-badged.

Acquisition Method

As requested, we have supplied vehicle costings for both hire purchase and contract hire, covering a period of three years.

Contract Hire

The benefits of our Master scheme that match your requirements are specified below:

- Inclusive full maintenance costs
- Priority booking service within our workshops
- Replacement tyres, batteries and exhaust
- Replacement vehicle in the event of a mechanical breakdown or accident up to a period of 28 days.

Contract Hire Cost

The cost of supplying the proposed vehicle, inclusive of the contract hire benefits, delivery costs and Road Fund Licence for the period is as follows:

Initial Contract Deposit	£1,860.48 + VAT
Monthly Cost	£570.16 + VAT

The initial contract deposit equates to three monthly payments and there would therefore be no payment due from you in the final quarter of this period. The cost assumes an annual mileage specified by yourselves of 20,000 miles.

Hire Purchase

As an alternative to contract hire, we are able to provide the following proposal for hire purchase:

• Cost of vehicle as specified, including VAT, delivery and Road Fund Licence for one year	£17,813.75
• Hire Purchase Interest Rate	8% flat (15.5% APR)
• Initial Deposit	£1,896.25
• 36 Monthly Payments	£587.84

Order and Delivery

An order may be placed by telephone, should you wish to do so prior to our next appointment, and delivery will be seven days from that date.
Upon order, we will visit you to complete the necessary agreements and to discuss other administrative arrangements.

About Our Company

Newtown Motors Ltd have been Pelegra dealers since 1974 and have specialised in providing high class facilities and automotive services to local businesses and retail customers.
Our service operatives are fully trained and well experienced in the servicing of Pelegra vehicles, using the latest diagnostic equipment available within the motor industry.
Service facilities are open 6 days a week.
Our investment in replacement part stock covers 6,000 lines and ensures that vehicle down-time is kept to a minimum.

Should you have any problems or questions concerning any aspect of your transport needs, the personnel below will be pleased to assist you quickly and efficiently:

Managing Director:	Barrie Reardon Smith
Sales Manager:	Paul Tavernor
Aftersales Manager:	Paul Rowlands
Replacement Parts Manager	Bob Clarke

Enhance the Proposal

- Put the proposal in a cover, complete with information about the vehicle(s) proposed.
- Personalise the proposal by putting the name of the person who it is for on the front cover, together with that person's company name and address as well as your own.
- Ensure that the reader can easily understand what the proposal is about.
- Include a covering letter that identifies the key points
- Consider all the features and benefits of your product and your method(s) of acquisition, but only use those in your proposal which will really mean something to your customer. This will ensure that your proposal will come across as a direct response to your customer's needs and circumstances and will show that you have been listening carefully.

Then Visit with Proposal

- Always take the proposal – never post it
- Have sufficient copies for all concerned
- Make sure that it is well-typed and correctly presented
- If you are presenting to one person, sit alongside him and go through the proposal
- Do not hand out all copies at once – your customer may be reading ahead of you
- Listen to reactions and take notes for future use

Gain customer commitment

Showing for Visual

- Use pictures and literature when your customer is 'visually orientated'. Build pictures in the customer's mind and use imagination.

Talking for Auditory

- Talk concisely and perhaps slower than usual when dealing with the 'auditory' person. Ensure that the customer understands and is happy with what you are telling him. Use voice intonation and the volume to make sure that you 'sound' interesting.

Feeling for Kinesthetic

- Respond using empathy when presenting to a person who is 'kinesthetically orientated'. Think about how he would feel when making a decision about such a purchase.

Use Third Party References

- Demonstrate that what you are recommending has worked well for other customers. It will add weight and credibility to your proposal.
- Show the customer how your products will satisfy stated needs, and include details of aftersales facilities that your company offers. Tailor this to individual circumstances.

Spend Time

- Take the time that it takes to get the results that you want

Make Sure Everything is Understood

- *"Are you happy about that, Mr Upsher?"*
- *"What else do you need to know?"*
- *"Do you want to run through that again?"*

Agreement of Proposal

- Get the customer to agree to each of the parts that make up the whole proposal

When, not If

- It is now just a question of 'when?'. You have done everything necessary to obtain the commitment already. It could still go wrong. That man is still 'down the road' but he no longer appears to be as professional as you are.

Complete the Paperwork

- Just as in retail selling, a full order form should be completed and a deposit should be asked for from customers with whom you have not done business before.

Confirm in Writing

- Again, this practice should be part of proactive selling as well as showroom selling. It certainly helps clarify everything and eliminates potential mistakes.

You Know the Rest

- Recap if necessary by reviewing *From Delivery to Repeat Business* (page 304).

End Result - Satisfaction

- For the customer
- For the company
- For you

The main points again

1 Open relationships and leave the door open and keep in touch.

2 Try to have a reason to re-contact potential customers.

3 The day could very well come when you get the 'Can you pop in and see me' call.

4 Re-qualify, present and demonstrate if necessary.

5 Give the customer all the time necessary before you get down to price.

6 Win some credibility and some time by completing a 'How to fund your purchase' matrix.

7 Give the customer a choice of two methods of funding to choose from.

8 Write a proposal, not a quotation.

9 Enhance the proposal.

10 Always visit with the proposal.

11 Gain customer commitment:

- Showing for visual
- Talking for auditory
- Feeling for kinesthetic
- Use third party references
- Spend time
- Make sure everything is understood
- Get agreement of proposal
- When, not If
- Complete the paperwork
- Confirm in writing

◆ ◆ ◆

SECTION ELEVEN
Endings

"A journey through sales time completed
... or has it just started?"

EPILOGUE

"Vision without action ... is just a dream.

Action without vision ... just passes the time.

Vision with action ... can change the world"

So there you are then: *The Complete Sales Guide* and your journey through sales time completed. Or has it just begun? The question is: what are you going to do next? Are you going to leave it there, stay where you are or continue to travel forwards and upwards?

The motor industry is a unique industry. It is relatively easy to enter and, let's face it, almost anybody can be a vehicle salesperson. You don't have to have lots of qualifications or experience to get in. Once you get used to the motor industry way of life, you will find it very hard to leave.

That gives you two choices: you can stay and bump along the bottom of the sales league, earn enough to get you by and have a relatively peaceful life; or you could decide to climb the odd mountain or two and really get somewhere.

The motor industry is wide open. Nearly anybody can enter, and anybody that does enter can get to the top. It is not a question of qualifications, it's a question of ability and determination that will take you on, ever upwards as far as you want to go.

- If you want to climb the motor industry mountain...
- If you believe that you can...
- If you know or find out how to do it...
- If you give yourself the chance to do it...

Then nothing can stop you.

David Upsher

Bibliography

Awaken the Giant Within	Anthony Robbins	Simon & Schuster, London W2 2AQ
Beliefs	Robert Dilts	Metamorphous Press, Portland, Oregon 97210
Frogs into Princes	Richard Bandler & John Grinder	Eden Grove Editions, London N7 8EF
Heart of the Mind	Connirae Andreas & Steve Andreas	Real People Press, Moah, Utah 84532
How to Walk your Talk	MaryAnn Reese	Southern Institute Press Inc., Florida 34635
Influencing with Integrity	Genie Laborde	Syntony Publishing, Palo Alto, California 94301
My Voice Will Go With You	Sidney Rosen	WW Norton & Company, London WC1A 1PU
NLP Practitioner and Master Practitioner Programme Notes	Ian McDermott	International Teaching Seminars, London NW3 1RS
Selling Cars	David Upsher	Mitac Ltd, Box, SN13 8AE
Successful Selling with NLP	Joseph O'Connor & Robin Prior	Thorsons, London W6 8JB
The Mind Map Book	Tony Buzan	BBC Books, London W12 0TT
The Secret of Creating Your Future	Tad James	Advanced Neurodynamics, Hawaii 96812
A Study in Scarlet	Sir Arthur Conan Doyle	First published in 1887
The Wok Cook Book	Kenneth Lo	Grafton Books, London W1X 3LA
Time Line Therapy™, Practitioner and Master Programme Notes	Tad James	Honolulu HI 96821
Training with NLP	Joseph O'Connor & John Seymour	Thorsons, London W6 8JB
Using your Brain – For a Change	Richard Bander	Real People Press, Utah 84532
Changing Belief Systems with NLP	Robert Dilts	Meta Publications, Cupertino, California

About the Author

David Upsher is a Director of Mitac and has been with the company since it was re-formed in 1985. On leaving school David and went straight into the motor industry as a trainee parts sales assistant. He was promoted to parts delivery driver on passing his driving test, and then went on to become a representative for an independent automotive component company.

Moving on to car and commercial vehicle sales, David spent time as a salesman with a major group, an old family firm and a large distributor of Rolls Royce and Bentley cars.

In 1971 David joined the new and pioneering BMW company, initially as a salesman at their Park Lane premises. He was soon promoted to Sales Manager and then General Manager, ending up as the Export Manager for BMW concessionaires.

Preferring people to paperwork, David decided to start a new career in training, in 1979. He joined Sewells as a Training Manager, and worked his way up to Director of Training by 1984. The following year he was offered the chance to join the newly refounded Mitac Ltd, and jumped at the opportunity.

David's responsibilities still revolve very much around training, and he prefers to run courses in selling, sales management, customer care and marketing rather than office based administration activities. He also attends courses – particularly relating to Neuro-Linguistic Programming (NLP).

He is a certified master practitioner of NLP and Time Line Therapy™.

David lives in Somerset with his wife Mira and their two children Katherine and James.

Mitac Performance Development

Mitac was established in 1978 and is currently the largest motor industry performance development company in the UK. Mitac also operates in European and international markets, from five divisions in four UK locations, as well as a European base in Brussels. Over 80 full time consultants are involved in these activities, and the company has been awarded an ISO9001 accreditation.

Services Offered

Mitac offers the motor industry a wide range of services that include:

- Integrated consultancy and training programmes
- Strategic business planning
- Electronic used car appraisal and pricing systems
- Used car/fleet management programmes
- Software development and installation
- Quality management and ISO 9000 implementation
- Mitac Online, complete motor industry information service
- Mitac Business College, offering a motor industry MBA programme

Strengths

Due to its policy of specialisation, Mitac offers an insight into analysing business requirements. The company understands, and can answer, clients' needs, and offers tailor-made solutions and assistance in applying quality management systems. Mitac utilises a wide range of expertise, based on hands-on industry experience. Coupled with the ability to respond to ever-changing markets, this offers the clients' companies training and skills that can enable them to grow, by removing the ubiquitous barriers of communication, co-operation and commitment.

◆ ◆ ◆

Services Menu

Training

Bespoke training programmes to meet the client's objectives:

- Business College
- Sales and Aftersales
- Finance and Commercial Awareness
- Personal Development
- Negotiation Tactics
- General Management
- Information Technology

Business College

Mitac Business School has been established because there are around 100,000 people in supervisory or management positions within the industry. The current training provision, despite all its efforts, is still failing to meet the industry's managerial and supervisory skills needs, particularly in the franchised sector.

To meet this need, Mitac, in partnership with a leading university, have developed an industry specific MBA in Retail Automotive Management.

The Masters degree may be completed full time over a 12-month period or through distance learning, which is not time bound, or through a mixture of both.

Other Training

Mitac's bespoke approach provides usable solutions to real problems. The objective is to improve individual and commercial performance standards and provide measurable methods of achievement. Training formulas include courses, seminars, workshops and conferences, as well as distance learning.

Training methods are focused firmly away from 'Chalk and Talk' and directed towards competitive and innovative syndicate work. Strong emphasis is based on problem solving and a constructive exchange of ideas between participants.

Mitac constantly updates both training methods and material to incorporate the latest thinking and technology. Best practices in all areas are established, and delegates attending Mitac training will have ample opportunity to study and model excellence. This is accomplished through demonstration, hands-on practice and computer-based simulations.

Consultancy

Mitac offers strategic solutions to business requirements:

- Network and Dealer Development Programmes
- Business Management/Financial Services
- Used Vehicle Management
- In-dealership consultancy
- ISO 9000
- National Vocational Qualifications (NVQ)

Network and dealer development programmes include customer service initiatives, quality management systems, bench marking and strategy and policy advice. Special expertise is offered in European dealer development, distance learning packages, integrated training and consultancy projects, and block exemption.

Business management and financial services include viability studies, performance profiling, financial modelling and business plan developments. In-dealership assistance is available in start-up management, management buy-outs and buy-ins and dealership restructuring.

Used vehicle management covers all the important areas of network profitability, brand awareness, residual value improvement and disposal strategies.

In-dealership consultancy activities are wide and various, and include training and development needs analysis and the development of fleet and used car operations. Help with staff appraisals, team profiling and recruitment is available, as well as design of customer prospecting systems, direct mail and point of sale materials.

ISO 9000 is a specialised area, and Mitac is well established as a consultancy who can assist dealers and importers gain accreditation based on developing workable and user friendly procedures and operation manuals.

Mitac has done much to pioneer NVQs within the motor industry, especially in sales. The company is an Approved Assessment Centre, recognised by both the Institute of the Motor Industry and City and Guilds.

◆ ◆ ◆

Information Technology

Practical application of bespoke systems for manufacturers, importers and dealers.

- Financial and modelling programs
- Planning systems
- Management reporting systems
- Training systems
- Electronic vehicle disposal
- Stock locators
- Mapping
- Dealer composite production
- Mitac Online

Financial and modelling programs include Motorplan profit and cashflow planning package, a dealer performance simulation program and a financial accounts analysis program. A retail labour rate calculation program is also available, in addition to labour efficiency control and cashflow forecasting.

Planning systems are available in sales prospecting, aftersales prospecting and pan-European network planning.

Management reporting systems include new and used car territory reports, aftersales performance reporting and operating standards control and reporting. Other systems are available relating to fleet and business user information and management accounts.

Training systems cover training and administration databases, business games for national and international conferences plus interactive distance learning.

Mitac's electronic vehicle disposal system is a leading-edge concept, and offers real time electronic auctions, automatic catalogue download and a satellite link facility.

The stock locator system provides on-line locator, sale and purchase facility as well as multi-level access and intelligent stock management.

Mapping facilities include geographical analysis and territory performance reporting as well as isochromes and multi-layer build dealer composite production covers, financial and statistical reporting, graphical representation and an interactive output module. Automated data input and flexible group reporting.

The benefit of having a Mitac composite is that it is validated by leading motor industry consultants, which means that the quality of output is enhanced. Mitac is a highly focused specialist consultancy company, and our understanding of the industry means that we can tailor the information that is required, to suit both imports/manufacturers and dealers. In addition, Mitac composites can incorporate financial, registration, CSI rating and mapping data, to provide a highly individual and relevant management report.

Mitac Online

Mitac Online is the first on-line modem based motor industry service. It has over 2,500 information sources on every topic needed in the motor industry. This information can be browsed through or, for specific items, subscribers can use a keyword search. It is an extremely powerful and convenient service available 24 hours a day, 365 days a year.

Mitac itself is a growing company, and constantly benefits from an inflow of up-to-date motor industry expertise. The services are ever-changing and expanding. For the latest brochure or information covering any or all of these services, please contact:

Mitac Ltd
Station House, Bath Road
Box, Corsham
Wiltshire
SN13 8AE

Telephone: 01225 743894
Facsimile: 01225 743544

SECTION TWELVE
Appendices

"An oral contract is not worth

the paper it is printed on"

Understanding Finance by John Walsh

Helping the Retail Customer to Buy

The customer has been showing increasing interest in our vehicle for the last hour, we are about to give him a price for his part-exchange, you are just about to tell him the difference to change, which in this case is £8,700... STOP!

Think about what £8,700 means to the customer. It could mean:

- Half a year's salary
- Three years of saving
- More than he paid for his house 20 years ago
- More money than he has ever saved in his life

The list is endless. We are all different and think differently. The point is, by presenting the cost of owning the vehicle in this way, we are leaving the interpretation of what £8,700 means to the customer. As you can see from the above, that can mean just about anything.

Lump Sums

How many people do you know that get paid their salary in a lump sum once a year? None, or at least not many. How many people buying vehicles from you get their salary paid in a lump sum? Chances are, none. Then why do we always make them think in those terms when we present the cost of owning the new vehicle in thousands of pounds? It is not suggested that we cover up the cost or avoid talking about it, but think about it: how do your customers get paid; how do they think of money? Our customers get paid a salary or wages in small chunks, normally monthly or weekly. When we present a figure of thousands of pounds, we are not talking the same language.

Everyone's a Customer

Who is a finance customer? Can you tell by looking at them, or do they give off a certain odour? Certainly not... they all are! Everyone manages their money on a monthly basis. Think about it: mortgages, rent, electricity, gas, telephone, rates, TV licence. All the companies involved in providing everyday services offer a monthly payment option – why? Because customers manage their money in small chunks.

Now ask yourself: do these major companies offer this monthly payment option to the customers that look like they are finance customers? No! Of course they don't, they offer it to every customer. We are probably not the only industry that doesn't offer this monthly payment option to our customers, but if we don't, we are not talking their language, we are not helping them to buy our product, our services, from us.

The Funding Options

We will start by covering the basic type of monthly payment options available to your customers. We will also look at ways to help your customers buy your vehicles using your loan product. If we don't, others will, and pretty soon we'll have no customers left. We'll be standing around talking to each other, saying something like: *"Stand back, give them plenty of room, they will be along in a minute"*.

On the other hand, if we do help people buy all our services, including finance, we will enjoy the sales experience far more and so will our customers.

What choice do your customers have?

- Hire Purchase/Conditional Sale
- Personal Contract Purchase
- Personal Lease

There are some common elements to all forms of borrowing.

All loans have three major elements:

- The amount borrowed
- The time taken to repay it
- The interest rate

Consider this example:

A customer wants to borrow £1,000 over 1 year	
If the current interest rate is 20% per year, this means the customer would pay back to the loan company:	
The amount of the loan	£1,000
The interest at 20%	£200
The total he would pay back is therefore	£1,200
As he would pay this back monthly, he would have a total monthly payment of £100 for 12 months.	

Say the monthly payment was too much for the customer and it needed to be about £50 a month, the first temptation may be to reduce the interest rate. Why? Because the first thing the customer will say is: "*What rate is that?*". When we say "*Twenty per cent*", he thinks that if he can negotiate a cheaper rate, then he will get a monthly payment nearer to his £50. Wrong!

Let's halve the rate to 10%.

The amount of the loan is	£1,000
The interest at 10%	£120
The total he would pay back is therefore	£1,120
As he would pay this back monthly, he would have a monthly payment of £91.66 for 12 months.	

We are still nowhere near his ideal payment of £50 a month, and what's more, we have just thrown all the profit out of the finance sale. The only way to get near a customer's ideal payment is to play about with the period or the amount of the loan.

Try this: using the same figures, let's offer him a two-year loan:

The amount of the loan is	£1,000
The interest at 20% per year x 2 years	£400
The total he would pay back is therefore	£1,400
As he would pay this back monthly, he would have a monthly payment of £58.33 for 24 months.	

The moral of this story is this: if you change the rate you will never get to the customer's ideal payment. If you change the length or amount of the loan, you will get near to his ideal payment.

The interest rates that we come across with retail customers are usually what are described as 'flat rates'. All that means is that a rate of interest is set at the beginning of the loan and will not be changed, which gives the customer the comfort that when they agree a payment today, it stays like that for the period of the loan. This makes monthly budgeting a lot easier.

The loan plans that we look at play about with the amount of loan or the period, in some plans both. Let us consider what each of these products is, and what is attractive to the customer.

Hire Purchase/Conditional Sale

This is the traditional monthly payment plan, where the customer agrees at the time he is buying the vehicle how much he wants to borrow, and how much he wants to pay monthly. From this we can work out how long the agreement needs to be to give him the monthly payment that he wants.

Here is an example:

Vehicle costing	£12,000
Part exchange value	£6,000
Balance amount of loan	£6,000
Interest rate of 10% per year x 3 years Balance	£6,000
Interest 10% x 3 years = 30%, therefore £6,000 x 30% =	£1,800
Total amount borrowed + Interest =	£7,800
3 years = 36 monthly payments	

Therefore £7800 divide by 36 monthly payments = £216.66

These are very straightforward forms of loan. In theory, the customer becomes the owner of the vehicle at the end of the agreement by paying a small fee to the loan company; in practice it is the same as owning the vehicle – he looks after it, enjoys it and decides when it's time to change.

If the customer wants to settle the agreement early, they can, at any time, and they will get a part-refund of the interest that is left to pay.

The law surrounding HP conditional sale is very comprehensive and protects both us and the customer; it's not all one way. The key benefit that the customer gets when buying a vehicle on finance through your approved dealership plan is that not only are they protected by your terms of business, they are also protected under the Consumer Credit Act. This means that should they have cause to complain about the goods or services, the loan company is jointly liable with the supplier of the goods. This can mean a lot to some types of customer. It is positive and should be put across carefully.

Personal Contract Purchase

The second type of loan to consider is the Personal Contract Purchase or, as it is commonly referred to, PCP.

This product has increased in popularity over the past few years for two main reasons:

- From the customer's viewpoint, the monthly payments are lower
- From the motor manufacturer's viewpoint, it encourages repeat business and cuts the average customer's buying cycle.

When PCP is presented to the customer, it offers them a lower monthly payment than a normal three-year HP loan, and they get to change vehicles every two years. Customers can't believe it – it's easy to sell PCP, you just have to overcome the customer's natural curiosity when they try to find the catch. The good news is, there is no catch!

So how does PCP work? It is such a simple concept, it works like this:

We now have the ability to predict reliably the future expected value of vehicles. In other words, we can anticipate the likely value of the vehicle the customer buys today if we know the likely mileage of the vehicle and its overall condition.

Say we take a vehicle costing £12,000. We know that the vehicle, when it is two years old, with 20,000 miles and one private owner, would be worth, say, 45% of its current value, or £5,400. If we know that this vehicle is likely to be worth that amount in two years' time, what PCP does is asks the customer to repay only the difference, that means the customer only repays 55% of the value of the vehicle over two years instead of repaying 100% over two or three years.

If you remember we looked at three components to any loan:

1. The amount borrowed
2. The time taken to repay it
3. The interest rate

With PCP we are playing about with the amount borrowed. The amount borrowed is the element that can effect the biggest change in monthly payments. The great thing is, we are playing about with the biggest change element without asking the customer to stump up any more money, either as a deposit or as increased payments. That's why the customers love it, and it is becoming even more popular.

Here are some examples of how it compares:

The vehicle costs £12,000
Part-exchange is £3,000
Interest rate is 10%

	HP 2 years	HP 3 years	PCP 2 years
Balance	£9,000	£9,000	£9,000
Future Value	N/A	N/A	£5,400
New balance	£9,000	£9,000	£3,600
Monthly payments	£450	£325	£225

The reason that the payments are so dramatically lower is simple: the customer is borrowing less. Now can you see why customers are choosing PCP.

At the end of the PCP the customer has three options:

1 Hand the vehicle back and walk away
2 Sell the vehicle privately or part-exchange it
3 Pay the future value amount (£5,400) and the vehicle is theirs

The customers greatest concern is:

"What if the vehicle isn't worth £5,400 at the end of two years?"

That's no problem: you can remind them that if that's the case, they can hand the vehicle back and walk away.

PCP is, in the main, undersold. Yet, let's face it, most customers work on monthly payments, and what customer wouldn't like a lower monthly payment for the same vehicle over a shorter period? Not many.

What's it doing for you? Well first of all, like HP, you make finance commission. However, the most important thing is that the customer comes back to you, quicker than before. You also know which PCP agreements are coming to an end, so you have a guaranteed flow of quality low mileage privately owned vehicles coming back to you.

Personal Lease

The new kid on the block is Personal Lease. This product grew out of the company car person that opted out and took money instead of a vehicle. They need a loan that offered them low deposit, because none of them has a vehicle to part-exchange. They also need low monthly payments, because the company will be giving them a monthly amount to compensate them for not having a company car. The product, however, whilst suited to the ex-company car driver, is open to everyone.

So how does it work? Well the deposit is typically three payments in advance, which is equal to about 10% deposit. This is lower than traditional HP, where often 20% is expected, although that is negotiable. Next, the capital cost of the vehicle is lower because the loan company gets to claim the VAT element in the cost of the vehicle back. Similar to PCP, the anticipated future value of the vehicle is calculated and deducted from the balance. The net result is that the customer gets the lower monthly payment that they are after.

Here is an example:

Vehicle costing £12,000
Assume there is £1,700 VAT in the cost
The figures used will be on £10,300, because the loan company will reclaim the VAT
The interest rate is still 10%
The vehicle costs £12,000
Part exchange is £3,000
Interest rate is 10%

	HP 2 years	HP 3 years	PCP 2 years	Personal lease 2 years
Cost	£12,000	£12,000	£12,000	£10,300
Deposit	£2,400	£2,400	£2,400	£900
Future value	N/A	N/A	£5,400	£5,400
New balance	£9,600	£9,600	£4,200	£4,000
Monthly	£480	£347	£255	£245

Wow! Less deposit and lower payments – every customer should have it. Before you get too excited, as it is a lease, (ie a service), the monthly payments attract VAT. That means the customer would really have to fork out £288 a month. Even so, he still hasn't had to put up 20% deposit, which for the company car driver opting out, could be a problem. As this is designed for the private individual, it's unlikely they would be able to claim the VAT back.

Credit Insurance

The last product to consider is Credit Insurance, because credit insurance can be offered with all these retail products. So what exactly is it? When customers are making the decision to buy a vehicle, they can be a little cautious because they want to be able to make the repayments that they agree. They may be worried about changing circumstances that could affect their ability to keep up the payments. This is where credit insurance comes in. In general terms, credit insurance insures the customer against any unforeseen events that may affect him.

The first and most basic is life cover. If the customer is worried about providing for his family should he die, then the basic level of cover provided would repay the balance in full, leaving the vehicle as an asset to his family. The second level of cover provides for the customer in the event that he is ill and cannot work. After a qualifying period, normally 14-30 days, the insurance takes over and makes the monthly payments on the customer's behalf, until they go back to work or the loan is repaid. The third level of cover is redundancy. That is, if the customer is made redundant, the insurance company will make payments on his behalf until he gets back into employment or the loan is repaid. Although nowadays most credit insurance companies put a limit to the number of payments they will make under redundancy, typically this is 12 months.

Credit Insurance works for you in two ways:

1 It earns you more finance commission
2 If your customer ever has to claim, you have a customer for life who tells everyone how good you are because you made their payments for them, not the insurance company.

As a final note on credit insurance, when my dad bought a new car on finance from me in 1985, I insisted that he take credit insurance, fearful that he could be made redundant. Six months later he had a heart attack, from which he fully recovered. He was off work for five months and all the five payments were made on his behalf. When he recovered, he and my mum disappeared to Austria for a two-week holiday courtesy of the credit insurance company. After that I was so convinced of the benefits of credit insurance that I made sure every customer at least knew about it.

What I've tried to do in this first section is whet your appetite and interest, by showing you that finance products are simple. It's finance companies that make them sound complicated. I've used generalisations in my descriptions of the products, but if it's got you motivated to find out more about them, well done! You're on your way to success. Your own loan company will be able to give you exact details of their specific products and will be more than willing to give you training on the products.

It is important for you to be able to present finance products confidently and professionally. Not because your boss says so, your customers are sophisticated 1990s shoppers who want to know all about how they can afford that new vehicle you've got.

Presenting Finance Products

Now that we have considered the products available let's consider how we can present them. As you know, every customer is different, however the choices open to them when looking for money to buy a vehicle are limited. They either pay cash or they borrow the money. Let us consider how to persuade the two groups of people why they should use your source of money.

The first group are the ones that borrow the money. They have already bought in to the concept of borrowing. What we need to do is convince them that our loan is better than the one they originally thought of. The second group of people are the few that pull the money out of their savings accounts. With these guys, we need to switch them onto the concept of borrowing.

A good business manager these days will get about 55-65% finance penetration, usually because the manufacturer is supporting the vehicle with a 0% product or something that costs the manufacturer or dealer money and the customer nothing. If you take this type of product out of your thinking, the good performing business manager would be achieving between 35-40% finance penetration. That is, of all the sales made in the dealership, 40% are through the dealer's preferred finance house. This means that, whatever you do, traditionally more customers say 'No' than 'Yes' when offered finance.

In this section, I will ignore the odd ones *like "Granny gave me the money" or "It's from a biscuit tin under the bed"*. Let's concentrate on the type of customer that you usually get.

Let's start with the people that always borrow the money to buy the vehicle.

Why do they borrow? Well it could be that they don't have the money. That may have been the case a few years ago; nowadays customers are more sophisticated, and recognise that it may be hard to save and, once they have got the money saved, they like the feeling of security that it gives them. Whatever their reason, don't assume that it's because they can't afford to buy it outright.

Early on we considered that most customers think of money in monthly lumps – that's the way the world is now. So when they start looking for a vehicle, they usually start by thinking can they pay for it out of their monthly salary, and if they know they have spare cash, they need to know what it will cost them per month.

Monthly figures are everywhere: your bank or credit card company writes to you on a regular basis offering loans and giving you typical monthly payments and the newspapers are full of adverts for loans, again giving typical monthly payments. So before the customer comes to see you, they have worked out how much they can afford and what price of vehicle they can consider.

Think about the loan products that we have to offer, where traditional HP offers a higher monthly payment than PCP or Personal Lease. The customer does not see examples of this type of product, that's why when we show the customer what we have got, they get a real surprise. The bank and loan companies products are designed for anything from a holiday to a computer or even a home extension; our products are designed specifically for vehicles. You can't get a PCP for a holiday for obvious reasons.

If a customer comes in to your dealership expecting to take advantage of your loan products, don't disappoint him, sell him the vehicle using the best finance product for his needs. If, on the other hand, the customer comes to your dealership knowing that he is going to borrow the money, the most common source of funding for money that is not borrowed through the dealership is the bank. The customer's own bank is normally the first place they think of going to borrow money. Let's face it, if you want a vehicle, you go to a vehicle dealership; if you want money you go to a bank, it's natural.

What we are going to do is look at ways of convincing the customer to choose our loan products over the bank. The good news is, it's easy!

Maximising Finance Opportunities

If you follow this track and these suggestions, you will convert a minimum of 50% of your bank customers to your dealership loan products.

The first thing you need to do is take action. Go to your local banks and get their up-to-date loan brochures, including the loan tables that let you calculate the bank monthly payments and the typical form work that is needed for the loan. You need to keep this up-to-date. Next, follow this sales track with every bank customer.

Credit line

Ask the customer if the bank was the first place that he thought of going. If it is the first place that he thought of going this time he needed a loan, would it be the first place that he would think of going again. Of course it would. By using the bank to give him the loan for the vehicle, he could be tying up that line of credit for the next few years.

Convenience

Show him the bank application form. It's scary! Even though the bank knows lots about you already, they still need a fully completed loan application form that asks a lot of personal information that's not always easy to answer. The customer has also got to make arrangements to get down the bank and tie it up, and all this has got to take place before they get their hands on the vehicle. We can take care of the loan here and now. We don't need to know as much information, and for many of us these days, we have the technology that lets us accept the customer in minutes. This is great for putting both the customer's and our mind at rest. Remember: our products are designed for vehicles; the banks are designed for any purpose.

Cost

Use the bank brochure again. Show the customer what it would cost at his bank to borrow the amount that they are after. At this stage, include the bank's credit insurance in the monthly payment. Then calculate what it would cost using your loan product including credit insurance. You are in control of the payment, so help your customer buy from you by calculating a payment that is lower than the bank payment. This means that the customer is protecting his bank loan facility for future, he's often getting better credit insurance cover, and we can take care of it all right now – no fuss, no time out and, best of all, it's cheaper than the bank.

This approach only works if you use up-to-date bank loan brochures that the customer will recognise (ie from their bank). Otherwise, if they can't see it with their own eyes, they will want to get down the bank to check out if what you are telling them is the truth.

This works half the time at least, and we haven't even looked at using the other loan products like PCP that are tailor-made for vehicles. Think back to the examples that compared PCP to traditional loans like bank loans: the payments were a lot lower per month. Best of all, banks don't usually have this kind of product.

This is probably the hardest bit to believe – once you have mastered using the bank conversion sales track, you can offer your loan product dearer than the bank, because you will have the confidence to back up a modest price difference with the benefits that your product offers – protection of their credit line and the convenience of taking care of business here and now.

There are no tricks here, just good solid customer benefits.

"I always pay by cash"

The customer who always pays cash is different. They need to be shown the benefits of borrowing. The chances are that they think of borrowing as bad news. All that interest and the fact that people will think that I can't afford the vehicle so I need to borrow, the shame of it. Be aware of the thought patterns that customers may be having, and be sensitive to their opinion of borrowing. Again, here is a simple track to follow. If you follow it, success will be yours.

The fact that the customer is aware of how to use their money to best effect is excellent. When you find out that the customer is really withdrawing their savings to pay for the vehicle, you need to outline for them the cost of using their savings. Get in a physical position where you and the customer can see the illustration that you are going to draw. Take a blank sheet of paper, a pen and a calculator and do the following steps.

Ask the customer two questions:

1 What rate of interest they are getting on their savings
2 How long they normally keep the vehicle.

Always calculate the example on £1,000; it's easier to understand.

1 Savings rate 4% net
2 Keeps the vehicle three years

	Savings	Dealership Loan
	£1,000	£1,000
Interest 1 year	£40	£80
Capital & Interest	£1,040	£1,080
Interest 2 years	£41.60	£80
Capital & Interest	£1,081.60	£1,160
Interest 3 years	£43.26	£80
Capital & Interest	£1,124.86	£1,240
Total Interest	£124.86	£240
Difference in Interest is £115.14 or £38.38 per year		

What is the customer getting for £38.38 per year? They get:

1 The new vehicle
2 They keep their savings intact
3 The savings have grown by £115.14

This is the traditional cash conversion that has worked in the UK since 1975. There are other methods of converting the cash customer; master this one first and then start improving your skills.

Borrowers and savers

These are the two kinds of customers: the borrowers and the savers. Identify which type the customer in front of you is, and try out the tracks that are outlined here. They have been incredibly successful for me. In the early days, when I missed bits out or got lazy, my performance dropped and, more importantly, so did my wages.

With the borrowing type of customer, you have a choice of products that you can offer. As we saw earlier, you can offer HP, PCP or Personal Lease. Each of the products offers customers different benefits:

- HP talks the customer's language – monthly payments
- PCP offers the customer lower monthly payments over a shorter time and a new vehicle every two years
- Personal Lease offers the customer low deposit and low monthly payments

Find out what's important to your customer and present the best one for them. If in doubt, present a brief description of all of them, and let the customer tell you which one suits them best.

Remember! Tell every single customer that your dealership has loan products that are specially designed for people buying vehicles. More than that, when you give the customer the price of a vehicle, or the difference to change, always work out a monthly payment and give them that at the same time. Try it – you will be amazed at the positive reaction that you get from customers when you talk to them in their language.

Credit insurance

When you are selling credit insurance, make sure that you present not only the benefits of protecting their family by having it, but also the dangers of not having it. Most of the major banks and building societies make you sign a disclaimer stating that whilst you have been made aware of the credit insurance product, you have decided not to take it. This is heavy, but it works. Make sure every customer knows that you offer credit insurance. If you are not quoting it assumptively, at least let every customer know how much it is going to cost. If you don't sell credit insurance to your customers, the loan company will sell it direct. The main reason that they are successful is because no-one mentioned it to the customer in the first place.

Helping the Business Customer to Buy

Loan products for our business customers are slightly more varied than those for our retail customer. Not so much in the way that the products work, which is mostly the same, but more so in the way that a loan product affects the customer's business. That could be in terms of cashflow or taxation. We are not accountants, and the best person to advise the customer on what product to choose is often their accountant, who has an intimate knowledge of their business. We can help our business customers to buy by offering them a choice of ways of paying for the vehicle that helps them run their business.

As the majority of new vehicles sold are to the business sector, it is essential that we can explain loan products and the effects they have on businesses.

In this section we will consider the options open to businesses and look at:

1 Hire Purchase
2 Lease
3 Lease Purchase
4 Contract Hire

We will be looking at how the products are put together and the effects that each product can have on a business. We will also be comparing them against each other. The first decision a company has to make is:

"Will we borrow or will we pay cash?"

There are few good reasons to pay cash and plenty of good ones to promote the use of someone else's money. Let's assume that the customer wants to use someone else's money. The next decision they have to make is:

"Do we want to own the vehicle or rent it?"

What's important to them?

The third decision is whether they want to rent it.

"Who do we want to take the risk of depreciation, ourselves or someone else?"

By answering three simple questions, most customers are guided to the loan product best suited to them.

Put simply, it looks like this:

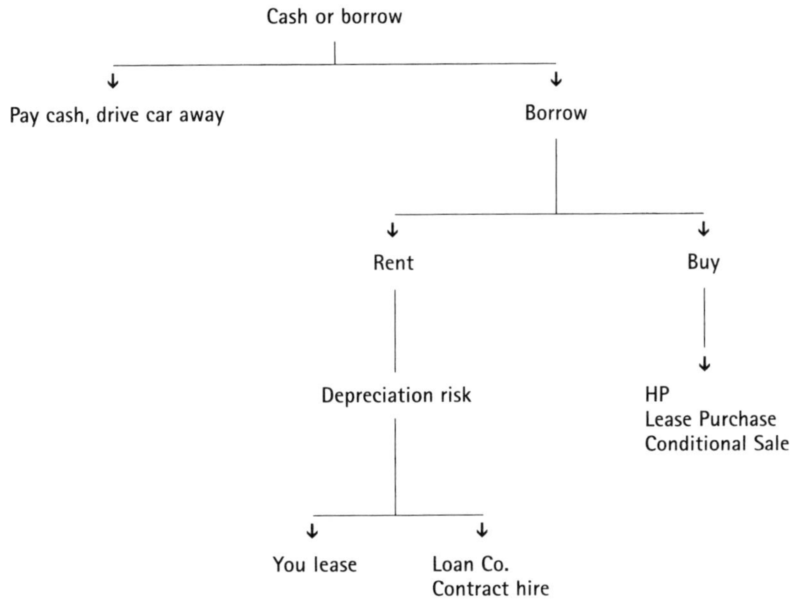

What we have to concentrate on is why customers should want to rent or buy and why they should take the risk of depreciation. Let's start by looking at each of the products.

Hire Purchase/Conditional Sale

This product is the same as we saw it with the retail customer. There are three variables:

1. The amount of loan
2. The loan period
3. Interest rate

The business application is that if the customer chooses HP, they can claim the normal writing down allowances. In practical terms, they are considered to be the owners of the vehicle. They are also allowed to write off as a business expense the interest charges, although this should be apportioned as a share of the 'private vs business mileage'. The vehicle running costs are normally treated as a legitimate business expense. As with the private customer using HP, the business can forecast cashflow and budget, since the payments are agreed at the outset and do not change during the life of the agreement.

Lease Purchase

Similar to HP, the Lease Purchase is made up of the same three elements. The tax treatment is the same – ie writing down allowances – and the business is allowed to write off the interest charges in the same way. The main differences are that some lease purchase agreements allow a future value to be deducted, giving the customer lower monthly payments. Most accept three months advance rentals, that's equivalent to about 10% deposit. It also sounds a bit more sophisticated than HP.

Lease

Like all loans, it's made up of the same three elements:

1 The amount of loan
2 The period
3 The interest rate

Similar to Lease Purchase, Lease offers the business customer low deposits – three months rental in advance; as we said, that's about 10%. The customer can also choose to have a future value which, when taken out of the cost of the vehicle, gives the customer lower monthly rentals.

With a lease, the customer takes the risk of depreciation. All this means is that if the vehicle is estimated to be worth, say, 45% of its original value (£5,400) and they only get £4,800, then the customer makes up the shortfall of £600. On the other hand, if the customer gets £6,000 for the vehicle, they get to keep the £600.

The biggest difference between lease and purchase plans is the tax treatment. As the business customer does not own the vehicle, he can write up to 100% of the rentals off against taxable profits, with a vehicle costing more than £12,000 this 100% starts to reduce. As the agreement is a lease, all the rentals attract VAT at the standard rate. However, the business customer is normally allowed to claim back 50% of the VAT.

Contract Hire

This is very similar to the lease described above: the same three basic elements, low deposit, low monthly payments, and future value. The biggest difference is that the loan company assumes the risk of the value of the vehicle at the end of the contract. So again, if the vehicle is predicted to have a value of 45% (£5,400) and it is actually worth £4,800, at the end of the contract, the loan company takes the loss.

Contract hire is normally associated with full maintenance. This is where servicing, running and maintenance costs are estimated and built into the rental. This can suit all types of company, from small to large. The main benefit is that it gives the company a fixed budget for the vehicle which will not change during the contract, and they do not have to worry about the value of the vehicle at the end of the agreement

Some Examples

Let us take a look at some examples of the different types of loan plan for businesses.

The writing down allowances for passenger vehicles are 25% of the value, up to a maximum of £3,000 per year
100% of lease rentals on vehicles costing up to £12,000 are allowable against taxable profit
Example vehicle costing £12,000
Interest rate 10%
Period 3 years
Annual mileage 15,000

	HP 3 years	Lease 3 years	Contract hire 3 years
Cost	£12,000	£12,000	£12,000
Deposit	£2,400	£900	£900
Maintenance costs	N/A	N/A	£1,620
Future value	N/A	£5,400	£5,400
Balance	£9,600	£5,700	£5,700
Monthly payments	£347	£247	£292
WDA Year 1	£3,000	£2,964	£3,504
WDA Year 2	£2,250	£2,964	£3,504
WDA Year 3	£1,687.50	£2,964	£3,504
Interest charges	£2,892	N/A	N/A
Total WDA	£9,829.50	£8,892	£10,512

As you can see from the table, it depends what the company wants and what is important to them.

If they want fixed budgeting, then contract hire is hard to beat. In a full maintenance agreement everything is covered, from servicing to wiper blades, and it's all included in the monthly rental.

If cashflow is important and they need a low deposit and lower monthly payments, then lease is a good option.

If they need to show the vehicle as an asset of the business, then HP/conditional sale or PCP may be the answer.

The Changing Face of Business

Businesses are diverse and dynamic, their needs change from month to month and year to year. Our job is not to be their accountant, but to advise them and inform them of the choices that are available. If we don't talk to the business customer about the different options and what they offer his business in broad terms, then we are leaving the customer to figure it out for themselves. Which could mean that they go to some other dealership who does take the time to explain confidently what each loan plan can offer.

Loan companies have loads of information on business user plans and run frequent training programmes on the business customer. Get yourself trained up on the subject and put yourself in a position where you can talk to business customers confidently about all the options that you can offer them. There are many people out there more than willing to help you... take the time and trouble to go and find them.

This is the 1990s. To be good you've got to be above-average and you've got to speak the same language as the customers. The language of funding options. Customers are more sophisticated: they want to know all about how they can pay for their vehicle. Grasp this challenge and make sure that when you pack your bag, you have all the knowledge and skills about loan products that are available to you.

After all, there are only three things that are certain in this life: you are born, you will die and if you buy a vehicle, most likely you will need finance.

Good luck.

Understanding Selling Law by Anthea Worsdall FIMI

Introduction

This section of the book is about the legal principles which affect the activity of supplying vehicles to customers, which we can call in its broadest sense 'consumer law'. The summary given here is not intended to be a detailed explanation of the law, or a substitute for obtaining legal advice in specific cases. It is, however, essential that everyone involved in the business of retailing vehicles does have some understanding of how the law may affect his activities. Increasingly, customers know – or think they know – a lot about their 'rights', and the professional salesperson should know at least as much as his customers.

First, the framework of how the law works. When you think about what legal rights a customer has you will probably be thinking in terms of his or her ability to sue you for some form of compensation if something goes wrong. This area of the law, which gives individuals rights which they can enforce by going to court, is 'civil' law. Aspects of the civil law which are important to the salesman are the law of contract and the law of 'tort' (which deals with other civil legal rights such as trespass, slander and negligence).

In addition to civil law, it is also important to realise the impact which the criminal law has upon civil law. The enforcement of the criminal law is not up to the individual, as a general rule, but instead is a matter for the state enforcement agency. In the case of consumer protection laws, this is the trading standards department of the local authority.

At first sight it may seem curious that the criminal law gets involved at all in the commercial relationship between the trader and his customer. Surely the fact that the customer has so many civil law rights these days means that the criminal law is not really relevant? In order to understand why both civil and criminal laws are of importance in consumer protection, you have to understand what the objective of each area of law is.

The civil law is, as we have seen, primarily concerned with protecting the rights of the individual. The customer who is sold a vehicle which is of unsatisfactory quality can bring a civil action against the person who sold it to him if he cannot resolve his problem amicably, and his remedy will be compensation in one form or another.

Where there has been a breach of the criminal law, then the main objective is to punish the offender by imposing a penalty which goes to the state rather than compensating any individual who may have been affected by the crime. So a retailer who sells a customer a clocked vehicle is liable to prosecution for a criminal offence, and faces the penalty of a fine or even imprisonment. Any compensation which the customer may be entitled to is a

◆ ◆ ◆

matter primarily for the civil law, and in theory the customer would have to bring a civil action. In practice, in criminal cases involving such an obvious and direct loss to someone identifiable – as with the sale of a clocked vehicle, the criminal court may be asked to use its special powers to make an order for compensation as well as imposing a penalty.

However, the basic principle remains: the criminal law seeks to deter conduct which is regarded as sufficiently anti-social to be criminal, whilst the civil law regulates the dealings between individuals. Where these two aspects of the law overlap, as they frequently do in consumer protection matters, it is because Parliament has decided that in those cases the civil law is not enough, because consumers may be deterred from enforcing the law in the courts for reasons of cost, complexity and so on.

This summary of the law looks at the different stages of customer transactions, highlighting the effect of both civil and, where relevant, criminal law at each stage.

The logical starting point, therefore, has to be to look first at the way in which the dealership promotes itself, its goods and services to its potential customers.

Advertising and Marketing

The control of the way in which a retailer or manufacturer describes his goods and services to the public is a classic example of the growth of consumer protection laws in the last 20 to 30 years. Despite this, the law still tends to focus more on incorrect factual statements and misleading price or credit information than on general statements about quality – eg *"The best vehicle in its class"* – which are generally left to voluntary control under the advertising industry's Code of Practice.

Examples of the effect of the law on advertising are given below:

- Specific promises made to the public in an advertisement may be enforceable by individuals as a *contract*. For example, an offer by a manufacturer to pay £100 to anyone who unsuccessfully tried his product, which was supposed to protect against contracting flu, was held by the court to be a "contractual offer" – ie it could be "accepted" by anyone who saw the advertisement, tried the product and caught flu, so entitling them to claim the £100.
- False or misleading statements of fact in an advertisement may be actionable under the criminal law, in this case the Trade Descriptions Act 1968, if the statement relates in some way to the qualities of the product or service being advertised. This may go beyond facts such as the mileage covered by a used vehicle, the engine capacity, or the number of owners, and extend into general adjectives such as 'beautiful', where the test of the

owners, and extend into general adjectives such as 'beautiful', where the test of the meaning of the word used will be the effect on the mind of the ordinary customer.

◆ Misleading statements not caught by the Trade Descriptions Act 1968 may be covered by the Misleading Advertisements Regulations. Under these provisions, the Director General of Fair Trading may require an advertiser to withdraw advertising which is regarded as "misleading".

◆ Statements about fuel consumption may not be made in any advertising or sales literature, unless the figures used are those obtained under the Government's fuel consumption testing regulations.

◆ Advertisements by a business must disclose that the advertiser is a trader.

◆ Consumer credit advertising is controlled by the detailed Regulations under the Consumer Credit Act 1974. Briefly, consumer credit advertisements:

- Must not give false or misleading information
- Must not offer to supply goods or services credit if they are not also available for cash
- Must fall within one of the categories of advertisement set out in the regulations.

◆ A consumer credit advertisement can sometimes be misleading even if it conforms with the Regulations – for example, a cash price calculated on the basis of a manufacturer's list price without a discount for cash.

◆ Price information in advertisements must not be misleading, and must conform with the requirements of the Price Marking Order if the advertiser is a retailer. This means, for example, that a retailer cannot show prices for goods in advertisements or elsewhere which exclude any non-optional sums the customer has to pay – for example, delivery charges – without showing those exclusions clearly and in the same size print as the main price indication.

◆ Sales literature used by the retailer, even if provided by someone else, is also caught by the legislation on trade descriptions, consumer credit and pricing.

Checklist on Advertising

◆ Even if you use an agency to prepare advertisements for you, or rely on copy or sales literature prepared by a manufacturer, it is still your legal responsibility to ensure you comply with the law. Under the trade descriptions and consumer credit legislation it is possible for the individual employee to be prosecuted for criminal offences as well as the dealership. Your defence to a criminal prosecution will depend on the proof of "due diligence" on your part. For your own protection, therefore, if you get involved in preparing or approving advertisements, you should:

- Familiarise yourself with the rules that apply (for details of user friendly guides, see appendix)
- Ensure that advertising copy is checked and signed off before printing
- Ensure information in advertisements is up-to-date and still valid at the time of publication
- Ensure that words like "while stocks last" and closing dates are included in advertisements which contain an offer made to the public, and ensure that any conditions which apply are made clear.
- In advertising used vehicles, follow the guidelines laid down in the Motor Industry Code of Practice.
- All prices advertised to consumers must include VAT

Displays in the Showroom

You hope that the customer, either having been attracted by your advertising or by the appearance and presentation of the dealership, will wish to come into the showroom so that you can attempt to sell him your product.

The law applies equally to the information displayed in the showroom. The following are some of the key points:

◆ Vehicles on display must either be marked with the selling price, including non-optional extras and VAT, or the price must be displayed clearly close by. If the price marked is incorrect (eg lower than the actual price), there is a potential criminal offence, even if the discrepancy is immediately corrected. The civil law does not entitle the customer to insist on being sold to at the lower price unless he can show that the seller was making an "offer" to sell at that price which the customer accepted. Generally a display of goods in a showroom will not legally be an "offer", but "an invitation to treat"

– ie an invitation to customers to make the seller an offer which can be accepted or rejected.

◆ New vehicles on display must carry the fuel consumption sticker required by the Government.

◆ The mileage reading on a vehicle is a "trade description" – an indication of how far that vehicle has travelled. If the mileage reading is incorrect, the retailer (and/or the salesman) commits a criminal offence just by having the vehicle on his premises, as well as by actually supplying it to a customer. The retailer's defence is to show "due diligence" and "all reasonable precautions" to avoid committing an offence. This will require the dealership to have in place a system for verifying mileages on used vehicles and the use of 'disclaimer' stickers on speedometers. No vehicles should be on display to customers without these checks having been carried out.

◆ Any vehicle displayed under a particular description (eg a manufacturer's used vehicle scheme) must comply with all the requirements of the scheme – as to checks made, for example – or else bear a prominent notice stating that the vehicle is "awaiting preparation" or similar.

◆ The Road Traffic Acts make it a criminal offence to display or sell an unroadworthy vehicle.

◆ Sales literature displayed in the showroom is also subject to the Trade Descriptions Act. It is the seller's responsibility to ensure that any updated information supplied by the manufacturer is passed on to the customer, and that if there are any differences between the vehicle as displayed and the brochure, these differences are pointed out to the customer.

Checklist in the Showroom

◆ Are all poster displays/sales brochures up-to-date and current? Old material should be amended or disposed of

◆ Are all vehicles on display priced with the total price the customer will have to pay?

◆ Are the prices shown correct?

◆ Are all used vehicles on display verified as to mileage? Are disclaimer stickers used?

Negotiating the Sale

Having caught the customer's interest, the salesman then has the job of converting that interest to a sale. What he says during this crucial period is of considerable legal significance.

- Any statement of fact about the vehicle he is selling which is false or misleading, even if only an oral statement made in conversation and written down, is caught by the Trade Descriptions Act 1968, and can therefore lead to a criminal prosecution.
- Any statement of fact (not opinion) which is incorrect may be treated in law as a "misrepresentation", entitling the other party to a remedy. This may mean getting out of the contract altogether, and/or in some cases obtaining compensation.
- If the customer tells the salesman the purpose for which goods are required, for example, a vehicle suitable to tow a caravan, then the law assumes that the seller will then sell goods which are suitable for that purpose. If they are not suitable, then the customer will be entitled to compensation.
- The discussions during negotiation are the point in the legal relationship where the customer should have all points of the agreement clearly explained. If the specification of the vehicle he is ordering differs from that in the sales brochure, or from the vehicle the customer has inspected, then it would be wise to ensure that information is written down rather than simply left to oral discussion.
- If during negotiation the customer wishes to have a written credit quotation, the information given must comply with the Consumer Credit Quotations Regulations.
- Any information given to a finance company about a customer or the transaction that is being proposed in order to obtain finance for the customer will, in law, be a representation. This means that any information given which is incorrect and influences the finance company's decision will be a misrepresentation. This could include, for example, a misrepresentation about the amount of deposit being paid by a customer. In the event that the customer defaults, this could entitle the finance company to recover all sums due under the agreement from the retailer.
- There have been a number of well publicised incidents where customers test driving vehicles have been involved in accidents. It is essential that the salesman takes steps to point out any particular features of the vehicle that the customer should be aware of, as well as the controls. Potentially, there is a liability in "tort" for negligence if insufficient warnings or guidance are given, causing an accident.

Checklist for Negotiations

- Ensure all information given to the customer is accurate
- Use only up-to-date sales literature and avoid using the handbook as a selling aid
- Record any specification details in writing (probably on the order form – see below)
- Ensure any information given to the finance company is accurate

Closing the Deal

The point at which the customer actually enters into a legally binding contract to buy a vehicle is, in theory, a rather grey area. Technically, a contract (subject to some exceptional contracts which must be in writing, eg consumer credit agreements), can be made when there has been an offer, an acceptance of the offer and the parties intend to be legally bound, plus of course agreement as to the "consideration" or price that is to be paid. In other words, an oral contract may come into effect before anything is put down on paper. In practice, this does not normally give rise to any difficulties, but it should be borne in mind in cases such as where a salesman discusses a deal with a customer and he goes away to "think about it". The law says that a contractual offer stays open for a "reasonable" period if no time limit is put on it. The prudent salesmen will therefore want to ensure that such a time limit has been stated, so that he is free to sell elsewhere after it has expired.

- For all practical purposes, the signing of the order form will constitute the binding contract between the parties. It is therefore important that this contains all the relevant information accurately stated (see *Negotiations* above).
- Where a vehicle is being traded in by the customer, the appraisal of it carried out by the dealer at this stage is vital. If the vehicle is defective or has a false mileage reading or has been stolen or is the subject of a total loss claim or is an undisclosed finance agreement, the retailer may be unable afterwards to recoup his losses from the customer. In fact, he may take on liabilities so far as, for example, a finance company is concerned. It is therefore vital that all the appropriate checks are carried out with HPI and elsewhere, and that the appraisal is carried out carefully.
- Where the customer is also entering into a finance agreement, it is essential that all the statutory requirements are completed properly. Failure to have all alterations initialled, for example, will make the agreement unenforceable.
- Where the customer pays a deposit in a transaction where he is paying by cash, it will normally be regarded as an "earnest of good faith" and will be forfeited if the customer

backs out of the deal. Where, however, the customer is buying under a regulated consumer credit agreement and has signed the finance agreement, he is entitled to pull out at any time up to the time the finance company has signed the agreement. If this happens, he is entitled to the return of any money paid to the retailer who has introduced him to the finance company. In practice, this means there is a sort of 'cooling off' period for all regulated consumer credit agreements up until the time it is signed by the finance company.

- The statutory cooling off period applies only where finance documents are signed off trade premises. You should **not** get finance documents signed off trade premises (for example, at the consumer's home) unless the finance company documentation you use is specifically designed for that purpose.
- Defects in goods pointed out before a contract is made are **not** the legal responsibility of the seller.

Checklist

- Has the customer been given the opportunity to examine the vehicle (if appropriate) and/or have any defects been pointed out (see below)?
- When preparing the order form for signature, are you satisfied that the customer knows exactly what he is buying? Do any points need to be noted on the order form?
- Has the finance document been completed accurately, with all signatures and alterations installed?
- If the customer leaves the showroom without placing an order, are there any "loose ends" which would enable him to come back later and "accept" an "offer" made earlier?
- If the customer is trading-in a vehicle, have sufficient details been recorded to enable any discrepancies to be identified when the vehicle is handed over later?
- On appraising the part-exchange, are there any concerns which you have about the genuineness of the vehicle's mileage and history as it has been represented to you? Have all the appropriate checks been carried out?

Handing the Vehicle Over

◆ The delivery of the vehicle to the customer completes the performance of the contract by the retailer provided that it does actually conform to the contract:

- It must meet any specific requirement in the contract
- It must meet any description applied to it – eg "New"
- It must be of "satisfactory quality" (see below)
- The retailer must pass on good title
- The vehicle must be fit for any specific purpose made known to the seller by the purchaser, or any implied purpose that he may have
- The retailer has met other contractual obligations, for example, delivery dates

Can the customer ever refuse to accept the vehicle? The answer is yes. If the vehicle does not meet one of the contractual terms as outlined above, the customer may be entitled to refuse to accept delivery. For example, the "new" vehicle has 600 miles on the clock, the "new" vehicle has unrepaired delivery damage, the vehicle does not have the power steering as specified and so on.

In practice, of course, handling these types of issue will generally be a matter more of customer relations than resorting to the letter of the law, but it is important to recognise that in some situations the customer may be in a strong legal position.

Can the customer be forced to accept the vehicle and take delivery? This, of course, is the other side of the coin, and the answer is yes if the vehicle is in accordance with the terms of the contract. It follows that in this situation the customer may lose his deposit if he refuses to complete the contract (but see the note above where he is buying on finance).

The Customer's Rights under the Contract

What is the customer entitled to when something goes wrong with the vehicle he has bought?

The most common legal remedy for breach of contract is compensation. In some cases the party who has suffered from the breach of contract may also be entitled to "reject" the goods he is buying and get his money back.

The consumer's right to get his money back depends on whether he has "accepted" the goods. He will be deemed to have accepted them if he retains the vehicle for a reasonable time without intimating to the seller that he has rejected them. He does not damage his right to reject simply by allowing the seller the opportunity to repair them, and the "reasonable time" will now include a reasonable opportunity to examine the goods to see if they conform with the contract. This is a change to the old law where customers could lose the right to reject even before they were aware there was a defect. "Acceptance" however only precludes a "money back" claim, it does not stop a claim from breach of contract.

However, in order for the customer to be entitled to a "legal" remedy, he has to show that there has been a breach of contract. The vehicle buyer may still have a remedy because he has the benefit of a warranty or guarantee of some sort (including manufacturer's 30-day exchange programmes). If his problem "fits" the warranty conditions, it does not matter whether or not there has been a breach of contract. In practice, most problems in the retail motor industry relating to vehicles sold will be resolved by a warranty.

The customer cannot, however, be forced to accept the solution offered to him by the warranty if there has been a breach of contract. The effect of the customer protection legislation in recent years has been to give the customer a choice as to his preferred solution in that situate. If, for example, a customer is claiming the cost of alternative transport when his vehicle is off the road for a day due to a defect, this may be a claim not covered by warranty (although the actual repair may be), but he may still be entitled to pursue it against the seller under the Sale of Goods Act.

◆ The key to understanding the customer's legal rights is therefore to understand when there has been a breach of the contract with the customer. The rights under the contract are summarised above. (See *Handing the Vehicle Over* – page 531)

In practice there are two main terms as to quality which operate in every contract for the sale of goods:

- That goods should be of satisfactory quality
- That they should be fit for any express purpose of the customer made known to the seller

"Satisfactory quality" is a new provision which came into effect on 3 January 1995 and replaces the old concept of "merchantable quality". Goods are "satisfactory" if they meet the standard that a reasonable person would regard as satisfactory, taking into account matters such as description, price and other relevant circumstances. "Quality" includes the state and condition of the goods, and the legislation sets out the following as being aspects of "quality" of the goods:

- Fitness for all the purposes for which goods of the kind in question are commonly supplied
- Appearance and finish
- Freedom from minor defects
- Safety
- Durability

Where specific defects are drawn to the buyer's attention before the contract is made, this term does not apply, nor where the buyer examines the goods before the contract is made.

Where the customer is a "consumer", ie someone buying goods for private use, these contractual rights cannot be excluded or diminished by the contract with the retailer, or any other means (eg the manufacturer's warranty). Where the customer is a non-consumer, these rights may be varied to the extent that it is reasonable, and the non-consumer's rights to reject unsatisfactory goods is subject to a test as to whether rejection is "reasonable".

The intention of the change in the law from "merchantable" to "satisfactory" quality is to strengthen the customer's position regarding "minor" defects, or those which appear after a period. It is too early to know how the courts will apply these provisions in actual cases, but it seems likely that despite the intention of giving the customer additional protection, the price paid will still be a significant test, particularly for used vehicles, where the courts have always taken the view that a used vehicle cannot generally be expected to be of the same standard as a new one.

Checklist on Handling Complaints

- Is the vehicle "satisfactory"? (see above)
- Does it conform with all other aspects of the contract, or representations made prior to the contract? (see above)
- If the answer to these two questions is probably yes, what right does the customer have outside the main contract, eg under the warranty?
- If the vehicle is not satisfactory, or otherwise not in conformity with the contract, has the customer "accepted" it?

For further essential guidance see:

The British Code of Advertising Practice

Code of Practice for Traders on Misleading Pricing

Consumer Credit Act – Office of Fair Trading Guide to the Advertising and Quotations Regulations 1989

The Motor Industry Code of Practice

The Legislation

Trade Descriptions Act 1968

Passenger Car Fuel Consumption Order 1983

Misleading Advertisements (Disclosure) Order 1977

Consumer Credit Act 1974

The Consumer Credit (Advertisements) Regulations 1989

The Consumer Credit (Quotations) Regulations 1989

The Sale of Goods Act 1979 (as amended)

Sale and Supply of Goods Act 1994

Further Reading

Consumer Law for the Motor Trade by Anthea Worsdall (Published by Butterworths)

Future Training and Personal Development Opportunities

If the content of this guide has, let's say, grabbed your imagination, been very clear to you or sounded like common sense, then perhaps would like to explore a little more. Specialised workshops will be held annually, designed specifically to review and expand on both the sales and psychological techniques outlined in this book.

'Journey Through Sales Time' workshops based on the content of *The Complete Sales Guide* take place every spring and autumn. They are residential and are run Monday to Friday. If you would like to know more, please contact David Upsher direct at:

Mitac Ltd
Station House
Box
Corsham
Wiltshire
SN13 8AE

Telephone: 01225 743894
Facsimile: 01225 743544

Index